Theology and Education have come together in recent years to form the discipline of "theological education". Dr Bernhard Ott brings a lifetime of reading and research, teaching, educational leadership and international collaboration to his book *Understanding and Developing Theological Education*. His professional involvement in three educational mega-systems (UK, EU, USA) reveals first-hand knowledge of their inner workings and interrelations. He also reveals to the reader the foundational Germanic tradition in theological education, often little known by non-German readers. Dr Ott also has broad international experience in the European Evangelical Accrediting Association (EEAA) and the International Council for Evangelical Theological Education (ICETE), and is well acquainted with ecumenical theological education.

The result: a clearly-written and comprehensive textbook for theological education, a resource for many years to come. A must-read for theological educators, students and leaders; for all who wish to understand better how theology can be educational and education theological.

Paul Sanders
International Director Emeritus, ICETE
Provost Emeritus, Arab Baptist Theological Seminary, Lebanon

ICETE Series

Understanding and Developing Theological Education

Understanding and Developing Theological Education

Bernhard Ott

© 2016 by Bernhard Ott

Published 2016 by Langham Global Library
An imprint of Langham Publishing

Previously published in German by Neufeld Verlag Schwarzenfeld in 2013,
ISBN: 978-3-86256-041-7.

Langham Partnership
PO Box 296, Carlisle, Cumbria CA3 9WZ, UK
www.langham.org

ISBNs:
978-1-90771-388-0 Print
978-1-90771-387-3 ePub
978-1-78368-120-4 PDF

Bernhard Ott has asserted his right under the Copyright, Designs and Patents Act, 1988 to be identified as the Author of this work.

All rights reserved. No part of this publication may be reproduced, stored in a retrieval system or transmitted, in any form or by any means, electronic, mechanical, photocopying, recording or otherwise, without the prior written permission of the publisher or the Copyright Licensing Agency.

All Scripture quotations, unless otherwise indicated, are taken from the Holy Bible, New International Version®, NIV®. Copyright ©1973, 1978, 1984, 2011 by Biblica, Inc.™ Used by permission of Zondervan.

British Library Cataloguing in Publication Data
A catalogue record for this book is available from the British Library

ISBN: 978-1-90771-388-0

Translated from German by Tom Keefer: tomkeefer126@gmail.com

Cover & Book Design: projectluz.com

Langham Partnership actively supports theological dialogue and a scholar's right to publish but does not necessarily endorse the views and opinions set forth, and works referenced within this publication or guarantee its technical and grammatical correctness. Langham Partnership does not accept any responsibility or liability to persons or property as a consequence of the reading, use or interpretation of its published content.

CONTENTS

Preface xi

1 Theological Education in Upheaval: An Introduction 1
   1.1 The Present Situation in Theological Education: An Initial Outline 1
   1.2 What Do We Mean by "Theological Education?": An Initial Definition . . . 6
   1.3 Special Challenges Demand Special Competencies: An Overview 7

2 The Battle for Reforms and Renewal in Theological Education:
   An Introduction to the International Discussion 15
   2.1 Impulses for Reform from the World of Missions and the Ecumenical
       Movement. 17
       2.1.1 From the Theological Education Fund to the Program on
             Ecumenical Theological Education. 17
       2.1.2 Impulses from the International Ecumenical Discussion 19
   2.2 Impulses for Reform within the International Evangelical Movement 22
       2.2.1 The Missionary Movement and Theological Education by
             Extension 22
       2.2.2 The International Council for Evangelical Theological Education
             and the Manifesto 23
   2.3 Voices from the Majority World 32
   2.4 Reform of Theological Education in North America 33
       2.4.1 H. Richard Niebuhr: Thinking Based in Ecclesiology 36
       2.4.2 Edward Farley: Overcoming Fragmentation 38
       2.4.3 Max L. Stackhouse: Rediscovering Apologetics. 49
       2.4.4 David Kelsey: Between Athens and Berlin 50
       2.4.5 An Alternative Based on the Bible. 59
       2.4.6 Warford: Wisdom Leading to Wisdom. 61
   2.5 Efforts to Reform Theological Education in German-Speaking Europe . . . 65
       2.5.1 Reform Efforts within the Context of Protestant Theological Studies
             at German Universities. 65
       2.5.2 Free Church and Evangelical Theological Education in German-
             Speaking Europe 78
   2.6 A New Agenda Leads to Paradigmatic Changes. 83

3 Foundations of Educational Theory: Traditions and Models of
   (Theological) Education 87
   3.1 Foundational Categories of Educational Theory 88

       3.1.1 Education and Training..88
       3.1.2 Formal, Non-formal, or Informal Training? 89
       3.1.3 Educational Levels 90
   3.2 An Overview of Typologies...94
       3.2.1 Historical Models..95
       3.2.2 Philosophy of Education: Top Down or Bottom Up..............95
       3.2.3 Dimensions of Theological Education Today....................98
       3.2.4 Athens – Berlin – Geneva – Jerusalem 100
   3.3 Secular Educational Models: An Overview..........................102
       3.3.1 The University-Based Educational Model 103
       3.3.2 The Dual Educational Model (Vocational Training).............105
       3.3.3 The Paradigm Shift in the Pedagogy of the Twentieth Century ...107
       3.3.4 The Adult Education Model 110
       3.3.5 The Technical University Model 114
   3.4 Traditions and Models of Theological Education: An Overview 117
       3.4.1 The Bible School Movement..................................118
       3.4.2 Theological Education as Academic Course of Study............122
       3.4.3 The American Seminary Model 126
       3.4.4 Alternative Models of Theological Education 131

4   Biblical-Theological Foundations: Toward a Theology of
    Theological Education... 137
   4.1 Biblical Building Blocks for a Theology of Theological Education 139
       4.1.1 Theological Education in Light of the Old Testament 141
       4.1.2 Theological Education in Light of the New Testament..........156
   4.2 On the Way to a Theology of Theological Education 170
       4.2.1 From the Bible to Present-Day Challenges.....................170
       4.2.2 God...173
       4.2.3 The Word of God 180
       4.2.4 God's Project..186
       4.2.5 The Power of God..192
       4.2.6 The Church as the Primary Place of Learning 194
   4.3 Midway Point: What Is Theological Education?.......................196

5   Integrating Theory and Practice in Theological Education 199
   5.1 Shedding Light on the Theory-Praxis Debate........................200
       5.1.1 The Problem and Suggestions for a Solution 200
       5.1.2 Praxis, Theoria and Poiesis....................................202
       5.1.3 Implications 205

    5.2 Spirituality and Character Development 207
        5.2.1 Theological Education and Spiritual Formation 207
        5.2.2 Encouraging Character Development. 224
    5.3 *Theoria*: Thought, Understanding, and Science 229
        5.3.1 Two Ways of Thinking. 232
        5.3.2 Cultural Differences in Thinking. 235
        5.3.3 Various Types of Theories. 237
        5.3.4 Truth and Understanding. 246
        5.3.5 The Capacity to Think and the Nature of Science 252
    5.4 *Poiesis*: Competencies and Skills. 256
        5.4.1 Key Qualifications, Key Competencies. 262
        5.4.2 Vocational-Specific Skills 267

6   **Curriculum Development in Theological Education** 269
    6.1 Foundational Considerations 269
        6.1.1 WHO? The Question of Responsibility and Support 269
        6.1.2 WHAT? The Question of Goals and Content 271
        6.1.3 HOW? The Question of Processes and Methods. 274
        6.1.4 WHERE? The Question of Context. 279
        6.1.5 WHO? The Question of Instructors 280
    6.2 Curriculum Development and Partnership. 283
        6.2.1 What Is Curriculum?. 283
        6.2.2 Developing Curriculum in Partnership 284
        6.2.3 Forms of Partnership. 287
    6.3 Where Are We Now? Entrance Requirements 290
        6.3.1 Formal Entrance Requirements and/or "Open Education" 290
        6.3.2 Open Access to Education: Possibilities and Limitations. 292
    6.4 Where Do We Want to Go? Graduation Requirements. 295
        6.4.1 Developing a Graduate Profile 296
        6.4.2 Defining Educational Goals 297
    6.5 How Do We Get There? Developing Curriculum. 301
        6.5.1 The Components of the Curriculum. 301
        6.5.2 The Course of Study. 303
        6.5.3 Courses and Course Descriptions 305
        6.5.4 Additional Organizational Structures and Measures 311
        6.5.5 Curriculum Integration. 325
    6.6 Two Examples 338
        6.6.1 "Reenvisioning the Theological Curriculum as If the *Missio Dei*
             Mattered" 338
        6.6.2 The Concordat Reform of the Reformed Church in Switzerland ... 340

| 7 | Ensuring Quality in Theological Education | 343 |

7.1 Quality Management, Evaluation, Accreditation – Definition of Terms. .345
    7.1.1 Terms and Concepts 345
    7.1.2 Purpose and Goal of Quality Management, Evaluation and
    Accreditation 348
7.2 Which Quality Management Model Should Be Used? 351
    7.2.1 Basic Categories and Basic Decisions 352
    7.2.2 Handling Externally Developed Quality Management Plans 358
7.3 Quality, Indicators and Standards. 362
    7.3.1 Definitions and Concepts 362
    7.3.2 Defining the Quality of Education. 363
    7.3.3 Indicators, Variables, Criteria. 365
    7.3.4 Quality Standards. 368
7.4 Implementation: Evaluation Instruments 371
    7.4.1 Instruments for Internal Quality Management 371
    7.4.2 Instruments of External Control 376

| 8 | Leading Theological Education with Head, Hand, and Heart | 379 |

8.1 What Leaders of Theological Schools Must Accomplish. 380
    8.1.1 Leadership Tasks 380
8.2 *Head*: Strategy → Orientation. 387
    8.2.1 The Vision 389
    8.2.2 The Profile 391
    8.2.3 The Implementation Program 394
    8.2.4 The Process of Developing Vision, Profile, and
    Implementation Program. 395
8.3 *Hand*: Structures → Coordination 398
    8.3.1 Creating Appropriate Organizational Structures. 399
8.4 *Heart*: Culture → Motivation 420
    8.4.1 What Do We Mean by Culture? 421
    8.4.2 What Determines the Culture of an Educational Institution? 422
    8.4.3 The Pedagogical Significance of the Institutional Culture 426

Bibliography. 429
    Magazines. 429
    Dictionaries and Lexicons 429
    Literature 430

Preface

The former rector of the University of Basel, theology professor Ulrich Gäbler, probably reflected the thinking of many when he said, "Our university currently looks like a construction site."[1] That has generally been the case in the world of theological education in recent decades. I've been at work on this construction site for more than thirty-five years. And because I originally worked as an architect before I became a theologian, I've had considerable experience with construction sites. However, I was thrown into the role of academic dean without having had the opportunity to receive any training for this task. In fact there was and is no course of study to train as an academic dean. I know that many others have had similar experiences. Being president of a theological seminary, or academic dean, or rector – these are jobs you learn by doing.

Friends and colleagues encouraged me to utilize my years of experience and reflection by writing this handbook of theological education during my sabbatical year in 2005–2006. I could make good use of many lectures that I had given and essays I had written over the years, not the least of which was my doctoral dissertation on this topic.

This handbook is about the leadership and curriculum development of theological education. The volume is written primarily for those who are in leadership roles at theological schools and training institutions, and more generally for those who serve as instructors, professors, and administrators, as well as those who serve as governing board and advisory council members. Students, too, may find it of value in their reflections on the purpose of their studies. This work intends to lay a theoretical foundation and give practical suggestions for the formation and design of theological education.

I write with a perspective that is intentionally broad, international, and diverse. I take my cue from a volume published by the World Council of Churches, *An International Directory of Theological Colleges 1997*, which

---

1. Ulrich Gäbler, "Universität Basel: Forschungspolitik und Universitätsleitung," in *Die neue Verantwortung. Anregungen aus dem internationalen Vergleich, der Hochschulforschung und Praxisbeispielen*, eds. Evelies Mayer, Hans-Dieter Daniel and Ulrich Teichler (Bonn: Lemmens, 2003), 82.

catalogues more than one thousand educational institutions on six continents. Included are theological faculties of universities, theological seminaries and colleges, as well as Bible schools and Bible institutes. These institutions are divided into six categories, from 1–2 year non-degree programs (Level 1) to doctoral programs (Level 6).[2] The entire spectrum is in view here. However the following chapters will more precisely define what theological education is – and is not.

The points of emphasis that may be evident in this handbook arise from my own sphere of knowledge and experience. In 2006 (first German edition) I was writing as the leader of a small free-church theological seminary in Switzerland (Theologisches Seminar Bienenberg). Non-university-based theological education in German-speaking Europe is therefore my starting point. However, theological education as a whole cannot be properly understood without awareness of the university system and tradition, therefore these will also be referenced.

In addition, my own theological education has had an international dimension, and I have always understood my teaching and leadership roles within an international context:

- Studies in North America (master's program) and England (doctoral studies).
- International network within the Mennonite World Conference. Visits to various theological schools in North America and in Paraguay. Regular inner-European contacts (Switzerland, Germany, France, the Netherlands). Participation in the Consultation on Theological Education on Five Continents of the Mennonite World Conference 1997, Calcutta, India.[3]
- Guest lecturer at Insituto Biblico Asunción and at Centro Evangélico Mennonita de Teologia de Asunción, both of which are part of the theological faculty of the Universidad Evangélica del Paraguay.

---

2. Alec Gilmore, ed., *An International Dictionary of Theological Colleges 1997* (London: SCM Press, 1997), 13–18.

3. Conference contributions in *Theological Education on Five Continents: Anabaptist Perspectives,* eds. Nancy R. Heisey and Daniel S. Schipani (Strasbourg: Mennonite World Conference, 1997).

- Doctoral study at the Oxford Centre for Mission Studies. Topic: "Mission Studies in Theological Education: A Critical Analysis of Mission Training in Evangelical Bible Colleges and Seminaries in German-Speaking Switzerland from 1960–1995."[4]
- Connections within the European Evangelical Accrediting Association (EEAA) and also with the International Council for Evangelical Theological Education (ICETE).
- In the 1990s, one of my main responsibilities was to lead our seminary through a number of accreditation processes. First was the accreditation of the bachelor's program by the EEAA. Following that was the validation of the master's program by the University of Wales. Both processes gave me familiarity with the mechanisms of accreditation and academic validation in an international context.

Six years after the first edition (2007) of this handbook a second edition was proposed (2013). It was the encouragement of colleagues as well as ongoing requests from students that convinced me that a revised edition would be worthwhile.

A critical reading of the first edition led me to consider a thorough re-working of the text. In the past seven years I have continued to develop many of the book's topics. Moreover, the whole field of theological education has undergone changes, and the contribution of a number of new publications needed to be included. And of course there were mistakes and weaknesses that needed to be corrected.

My further study of the topic of theological education is closely connected with two professional assignments that I have grown into during the past seven years:

- In 2007 I joined the accrediting council of the European Evangelical Accrediting Association (EEAA). Since 2009 I've served as Accreditation Director and thus been responsible for the implementation of accreditation processes. Since 2013 I also serve as chairman of EEAA. These responsibilities not only enabled me to gain extensive experience in the areas of quality control,

---

4. Published under the title: *Beyond Fragmentation: Integrating Mission and Theological Education* (Oxford: Regnum Books International, 2001).

evaluation, and accreditation, it also challenged me to deepen my own knowledge and expertise in these disciplines.
- Also in 2007, I accepted the invitation of the European School of Culture and Theologie (at the Akademie für Weltmission), in conjunction with their partnership with Columbia International University, to develop a Doctor of Education degree program, with an emphasis in Leadership in International Theological Education. Developing this doctoral curriculum, planning various topics for the courses to be offered, and interacting with the professors and more than thirty doctoral students from all over the world, broadened my perspective and deepened my understanding of theological education. Since 2013 I have also served as Academic Dean of the European School of Culture and Theology.
- Through my work with the EEAA, I also became involved in the activities of the International Council for Evangelical Theological Education (ICETE). Participation in a three-year project to discuss and define global standards for doctoral studies in theology proved particularly instructive. Four consultations (in Beirut, Bangalore, Boston and Nairobi) with experts from all over the world enriched my understanding of international developments in the field of theological education enormously.

Despite all the latest developments and my own expanded experience and expertise, I did not find the time for a thorough revision of the entire book. We opted for a limited revision instead. The readers may take note of the following feature of this revision: Additional bibliographical information was added at the end of some chapters. These additional references have *not* been included in the bibliography at the end of the volume.

Many thoughts, ideas, and insights that I have newly acquired or newly formulated in recent years have been woven into a number of papers and lectures and can be found in the following sources:

1) "Tradition and Transformation: Anstöße zu transformativer theologischer Ausbildung." In *Die Welt Verändern: Grundfragen einer Theologie der Transformation*, edited by Tobias Faix, Johannes Reimer, and Voker Brecht, 296–302. Marburg: Francke, 2009.

2) "Training of Theological Educators for International Theological Education: An Evangelical Contribution from Europe." In *Handbook on Theological Education in World Christianity. An Edinburgh 2010 Publication Project*, edited by World Council of Churches, 697–708. Oxford: Regnum, 2010.

3) "Doing Theology in Community: Reflections on Quality in Theological Education." In *History and Mission in Europe*, edited by Peter Penner. Schwarzenfeld: Neufeld Verlag and Elkhart: Institute of Mennonite Studies, 2011.

4) "Fit für die Welt – Neuere Entwicklungen in freikirchlicher theologischer Ausbildung." UNA SANCTA 66, no. 2 (2011): 113–122.

5) "Die Bedeutung des 'Fremden' in der theologischen Ausbildung. Erkenntnistheoretische und pädagogische Impulse von Lesslie Newbigin." In . . . *So ganz anders. Fremdheit als theologisches und gesellschaftliches Phänomen* (GBFE Jahrbuch 2013), edited by Robert Badenberg, Rainer Ebeling, and Elke Meier, 75–105. Marburg: Francke, 2013.

6) "Accreditation: Importance and Benefits for the Institution." In *Foundations for Academic Leadership*, edited by Fritz Deininger and Orbelina Eguizabal. Nürnberg, Germany: VTR Publications, 2013.

For the *Encyclopedia of Christian Education*, edited by George Thomas Kurian and Mark A. Lamport (London: Rowman & Littlefield, 2015):
- "Theological Education and the Bologna Process in Europe"
- "Theological Education, Theology of"
- "Theological Education Traditions (Orthodox, Roman Catholic, Mainline Protestant, Evangelical)"

Many thanks to Langham Partnership and all the individuals who have initiated and facilitated this English translation. Now I entrust this handbook into the hands of the readers in the hopes that it will continue to strengthen theological education and thereby advance the mission of the church even beyond the initial German-speaking context.

Bernhard Ott
Liestal, October 2015

1

Theological Education in Upheaval: An Introduction

1.1 The Present Situation in Theological Education: An Initial Outline

The whole field of education is in upheaval. That is a worldwide phenomenon. The underlying causes take many forms. The term "globalization" is often used and refers to various mechanisms: liberalization (free market), information technology (internet) and mobility certainly come to the fore.[1] In Europe these forces for change in higher education have been unleashed and continue to be governed by the so-called Bologna process.

All these paradigmatic changes create enormous challenges for educational institutions, including institutions of theological education. Traditionally, education has been driven primarily from *behind* and from *above* (i.e. from history and from the institution). Western educational traditions and governmental requirements have led to a level of stability. Schools have been above all else *administered*. It is not without cause, therefore, that Peter Senn speaks of a model of school leadership that is administration oriented and marked by educational politics. By contrast, today's world needs an educational system that is driven from *below* and from the *front* (i.e. shaped by the grass roots and by the future). The needs of the people and the needs

---

[1]. Cf. Wadi D. Haddad, "Tertiary Education Today: Global Trends, Global Agendas, Global Constraints." Lecture given on 19 August 2003 on the occasion of the ICETE Consultation for Theological Educators, High Wycombe, UK (http://www.icete-edu.org).

of the future become the determining factors. Senn describes this model, which has been called for in the framework of what is known as New Public Management, as market driven and entrepreneurial.[2]

In addition there has been a paradigm shift away from an institution-centred and teacher-oriented view to a perspective that is wholly focused on the students. The centre point of any education is the individual who gets what he or she needs at the time from the marketplace of educational opportunities. Such a model necessitates curricula and programs of study that are flexible, open, modular, and customized to the individual's needs and desires. Education is a product in a marketplace, not simply a tradition to be maintained or administered.

Certainly educational offerings must be able to withstand scrutiny when it comes to quality. What has long been the case in the business arena is increasingly expected in the world of higher education: quality assurance, evaluation, and accreditation.[3]

Even this brief introductory outline suggests that a new set of qualifications is now expected of leaders of educational institutions. Nigel Bennett, Megan Crawford, and Marion Cartwright make it clear that three big questions must be answered today within the context of New Public Management:[4]

- What *is* institutional (school) leadership in the first place, and what are its responsibilities?
- What kind of training and preparation must those in positions of educational leadership have?
- What constitutes "good" and "proper" leadership in education?

It's not surprising that a flood of literature has been produced in recent years dealing with educational management and curriculum development. Nor is it surprising that there is hardly a college or university that does not

---

2. Peter T. Senn, *Führung Pädagogischer Hochschulen* (Zürich: Rüegger, 2004), 25–28.
3. Cf. Rolf Dubs, *Qualitätsmanagement für Schulen*, 1st ed. (St Gallen: University of St Gallen Institute, 2003).
4. Nigel Bennett, Megan Crawford, and Marion Cartwright, *Effective Educational Leadership* (London: SAGE Publications, 2003), ix. The situation is also accurately summarized by Katharina Cortolezis-Schlager and Reinhart Nagel in "Und sie bewegt sich doch!: Steuerung und Organisation der Schulprozesse," *Organisationsentwicklung* 2 (1999): 4–15. See also John MacBeath, ed., *Effective School Leadership. Responding to Change* (London: SAGE, 1998). This volume compiles studies from Denmark, Scotland, England, and Australia, all of which deal with the new role of leadership that is required in light of the New Public Management.

offer continuing education or post-graduate courses for leaders of institutions of higher learning.

This change is observable at all levels of the educational system: in primary and secondary education, one refers to "semi-autonomous schools." It is no longer the case that primary and secondary schools simply carry out detailed instructions dictated from above, uniformly binding on all schools. They are now expected to create their own identity within general guidelines set down by the state. To name just one example, in an increasing number of cities students can choose which high school they want to attend. There are, in effect, free market forces in play. Individual schools must "sell" themselves and their product to the students and their parents. Schools that fail to do this will lose market share. This presents a new challenge to school leaders and administrators.

The situation is the same at the college and university level. The "unleashed" university (Müller-Böling) requires a new kind of management. Job descriptions for chancellors and principals must be rewritten. Those who lead colleges and universities must become "actors" in the evolution of higher education.[5] The age of a "scholars republic," administered by governmental bureaucrats, is over.[6]

This changing trend can be observed worldwide and is documented by a variety of studies.[7] In the past twenty years in America and Great Britain an increasing amount of social science research has been conducted in the area of school/university leadership. For about the past ten years there has been a similar development on the continent.[8] School leadership and educational

---

5. Evelies Mayer, "Dekane als Akteure der Hochschulentwicklung," in *Die neue Verantwortung der Hochschulen*, eds. Evelies Mayer, Hans-Dieter Daniel and Ulrich Teichel, 155–156 (Bonn: Lemmens, 2003).

6. Detlef Müller-Böling, *Die entfesselte Hochschule* (Gütersloh: Bertelsmann Stiftung, 2000), 20–21.

7. Cf. Brian J. Caldwell, "Autonomy and Self-Management: Concepts and Evidence," in *The Principles and Practice of Educational Management*, eds. Tony Bush and Les Bell (London: Sage Publications, 2002), 34: "Debates on the merits of school-based management, local management and self-management have been robust and inconclusive for most of the last two decades since these elements of school reform made their appearance in a small number of nations. It is now apparent that these phenomena are a feature of school reform in virtually every nation that is seeking to improve the quality of learning."

8. Senn, *Führung*, 26–27.

management have become key themes of educational philosophy.⁹ The growing interest of social scientists in educational management and leadership is one expression of the changes described above.

These developments in the West stand in stark contrast, however, to the fact that there are still millions upon millions of people who have no access to basic education. The most significant efforts of UNESCO continue to be directed toward the goal "Education for All." Yet despite enormous effort, it will be difficult to achieve the ambitious "Dakar Goals" by 2015.¹⁰

The question may be raised whether all of the above applies to educational institutions, which are privately funded rather than state (tax) supported, and also whether it applies to theological schools?

The fact is that private schools, too, must increasingly operate autonomously and within the framework of the competition of the marketplace. But theological schools in particular have traditionally served a stable and reliable constituency and therefore have not, until recently, been forced to think in terms of market-driven management. These institutions have tended to function largely under the administration of tradition.

Perhaps it can be expressed this way: whereas for public schools the shift is qualitative, for private schools it is merely quantitative. Nevertheless, even for private schools the new challenges for chancellors, principals, and others in leadership are enormous.

These changes can be verified in the United States by a look at the journal *Theological Education*. A study by Roy A. Andrews demonstrates that the topic of Seminary Presidency in Theological Education has grown in scope and importance.¹¹ In this article Andrews makes plain the struggle to arrive at a clear understanding of the role of a seminary president (rector). It has become increasingly clear that the top leadership role in a seminary is comparable to that of a CEO in the business world. Not all will agree. Andrews suggests that we use the role of a pastor in a church (pastorate) as a metaphor

---

9. Stefan G. Huber provides an overview of the international research in *Qualifizierung von Schulleiterinnen und Schulleitern im Internationalen Vergleich*, 1st ed. (Kronach: Link, 2003), 28–66.

10. More about the state of education internationally and the efforts of UNESCO can be found at http://www.unesco.org

11. Roy A. Andrews, "The Pastorate as a Metaphor for the Seminary Presidency: A Focus Study in the Theological Education Journal," *Theological Education* 49 (2005): 115–127. (Supplement).

for the leadership of a seminary. It is precisely this comparison – there the CEO, here the pastor – which fuels the debate about seminary leadership and makes it interesting. Is a theological training institution more like a church community, or is it a business whose mission is learning? Or does it need to be both, which doesn't make the leader's job easier?

A glance at the developments of the past two or three decades in the private (not publicly funded) theological schools in German-speaking Europe shows much the same thing. Both the evangelical schools within the Konferenz Bibeltreuer Ausbildungsstätten (KBA) and the seminaries of the classical free churches (Baptists, Evangelical Free, Methodist, etc.), were able to sail through fairly calm seas throughout the 1970s and 1980s. Student enrollment remained stable. Donors were faithful and reliable. Young people tended to choose the schools that were recommended by their denominations or by mission agencies. All of that has changed. New schools, with new forms of learning, have shaken things up. Efforts to achieve accreditation led to increased competition. Master's degree programs sprang up everywhere, increasing the competition even further. Printed flyers, advertisements in Christian magazines, and info-booths at large youth gatherings now no longer consist of unpretentious presentations of information. Instead, these have given way to polished, professional, even aggressive forms of marketing. Schools have to fight for students. They must compete similarly to win the favor of mission agencies, churches, and donors. The storm that "Bologna" unleashed in the world of higher learning has created new challenges for those who lead theological training schools. The leadership of a theological training institution has become a demanding business – somewhere between pastoral presence and management.

We can be sure of this: theological education is not immune to all these developments. That is true for public or private institutions, whether funded by the state, by churches, or by private citizens. But theological education is faced with additional questions: How do we justify theological education in the first place? Is there such a thing as a theology of theological education? Since the church relies on the Bible as its source, and since the Christian faith has been transmitted from generation to generation for centuries, theology and theological education are in their very essence bound up with the Bible and tradition. Thus the tension between market principles and tradition is especially great when it comes to theological education.

One of the greatest challenges for theological education is certainly the fact that more than half of all Christians today live in parts of the world that were first reached with the gospel during the modern missionary movement. These African, Asian, and Latin American Christians have for decades been saying quite clearly that the traditional Western model of theological education is not appropriate for their context. The church around the globe has, therefore, developed a variety of alternate forms of education in recent decades. Further, traditional Western models have been called into question.[12]

These challenges demand a great deal from those who teach and lead at theological training institutions. The reality shows a three-fold context of (1) a widespread market orientation in educational philosophy, (2) the Bologna process in the realm of European higher education, and (3) the need for education and training within the worldwide church in light of its mission. In this context theological education must be made relevant and future oriented. This book offers a base of knowledge and practical application to assist in this effort.

1.2 What Do We Mean by "Theological Education?": An Initial Definition

A precise clarification of the term "theological education" will follow in the course of the presentations made in this book. Nevertheless an initial definition, brief and preliminary, should be given at the outset, in order to avoid misunderstandings in the subsequent chapters and to enable a rational treatment of the material.

I suggest that it is helpful to distinguish between "education for discipleship" and "education for apostleship."[13] In other words, there is a training that is foundational for all of Christianity, which all who grow up and live in the church should receive. This includes everything we call "Christian education" – catechism, church teaching, Sunday school (both for children

---

12. In particular all forms of training that fly under the banner of *Theological Education by Extension* and in particular the writings of Kinsler.
13. In this I follow Daniel Schipani, "The Church and its Theological Education," in *Theological Education on Five Continents,* eds. Nancy R. Heisey and Daniel Schipani (Strasbourg: Mennonite World Conference, 1997), 5–33.

and for adults). Beyond this there is training for those who exercise pastoral or leadership functions.

The term "church teaching" can be used to encompass everything intended for the basic foundational training intended for all Christians. I suggest that the term "theological education" be reserved for the specialized training for pastors and leaders. This is how I use the term in the following chapters. Distinctions and nuances will emerge. These will be captured in a summary (4.3) at the end of chapter 4.

1.3 Special Challenges Demand Special Competencies: An Overview

What will be discussed in this book? The following seven chapters (2–8) attempt to offer responses to the current challenges. It is assumed that those who teach and lead at theological training schools must have a whole range of competencies. These are *foundational competencies* in the areas of education, history of theological education, theological foundations for theological education, as well as models and paradigms of theological education. These areas of knowledge and competency form a kind of matrix, a system of coordinates, which provides the necessary orientation throughout the course of theological education. Chapters 2–4 deal with these foundational competencies.

In addition, *skill competencies* will be discussed. The goal of these competencies is to acquire the abilities and proficiencies needed to carry out leadership responsibilities. Chapters 5–8 deal with these more practical topics.

There follows here an introduction to the content of the individual chapters:

Chapter 2: The Battle for Reforms and Renewal in Theological Education: An Introduction to the International Discussion

When we battle for renewal in theological education today in the context of all the aforesaid upheaval and change, we are not doing so in a historical vacuum. Although the current upheavals may seem particularly severe, we must remember that theological education has, in the course of history, undergone any number of changes. In the span of time since the end of the

Second World War, there have been particularly intensive efforts to reform theological education. These efforts have been exerted on a number of levels:

- Within the World Council of Churches, especially through the *Theological Education Fund* and its successor commissions *Programme on Theological Education* and *Ecumenical Theological Education*.
- Within evangelicalism through the work of ICETE.
- In North America through a variety of studies, often in connection with the Association of Theological Schools.
- The efforts to reform theological education within the universities in Germany and Switzerland.
- The development of free church and evangelical theological training institutions in German-speaking Europe, many of which are connected through the EEAA and/or through the Konferenz Bibeltreuer Ausbildungsstätten (KBA).

Chapter 2 outlines these reform efforts in order to gain a better understanding of the battle for the renewal of theological education, particularly in an international context and with a historical perspective.

Chapter 3: Foundations of Educational Theory: Traditions and Models of (Theological) Education

When we take a broad overview of the field of theological education, we see a multiplicity of forms and models. There is a notable variety available today in theological education – theological faculties at state universities, seminaries and academies run by churches and denominations, training courses offered for missionaries and preachers, evangelical Bible schools, and what is called Theological Education by Extension. Each form represents a distinct educational tradition, which has arisen in a specific historic context.

Those in positions of leadership in institutions of theological education need to understand which models and traditions have influenced the current situation. In addition, each training institution must find its identity among the many models and traditions. Three primary questions arise:

1) Which approaches and models, past or present, have shown that they can be effective in today's world?

2) Which secular educational traditions and models influence theological education today?

3) Which historic or more recent models of theological education do we see at work today?

Chapter 3 offers clarity in these areas.

Chapter 4: Biblical-Theological Foundations: Toward a Theology of Theological Education

Theological education happens within the tension between the theological-pedagogical ideals and the challenges of everyday reality. Within that tension it is all too easy for the challenges of the everyday world to overrun other considerations. That is why, in the midst of the battle for the renewal of theological education, theologians and educators have consistently called for us to avoid being so strongly ruled by pragmatic constraints that we lose sight of foundational theological coordinates.

In America in the years following the Second World War, it was H. Richard Niebuhr who, along with others in the aforementioned study, strongly insisted that basic theological considerations must be the starting point for the necessary reforms.[14] Later Edward Farley and David Kelsey also insisted that theological education must be anchored in theology.

For Robert Banks, none of these efforts go far enough. In *Reenvisioning Theological Education* he demands a truly radical reorientation of theological education based on the New Testament. His proposal, which he draws from Jesus and Paul, breaks with every tradition of theological education.

Within ICETE as well, the topic of "a theology of theological education" has received considerable attention. As early as the Manifesto of the 1980s we read in article 4: "Evangelical theological education as a whole today needs earnestly to pursue and recover a thorough-going theology of theological education." This concern continued to be voiced in the succeeding years and finds its latest expression in Volume 29, no. 3 of the *Evangelical Review of Theology* that is devoted in its entirety to the topic of a theology of theological education.

---

14. H. Richard Niebuhr, *The Purpose of the Church and Its Ministry: Reflections on the Aims of Theological Education* (New York: Harper, 1956).

There is, however, still much work to be done to arrive at a theology of theological education. Two questions dominate the horizon:

1) To what extent and under what hermeneutical assumptions can theological education lay its foundations in and be shaped by the Bible?

2) What might a thoughtful systematic theology of theological education look like?

Chapter 4 introduces some building blocks of a theology of theological education and proposes a possible synthesis. The last part of the chapter consists of conclusions based on the results of chapters 2–4, yielding a solid definition of theological education.

Chapter 5: Integrating Theory and Practice in Theological Education

A dominant characteristic of our modern culture, shaped as it is by analytical thinking, is the fragmentation of life as a whole. That holds true for theology and theological education as well. It is telling that Gerhard Ebeling begins his introduction to the study of theology with the following statement:

> The study of theology is beset by a crisis in orientation. Because our access to the unity and totality that constitutes the subject matter of theology is disrupted, the main domain of its subject matter and task has broken apart and crumbled into a bewildering conglomeration of individual items.[15]

But it's not just that theology as a field of study is fragmented. Fragmentation is evident at all levels:
- Mission and theology have been broken apart.
- Church goers and institutions are estranged.
- Theory and practice stand as enemies opposed to one another.
- And, as Ebeling so strongly expressed, curricula have split apart and crumbled into a confusing conglomeration of unconnected pieces.
- Spirituality (faith) and intellectual work (thought) are largely estranged.

---

15. Gerhard Ebeling, *The Study of Theology*, trans. Duane A. Priebe (Philadelphia: Fortress, 1978), 1.

- Training to think and training to do are often in conflict with one another.
- The chasm between the past (Bible, tradition) and the burning questions of the present and the future often seems insurmountable.
- Market-driven thinking has brought with it the effort to make curricula more flexible and more modular. This in turn, however, has undermined almost every effort to integrate curricula and has only increased fragmentation.

In light of such fragmentation it's not surprising that the call for integration and wholeness has grown louder. Consequently an entire chapter is devoted to the topic of "Integration in Theological Education," which will deal with the following:

- The current theory-practice debate can be re-examined based on the Greek concepts *Theoria*, *Praxis*, and *Poiesis*.
- The term *Praxis* leads us to the areas of "spirituality" and "personality development."
- The term *Theoria* causes us to rethink the intellectual sides of learning and education.
- In conjunction with the term *Poiesis* we will discuss competencies and skills.

These things are covered in chapter 5.

Chapter 6: Curriculum Development in Theological Education

One of the greatest vices in the leadership of institutions of higher learning is what I call "additionalism." Additionalism is an unmistakable sign that an institution is being poorly led. What is additionalism?

Let's look at current practice. All too quickly academic deans can get to the place where they simply maintain the curriculum. The core curriculum and the overall structure of the program have arisen over time and are more or less "given." Everything must merely be properly organized, assigned, and administered.

The calm that is created by merely maintaining and administering a given program of study will, however, be frequently disrupted by new demands. Both faculty and students may cite inadequacies in the curriculum and demand changes or additions. Some of these demands arise from the area of praxis: more training in counselling or missions, additional areas of pastoral theology, etc. Other requests may come from the faculty – the Old Testament professor wants more class hours devoted to Hebrew, the systematic theology professor wants more courses in ethics.

The academic deans soon find that they are in a reactive mode. And this situation leads to additionalism: add something here, place additional hours there, expand this course, supplement that course. And because the core curriculum must, of course, be maintained, the scope and length of study grows. The "conglomeration of individual items" becomes larger. And the essence fades and becomes more difficult to recognize. The crisis in orientation, of which Ebeling spoke, is taking its course.

The solution can only be found in ongoing proactive curriculum development. This requires that those responsible for the curriculum re-take control. They must shape and develop the curriculum with foresight, wisdom, and a panoramic perspective. To do this, they must master the 'craft' of curriculum development. Chapter 6 delivers the needed skills.

Chapter 7: Ensuring Quality in Theological Education

Quality control, evaluation, assessment, and accreditation are much used terms in the field of education as elsewhere. That's a new development and is something of a revolution. The September 2005 edition of the journal *Qualität und Zuverlässigkeit* includes, for example, the following:

> In Germany, quality control first became a topic in universities in the late 1990s. As a result of the Bologna process, the standardizing of educational systems throughout Europe, topics such as accreditation, evaluation, and quality assurance for curricula received great emphasis. As is common in times of budgetary stress, so-called output control was introduced into the landscape of higher education. The idea of managing budgets based on measurable outputs and results was like a revolution to many in academia.[16]

---

16. Hermann Wehr, "Die hohe Schule, Hochschul QM heute: Chancen und besondere Herausforderungen," *Qualität und Zuverlässigkeit* 50, no. 9 (2005): 28. Please note that all quotes from German works have been translated into English by the translator of this publication.

This revolution reached the world of theological education as well. Even earlier than was the case in the public universities, denominational/free-church seminaries and evangelical Bible schools were forced to face these challenges. As early as the 1970s these schools were seeking international recognition, and to this end they founded the European Evangelical Accrediting Association (EEAA) in 1979. This enabled them, in conjunction with other accrediting associations on the continent, to submit themselves to a recognized, standardized measure of quality. The result was that their bachelor's and master's degree programs achieved international recognition.

Along with the efforts to achieve quality assurance and receive accreditation, these institutions have sought to attain similar recognition to enable them to issue post-graduate degrees and recognized occupational certificates.

However, it is easy for the emphasis on quality assurance and evaluation to be overshadowed by the accreditation process and the pursuit of academic titles. It really comes down to this: that an education delivers what it promises. The first goal of quality control is not accreditation but remains to constantly improve the quality of education and learning. Accreditation, if it does its job, simply verifies that an institution pays attention to the quality of its academic program, makes ongoing improvements, and delivers what it promises.

Those who lead educational institutions must acquire the following skills and competencies:
- They must understand the terms quality assurance, evaluation, and accreditation.
- They must be familiar with a variety of quality assurance models and be able to choose those that are appropriate.
- They must understand how quality is defined in the field of higher education. They must also understand indicators and standards of quality.
- They must master a variety of evaluation tools and use them appropriately.
- They must be familiar with the advantages, limits, and processes associated with various accreditation models.

Chapter 7 introduces these questions and competencies.

Chapter 8: Leading Theological Education with Head, Hand, and Heart

As has already been mentioned, leadership skills become increasingly important in the context of higher education today, a context that is shaped by the methods and values of the business world and the marketplace. "Leadership" and "management" are terms that have become quite fashionable. In the early phases of this development, business management tended to become the example that was looked to. Only with the passage of time were models of leadership and management developed that were tailored to the needs of educational institutions. Indebted to the work of Peter Th. Senn, this book introduces a leadership model for theological schools that is built on the words *head*, *hand*, and *heart*. Specifically, this model is about:

Head	Strategy: Mentors and Models
	→ Orientation
Hand	Structures: Organization and Resources
	→ Coordination
Heart	Culture: Relationships and Climate
	→ Motivation

Chapter 8 delves into this model.

2

The Battle for Reforms and Renewal in Theological Education: An Introduction to the International Discussion

Anyone in the present day who proposes to make theological education relevant and future oriented, stands in the stream of history. No one starts at zero. No one stands in an historical vacuum. For this reason, it would seem essential at this point to offer an introduction to the history of theological education. This is not feasible, however, for a number of reasons. For one, there are scarcely any written histories of theological education that can be referenced.[1] One would have to undertake a thorough examination of the sources. This, however, would go far beyond the scope of this handbook.

Nevertheless this chapter will attempt to provide a glimpse into the history of theological education. We'll undertake this from the perspective of

---

1. Edward Farley, who has produced a typological outline of the history of theological education, writes: "There is nothing that even approaches a comprehensive history of theological education," in *Theologia. The Fragmentation and Unity of Theological Education* (Philadelphia: Fortress Press, 1983), 45. The few sources which he then cites deal with only portions of this history. A comprehensive representation of the history of theological education has yet to be written.

the present and will examine the recent discussion of the future of theological education. That will necessitate any number of side trips through history.[2]

A glance at the literature published over the past fifty years on the topic of theological education reveals a frequent use of terms like "reform" and "renewal." In 1999 Robert Banks spoke of *Reenvisioning Theological Education* and pressed for a completely new view of theological education, grounded in the New Testament. A few years earlier the same line of thinking was to be found in Robert W. Ferris' *Renewal in Theological Education: Strategies for Change*. Yet the call for reform and renewal of theological education can be dated much earlier and is in no way limited to the English-speaking world. In 1965 Wolfgang Herrmann and Gerd Lautner introduced their work, *Theologiestudium: Entwurf einer Reform* [The Study of Theology: a Reform Proposal], and made the case that in the (then) present situation, not just "repairs" were needed but rather far-reaching "reforms".[3] Almost forty years later (2002) Hans-Günter Heimbrock and Matthias von Kriegstein published their work, *Theologische Bildungsprozesse gestalten: Schritte zur Ausbildungsreform* [Processes of Theological Training: Steps to Educational Reform]. For more than fifty years[4] efforts have been underway to reform, renew and restore theological education. Anyone who is leading the way today in the renewal or reform of theological education is standing in the line of succession of earlier reform efforts.

---

2. The presentation in this chapter will omit two streams which are certainly worthy of inclusion. (1) First, the history and contribution of Catholic theological education. Catholic perspective and experience is represented in some ecumenical writings as well as in some contributions from the Association of Theological Schools (ATS). For the European context Adrian Loretan, ed., *Theologische Fakultäten an europäischen Universitäten* (Münster: LIT Verlag, 2004), is a valuable source. (2) The situation is similar when it comes to the more recent contribution of the Pentecostal-charismatic churches and movements. Given the size of the movement and its missionary dynamic, together with the tremendous need for leadership training, the Pentecostal contribution to theological education must not be overlooked. There are, however, very few studies to date which make this contribution accessible. One example is Cheryl Bridges Johns, *Pentecostal Formation: A Pedagogy among the Oppressed* (Sheffield: Sheffield Academic Press, 1993). As well as Matthias Wenk, "Do We Need a Distinct European Pentecostal/Charismatic Approach to Theological Education?" (unpublished manuscript).

3. Wolfgang Herrmann and Gerd Lautner, *Theologiestudium. Entwurf einer Reform* (Munich: Kaiser, 1965), 11.

4. The material will show that it is legitimate to begin our presentation after the Second World War. The trail of reform can be traced much farther back than that, however. Interestingly, within the tradition of Western evangelical theological education, the trail always leads back to the Pietistic movement (Spener) and to Schleiermacher.

This chapter introduces us to the discussion of recent decades. With an eye to brevity, no attempt at a comprehensive presentation of the developments and debates will be made. Instead an introduction to a variety of important contributions to those debates will be presented. Those who are interested will receive here an introduction to the literature and are encouraged to pursue further study on their own.

We begin this overview with an outline of the international discussion, in both ecumenical and evangelical circles. We will then turn to recent developments in North America, and in conclusion we will look at German-speaking Europe.

We will then attempt to present the important contribution of the literature and to summarize the paradigmatic changes in the midst of which we find ourselves.

2.1 Impulses for Reform from the World of Missions and the Ecumenical Movement

On the international scene after World War II, movement toward reform of theological education came from the world of missions. The paradigm shift in world missions which occurred in the twentieth century – from a colonial to a post-colonial paradigm – caused a fundamental re-thinking of theological education. On the one hand it was clear that the so-called young churches desperately needed solid theological training to sustain their continued expansion. On the other hand theological education was distinctly Western, and the introduction of theological education into the Majority World occurred through the export (or import) of Western models.

2.1.1 From the Theological Education Fund to the Program on Ecumenical Theological Education

It was from this perspective that "theological education" was included in the agenda of the International Missionary Council – specifically in 1958 on the occasion of the World Missions Conference in Accra, Ghana. The Theological Education Fund was founded at that time with the goal of bringing a number of theological seminaries in the former "mission fields" up to Western standards, which for the most part was accomplished.⁵

In 1978 the Theological Education Fund (TEF) was renamed the Programme on Theological Education (PTE). This nomenclature was later expanded to Programme on Ecumenical Theological Education (ETE). In 1978 on the occasion of the name change from TEF to PTE Lesslie Newbigin wrote:

> It was not just that the theological schools of the Third World needed to be brought up to the "best" Western standards. It was the question whether these standards really are the best, whether the models of ministerial formation in Europe and North America are really the right ones for the Third World – or even for the areas where they have been developed.⁶

Newbigin hit the nail on the head. Are Western models of education really helpful for the churches in the Majority World? And as a corollary question for the Western churches: Are these models even helpful for the churches in Europe and North America?

Since the integration of the International Missionary Council into the World Council of Churches occurred during this same period – between 1952 and 1961 – a second thing became clear: missions and the church belong together. Therefore a division in theological education was untenable: here in the West theological education for the church, and there in the Majority World theological education for missionary activity. Rather the focus must always be on the church and its mission and on theological education as a function of this missional church.

As a result, it became less important to ensure "development aid" in terms of theological education but rather to ensure that theological education was encouraged and supported all across the entire spectrum of the ecumenical movement and missions worldwide. In this regard the voice and the contribution of the churches in the Majority World were deemed essential.

---

5. Cf. Lesslie Newbigin, "Theological Education in a World Perspective" in *Ministerial Formation* 4 (1978): 3.
6. Ibid.

The direction of the growing trend is appropriately captured in the title of Christine Leinemann-Perrin's work: *Training for a Relevant Ministry*.[7] That was and is the point. Theological education must be relevant for the church and its mission, even if that means painful changes for some Western-style schools. And when Leinemann-Perrin points in her summary to the amount of work still to be done ("The Unfinished Task")[8], she is certainly right, even though thirty years have since passed.

2.1.2 Impulses from the International Ecumenical Discussion

The impulses that came from the international ecumenical process are to a great degree connected with the English-language journal *Ministerial Formation*. This publication provides an inspirational platform for an international network of educators. Especially for those who work internationally, *Ministerial Formation* is a rich source of reflection and stimulating ideas.

What specific ideas shaped the international discussion about theological education? In his previously cited 1978 article Newbigin mentions three areas:

1) Regarding the **structure** of theological education – sociological questions: The mere introduction of the new term *ministerial formation* indicates a new direction. It is no longer just about mere academic theological education. Rather it is about training for ministry in the church and in missions. The elitist Western model of theological education as training for professional clergy is called into question. The young churches are not well served when an elite group is trained to high Western academic standards using Western finances. Instead ways must be found to train leaders and volunteers at the grassroots level, right where they are. What's at stake is the equipping of the people of God to minister in this world.[9]

2) Regarding the **methods** of theological education – pedagogical questions: The goal of accomplishing this kind of *ministerial formation* at the grassroots level demands, of necessity, new methods. Formal training

---

7. Christine Leinemann-Perrin, *Training for a Relevant Ministry* (Geneva: WCC, 1981). The complete study by Leinemann-Perrin analyzes the work of the TEF/PTE from 1958–1978.
8. Ibid., 232–233.
9. This perspective is well-expressed in the title of a book by Ross Kinsler, *Ministry by the People: Theological Education by Extension* (Geneva: WCC, 1983).

at educational institutions geographically far removed from where the students normally live simply will not do. In the final analysis such Western models encourage an elitism within the people of God that is anything but desirable. Pedagogical models and methods are needed that bring training and education to the people where they are. The solution has become known as Theological Education by Extension (TEE). TEE is an educational concept that is not institution-centred (a "come" structure) but rather person-centred (a "go" structure). This has raised any number of foundational pedagogical questions. Central among these is the relationship between and sequencing of theory and practice. The idea behind and the introduction of TEE is closely tied to F. Ross Kinsler. One cannot study TEE without encountering his books and articles.

3) Regarding the **content** of theological education – theological questions: Newbigin sees the critical questioning of Western theological education in the realm of content.[10] What justification is there for teaching Western theology as normative around the world? Do Christians of the so-called young churches have the right to read the Bible – independently, in their own context, without patronizing from the West – and in so doing possibly set their own distinct theological accents? The answer is called "contextualization," not in the sense of application to a foreign context, but rather in the sense of a theology developed within a specific context. It cannot be overlooked that these developments of the 60s and 70s were inspired to a great extent by the thinking of liberation theology, including the teaching of Paulo Freires.[11]

Newbigin is certainly right about the scope and importance of this paradigmatic change in theological education when he contends that it is not simply about finding new models of education for the Majority World. Instead, it is more about a radical questioning and re-thinking of traditional Western theological education.

It would be beyond the scope of this volume to try to outline all the thinking and discussion about theological education within the ecumenical movement from that point to the present day. A significant contribution

---

10. Newbigin, "Theological Education," 5.
11. Ibid., 4. Newbigin recognizes this connection. As do the early writings of Ross Kinsler, *The Extension Movement in Theological Education* (Pasadena: William Carey Library, 1981).

came with the multi-year study "Viability of Ministerial Formation and Ecumenical Theological Education Today," which concluded with the Global Consultation on Theological Education in Oslo in 1996. Excerpts from this consultation were published in German-speaking Europe by the Evangelisches Missionswerk. Prior to the 1996 consultation Dietrich Werner published a pamphlet entitled *Theologie zum Leben bringen: Anforderungen an eine zukunftsorientierte Ausbildung* [Bringing Theology to Life: The Call for a Future-oriented Education].[12] Later the comprehensive *Impulse für eine Kirche von morgen: Beiträge zur ökumenischen-theologischen Ausbildung* [Ideas for a Church for Tomorrow: Suggestions for Ecumenical Theological Education] was published.[13]

The office of Ecumenical Theological Education within the World Council of Churches began a number of meaningful projects as part of the events in Edinburgh marking the Council's hundred-year anniversary 1910–1920. Worth special mention are the "Global Survey on Theological Education" and the momentous collection of one hundred essays, *Theological Education in World Christianity*.[14]

In summary it can be stated that a paradigm shift has occurred since the 1950s internationally and in the ecumenical sphere. We will come back to this at the end of this chapter. The following points can now be made:

- There is a new perspective in theological education, focusing on the church and her mission. Critical voices from the Majority World have become increasingly loud, insisting that traditional Western forms of education are inadequate and incapable of accomplishing what they intend. The chasm between academic theology and the real grass roots world is simply too vast.
- Theological education is therefore now consciously understood as *ministerial formation* (which is also the title of the corresponding journal of the Ecumenical Council of Churches).

---

12. Dietrich Werner, *Theologie zum Leben bringen. Anforderungen an eine zukunftsorientierte Ausbildung*, EMW Informationen 105 (Hamburg: Evangelisches Missionswerk, 1995).

13. Evangelisches Missionwerk, *Impulse für eine Kirche von morgen. Beiträge zur ökumenischen-theologischen Ausbildung*, Weltmission heute 27 (Hamburg: Evangelisches Missionswerk, 1997).

14. Information about the activities and the resources of the World Council of Churches devoted to theological education can be found at www.oikoumene.org/en/what-we-do/ecumenical-theological-education.

- Because the church is missional by nature, theological education that wants to serve the church must also be missional by nature.
- Known as Theological Education by Extension, a revolution began that said farewell to a centralized structure of education limited to an institution in a specific location (come structure), in favor of a decentralized system that takes the training to the people where they live (go structure).
- Theology can no longer be formulated and taught without taking into consideration the contextualization of all theology.
- The call for holism has grown ever louder. Faith and thought, theory and practice, science and spirituality dare not be separated any longer. They must be integrated.

Additional Literature

Dietrich Werner, David Esterline, Namson Kang, and Joshva Raja, eds. *Handbook of Theological Education in World Christianity*. Eugene, OR: Wipf and Stock Publishers, 2010.

Dietrich Werner. *Theological Education in World Christianity: Ecumenical Perspectives and Future Priorities*. Tainan, Taiwan: Programme for Theology and Cultures in Asia, 2011.

2.2 Impulses for Reform within the International Evangelical Movement

By 1961 at the latest, after the integration of the International Missionary Council into the World Council of Churches, there was an independent movement within the world of evangelical missions. This next section deals with the evangelical contribution to the renewal of theological education.

2.2.1 The Missionary Movement and Theological Education *by Extension*

How strongly theological education was seen from a missions perspective within the evangelical movement is readily apparent in the writings of people like Ralph D. Winter, Ted Ward, Kenneth B. Mulholland, Robert W. Ferris, Robert L. Youngblood, and Robert Banks. These evangelical educators are not so much concerned with what theological education should look like in the context of Western educational traditions. Instead these authors are moved by the burning question of what theological education should look like in light of the needs of the Majority World and world missions.

All of these evangelical educators have themselves worked in international missions, and they plead for forms of theological education along the lines of TEE and other alternative models. Their central concern is for training that is highly practical for the work of missions (*mission training*).[15]

2.2.2 The International Council for Evangelical Theological Education and the Manifesto

Within the framework of the World Evangelical Alliance, the International Council for Evangelical Theological Education (ICETE) is dedicated to the topic of theological education.[16] ICETE was founded in 1980 and can be understood as part of the self-definition that was necessary within the evangelical movement in the 1960s following the break with the World Council of Churches. The Congress for World Evangelism in Lausanne in 1974 and the Lausanne movement that grew out of it may be seen as essential steps in the journey of evangelicalism to establish its own identity. From the 1974 Lausanne congress arose calls for the encouragement and renewal of theological education.

The thinking within ICETE during the 1980s can be traced in the pages of *Theological Education Today*, a supplement to the *Theological News*, published by the Theological Commission of the World Evangelical Alliance. The "Manifesto on the Renewal of Evangelical Theological Education" that was drafted in the 1980s may be seen as an early high point of the thinking within ICETE.[17]

---

15. See, for example, the contributions in William Taylor, ed., *Internationalizing Missionary Training. A Global Perspective* (Exeter: Paternoster Press; Grand Rapids: Baker Book House, 1991).

16. Until 1996 under the name of *International Council of Accrediting Agencies*. Information about ICETE can be found at http://www.icete-edu.org/.

17. Cf. Robert W. Ferris, "Renewal of Theological Education: Commitments, Models, and the ICAA Manifesto," *Evangelical Review of Theology* 14, no. 1 (1990): 64–77.

ICETE Manifesto on the Renewal of Evangelical Theological Education[18]

Preface

The origins of the Manifesto go back to the meetings of the International Council for Evangelical Theological Education (ICETE), held at Chongoni, Malawi, in 1981. As a new body linking programmes of evangelical theological education worldwide, ICETE determined to draw up for public consideration a "Manifesto on the Renewal of Evangelical Theological Education." After wide consultation and several revisions, the following statement was unanimously adopted by ICETE in 1983, and was subsequently published in *Theological Education Today* 16:2 (April–June 1984) 1–6, and in the *Evangelical Review of Theology* 8:1 (April 1984), 136–143. This second edition (1990) incorporates minor changes in wording and presentation, together with a revised preface.

ICETE wanted a very specific kind of statement for its Manifesto. It wanted a statement that would clearly articulate the broad consensus on renewal which it believed already exits – often unrecognized – among evangelical theological educators worldwide. And, realizing how far short evangelical theological education often falls with respect to such renewal, ICETE also wanted a document which could provide encouragement, guidance and critical challenge in pursuing renewal.

In using the Manifesto one must therefore carefully recognize both what it is trying to do, and what it is not trying to do. The Manifesto is trying to define those aspects of the renewal agenda for evangelical theological education which appear already to have gained very broad agreement, but which nevertheless have not yet been attained in large measure in practice. The Manifesto is not trying to present a comprehensive model for quality theological education. Rather it is attempting to identify certain specific gaps in our achievement of such a model. Nor is the Manifesto seeking to designate every form of renewal which ought to be pursued. Rather it is attempting to identify those particular aspects on which consensus now seems to exist. The expectation is that, once we recognize how much agreement already exists among us in what we have yet to achieve, we will be able to work together for its implementation in a better climate of understanding, with more attentiveness, with a greater precision of focus, and with an increased motivation to explore additional points of agreement. The Manifesto is intended therefore not as a final step, but as a specific, practical first step in an ongoing cooperative venture in renewal. Through republication of this Manifesto in a second edition, ICETE and its constituent movements seek once again to

---

18. http://www.icete-edu.org/manifesto.html

declare publicly their commitment to the renewal of evangelical theological education, and to secure for themselves and for others a continuing sense of common direction in pursuing such renewal.

Introduction

We who serve within evangelical theological education throughout the world today, and who find ourselves now linked together in growing international cooperation, wish to give united voice to our longing and prayer for the renewal of evangelical theological education today – for a renewal in form and in substance, a renewal in vision and in power, a renewal in commitment and direction.

We rightly seek such renewal in light of the pivotal significance of theological education in biblical perspective. Insofar as theological education concerns the formation of leadership for the church of Christ in its mission, to that extent theological education assumes a critically strategic biblical importance. Scripture mandates the church, it mandates leadership service within that church, and it thereby as well mandates a vital concern with the formation of such leadership. For this reason the quest for effective renewal in evangelical theological education in our day is a biblically generated quest.

We rightly seek such renewal in light also of the crisis of leadership facing the church of Christ around the world. The times are weighted with unusual challenge and unusual opportunity, demanding of the church exceptional preparation of its leadership. In many areas the church is faced with surging growth, of such proportions that it cannot always cope. In many areas the church is also faced with open hostility without and hidden subversion within, distracting and diverting it from its calling. Everywhere the opportunities and challenges take on new and confusing forms. The times demand an urgent quest for the renewal of theological education patterns, that the church in its leadership may be equipped to fulfill its high calling under God.

We rightly seek such renewal also in light of the condition of evangelical theological education in our day. We recognize among ourselves exciting examples of that renewed vitality in theological education which we desire to see everywhere put to the service of our Lord. Things are being done right within traditional patterns and within nontraditional patterns, which need attention, encouragement and emulation. We also recognize that there are examples in our midst, usually all too close at hand, where things are not being done right. We confess this with shame. Traditional forms are being maintained only because they are traditional, and radical forms pursued only because they are radical – and the formation of effective leadership for the church is seriously hindered. We heartily welcome the wise critiques of evangelical theological education which have arisen in recent times, which have forced us to think much more carefully both about our purposes in theological education and about the best means for achieving those purposes. We believe that there is now emerging around the world a wide consensus among evangelical theological educators that a challenge to renewal is upon us, and upon us from our Lord. We believe that there is also emerging a broad agreement on the central patterns that such a renewal should take. New times are upon us, and new opportunities. We wish to pursue these opportunities, and seize them, in obedience to the Lord. Therefore, in order to provide encouragement, guidance and critical challenge to ourselves and to all others who may look to us for direction, we wish to assert and endorse the following agenda for the renewal of theological education worldwide today, and to pledge ourselves to its practical energetic implementation. We do not presume that we are here setting forth either a full or a final word on these matters. But we do make this expression after extended prayerful reflection, and we wish to offer the hand of warm fellowship to all those who may likewise feel led to endorse these proposals, and to express to them an invitation to practical collaboration in this quest, for the sake of Jesus Christ our Lord, the evangelization of the world, and the establishment and edification of the church.

Therefore, we now unitedly affirm that, to fulfill its God-given mandate, evangelical theological education today worldwide must vigorously seek to introduce and reinforce . . .

1) Contextualization

Our programmes of theological education must be designed with deliberate reference to the contexts in which they serve. We are at fault that our curricula so often appear either to have been imported whole from abroad, or to have been handed down unaltered from the past. The selection of courses for the curriculum, and the content of every course in the curriculum, must be specifically suited to the context of service. To become familiar with the context in which the biblical message is to be lived and preached is no less vital to a well-rounded programme than to become familiar with the content of that biblical message. Indeed, not only in what is taught, but also in structure and operation our theological programmes must demonstrate that they exist in and for their specific context, in governance and administration, in staffing and finance, in teaching styles and class assignments, in library resources and student services. This we must accomplish, by God's grace.

2) Church-Focused Orientation

Our programmes of theological education must orient themselves pervasively in terms of the Christian community being served. We are fault when our programmes operate merely in terms of some traditional or personal notion of theological education. At every level of design and operation our programmes must be visibly determined by a close attentiveness to the needs and expectations of the Christian community we serve. To this end we must establish multiple modes of ongoing interaction between programme and church, both at official and at grassroots levels, and regularly adjust and develop the programme in the light of these contacts. Our theological programmes must become manifestly of the church, through the church and for the church. This we must accomplish, by God's grace.

3) Strategic Flexibility

Our programmes of theological education must nurture a much greater strategic flexibility in carrying out their task. Too long we have been content to serve the formation of only one type of leader for the church, at only one level of need, by only one educational approach. If we are to serve faithfully the leadership needs of the body of Christ, then our programmes singly and in combination must begin to demonstrate much greater flexibility in at least three respects. Firstly, we must attune ourselves to the full range of leadership roles required, and not attend only to the most familiar or most basic. To provide for pastoral formation, for example, is not enough. We must also respond creatively, in cooperation with other programmes, to the church's leadership needs in areas such as Christian education, youth work, evangelism, journalism and communications, TEE, counselling, denominational and parachurch administration, seminary and Bible school staffing, community development, and social outreach. Secondly, our programmes must learn to take account of all academic levels of need, and not become frozen in serving only one level. We must not presume that the highest level of training is the only strategic need, nor conversely that the lowest level is the only strategic need. We must deliberately participate in multi-level approaches to leadership training, worked out on the basis of an assessment of the church's leadership needs as a whole at all levels. Thirdly, we must embrace a greater flexibility in the educational modes by which we touch the various levels of leadership need, and not limit our approach to a single traditional or radical pattern. We must learn to employ, in practical combination with others, both residential and extension systems, both formal and non-formal styles, as well, for example, as short-term courses, workshops, evening classes, holiday institutes, in-service training, travelling seminars, refresher courses, and continuing education programmes. Only by such flexibility in our programmes can the church's full spectrum of leadership needs begin to be met, and we ourselves become true to our full mandate. This we must accomplish, by God's grace.

4) Theological Grounding

Evangelical theological education as a whole today needs earnestly to pursue and recover a thorough going theology of theological education. We are at fault that we so readily allow our bearings to be set for us by the latest enthusiasms, or by secular rationales, or by sterile traditions. It is not sufficient that we attend to the context of our service and to the Christian community being served. We must come to perceive our task, and even these basic points of reference, within the larger setting of God's total truth and God's total plan. Such a shared theological perception of our calling is largely absent from our midst. We must together take immediate and urgent steps to seek, elaborate and possess a biblically informed theological basis for our calling in theological education, and to allow every aspect of our service to become rooted and nurtured in this soil. This we must accomplish, by God's grace.

5) Continuous Assessment

Our programmes of theological education must be dominated by a rigorous practice of identifying objectives, assessing outcomes, and adjusting programmes accordingly. We have been too easily satisfied with educational intentions that are unexpressed or only superficially examined, or too general to be of directional use. We have been too ready to assume our achievements on the basis of vague impressions, chance reports, or crisis-generated inquiries. We have been culpably content with evaluating our programmes only irregularly, or haphazardly, or under stress. We hear our Lord's stern words about the faithful stewardship He requires in His servants, but we have largely failed to apply this to the way we conduct our programmes of theological education. Firstly, we must let our programmes become governed by objectives carefully chosen, clearly defined, and continuously reviewed. Secondly, we must accept it as a duty, and not merely beneficial, to discern and evaluate the results of our programmes, so that there may be a valid basis for judging the degree to which intentions are being achieved. This requires that we institute means for reviewing the actual performance of our graduates in relation to our stated objectives. Thirdly, we must build into the normal operational patterns of our programmes a regular review and continual modification and adjustment of all aspects of governance, staffing, educational programme, facilities, and student services, so that actual achievements might be brought to approximate more and more closely our stated objectives. Only by such provisions for continuous assessment can we be true to the rigorous demands of biblical stewardship. This we must accomplish, by God's grace.

6) Community Life

Our programmes of theological education must demonstrate the Christian pattern of community. We are at fault that our programmes so often seem little more than Christian academic factories, efficiently producing graduates. It is biblically incumbent on us that our programmes function as deliberately nurtured Christian educational communities, sustained by those modes of community that are biblically commended and culturally appropriate. To this end it is not merely decorative but biblically essential that the whole educational body

– staff and students – not only learns together, but plays and eats and cares and worships and works together. This we must accomplish, by God's grace.

7) Integrated Programme

Our programmes of theological education must combine spiritual and practical with academic objectives in one holistic integrated educational approach. We are at fault that we so often focus educational requirements narrowly on cognitive attainments, while we hope for student growth in other dimensions but leave it largely to chance. Our programmes must be designed to attend to the growth and equipping of the whole man of God. This means, firstly, that our programmes must deliberately foster the spiritual formation of the student. We must look for a spiritual development centred in total commitment to the lordship of Christ, progressively worked outward by the power of the Spirit into every department of life. We must devote as much time and care and structural designing to facilitate this type of growth as we readily and rightly provide for cognitive growth. This also means, secondly, that our programmes must foster achievement in the practical skills of Christian leadership. We must no longer introduce these skills only within a classroom setting. We must incorporate into our educational arrangements and requirements a guided practical field experience in precisely those skills which the student will need to employ in service after completion of the programme. We must provide adequately supervised and monitored opportunities for practical vocational field experience. We must blend practical and spiritual with academic in our educational programmes, and thus equip the whole man of God for service. This we must accomplish, by God's grace.

8) Servant Moulding

Through our programmes of theological education students must be moulded to the styles of leadership appropriate to their intended biblical role within the body of Christ. We are at fault that our programmes so readily produce the characteristics of elitism and so rarely produce the characteristics of servanthood. We must not merely hope that the true marks of Christian servanthood will appear. We must actively promote biblically approved styles of leadership through modeling by the staff and through active encouragement, practical exposition, and deliberate reinforcement. This we must accomplish, by God's grace.

9) Instructional Variety

Our programmes of theological education must vigorously pursue the use of a variety of educational teaching methodologies, evaluated and promoted in terms of their demonstrated effectiveness, especially with respect to the particular cultural context. It is not right to become fixed in one method merely because it is traditional, or familiar, or even avant-garde. Lecturing is by no means the only appropriate teaching method, and frequently not the best. Presumably the same may be said of programmed instruction. Our programmes need to take practical steps to introduce and train their staff in new methods of instruction, in a spirit of innovative flexibility and experimentation, always governed by the standards of effectiveness. This we must accomplish, by God's grace.

10) A Christian Mind

Our programmes of theological education need much more effectively to model and inculcate a pattern of holistic thought that is openly and wholesomely centred around biblical truth as the integrating core of reality. It is not enough merely to teach an accumulation of theological truths. Insofar as every human culture is governed at its core by an integrating world view, our programmes must see that the rule of the Lord is planted effectively at that point in the life of the student. This vision of the theologically integrated life needs to be so lived and taught in our programmes that we may say and show in a winsomely biblical manner that theology does indeed matter, and students may go forth experiencing this centring focus in all its biblical richness and depth. This we must accomplish, by God's grace.

11) Equipping for Growth

Our programmes of theological education need urgently to refocus their patterns of training to encouraging and facilitating self-directed learning. It is not enough that through our programmes we bring a student to a state of preparedness for ministry. We need to design academic requirements so that we are equipping the student not only to complete the course but also for a lifetime of ongoing learning and development and growth. To this end we must also assume a much greater role in the placement of our students, as part of our proper duty, and experiment in ways of maintaining ongoing supportive links and services with them after graduation, especially in the early years of ministry. By these means each student should come to experience through the programme not the completion of a development but the launching of an ongoing development. This we must accomplish, by God's grace.

12) Cooperation

Our progammes of theological education must pursue contact and collaboration among themselves for mutual support, encouragement, edification and cross-fertilization. We are at fault that so often in evangelical theological education we attend merely to our own assignments under God. Others in the same calling need us, and we need them. The biblical notion of mutuality needs to be much more visibly expressed and pragmatically pursued among our theological programmes. Too long we have acquiesced in an isolation of effort that denies the larger body of Christ, thus failing both ourselves and Christ's body. The times in which we serve, no less than biblical expectations, demand of each of us active ongoing initiatives in cooperation. This we must accomplish, by God's grace.

May God help us to be faithful to these affirmations and commitments, to the glory of God and the fulfillment of his purposes.

This evangelical Manifesto sets accents that are typical for evangelicalism (Bible, spirituality, missions), yet its assessment of the challenges and urgency of the global situation is similar to that articulated in the ecumenical documents cited earlier. Thus the Manifesto provides further evidence documenting the paradigm shift in theological education.

In the 1980s Robert W. Ferris conducted an international research study of educational institutions based upon the criteria of the Manifesto. This study has been published under the title *Renewal in Theological Education: Strategies for Change*.[19] The study shows that the Manifesto is a suitable instrument to serve as an orientation point for the renewal of theological education.

Flowing out of this, the global discussion points within the evangelical movement are evident especially at the conferences of ICETE which occur every three years. Topics such as "Theological Education in Global Partnership" and "Theological Education in the tension between Bible and Cultural Context" dominate the agenda.[20]

Of special significance is the ICETE's consultation which, from 2009–2012, concerned itself with the global standards for theological studies at the doctoral level. The result, documented in three statements, is a milestone in future-oriented global partnership in theological education.[21]

Another international conference held in Boston in 2012 also dealt with the topics "The Future of Theological Education" and "Global Partnership." This conference took place within the framework of the Lausanne movement

---

19. Robert W. Ferris, *Renewal in Theological Education: Strategies for Change* (Wheaton, IL: The Billy Graham Center, 1990).
20. Documents from the conference can be found at www.icete-edu.org/consultations/index.htm.
21. The key document of the ICETE doctoral consultation, the *Beirut Benchmarks* can be found at www.icete-edu.org/beirut. This document and the other two documents on the topics of Professional Doctorate and ICETE Best Practice Guidelines for Doctoral Programs has now been published. See Ian Shaw, *Best Practice Guidelines for Doctoral Programs* (Carlisle: Langham Global Library, 2015).

and under the banner of the conference title Consultation on Global Theological Education. It sought to deal yet again with critical questions arising in light of a global Christianity in the throes of change. How must theological education adapt if the gravitational centre of Christendom is no longer in the North or the West but in the global South?[22]

2.3 Voices from the Majority World

Within both of the processes already addressed, in the evangelical and the ecumenical worlds, the influence of Christians in the Majority World has been evident. The following section seeks to make clear that theologians from the Southern hemisphere have also raised their voices independently beyond the scope of what has already been referenced.

This is documented by many contributions in the journal of the World Council of Churches mentioned above, *Ministerial Formation*.

A strong contribution came from the Fraternidad Teologica Latinoamerica, documented in a volume edited by René Padilla, *New Alternatives in Theological Education*.[23]

The British missions theologian Andrew Kirk, informed and motivated by many years of experience in Latin America, suggests an alternative model of theological education in his work *The Mission of Theology and Theology as Mission*.[24]

The more recent discussions and developments within theological education can also be traced in the activities of the continental and regional associations of seminaries. In the ecumenical world these are the members of the World Conference of Associations of Theological Institutions (WOCATI; www.wocati.org). In the evangelical world these are the members of the International Council for Evangelical Theological Education (ICETE; www.icete-edu.org).

---

22. Reports and documents from this consultation can be found at www.lausanne.org/en/gatherings/issue-based/event/4-consultation-on-global-theological-education.html

23. René Padilla, *New Alternatives in Theological Education* (Oxford: Regnum, 1988).

24. Andrew Kirk, *The Mission of Theology and Theology as Mission* (Valley Forge, PA: Trinity Press International, 1997). Kirk later described his proposal more precisely in "Reenvisioning the Theological Curriculum as if the Missio Dei Mattered," in *Theological Education as Mission*, ed. Peter Penner (Schwarzenfeld: Neufeld, 2005), 15–38.

2.4 Reform of Theological Education in North America

Thus far our attention has been on the ecumenical and evangelical movements respectively, as well as the voices from the Majority World and the world of missions. Now this chapter and those that follow will have a geographic focus. We will begin with North America and then turn to the European and the German-speaking context.

The development of academic theological education in North America in the twentieth century is closely connected with the Association of Theological Schools (ATS).[25] The ATS has its origins in a series of conferences of theological schools that were convened every two years, beginning in 1918. The Association was formally founded in 1936 and set definitive standards for quality assurance and accreditation. Today more than 250 schools belong to the ATS, most of these in the USA, but some in Canada as well. About a third of these schools are the theological faculties of larger colleges or universities. Two-thirds are independent theological seminaries. Evangelical, Catholic and Orthodox schools belong to the ATS. Included are schools associated with the so-called mainline churches and denominations, as well as those associated with other churches of evangelical, liberal, or Pentecostal bent (given the name "free church" in many parts of Europe).[26]

Even this brief description of the ATS suggests that the situation in North America (particularly in the USA) is different from that of German-speaking Europe. The majority of theological schools are not associated with state/public universities. They are in fact private institutions, in many cases church- or denomination-funded. Early on, the ATS became an umbrella organization that spanned across theological and denominational boundaries. Its purpose is to oversee the accreditation of schools, that is, to ensure quality, to maintain comparable standards, and to grant academic degrees and titles.

The reform process in theological education over the past fifty years in North America can, therefore, be readily traced by examining the developments in the ATS. It is not possible, of course, to do that here in any

---

25. Information about the ATS available at http://www.ats.edu/
26. Along with the ATS, which includes theological schools that offer academic programs to train pastors, there is also within the evangelical spectrum the Accrediting Association of Bible Colleges (AABC), which changed its name in 2004 to the Association for Biblical Higher Education (ABHE). More information is available at http://www.abhe.org/. Cf. Robert Banks, *Reenvisioning Theological Education* (Grand Rapids: Eerdmans Publishing, 1999), 7–8.

great detail. The journal *Theological Education*, which has been published by the ATS since 1964, documents the discussions about reform and the processes of change.[27]

The reform process is marked by one great tension. On the one hand is the pressure upon the seminaries to "produce" qualified graduates for professional ministry who work pragmatically and efficiently in the church. This pragmatic orientation of theological education began to arise after the Second World War in conjunction with a shift in emphasis within higher education generally from "*liberal* education" to "*relevant* education."[28]

This pragmatic quest for efficiency stands in contrast to the call for more fundamental theological considerations. Ever since the 1950s a considerable number of renowned authors have demanded that the reform of theological education must grow out of the soil of fundamental theological discussions and must not be shaped primarily by the pursuit of pragmatism. Some of these voices will be introduced more fully in what follows.

At the top of the list stands a study by H. Richard Niebuhr published in 1956. We begin the more detailed presentation (2.4.1) with Niebuhr.

Between 1983 and 2006 a number of seminal works were published. The initial spark, as it were, for this decade of reflection may be found in Edward Farley's *Theologia*. After that came:[29]

1985	Joseph C. Hough Jr. and John B. Cobb Jr., eds. *Christian Identity and Theological Education*. Chico, CA: Scholars Press.
1985	The Mud Flower Collective. *God's Fierce Whimsy: Christian Feminism and Theological Education*. New York: Pilgrim Press.

---

27. Past issues of *Theological Education* as well as many additional texts may be downloaded in their complete versions at http://www.ats.edu/Resources/PublicationsPresentations/Pages/default.aspx.

28. The parallels to the German terms *bildung* (education) and *ausbildung* (training) are obvious. Regarding this upheaval in North America see Nancy Murphy, "A Theology of Education," in *Mennonite Higher Education in a Post-Christian World*, ed. Harry Huebner (Winnipeg: CMBC Publications, 1998), 1–3.

29. The list could be longer. See the literature that Robert Banks discusses in *Reenvisioning Theological Education*, 17–70.

1985	Charles M. Wood. *Vision and Discernment.* Decatur, GA: Scholars Press.
1988	Edward Farley. *The Fragility of Knowledge: Theological Education in the Church & the University.* Philadelphia: Fortress Press.
1988	Joseph C. Hough Jr. and Barbara G. Wheeler, eds. *Beyond Clericalism: The Congregation as a Focus for Theological Education.* Atlanta, GA: Scholars Press.
1988	Max L. Stackhouse. *Apologia: Contextualisation, Globalization and Mission in Theological Education.* Grand Rapids: Eerdmans.
1991	Barbara G. Wheeler and Edward Farley, eds. Shifting Boundaries. *Contextual Approaches to the Structure of Theological Education.* Louisville: Westminster John Knox Press.
1992	David H. Kelsey. *To Understand God Truly: What's Theological about a Theological School?* Louisville: Westminster John Knox Press.
1993	David H. Kelsey. *Between Athens and Berlin: The Theological Education Debate.* Grand Rapids: Eerdmans.
1999	Robert Banks. *Reenvisioning Theological Education. Exploring a Missional Alternative to Current Models.* Grand Rapids: Eerdmans.
2005	Malcolm L. Warford. *Practical Wisdom on Theological Teaching and Learning.* New York: Peter Lang.
2006	Charles R. Forster et al., eds. *Educating Clergy: Teaching Practices and Pastoral Imagination.* San Francisco: Jossey-Bass.
2006	Linda Cannell. *Theological Education Matters.* Newburgh, IN: EDCOT Press for MorgenBooks.

In relation to the international discussion and in view of the context of German-speaking Europe, we can limit ourselves to a more detailed look at the contributions of Niebuhr, Farley, Stackhouse, Kelsey, Banks, and Warford.

2.4.1 H. Richard Niebuhr: Thinking Based in Ecclesiology

In 1956 a study was presented by H. Richard Niebuhr (in collaboration with Daniel D. Williams and James M. Gustafson), financed by the Carnegie Corporation, and bearing the title *The Purpose of the Church and Its Ministry: Reflections on the Aims of Theological Education*. The study played an important role in the early phase of the reform discussion after the Second World War.

The starting point of the study is intentionally and fundamentally theological. The first question that must be asked is the question of the church. Part 1 is entitled "The Church and Its Purpose." Niebuhr's thesis is that all training must always keep in mind the community that will be served.[30] Therefore the church must first be defined. The scope of theological education must not be shortsightedly limited to the profession of pastor. It must always keep in mind the entire mission of the church in society.[31] That is why theological education must *first* be thought through theologically, not methodologically, technically, or structurally – although all of these have their importance.[32]

The study then moves on from ecclesiological considerations and takes up foundational questions of ministry and ministerial office in Part II, entitled "The Emerging New Conception of the Ministry."[33] The study asserts that American theological education is too one-sided in that, for the most part, it offers training only for the traditional and professional office of pastor. Because the office of pastor (*the ministry*) has, in recent times, been divided into many different tasks, pastoral education has also been splintered into a wide array of seemingly unconnected praxis-oriented courses. The loss of the single task of the ministerial office led to the loss of a unified course of study. In addition, the New Testament understanding of the ministry of all believers requires renewed emphasis.

Niebuhr's study insists that an overall redefinition of spiritual ministry is needed, a redefinition based in ecclesiology. Starting from that redefinition,

---

30. H. Richard Niebuhr, *The Purpose of the Church and Its Ministry: Reflections on the Aims of Theological Education* (New York: Harper Collins, 1956), 1.
31. Ibid., 3.
32. Ibid., 3–5.
33. Ibid., 48ff.

then, theological education can be reconceived. The study states that the task of the pastor is to lead the church to be the church (according to the principles of the church), with a view toward the growth and the mission of the church.

Once that happens, theological education can be taken under consideration. The report card given by the study is devastating: "The first impression many observers receive is one of inertia and conservatism."[34] More concretely: the "old" curriculum is retained, and new elements are added on, in an effort to be relevant for today's world.[35] The confusion in relation to church and ministry is carried over to the curriculum. Instead of a focused education, we are left with a curriculum made up of many unconnected parts.

> Such is the first superficial impression: our schools, like our churches and our ministers, have no clear conception of what they are doing but are carrying on traditional actions, making separate responses to various pressures exerted by churches and society, contriving uneasy compromises among many values, engaging in little quarrels symptomatic of undefined issues, trying to improve their work by adjusting minor parts of the academic machine or by changing the specifications of the raw material to be treated.[36]

Niebuhr's study proposes to focus the task and the goals of theological schools as follows: "... defining the theological school as intellectual centre of the church's life."[37] Theological education should be completely defined by ecclesiology: "To speak in Aristotelian language, the efficient, material, formal and final causes of the theological school are identical with those of the church." And, "Its motivation is that of the church – the love of God and neighbor."[38]

A two-fold function of the theological school results:

> On the one hand it is that place or occasion where the church exercises its love of God and neighbor; on the other hand it is the community that serves the church's other activities by bringing

---

34. Ibid., 95.
35. Ibid., 98.
36. Ibid., 101.
37. Ibid., 107.
38. Ibid., 107, 108 respectively.

reflection and criticism to bear on worship, preaching, teaching and the care of souls.[39]

Not everyone will want this. In particular the anti-ecclesial forces in the academic world as well as the anti-intellectual forces in the church will not like this definition. That dare not deter us "to love God with the whole understanding has never been accepted by the great church."[40]

Whether or not one agrees with the definitions and proposals of Niebuhr's study, the great significance of Niebuhr's work and that of his colleagues lies in their starting point, the way they proceed to make their case: Theological education must be conceived, thought through, theologically, and that includes the perspective of ecclesiology and an ecclesiological understanding of ministry and ministerial office. That summarizes, in my opinion, the lasting significance of this work which was written more than fifty years ago.

2.4.2 Edward Farley: Overcoming Fragmentation

Second it is important to note the contributions of Edward Farley. At the centre stands his book, published in 1983, *Theologia: The Fragmentation and Unity of Theological Education.*[41]

Historical Paradigms of Theological Education

The core of Farley's book consists of a critical historical analysis. He sees three eras and identifies paradigm shifts at their transition points. These eras do not coincide with those generally used to divide history or church history (Antiquity, Middle Ages, Modern Age). Instead their boundaries are linked to the birth and development of the universities, resulting in the following framework:

1) The pre-university era of the early church extending into the early Middle Ages (11th century). Farley calls this period the "Early Christian Centuries." This is the era of the *monastic* paradigm of theological education.

---

39. Ibid., 110.
40. Ibid., 117.
41. Farley expanded on his thinking in later publications. Particularly noteworthy is his 1988 work mentioned earlier, *The Fragility of Knowledge: Theological Education in the Church and the University* (Philadelphia: Fortress Press, 1988), as well as the collection edited together with Barbara Wheeler, *Shifting Boundaries: Contextual Approaches to the Structure of Theological Education* (Louisville: Westminster John Knox Press, 1991).

2) The second era dates from the birth of the universities in the Middle Ages to the development of modern universities during the Enlightenment, from the twelfth to the seventeenth century. For Farley this is the era of the *scholastic* paradigm.[42]

3) Farley sees a third era from the seventeenth or eighteenth centuries to the present day. It is the era of the modern university, influenced by the Enlightenment. Farley contends that this era produced two new paradigms: the *academic* paradigm and the *clerical-professional* paradigm.

Theologia: The Heart of Theological Education

The key concept which undergirds Farley's analysis is the term *theologia*, which gives his book its title. In defining *theologia*, Farley insists it is important to distinguish between faith as an act of trust, on the one hand, and understanding as a result of reflection, on the other. He terms the former *faith's pre-reflective insightfulness* or *belief-ful knowing*. People experience this in their personal trust in God. This is the existential and essential starting point for *theologia*, but is not yet *theologia* itself. The latter, *theologia* proper, is conscious reflection which leads to knowing God, a holistic heart recognition. Farley calls this conscious reflection of belief that springs from an existential experience of faith and that leads to the knowledge of God *theologia* or *theology as understanding*.[43]

Farley also argues that *theologia* or *theology as understanding* is to be clearly distinguished from *theology as discipline*.[44] *Theology as discipline* is the systematic and theoretical presentation of the contents of the Christian faith in the context of study and education. This encompasses portions of curriculum design, the course of study and the goals of study. This is what later is termed *Encyclopedia*, defining the discipline of theology as a science.

Accordingly the following graph (figure 1) can be made of Farley's framework: in the centre is *theologia*, the heart, if you will, the knowing reflection of faith. Here Farley sees the *ratio studiorum*.[45] He understands

---

42. One may ask at this point why Farley does not assign the Reformation its own paradigm. Farley discusses the influence of the Reformation in some detail but does not see the Reformation as a paradigm shift within the context of the framework that he develops.
43. Farley, *Theologia*, 29ff., 156f.
44. Ibid., 29–33.
45. Ibid., 16–18.

this to be the core that gives theological education its meaning and direction. If the *ratio studiorum* is lost, theological education becomes fragmented, disoriented, aimless. It's here on this point that Farley begins his critique. His thesis is that the root of the problem with theological education can be found in the loss of *theologia*, because with it the *ratio studiorum* is also lost. Put another way, theological education is no longer the reflection of faith that leads to the understanding of God but rather has become nothing more than an intellectual exercise in fulfilling an academic curriculum. And thereby the heart of theological education has been lost.

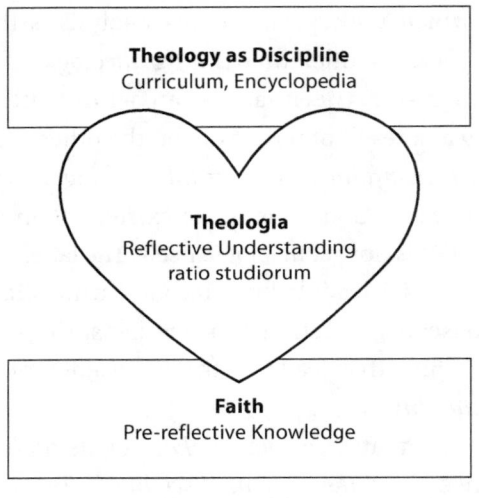

Figure 1

The Loss of Theologia through the Centuries

Farley went on to explain how the concept of *theologia* developed through the three historical eras. It is worthwhile to examine Farley's analysis more closely.

1) Farley asserts that in the first era, the pre-university era of the *monastic* paradigm, the concept of *theologia* remains largely intact. Theological education occurs within the community of cloister and the *ratio studiorum*, the goal of theological education, is clearly focused on living a holistic life pleasing to God (divinity). *Theology as discipline*, as a structured course of study, is completely directed toward *theologia*, toward knowing God. Study methods include reading, memorizing, discussing, and meditating

on the Bible. Furthermore the foremost teachers of the church reflect upon and articulate the Christian faith in their writings for apologetic and catechistic purposes.

2) A first great paradigm shift came, according to Farley, with the birth of the universities in the Middle Ages. It led to a transition from a *monastic* to a *scholastic* model of theological education. Theology as science (as in *scholastic* science) became the motto. The university became venue for theological work and theological education. The *ratio studiorum* was now thought to lie in a logical, persuasive presentation of the Christian faith in a system of thought under the influence of Aristotelian philosophy.

The term *scientia*, as understood in the Middle Ages, is the Latin translation of the Greek *episteme*. Aristotelian thinking understood *scientia* to mean both a comprehending, understanding knowledge and a structured discipline of research and study. Theology as science can therefore contain both dimensions, on the one hand theology as a *habitus* of the soul, a faith-filled and reflective knowledge of God, and on the other hand theology as a discipline of systematic study of the Christian faith.

However Farley points out an important shift in emphasis: theology as understanding (of God) was understood less and less as a divine enlightenment, but instead, influenced by Aristotelian anthropology, was seen as a natural ability of the human soul. In terms of the existential dimension of theology and theological education, that shifted the starting point from God to man. According to this view of things, religiosity has its origins in the human soul and not in the revelation of God. This paves the way for a naturalistic, humanistic theology.

A further significant shift in emphasis that occurred with the transition to the second (*scholastic*) era is described by Farley as a move away from the study of the Holy Scripture (*sacra pagina*) and toward an Aristotelian science of faith (*sacra doctrina*). Accordingly, new methods are introduced into theological education. Farley sees the difference between *lectio* (explanatory reading of the Scriptures) and *quaestio* (rational examination and philosophical argumentation) as a dramatic change. This is really the birth of *theology as discipline*. *Sacra doctrina* becomes a science of thought that presents the Christian faith in terms of philosophical categories.

Even if the theologians of the Middle Ages largely retained both *theology as understanding* and *theology as discipline* without seeing them as distinct, Farley insists that a decisive shift in emphasis occurred. The *ratio studiorum* clearly shifted from the holistic knowledge of God (divinity) to a philosophical system of teaching. That began the trajectory that dominated the Enlightenment. And that brings us to the second great paradigm shift, from the *scholastic* model of the Middle Ages to the Enlightenment.

3) What follows is a third period, which covers, according to Farley, the time from the seventeenth century to the present day. Farley identifies two movements which shape theology and theological education during this era: the Enlightenment and pietism. These two movements also serve to reveal two paradigms during this third era. The Enlightenment leads to the *academic* paradigm of the modern university, and pietism leads to the *clerical-professional* paradigm that is encountered primarily in seminaries and pastoral training institutions. These two paradigms of the modern age are closely connected with one another and yet their emphases are polar opposites.

This becomes evident in the matter of the *ratio studiorum*. Pietism, originating in the Reformation, places the meaning and the aim of theological education in ministry in the church. Thus theological education receives an emphasis in practical training for the role as pastor. The theology of the Enlightenment also sought answers to the question of the purpose and the goal of theological education. And here is where *theological encyclopedia* comes into play. Schleiermacher justified theological education functionally as well, with roles of church leadership in mind. This, however, was not an easy sell in the context of the universities, where scientific study was seen to be an end in itself, free of any purpose. This ambivalence is still evident today in theological studies in the universities.

Farley's thesis is that both of these paradigms neglect *theology as understanding* – or what Farley calls *theologia* – and that is crucial. In the academic paradigm, *theologia* gets completely lost amid pure science, religious criticism, agnosticism, and atheism.[46] In the *clerical-professional* model of the seminaries (Farley speaks particularly about seminaries in

---

46. This doesn't mean that the individual theologian cannot be a person of faith, but as a scientist he operates with a methodological atheism.

North America) knowing God in the comprehensive sense of *theologia* fades into the background and makes room for an increasingly pragmatic striving for praxis know-how.

A summary of Farley's analysis of the two paradigms of the third era is illustrated in figure 2.

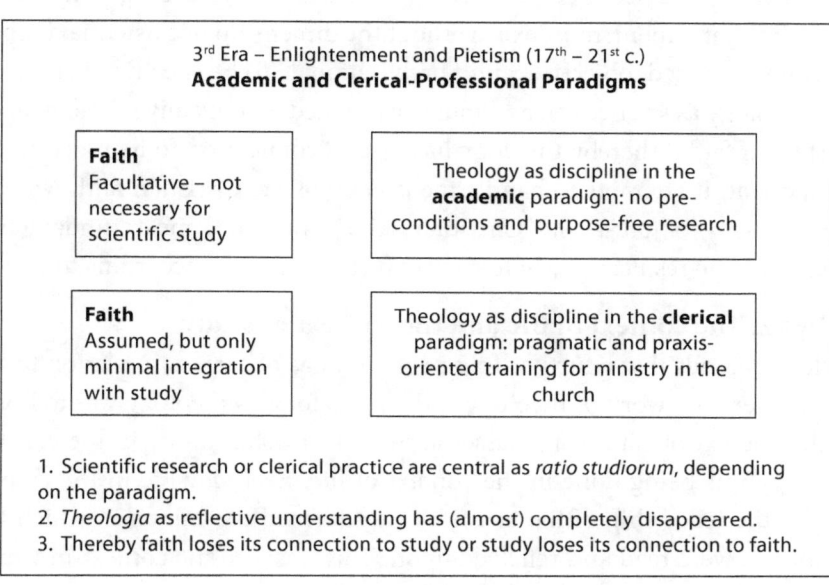

Figure 2

The Result: Fragmentation of Theology and Theological Education

Because of these historical developments, Farley sees the fragmentation of theology and theological education as the greatest problem in the present day. The dismembering and splintering of the one whole has more dimensions than may be apparent at first glance:

Split #1: The knowledge of God and study

As described above, Farley sees the core problem in the fact that the two perspectives, *theology as understanding* (holistic knowledge of God, divinity) and *theology as discipline* (a specialized area of science), with the passage of time have drifted further and further apart.[47] To use other terms that might

---

47. Farley, *Theologia*, 29ff.

be more familiar to us, the study of theology and the knowledge of God have gotten separated from one another. Farley pointed out how, starting out in the early church and through the scholastic theology of the Middle Ages and finally through the establishment of theology as a scientific study as a result of the Enlightenment, these two dimensions of theology have clearly gotten more and more disconnected. Theology as a science, according to the views of the Enlightenment, must exist without the dimension of existential faith. It must be distanced, objective, and purely rational. To be specific, that means that theology as science can and must be pursued *without* any relationship to existential faith. Thereby theology has lost its connection to its most innate component. It attempts to handle the *content* of the Christian faith without the necessity of *possessing* Christian faith. This first, most fundamental fragmentation results in a whole array of further fractures according to Farley:

Split #2: The context of life and the context of study

Farley contends that a further fragmentation has occurred in relation to the place where the work of theology is done. As long as theology was at home in the context of catechism classes and the fellowship of life in the cloister, theology was being done in the context of life. Everyday life in the church and/or the fellowship of life in the cloister formed the milieu in which the Scriptures were read and reflected upon. This was also the context in which theological education happened.

When theology and theological education were relocated to the universities (and later to other institutions disconnected from the context of church life), the context for doing theology was fundamentally changed. The milieu for study became its own world, with its own rules, vocabulary, rituals and values. Anyone who wanted to study theology moved into the artificial world of academia, a world that was (and is) often separated from the life context of family, society and church by a huge chasm.

That fact has far-reaching pedagogical consequences. If we assume that in a course of training and study certain skills are to be learned,[48] the gap between the context of study and the context of life proves fatal. The declared goal of university study is to learn how to conduct scientific research. This is, however, not the skill people need to live the Christian life, nor is it the

---

48. *Skills* in the sense of the abilities to successfully solve problems and challenges in real life, in the real world, in the same way they were solved during training.

skill needed by those who will later serve in the church or in missions. Thus the student learns neither knowledge and wisdom (in the sense of Farley's *theologia*) nor practical pastoral skills.

Split #3: The Bible as God's Word and the Bible as a document of religious history

The first two developments also brought with them a far-reaching change in how the Bible was viewed. Whereas theology rooted in religiosity, as was practiced in the early church, held an interpretation of the Bible that was shaped by devoted spirituality, Bible study in the academic paradigm of theological education increasingly gave way to historical-critical textual analysis employing correct methodology and preserving appropriate (personal, emotional) distance. Farley explicitly points out the shift in methodology. In the monastic model, Bible study consisted of reading, memorizing, discussing, and meditating upon the text.[49] By contrast, in the scholastic model, debate using Aristotelian logic moved to the fore, until finally, after the Enlightenment, the methodical, professional, objective, scientific analysis of the text became the accepted approach. With this approach, the personal faith of the student was not necessary. In fact, such personal faith could be seen as subjective bias that gets in the way of scientific work with the text.

Here, too, the consequences were predictable. It goes without saying that hand in hand with this process the Bible as God's Word faded increasingly from view. What remains is the objective analysis of the Bible as a document of religious history. A theology student who believes in Christ, who knows the Bible and lives with the Bible from a personal experiential faith – that student is hit head-on at the very outset of his or her course of study by the fragmentation we've just described.

Split #4: Dismemberment of the theological curriculum

Because of the Enlightenment and the increasing specialization of the sciences that followed, the single entity of theology was completely shredded. During and after the Enlightenment the study of theology at the universities was increasingly faced with the question of whether and to what extent theology was related to the other sciences. Thus the agenda of theological study at

---

49. Farley, *Theologia*, 33.

the universities was determined not by the needs of the church or by those of personal faith but instead by the scientific disciplines of the university. The study of the Bible had to appear meaningful and credible in the eyes of the historical and literary sciences. Systematic theology began to orient itself around philosophy. Church history was studied using the methods of historical science. And practical theology leaned heavily on the social sciences – psychology, sociology, and pedagogy.

Here too the consequences are well known. We don't need to go into detail about how, over time, the large subdivisions such as Old Testament, New Testament, dogmatics, ethics, etc., were split into dozens of smaller specialty areas. For centuries now, especially in German theology, no theologian has had the expertise and the courage to present an overview of his discipline. And that is an evident symptom of this analytical splintering.

Split #5: Theory and practice

Because theological education underwent a one-sided development favoring *theology as discipline* (to the neglect of *theology as understanding*), it completely lost its praxis orientation. Through the influence of Aristotle in scholasticism and through Descartes' definitive prioritizing of thought, theology has become a theory, and theological education has become an exercise in theoretical, academic reflection. Praxis, if it is mentioned at all, is seen to belong to the category of application, and this certainly takes second place to theory. Thus, as the fifth fragmentation, a fundamental chasm between theory and practice is formalized. And the superior theory is placed above the subordinate practice.

The pedagogical/educational consequences are significant: a course of study that concentrates on theory alone must somehow give attention to application. If graduates cannot put the theories they have learned into practice, their study proves worthless. Traditional theological education has seldom paid enough attention to this. Moreover, a curriculum that is one-sidedly theoretical, tends to promote deductive learning. Inductive learning, which leverages praxis and experience as a source of understanding, has no place in this model.

Split #6: Decoupling of practical theology

Pietism and Schleiermacher introduced a focus on pastoral praxis. This emphasis is particularly strong in North American seminaries. This focus does not, however, solve the problem. Neither does a well-developed curriculum of practical theology. At first glance it would appear as if the *clerical-professional* paradigm included by definition an appropriate measure of praxis orientation. But appearances are deceiving. Practical theology remains within the area of theory. It is the *theory* of pastoral activity. That is certainly true for European higher education as well. But even the North American seminaries with their considerably stronger emphasis on praxis are not able to successfully integrate theory and practice. There too practical theology remains within the realm of theory, even though methods of psychology, sociology, and pedagogy are amply employed. It would appear that practical theology feels compelled to fight for its place among the accepted theoretical disciplines of Bible, history, and systematics. To accomplish this, practical theology behaves just as theoretically and scientifically as the three "theoretical" disciplines.

This tendency toward scientific theory found in practical theology is nothing more than a symptom of a sixth fragmentation, the split between the so-called *theoretical* disciplines (Bible, history, and systematic theology) and so-called *practical* theology.

Split #7: Clergy and laity

Far more serious in the development of practical theology is the fact that the term praxis is used narrowly for pastoral praxis. Thereby theology and theological education become something for professional church staff. Seen in this light, the loss of *theologia* is painfully obvious. The concept of *theologia* (theology as understanding) is about wisdom. It is about a fundamental understanding that has authentic living in view. The study of theology is thus intended to communicate insight for living that enables the student to live his life of faith in God more intensively and comprehensively. That applies to every Christian. However, theological education that reduces the term praxis to the theory of pastoral activity deceives the church (and the students) in two ways: it withholds from the church and from the students true practical training for living the Christian life, and implies that Christian praxis is in reality *professional-pastoral* praxis. That is why Farley uses the term *clerical paradigm*, because it re-introduces the clergy/laity divide, which, in theory at least, was done away with in Protestantism through the priesthood of all believers. Thus this is a particularly serious fragmentation of theological education because its ripple effects extend so deeply into the life of the church.

That is the diagnosis. Does Farley see any possible therapies to overcome the illness?

The Way Out of the Crisis

Farley has been accused of being a brilliant diagnostician but a mediocre therapist.[50] His accusers also say that his concept of *theologia* is not clearly enough defined to work with.[51] It seems to me that the greatest weakness of his work is that it deals exclusively with the Western academic educational tradition. Farley doesn't mention the burning questions and concerns within the international discussion that were touched on earlier. One almost has the impression that Farley is having a conversation that excludes input from the recent international, missional and ecumenical discussions.

Nevertheless I would appeal to the reader not to underestimate Farley's value. I have devoted so much space to his analysis because I am convinced that his assessment addresses the root problems in Western theological education. Farley is concerned about *one* thing – about *theologia* as thoughtful faith, as a habit of the soul, as wisdom. And on this point Farley is quite concrete. We must rediscover *theologia*.[52] What does that mean? *Theologia, theology as understanding*, aims to understand God and life more completely through thought and reflection in such a way that we are able to understand (love) God more deeply, and to live as Christians in this world, more wisely and more fully engaged. That being the case, theological education must accomplish exactly this goal.

Like Niebuhr before him, Farley has provoked a discussion that goes beyond the pragmatic and operational questions and encourages us to consider foundational questions of theology and philosophy. If Robert Banks is correct in his review, then Farley has been for the most part ignored.[53] The pragmatism of the day tends to repress any such foundational reflection – not only in North America.

One thing is certain: Farley's 1983 volume generated much discussion in North America and spawned a number of notable contributions from others.

---

50. Ferris, *Renewal in Theological Education*, 18–20.
51. Banks, *Reenvisioning Theological Education*, 31–33.
52. Farley, *Theologia*, 151–173.
53. Banks, *Reenvisioning Theological Education*, 8–11.

2.4.3 Max L. Stackhouse: Rediscovering Apologetics

In 1988, a volume by Max L. Stackhouse was published under the title *Apologia: Contextualization, Globalization, and Mission in Theological Education*.[54] Stackhouse writes within the context of conversations about the reform of theological education at the Andover Newton Theological School (USA). In addition his study reflects a lively dialogue with the World Council of Churches.[55]

In Part I Stackhouse and his Andover colleagues analyze the situation as follows: theological education has lost a "metaphysical-moral vision" (ch. 1). At the same time theological education faces the challenges of an increasingly complex and interdependent world (ch. 2). Theological education faces growing problems when it comes to defining the relationship between text and context (ch. 3). And finally theological education faces challenges stemming from the reorientation of missions (ch. 4).[56]

Part II discusses four proposals that have arisen in recent years. Within the ecumenical discussion during the 1980s, greatest emphasis was given to the idea that theological education must take place on the global horizon (ch. 5). Liberation theology challenged theological education to understand theology as *praxis*, a socio-political praxis in solidarity with the poor and disadvantaged (ch. 6). The paradigm shift in missions demands the contextualization of theology (ch. 7). And finally, Farley's question is discussed – how *theologia* in its original form can be recaptured (ch. 8).

In Part III Stackhouse contends that all these reform initiatives have merit and yet miss one key thing. Stackhouse and his colleagues offer the diagnosis that all previous reform proposals avoid, repress, or fail to answer one essential issue – the fact that ever since the Enlightenment, religion has been considered a *second-order reality*. Stackhouse asserts that the primary challenge for theology and theological education is to contend and defend

---

54. Max L. Stackhouse, *Apologia: Contextualization, Globalization, and Mission in Theological Education* (Grand Rapids: Eerdmans Publishing, 1988).
55. Two studies in particular are noteworthy: A. Sapsezian, S. Amirtham and F. Ross Kinsler, *Global Solidarity in Theological Education* (Geneva: World Council of Churches, 1981); and S. Amirtham and S. Weley Ariarajah, *Ministerial Formation in a Multifaith Milieu* (Geneva: World Council of Churches, 1986).
56. This brief outline is derived from Stackhouse's own summary, *Apologia*, 78.

"that religion makes a fundamental, objective difference in the real world,"[57] that is, that religion belongs to the *first-order realities*. Hence the programmatic title of his book: *Apologia*. Stackhouse articulates his case as follows:

> The problem can be stated this way: Religion is based on a fundamental presupposition that there is a metaphysical-moral realm that is real, transcendent to the empirical world, and simultaneously sufficiently present to human reflection and experience that it can be taken as the decisive point of reference for the understanding and guidance of empirical life and historical existence. Further, religion (all religions) presuppose that this metaphysical-moral reality has been sufficiently unveiled (that is either revealed or discovered) so that humans can know something about it with enough clarity and security to take it as foundation for belief and action without intellectual fraud or ethical duplicity. Thus, religion presumes a first-order reality of a metaphysical-moral sort, epistemologically accessible, that can be used to interpret and guide all second-order matters, cultural cohesion, and political-economic programs.[58]

Stackhouse took the discussion a step further. He critically honored and accepted the conversation of the previous twenty years. At the same time he introduced the realm of apologetics on a higher plane, as it were. Theology and theological education must, on the intellectual plane, regain ground that was lost in the Enlightenment: Religion is a first-order reality. Because of that, theological education has a challenging task, especially in the enlightened, secularized, and predominantly post-Christian West.

2.4.4 David Kelsey: Between Athens and Berlin

Attention must also be drawn to David Kelsey, a professor at Yale Divinity School. His books, *To Understand God Truly: What's Theological about a Theological School?* (1992) and *Between Athens and Berlin: The Theological*

---

57. Stackhouse, *Apologia*, 141.
58. Ibid., 143.

Education Debate (1993) present two studies[59] that have sparked a significant amount of further thought and discussion.[60]

Whereas Stackhouse went beyond Farley in thinking, drawing upon his intensive conversations with representatives of ecumenism and missions, Kelsey starts where Farley left off and attempts to more precisely clarify the situation of Western educational traditions. In so doing he contrasts the model of classical education (which he calls "Athens") with the model of professionally oriented science (which he calls "Berlin").

Metaphorically speaking, theological education always occurs at the intersection of different roads. According to Kelsey, it happens at the intersection of three roads: the Athens road, the Berlin road, as well as a denominational road.[61] In Kelsey's concept, church tradition defines the content (the subject matter), that which Farley calls "the Christian thing." Athens and Berlin represent two kinds of schools, two forms of pedagogy, two ways of learning and understanding.

The "Athens" Model of Theological Education

The key word in the Athens model is *paideia*. Kelsey works from the historical meaning of *paideia*, which he articulates as:

> The Greek word *paideia* meant at once "schooling," "culturing," and "character formation." Although, as we shall note, it underwent important changes between the fourth century BC and the fourth century AD, the concept of *paideia* retained important continuities through this history. Its aim was to form in the souls of the young the virtue or arête they needed to function as responsible citizens. In its earliest form this schooling had focused on athletics and on the study of the poetry ascribed to Homer. The assumption was that by simultaneously subjecting

---

59. David H. Kelsey, *To Understand God Truly: What's Theological about a Theological School?* (Louisville: Westminster John Knox Press, 1992); *Between Athens and Berlin: The Theological Education Debate* (Grand Rapids: Eerdmans Publishing, 1993). Both books can be found in their entirety at http://www.religion-online.org. Further references to these two volumes are drawn from these online versions and will indicate only the chapter cited.

60. For example, Brian Edgar uses Kelsey's study as the starting point for his typology in "The Theology of Theological Education," *Evangelical Review of Theology* 29, no. 3 (2005): 208–217.

61. Kelsey, *Understand God Truly*, ch. 2.

the bodies of the young to physical discipline and their souls to the traditions and customs of ancient Greece as conveyed by literature, they would emerge deeply shaped by those dispositions or habits, that is, virtues that make the good citizen. At the same time it meant that the ruling class were all genuinely "cultured" in the same way so that, whatever their differences of judgment on particular matters, they were unified by a shared picture of the good life and of what was to be most valued in it.[62]

Although the meaning of *paideia* underwent a change over time, which Kelsey describes in some detail, he nevertheless sees in the concept a trans-historical pedagogical paradigm which for him typifies "Athens":

We will abstract them as an ahistorical construct, a type of excellent education, for which "Athens" will be the emblem:

1) The goal of *paideia*, which is the cultivation of the excellence or arête of the soul, consists not in acquiring a clutch of virtues but in knowledge of the Good itself. Education as *paideia* is defined as a single underlying principle of all virtues, their essence. To be shaped by arête simply is to know the Good.

2) The Good is not only the underlying essence of the moral and intellectual virtues; it is the highest principle of the universe. It is the divine. Plato came to be understood as the founder of a religion, and *paideia* was understood to be an education whose goal was in some way religious as well as moral.

3) The goal of *paideia* cannot be taught directly – for example, by simply conveying information about various philosophers' doctrines regarding virtue. Knowledge of the Good only comes through contemplation, the ultimate fruit of which is an intuitive insight, a *gnosis* of the Good. Accordingly, all a teacher can provide a student is indirect assistance, intellectual and moral disciplines that will capacitate the student for the student's own moment of insight. This can be accomplished by the study of texts – not merely Homer now, but the philosophers as well, especially Plato.

---

62. Ibid., ch. 3. Cf. Kelsey, *Between Athens and Berlin*, ch. 1.

The Battle for Reforms and Renewal in Theological Education 53

4) Insightful knowledge of the Good requires a conversion, a turning around of the soul from preoccupation with appearances to focus on reality, on the Good. This conversion results from a long educational process that Jaeger characterizes as "slow vegetable growth." It requires, like vegetable growth, a climate and nutrients that can only be provided by a society and its culture, by the right *polis*. Education as *paideia* is inherently communal and not solitary.[63]

Theological training on the Athens road is therefore character formation, education toward wisdom, instruction of the whole person. Elsewhere Kelsey summarizes this as follows:

> According to the "Athens" model, theological education is a movement from source to personal appropriation of the source, from revealed wisdom to the appropriation of revealed wisdom in a way that is identity forming and personally transforming. This is true whether theological education is understood broadly as education in "the faith" or more narrowly as education for church leadership. In either case, it is understood that appropriation does not come about through direct instruction. Rather, it comes about indirectly by inquiry into other matters whose study is believed to capacitate persons to appropriate this wisdom for themselves. This means that theological education of the "Athens" type tends to focus on the student, on helping the student undergo a deep kind of formation. To be sure, study focuses on various subject matters. However, this study is ordered to something more basic, the students' own personal appropriation of wisdom about God and about themselves in relation to God.
>
> This has implications for the relationship between teacher and learner. It must be an indirect relationship. Teachers themselves are also seeking personally to appropriate wisdom about God and about themselves in relation to God. At most the teacher "teaches" only indirectly by providing a context in which the learner may come to that combined self-knowledge and

---

63. Kelsey, *Between Athens and Berlin*, ch. 1.

God-knowledge that is a "personal appropriation" of revealed wisdom. Central to this context are those texts and practices, such as Scripture and the practice of the Christian life, whose study is believed to lead to understanding God.

This, in turn, has implications regarding who is qualified to teach in theological education in the "Athens" model. There are two very different sorts of capacities required to do such teaching. One is extraordinary learning in regard to the relevant texts and practices. The other is a set of personal gifts for the indirect "teaching" that, as midwife, helps another come to personal appropriation of revealed wisdom. The two sets of qualifications are in tension with each other, and the tension creates the possibility of serious deformity in this type of education. If "learnedness" is overstressed, education tends to slip into direct communication of information, subverting the basic character of this type of education. On the other hand, if the personal gifts for this sort of teaching are overstressed, education tends to slip into manipulation or therapy, technique tends to become dominant, and the substance by which the student was indirectly to be "formed" gets lost.

All of this has implications regarding the communal context of education. Theological education of the "Athens" type is inherently communal. The learning is in one way "individualistic," in that each must do it for herself or himself. Yet, by definition it cannot be solitary. Teachers and learners together constitute a community sharing the common goal of personally appropriating revealed wisdom. It is, then, a community ordered to the same end, a community under orders. Some members of the community, presumably the teachers, have been engaged in this common quest longer than others, presumably the learners; but it is a shared quest.[64]

Nothing need be added to Kelsey's summary. This is about character formation in the best sense of that term.

---

64. Ibid.

The "Berlin" Model of Theological Education

In contrast, the key word *research* is at the centre of the Berlin model, according to Kelsey. He points thereby to the Humboldt University and the place that Schleiermacher gave to theology there. Kelsey identifies the basic pedagogical principles as the scientific method and professionalism.[65]

Kelsey engages in an intense study of Schleiermacher's work. He is convinced that Schleiermacher accomplished something great by securing a place for theology in the context of the modern university. At the same time, however, Kelsey notes that this came at a price.

Schleiermacher faced the following challenges:

- The idea of a critical science in which everything must be subjected to methodical research and human reason is diametrically opposed to the traditional understanding that theology has a revealed and therefore normative text. How can one do theology if it is no longer acceptable to recognize authoritative revelation?
- In the wake of the Enlightenment, theology lost its place, ranked before and above all other sciences. What place does theology now occupy if it is no longer the normative starting point for all other sciences?
- The freedom to teach and to learn would seem to include the freedom to judge even the Scriptures critically. Does the gospel permit such freedom?[66]

Kelsey reaches the conclusion that theological education, as understood within the Athens paradigm, really has no place in the university of the Enlightenment era. We recall: "According to the 'Athens model,' theological education is a movement from source to personal appropriation of the source, from revealed wisdom to the appropriation of revealed wisdom in a way that is identity forming and personally transforming."

Despite this tension, Schleiermacher succeeded in securing a place for the study of theology at the universities, but only as a result of the following concessions:

- Theology is not a pure science that deals with questions of ultimate truth. Rather it is a "positive" science that deals with what is

---

65. Kelsey, *Understand God Truly*, ch. 4.
66. Kelsey, *Between Athens and Berlin*, ch. 1.

historically given. Theology is thus primarily an historical science. Using scientific methods, theology examines the testimonies of faith of the people of God as they are presented in the Bible and by tradition.

- Theology is functionally directed toward church leadership. Just like the judge and the doctor, as leading figures in the community, need the best academic education, so also the pastor.

Under these new conditions, theological education underwent fundamental change. Kelsey summarizes the consequences as follows:

> According to the "Berlin" model, theological education is a movement from data to theory to application of theory to practice. This movement correlates with its bipolar structure: *Wissenschaft* (science) for critical rigor in theorizing; "professional" education for rigorous study of the application of theory in practice.
>
> [. . .]
>
> This has implications for the relation between teacher and learner. The teacher does not exist for the student, as is the case in *paideia*. Instead, the teacher is basically a researcher who needs the student to help achieve the goal of research in a cooperative enterprise. Humboldt said that this cooperation proceeds by "combining a practiced mind, which is on that account apt to be more one-sided and less active [the teacher's] with one which, though weaker and still neutral, bravely attempts every possibility [the student's]."
>
> Given the bipolar structure of the "Berlin" type, this has a further implication for theological education that is of momentous importance. When theological education conforms to the "Berlin" type of education, what makes it theological is its professional pole, not its *Wissenschaft* pole. The *Wissenschaft* pole is governed by research agendas, by sets of topics to be researched. For Schleiermacher it was to be a historian's research agenda, followed by a philosopher's agenda. Biblical texts, church institutions, practices of worship, moral standards, and the like are all equally to be studied to discover their origins, how and why they changed through time, what their influences have

been, etc. Then, of that entire, utterly heterogeneous array of phenomena, the question of their underlying Christian "essence" was to be asked. Inquiry is governed not, as in the "Athens" type, by an interest thereby indirectly to come to know God, but by an interest to discover as directly as possible the truth about the origin, effects, and essential nature of "Christian" phenomena.

There is nothing "theological" about all of that. Nor need there be. Neither intuitive experience of God nor capacities for such experience are cultivated, not even indirectly, by engaging in *Wissenschaft*. Such experience is cultivated only in religious communities of whose inward experience all these Christian phenomena are but outward expressions. What makes theological education of the "Berlin" type theological is that it aims at preparing leaders for just those communities, leaders capacitated to help those communities nurture consciousness of God.

Note, then, that what makes theological education of this type *theological* is that it is ordered not theocentrically, but ecclesiocentrically – to understanding church, or more exactly, to understanding church leadership, not to understanding God. There may be excellent theological reasons for adopting just this view; at this point it is important simply to note what the view is. Note secondly a deep irony in the "Berlin" type of excellence in theological education: Although what makes it properly "theological" is its goal (as professional education) of nurturing the health of the church by preparing for it excellent leadership, what entitles it to a home in the *wissenschaftlich* education it needs is the rather different goal of nurturing the health of society as a whole (for which professional church leadership is a "necessary practice").

Clearly, this has important implications regarding faculty. The major criteria governing selection of persons for faculty positions in accord with this type of theological education is not simply great learning in already established knowledge, but demonstrated capacity to engage in scholarly research; and it is not so much personal capacities to be midwife of others' coming to an understanding of God and of themselves in relation to God as it is the ability to cultivate capacities for scholarly research in others. The normal way of demonstrating capacity for research, of course, is by publication of results of critical inquiry that make original contributions to the fund of knowledge.[67]

This summary as well needs no elaboration.

Kelsey is not at all suggesting that one model is preferable to the other, nor is he suggesting that both are wrong. Kelsey assumes that the church in every generation has strived for excellence in the given context of that day. He sees "Athens" and "Berlin" as two expressions of this pursuit of excellence within a particular cultural context. In the setting of the Greek world, the church found excellence in theological education in the Athens model. In the setting of the Enlightenment, the church found excellence in the Berlin model.

Kelsey asserts that theological education in North America today is indebted to both models. As has been previously stated – where the Berlin road and the Athens road cross, that's where theological education happens. Indeed, theological education must happen there.

Three thoughts in conclusion:

1) Farley's *Theologia* elicited very extensive discussions. Impressively, Kelsey successfully manages to bring these discussions to the point. Academic theological education, in the form that has established itself in the West since the Enlightenment, struggles to do justice to the scientific method of the Berlin model without losing the *paideia* of the Athens model. Kelsey introduces basic categories into the present debate over reform in theological education that we cannot do without.

2) Yet the debate from Farley to Kelsey is a Western, academic debate. What are we to do with all the burning questions raised by those in cross-cultural missions and by the churches of the Majority World?

3) And finally, Kelsey asks, almost as an afterthought, whether it might not be appropriate for the Christian church to pursue a Jerusalem

---

67. Kelsey, *Between Athens and Berlin*, ch. 1.

model, that is, a model of theological education that is anchored in Jewish and early church thought patterns.⁶⁸

That's a good question, one which Robert Banks addresses.

2.4.5 An Alternative Based on the Bible

Robert Banks' book *Reenvisioning Theological Education* explicitly takes up the debate that has been going on since Niebuhr. In the first seventy pages of his book he gives an overview of the entire discussion thus far. And while he appreciates and respects the analysis and suggestions for reform, he criticizes that none of the studies have been radical enough. Neither Athens nor Berlin should be our orientation, but rather Jerusalem, that is, the Bible. Thus Banks echoes Kelsey, who suggested that in addition to the Athens and the Berlin model, there could well be a Jerusalem model, oriented around the Jewish and early church tradition.

Banks argues that it is legitimate, not only to look back to Berlin or Athens historically, but rather to begin with the Bible and in particular with Jesus and with Paul. He rejects the notion that such an orientation is a naïve "back to the Bible" mentality. He sees it rather as a courageous "forward with the Bible" mindset.⁶⁹

The question, whether and to what degree a model of theological education can and must be derived from the Bible, is indeed justified, and for evangelical theology it is a foundational question that is still relevant today.

Banks proposes, based on his biblical studies, what he calls a "missional alternative to current models." To be precise, Banks states, "By 'missional' I mean theological education that is wholly or partly field based, and that involves some measure of doing what is being studied. This may take the form of action-reflection or reflection-action."⁷⁰

---

68. "Although persuasive theological arguments can be given for adopting each of these types, neither of them can be said to be somehow theologically mandated by the very nature of Christianity. Indeed, Tertullian's ancient question, "What has Jerusalem to do with Athens?" might suggest that, with its roots in Jerusalem, Christianity in fact theologically mandates a third type of excellent schooling altogether, one hitherto ignored by major Christian communities. Whatever the theologically normative case might be, however, it is the case de facto that modern North American Christian theological education is committed to "Athens" and "Berlin," and it is committed to both of them for historical reasons." (Kelsey, *Between Athens and Berlin*, ch. 1).
69. Banks, *Reenvisioning Theological Education*, 81.
70. Ibid., 142.

Banks envisions a biblically based alternative to all other models that have been discussed in the North American scene in the past fifty years or more. He summarizes this alternative as follows:[71]

1) The "classical" model (Farley), which seeks to recapture the best of classical education, namely the formation of people of wisdom through the holistic and experiential study of the Bible and Christian tradition.

2) The "vocational" model (Hough and Cobb, and also Stackhouse), which seeks to equip people to meaningfully relate Christian tradition to the questions of the day, and thus prepare them for pastoral ministry.

3) The "dialectical" model (Kelsey, Wood), which seeks to combine the two previous models, that is, hold them in creative tension.

4) The "denominational" model (Schner and Muller), which emphasizes the mastering and applying of denominational/confessional traditions.

Banks finds all four models too cognitive, too far removed from praxis. Even where character formation and preparation for ministry are the focus, it is assumed that these goals can be achieved cognitively. Banks, on the other hand, contends that theological education must bring the person in contact with the real-life context in which s/he will later minister. Basing his approach on Paul and on Jesus, Banks argues for training *in* ministry not a preparation *for* ministry.

Banks' proposal is indeed an alternative. These are two very different approaches to education. One approach proposes to prepare students for a task without asking them to perform the task vocationally. The other approach proposes learning skills while doing, while functioning vocationally. We will come back to these two basic models again in chapter 3.

The other question arising from Banks is one we will look at again in chapter 4: To what extent can a model for theological education be derived from the Bible? And, if it can, is Banks' proposal the result?

---

71. Ibid., 143–144.

2.4.6 Warford: Wisdom Leading to Wisdom

It appears that the theoretical reflections on the foundational questions of theological education reached a certain high point with the two studies by David Kelsey. What needed to be said seems to have been said. Banks added another alternative, which has, however, scarcely been addressed in the ongoing debate.

The conversation in recent years has been less about the foundational questions of theological education and more about the practical formation of theological education. The articles in *Theological Education* as well as those in newer publications confirm this.

Initiatives for the renewal of theological education that have come from institutes and study centres are also notable:

- Notable is the Center for the Study of Theological Education, led by Barbara Wheeler, at Auburn Theological Seminary in New York. This institute regularly publishes the results of research in the field of theological education and cites initiatives for the renewal of theological education. The texts are available on the internet at http://www.auburnseminary.org/CSTE.
- An extremely creative project called The Lexington Seminar was launched by the Lexington Theological Seminary. The Lexington Seminar is an ongoing conversation among various theological seminaries with the goal of better understanding the current problems through dialogue and taking steps toward a better future through creative reciprocal inspiration.[72] Every year five seminaries are invited to a meeting. In a three-year process of reflection, innovations for the future are proposed, based on the collective thinking. These innovations are then implemented at the participating schools. Thirty-five theological schools have participated in the process thus far. The thing that is new and promising in this process is that a manageable number of seminaries embark on a journey together. The thinking that is done remains

---

72. The philosophy and process of the Lexington Seminar are presented in Malcolm L. Warford, *Practical Wisdom on Theological Teaching and Learning* (New York: Peter Lang, 2005), ix–xiv. All essays in the book are available online at www.lexingtonseminar.org/links/documents.php.

therefore closely connected to the reality of the participating seminaries, and a high level of application and implementation becomes possible.

The experiences of the Lexington process were publicized in 2005 in Malcolm L. Warford's volume *Practical Wisdom on Theological Teaching and Learning*. The title suggests Warford's purpose. He is looking for practical wisdom as it relates to the process of teaching and learning. The essays in Warford's book revolve around four realities which pose practical challenges to theological education in North America today.[73]

Formation: Addressing Essential Questions

The first reality is that it can no longer be assumed that students have a thoroughly Christian background in their families and churches. That means, "The seminary is now required to be in itself a place of basic formation in the gospel as well as a community that equips men and women for the church's ministries. . . . Seminaries, therefore, are increasingly responsible for an even larger proportion of students' spiritual formation."[74]

This need to introduce students more thoroughly into the knowledge and practice of the Christian life faces a number of hurdles from opposing forces:

1) The presence of information technology in theological education makes it possible for students to acquire knowledge from a distance, in virtual communities, through technology. But how can spirituality, a life of discipleship, and character development be taught when relationships and community are reduced to a minimum or disappear entirely?

2) The great variety in the backgrounds, needs, and desires of the students have led to a multiplicity of progamme offerings that are, as much as possible, tailored to the individual, modular and flexible. The result is a further loss of a stable community, less ongoing contact among students, and an even weaker integration of curriculum in the sense of a holistic, homogeneous program. How can discipleship and spiritual formation be encouraged given these conditions?

---

73. Cf. Warford, *Practical Wisdom*, in the Introduction, 1–12.
74. Ibid., 3–4.

3) A third complicating factor, according to Warford, is that the study of theology has become more comprehensive, complex, critical, and diverse. Students are expected to take a number of courses that introduce them to a variety of theological questions.

4) Finally, there is a difference in the professors/instructors as well. Whereas in the past most professors came from a background in pastoral studies (BD or MDiv) and many had pastoral experience, today most have a purely academic background (religious studies) and little or no pastoral experience. That results in instruction that is decidedly less pastoral.

Institutional Identity: Engaging Multiple Aims

The diversity among students described above, coupled with pragmatic expectations of churches, has led to an increased diversification on the part of the institutions themselves. Schools have become more heterogeneous. A diversity of needs must be met by a diversity of programs and offerings.

That has led to school administrations that are more complex and require more personnel. More importantly, the identity, purpose, and aims of the schools have become less focused.

Whereas for many years theological seminaries had a single, precise aim – to train pastors for a denomination, for example – today many schools offer a wide variety of curricula to a broad spectrum of students.

It has become significantly more difficult for schools to formulate a relatively homogeneous vision that is embraced by all.

Assessment: Fidelity to Our Intention

In addition to all this, theological seminaries are under enormous pressure to survive in a competitive market. This pressure brings with it the need to ensure credibility, employing mechanisms which have become common in Western culture – quality assurance and accreditation. Assessment has therefore become as much the norm in theological seminaries as elsewhere in society.

Quality assurance in its ideal form seeks nothing more than to help institutions to articulate clear goals and to achieve those goals. It is about institutions of higher learning themselves becoming learners, whose very culture includes a commitment to ongoing development through evaluation and improvement.

This ideal, however, faces significant obstacles: to effectively administer quality assurance requires considerable time and money, and that creates resistance among employees, especially among teaching faculty. Evaluation can quickly come to be seen as a necessary evil, which does not enhance the learning process.

Moreover, accreditation is often seen as the only reason for evaluation. When that is the case, the certification of curricula and degrees becomes the focus, rather than the creation of a culture of ongoing institutional learning and improvement.

Theological schools face the sizable challenge of incorporating assessment into their culture of institutional learning.

Faculty Work and Calling

These centrifugal and fragmenting forces that seem to be at work at every level affect the community of the teaching faculty as well. Warford describes the situation with a quote from Timothy Fuller: "Academic institutions, it would appear, are in varying degrees disintegrated communities of scholars."[75] Certainly professors at North American seminaries do not experience themselves as part of a mutually inspiring community of learning, into which students may be invited.

If education is above all else conversation, and schools therefore are above all else places of conversation – as the British philosopher Michael Oakeshott has said – then today's theology schools are wide of the mark. Instead of a community of learning, there is individualism and vocational competition.

Changes in societal and vocational realities only exacerbate the problem. A growing number of teachers see their vocation as part of a career in academia. More than a few live far away, work part-time, and as a result are only on campus now and again. For them, teaching is simply one activity in this phase of their lives.

The effect on students is easily recognized. They follow the same pattern or they distance themselves from their school after graduation, because they haven't experienced it as a place of community, where conversations of teaching and learning occur.

---

75. Warford, *Practical Wisdom*, 9.

According to Warford this situation has everything to do with the calling (vocation) of those who teach. Many lack the inner conviction that they are teachers of the church who are introducing the next generation of pastors to the Christian tradition. That gives Warford the title for his book: we need teachers of wisdom.

The shift in emphasis from the Farley-Stackhouse-Kelsey debate to the Lexington process to Warford's book is worth noting.[76] It appears that the era of espousing new theories of theological education is past. Now the concern seems to be the challenges and questions of implementation. Farley, Stackhouse, and Kelsey certainly hint at what is to follow. Between Athens and Berlin, that is, in the tension between classical education, the scientific method, and vocational pragmatism, wise teachers are needed who can lead the next generation into the wisdom of the Christian faith and of pastoral praxis. Along the way, however, strong headwinds are blowing in the form of the diverse, disintegrating forces of a postmodern culture. We will deal with this again with the European context in view.

We have now gained an international perspective – ecumenical and evangelical voices, voices from the arena of missions and the Majority World, as well as from North America. With this background we now turn our attention to recent developments in German-speaking Europe.

2.5 Efforts to Reform Theological Education in German-Speaking Europe

2.5.1 *Reform Efforts within the Context of Protestant Theological Studies at German Universities*

The Study of Theology: A Reform Proposal

We begin our overview with a document published in 1965 by Wolfgang Herrmann and Gerd Lautner entitled *Theologiestudium: Entwurf einer Reform* [The Study of Theology: A Reform Proposal].[77] It comprises a report

---

76. Ibid.
77. Wolfgang Herrmann and Gerd Lautner, *Theologiestudium. Entwurf einer Reform* (Munich: Kaiser, 1965).

that was commissioned by the Fachverband Evangelische Theologie, part of the Verband Deutscher Studentenfachschaften.

Hans-Joachim Haubold's description of the situation in the forward to the report is telling:

> The situation among the church seminaries and theological faculties remains essentially unchanged: "Reforms" are undertaken as insufficient accommodations to the changing situation of the students. But reform means a fundamentally new structure that will do justice to the current situation.

The two authors of the report distinguish shortly thereafter between "repair" and "reform."[78] They have no desire to propose further "repairs" (cosmetic changes and improvements). Rather a "…reform in the unified sense of a course of study with entirely new accents – with our specific specialty in view – in the sense of a new scientific (rational, methodical) communication of theology and church."

The background of these reform proposals can be outlined as follows:

1) Initial context can be found in the emancipation movement among the students in the 1960s. The pressure for reform came first of all from the bottom up. A revolution began. Study at a university was no longer to be a top-down one-way street but rather was to be participatory. How controversial and emotional this palace revolution was, is evident in the tone struck by the authors in stating their central thesis: "The dictatorship is unmistakably overthrown, and just as unmistakable is the students' demand for the right of co-determination."[79]

2) Second, the report wrestles with the old basic question, whether and in what way the study of theology should be directed toward the church, that is, toward the vocational training of pastors.[80] The report addresses this question quite thoroughly. It is shown that, rooted in pietism and Schleiermacher, Protestant theological education at the universities was geared toward vocational service in the church and the pastorate. At the same time the

---

78. Ibid., 11.
79. Ibid., 13.
80. Ibid., 15.

report emphasizes the significance of the university ethos of scientific study. The authors seek to maintain the value of both: the basic orientation toward pastoral ministry and the academic education detached from any purpose. The two poles are held in tension by the authors' definition of the purpose of studying. It is worthwhile to read the text in its original wording:[81]

The Meaning of Studying

The etymology of the word "*Sinn*" [meaning, sense] indicates via the old high German meaning – travel, pursuit – the roots in the word "to send." Even with an appropriate hesitancy to draw too much from a word's etymology, this finding is useful. For the meaning here of being underway, on a mutual adventure, moving toward a goal not fully certain or sure, clearly and adequately characterizes the ethical destination of studying.

Studying is an attempt, aimed at understanding. It is a risk and carries no guarantee. Even today when theology students are increasingly after quantity in their studies, when they cram, strain, pursue, toil, but don't really study, success is not guaranteed. Because high marks on one's exams is not the goal. A course of study that only has the exams in view is perhaps expedient, but not very meaningful. The meaning of studying cannot be equated with exam grades.

The journey itself is the meaning, not the goal. The meaning reveals itself only in the fulfilled present, in the dedication to the task. The hours and years of study must themselves be meaningful, fulfilling. These 5–6 years must never be dismissed and neglected as a "not yet" on the way to a purpose in the future.

If studying is primarily or exclusively directed toward the goal of training pastors, it will remain empty, be sucked down by the pull of "exam-phobia," and squeezed in the vise of despair, never having learned enough. Then the high demands of one's future vocation become the ghost of one's study. The acquiring of knowledge becomes dominant. All that is important is achieving one's potential, which will later serve as a resource to be drawn

---

81. Ibid., 24–26.

from. But the time of studying itself is lost time, time that must be killed, time that is sacrificed to the insatiable purpose. Studying falls under the power of worry. It becomes joyless, dry, and stressful.

In short, it becomes a training ground for leaders in the church. Tomorrow's men are missing their today. And for the student that means his study. He should seek fulfillment not in his future as a pastor, but rather in his present as a student.

We must energetically defend against pragmatic, utilitarian thinking. The job of the student is to study, to stay true to the course of being on a journey.

The purpose must grow out of the meaning, and in a way only arrive at the end of the journey. But the purpose must never skip over the journey, must never forget the detail in pursuit of the image, must never forget the devotion to the individual in the pursuit of the whole.

The Purpose of Studying

We in no way deny that studying has a purpose. Who would seriously want to deny the connection between theological education and pastoral training? Yet this connection must be looked at critically. Both terms must be sharply differentiated in order for them to be positively connected. This connection occurs under the term *relational distance*. Distance is the prerequisite for reflection concerning the job description, the vocational goal that must not be blindly, uncritically pursued. Relationship maintains the critical questioning of the direction of the goal. During the time of study, the accent is on the distance. During the time of pastoral training, the accent is on relationship. The term *relational distance* makes it possible to resolve the conflict between "education" and "training" as the goal of studying. Studying has education in mind when it is engaged in practicing a scientific approach. A theologian thus educated is a prerequisite of a properly trained pastor. Education is an essential component of training. Training teaches science and praxis together. And it does this, in turn, in the name of scientific critical thinking, which has made "praxis" a subject of reflection.

3) The style of this lengthy passage hints at yet a third context of the authors' reform proposal: It is "the changed preaching environment in the modern world" and the resulting "pursuit of pedagogy, psychology, and social sciences within framework of practical theology."[82] When this report was published, secularization and estrangement from the church were becoming a reality to a degree never before seen. The church faced the enormous question of whether (and how) the gospel could still be communicated to people of the modern world. It was in those years that the paradigm shift in practical theology occurred. This shift is often described with terms such as empirical change, practical theology as the science of action, or the paradigm of empirical social sciences. The authors of the 1965 report seek to take seriously the intense demand for a vocational orientation, a greater emphasis on praxis in theological education at the universities. But they fear that education in the classical sense will fall victim to the "insatiable purpose," to use their phrase. They want to avoid that loss at all costs and seek to maintain at least some measure of the ideals of a university education.

4) The report addresses a further problem that arose as a direct result of the developments in university theological study just described. "The effort to include the helping sciences [social sciences] leads necessarily to an expansion of content." From there it's not long until suggestions are made to make cuts in areas of history or Hebrew.[83] Shortsighted transfer mechanisms like these are rejected by the authors. They seek instead to thoroughly rethink and redefine the term "content"[84] and above all to avoid a situation in which the reform debate devolves into a content debate, in which the quality of study is choked by the quantity of the content, or in which haggling over territory and a tug-of-war over curriculum poison the academic atmosphere.

Four descriptors outline the topics addressed by the 1965 reform proposal: (1) emancipation movement among the students, (2) the study of theology and the training of pastors, (3) the challenge of reaching a secularized society

---

82. Herrmann and Lautner, *Theologiestudium*, 15.
83. Ibid.
84. Ibid., 35–37.

(introduction of social sciences into practical theology), and (4) expanded content and territorial battles in curriculum planning.

From the perspective of forty years later, several comments and questions seem obvious:

1) The study sees theological education as based in the context of the universities. It raises Schleiermacher's question about whether theology can justify its place in the modern university. Following the historical representation of pietism and Schleiermacher, the report starts the unfolding of the program of reform with foundational chapters on the scientific method (ch. 4), on theology as science (ch. 5), and on practical theology as the science of the church (ch. 6). Theology can only find its place at the university if it subjects itself methodically to the dictates of science. These chapters make clear that the report is strongly influenced by the unbroken dominance of historical-critical, form-critical methodology and by kerygma theology. What Farley calls *theologia* is scarcely mentioned at all.

2) In addition, it is noteworthy that the question of the nature of the church and the vocation of the pastor are not touched upon until chapter 7 and are discussed but briefly. I would like to point out here that a reform proposal with this starting point – first science, then ecclesiology, then pastoral ministry – has a trajectory and an emphasis diametrically opposed to the path that Richard Niebuhr proposed ten years earlier in North America.

3) It seems clear as well that the scope of the discussion in the 1960s was limited to the situation in the European (or even the German) universities and the training of pastors. The developments in North America, the enormous widening of perspective that came through ecumenical, international and missionary voices in the following decades, globalization, pluralism in a postmodern society, and the revolution in education within Europe – all these factors are missing from the discussion.

The Work of the "Mixed Commission"

Later the reform process within Protestant theological study in Germany can be traced by following the work of the so-called "Gemischte Kommission"

[Mixed Commission].⁸⁵ Since 1965 this commission, made up of representatives of the university theological faculties and of the member churches of the Evangelische Kirche in Deutschland, has overseen the task of evaluating and guiding the process of reform in theological education.⁸⁶

The reform processed has been documented in fourteen volumes published between 1967 and 1993 under the title *Reform der theologischen Ausbilding* [Reform of Theological Education]. It's not necessary to summarize the entire process here. Those who wish further information can consult Michael Ahme's dissertation *Der Reformversuch der EKD 1970-1976* [The Reform Efforts of the EKD 1970-1976]⁸⁷ and the collection edited by Michael Ahme and Michael Beintker, *Theologische Ausbildung in der EKD. Dokumente und Texte aus der Arbeit der Gemischten Kommission/ Fachkommission zur Reform des Theologiestudiums 1993-2004* [Theological Education in the Evangelical Church in Germany. Documents and Texts from the Work of the Mixed Commission/Special Commission for the Reform of Theological Study 1993-2004].⁸⁸

I only want to emphasize a few things here. Particularly noteworthy are the "Grundsätze für die Ausbildung und Fortbildung der Pfarrer und Pfarrerinnen der Gliedkirchen der EKD"⁸⁹ [Principles for the Education and Continuing Education of Pastors in the Member Churches of the EKD]. They still provide orientation today especially in the midst of the challenges of the

---

85. See the entire report edited by H. E. Hess and H. E. Tödt, *Reform der theologischen Ausbildung*. Vol. 1: "Untersuchungen, Berichte, Empfehlungen" (Munich: Kreuz, 1967).

86. Otto Kaiser and Hans Eduard Tödt, "Zum Stand der Reform des Studiums der Evangelischen Theologie," in *Reform der theologischen Ausbildung*, eds. H. E. Hess and H E. Tödt, (Munich: Kreuz, 1967): 14–15.

87. Michael Ahme, *Der Reformversuch der EKD 1970-1976* (Stuttgart: Kohlhammer, 1990).

88. Michael Ahme and Michael Beintker, *Theologische Ausbildung in der EKD. Dokumente und Texte aus der Arbeit der Gemischten Kommission/Fachkommission zur Reform des Theologiestudiums 1993-2004* (Leipzig: Evangelische Verlagsanstalt, 2005). Eilert Herms, the chairman of the commission from this period, gives a good overview of the process from 1985-1998 in a report entitled "Die Arbeit der Gemischten Kommission 1985-1998. Bilanz und Ausblick". Michael Beintker gives a good overview from 1999–2003 in *"Zwischen Bologna und Pisa. Die Arbeit der Gemischten Kommission zur Reform des Theologiestudiums / Fachkommission I von 1999-2003"*. Both reports can be found in Ahme and Beintker, *Theologische Ausbildung*, 159–177 and 179–203 respectively.

89. These "Grundsätze" [Principles] have been re-published in Ahme and Beintker, *Theologische Ausbildung*, 11–68.

Bologna process.[90] The "principles" are, according to Herms, characterized by the following points:[91]

1) The educational concept consists of three steps which include university studies, a period of internship in the role of pastor, and continuing education.

2) The first phase, a scientific study of theology, serves a key function.

3) Concentration on the text is absolutely essential.

4) Exegesis must be about determining the real meaning of the text.

5) The search for truth is paramount, absolutely essential.

6) Study must be linked with praxis.

7) Life experience must be incorporated and integrated into study.

In conversations with the churches of other European countries, two characteristics of European Protestant theological education have been identified:

- The scientific study of theology as the first phase of theological education – normally at a state university – is an integral component of a pastor's training.
- The first (scientific study) and second phase (experiential training in the role as a pastor) must be closely connected, that is, they must be reciprocally challenging and there must be cross-fertilization between the two.[92]

Here we have articulated two axiomatic principles of German Protestant theological education: (1) the commitment to theological education in the context of a state university and (2) the commitment to the church. This educational model stands fully in the tradition of Schleiermacher. The model must, however, be newly contextualized in a postmodern, pluralistic and secularized environment. I see that as the decisive accomplishment of the Mixed Commission.

---

90. See Ahme and Beintker, *Theologische Ausbildung*, 7–8.
91. Herms, "Die Arbeit der Gemischten Kommission," 167.
92. Ahme and Beintker, *Theologische Ausbildung*, 170.

It is apparent, however, that the entire discussion is taking place in the rather limited world of the university and the EKD. International input is mostly lacking. Critical questioning of the classical theological education – like the questions posed by Farley, Kelsey and others in the US – is not part of the consideration. And what about input from the international ecumenical discussion? And what has the Bologna process set in motion? These questions must still be answered.

Receiving Input from the Ecumenical Movement into University-Based Theological Education in Germany

Lothar Engel lists eleven challenges which university-based theological education in Germany faces, arising from input from the ecumenical movement:[93]

1) Theological education aims at a holistic theological training process.

2) Theological education is a genuine responsibility of the church.

3) Because theological education happens for the future of the church, it must operate under missiological premises.

4) The scientific dimension of theological education is absolutely essential. This includes the critical consideration of the limits of one's own context and perspective.

5) Communication with the entire people of God is assigned a foundational hermeneutical function within theological education.

6) Spiritual direction during the time of theological education is of great importance.

7) Academic education must be linked with relevant, real-life experience.

---

93. Lothar Engel, "Ökumenische Impulse und die Wirklichkeit von Fakultäten und kirchlichen Hochschulen," in Evangelisches Missionswerk, *Impulse* (1997): 52–57. Engel's article is based on the previously cited paper by Dietrich Werner, *Theologie zum Leben bringen. Anforderungen an eine zukunftsorientierte Ausbildung*. Engel summarizes and comments upon Werner's findings.

8) Theological education must keep the global sending of the church in view (the Great Commission) and must equip students to participate in the *missio Dei*.

9) The credibility of theological education increases when the church lives in solidarity with the poor.

10) Ecumenical openness and cooperation between denominations must be practiced and learned.

11) Theological education needs to be networked internationally and ecumenically.

That's the vision. Yet the reality is discordant. On the one hand there are examples of innovative and cooperative implementation of ideas from the ecumenical movement. Many good ideas are summarized in the previously mentioned volume, *Impulse für eine Kirche von morgen. Beiträge zur ökumenisch-theologischen Ausbildung* [Ideas for a Church for Tomorrow: Suggestions for Ecumenical Theological Education], published by the Evangelisches Missionswerk. The content documents the outcome of discussions held at a conference sponsored by the World Council of Churches, "Ecumenical Theological Education – Its Viability" (Oslo 1996).

One other document that takes ideas from the ecumenical dialogue in recent decades and translates them into a praxis-oriented and contextualized model of theological education is entitled *Theologische Bildungsprozesse gestalten. Schritte zur Ausbildungsreform* [Shaping Theological Educational Processes: Steps to Educational Reform].[94]

One innovative, practical step forward in one area is the opening of the Greifswalder Institut zur Erforschung von Evangelisation und Gemeindeentwicklung [Greifswald Institute for the Research of Evangelism and Church Development], founded by Michael Herbst.[95]

However, there is a noticeable discrepancy between the extremely creative and inspiring process within the World Council of Churches on the one hand

---

94. Edited by Hans-Günter Heimbrock and Matthias von Kriegstein (Frankfurt: Spener, 2002). This paper documents the reform process within the school of theology at the Goethe University in Frankfurt.

95. Cf. Michael Herbst, "Mission in der theologischen Ausbildung," *Theologische Beiträge* 36 (2005): 202–216.

and the reform efforts within the theological schools of German universities on the other. Lothar Engel and Dietrich Werner, who for years were catalytic agents for the ecumenical process in the German context, express frustration again and again.

In a 1992 opinion Werner writes: "Encouragements from the ecumenical movement for the reform of theological education have thus far had little effect on the theological schools of the state universities." He complains that too much time is spent occupied with the classical texts of the Bible and with history of dogmatics while not enough time is devoted to the analysis of the current context. The topics of church renewal and church growth are scarcely addressed in the theological schools of the universities. They are postponed until the student gathers experience in a time of internship in a pastoral role. As a rule, theological education in Germany is still too one-sidedly geared to the role of full-time pastor. The multiplicity of ministries and the multiplicity of tasks within the church are given little consideration, according to Werner.[96]

Later Werner decries the fact that many good initiatives for giving more attention to areas like the theology of missions and ecumenical science have fallen victim to budget cuts, time pressures, and overcrowded curriculum plans.[97]

One cannot avoid the conclusion that many topics vital to theological education – topics which have been part of the international and ecumenical discussion for years – have found only limited attention in the theological schools of German universities.[98]

Evelies Mayer was right when she wrote (2003) about the theological faculties, "German universities, when compared with their international counterparts, are neither innovative nor reform minded. There are many indications that the modernization of higher education is making little progress, despite many ideas and concepts that have been proposed."[99]

---

96. Dietrich Werner, "Ecumenical Renewal of Congregations," *International Review of Missions* 71 (1992): 78.
97. Werner, *Theologie zum Leben bringen*, 12.
98. Jacques Nicole reported similar findings in Switzerland: "Brief History of the So-Called 'Classical' Model for Theological Education," *Ministerial Formation* 67 (October 1994): 33–34.
99. Evelies Mayer, "Hochschule innovativ: Das ursprüngliche Programm," in *Die neue Verantwortung der Hochschulen*, eds. Evelies Mayer, Hans-Dieter Daniel, Ulrich Teichler (Bonn: Lemmens, 2003), 15.

Pressure to Reform, Resulting from the Bologna Process

In Europe in the late 1990s, efforts to reform theological education received an additional boost from the so-called Bologna reform.[100] In the text of a report from the Conference of Rectors of Swiss Universities (CRUS) it is described as follows:

A European "Reform of the Century"

> In the universities in Europe a "reform of the century" is in progress. The goal is transparency and structural compatibility within the world of European universities, while keeping in mind cultural, linguistic, and educational/political diversity.
>
> To this end the education ministers from key European governments met at the ancient and venerable University of Bologna in 1999 and approved a program of political action, the so-called "Bologna Declaration." This document committed them to promoting compatibility and transparency in the structures of European higher education, making mobility easier, and strengthening European competitiveness. These goals are to be reached by means of mutual adaptation to achieve similarity/compatibility in educational structures (based on a two-step system), in degree nomenclature, in awarding of academic credits (on the basis of the ECTS), in the tools used for quality assurance, as well as in increased attention given to the European dimension of curricula.[101]

The Bologna process is nothing less than a farewell to the elitist educational monopoly of the state universities – and in the case of theology, a farewell to the monopoly of the state church. The Bologna reform must be seen not only in the context of a united Europe and globalization but also as an expression of liberalization and the free market. Detlef Müller-Böling put it well in his provocative book, *Die entfesselte Hochschule*: "From a Republic

---

100. A summary of the most important developments and documents from 1988 to 2006 can be found in Bob Reinalda and Ewa Kulesza, *The Bologna Process – Harmonizing Europe's Higher Education* (Opladen: Barbara Budrich Publishers, 2006), 2nd revised edition.

101. "Zur Erneuerung der universitären Lehre im Rahmen der Bologna-Reform," 1 at http://www.bolognareform.ch/

of Academics to a Service Industry?"[102] That means that institutions of higher education can no longer survive on their historically won reputations alone. Their "product" must now compete on the open market through verifiable quality. That is new territory for traditional universities. But for smaller, specialized seminaries that have long been part of an international network, it provides new opportunities.

Theological faculties – and the humanities as a whole – received the initiatives of the Bologna process only with reluctance and aversion. There is simply too much friction between the classic educational ideals of Humboldt and the liberal, market-driven concept of Bologna.

This is especially true in Germany. The following sentences from Ahme and Beintker make the scepticism abundantly clear:

> German universities are currently experiencing by far the most radical changes in their entire operation of teaching and studying. The results of this process, which bears the name of the world's oldest university, cannot yet be foreseen. The Special Commission was guided by the wisdom that in a situation like this principles must be determinative. They offer, of course, a solid foundation for the design and construction of a theological curriculum and a reliable orientation in the reform activism grown rampant in the politics of higher education. Conceptual knowledge alone is able to provide promising perspective for what is taking shape.[103]

The direction that the EKD would take in response to the Bologna reforms was clear: Equipped with the principles of the Mixed Commission introduced earlier, the EKD would seek to survive the unavoidable with minimum damage. University-based theological education was, indeed, faced with significant problems because of the Bologna structures. We are unable to deal with these in detail now.[104]

---

102. Detlef Müller-Böling, *Die entfesselte Hochschule* (Gütersloh: Bertelsmann Stiftung, 2000), 16ff.
103. Ahme and Beintker, *Theologische Ausbildung*, 7–8.
104. More thoroughly, Michael Beintker, "Zwischen Bologna und Pisa," in *Theologische Ausbildung in der EKD. Dokumente und Texte aus der Arbeit der Gemischten Kommission/ Fachkommission zur Reform des Theologiestudiums 1993-2004*, eds. Michael Ahme and Michael Beintker (Leipzig: Evangelische Verlagsanstalt, 2005), 188–195.

However it would appear that in Germany the churches of the EKD may well reject in principle any implementation of the Bologna process in the area of university-based theological education for the vocational training of pastors.

The changes set in motion by the Bologna process can be seized upon constructively as a chance to achieve an overall restructuring of theological education. This is demonstrated by the so-called Concordat Reform undertaken by the Reformed Churches of Switzerland. As a part of this reform, a new concept was introduced which integrates theory and practice in the vocational education of pastors. This concept will be presented at the end of chapter 6 (6.6.2).[105]

2.5.2 Free Church and Evangelical Theological Education in German-Speaking Europe

In this section various types and groups of schools will be discussed. What they have in common is that they offer theological education outside the framework of the state universities. To study theology at the universities remains a privilege of the state church in German-speaking Europe. Free church and evangelical seminaries and Bible schools are supported by private donations or by churches or denominations (i.e. those churches outside the state church, hence the moniker free church).

At the same time, however, these schools are very heterogeneous. A number of evangelical Bible schools and seminaries are members of the Konferenz Bibeltreuer Ausbildungsstätten (KBA). Based on background and donor base, one can identify some three types of schools within the ranks of the KBA: (1) non-denominational schools and seminaries whose origins can often be traced to North American missionaries (e.g. Bibelschule Brake and Freie Theologische Akademie, now called Freie Theologische Hochschule, in Giessen). (2) Schools in the pietistic tradition within the Protestant state church (e.g. Theologisches Seminar Bad Liebenzell, Theologisches Seminar St. Crischona). (3) Schools of the free-church tradition (e.g. Bibelschule Wiedenest, Bibelseminar Bonn).

A second group of schools are those supported and run by free-church denominations. Of particular note are the schools of the classical free

---

105. Further information available at http://www.konkordat.ch

churches: the Baptists (Elstal/Berlin), Methodists (Reutlingen), Evangelical Free Church (Ewersbach), Mennonites (Bienenberg/Liestal), and Pentecostal churches (Beröa/Erzhausen). The majority of these schools are within the revivalist-evangelical tradition but would be hesitant to use the term evangelical (as it is often understood today) to describe themselves, at least without qualifiers.

Schools from both of the above groups are connected with one another through the EEAA. This organization is, however, not limited to German-speaking Europe.[106]

The Schools and Seminaries of the KBA

The KBA was founded in 1963/64 with the aim of strengthening the Bible-believing seminaries and Bible schools, as opposed to the university-based theological faculties which were viewed as liberal and as critical of the Bible.[107]

The KBA lives from its annual conference. The developments within these schools and the topics important to them can also be traced by means of the annual KBA conference. A study of the conference files quickly reveals, however, that foundational questions of theological education were handled only occasionally.[108] The late 1990s saw a more thorough discussion of the future of schools in the KBA. An extensive survey was intended to provide an analysis of the current situation and be the basis for the reforms needed to move into the future. The results of the survey as well as interpretation and proposals for reform were presented at the 1997 conference and published in *Theologische Ausbildung zu Beginn des 21. Jahrunderts* [Theological Education at the Beginning of the 21st Century].[109] Wilhelm Faix summarized the central points in the following theses:[110]

---

106. A special category is occupied by the Staatsunabhängige Theologische Hochschule (STH) in Basel. It belongs to none of the previously described groups but offers a government-recognized university-level degree program that is a biblically-based, Bible-believing alternative to theology schools at state universities. In this sense, this school belongs with those discussed in this chapter.

107. Regarding the beginnings of the KBA, see Ott, *Beyond Fragmentation*, 60–61.

108. As part of my dissertation I studied these conferences, especially regarding themes of missions and missiology, and thus accessed their files for the years from 1963 to 1995.

109. Tobias Faix, et al., *Theologische Ausbildung zu Beginn des 21. Jahrunderts* (Bonn: Verlag für Kultur und Wissenschaft, 1998), 31–37.

110. Faix et al. "Theologische Ausbildung im Umbruch," in *Theologische Ausbildung*, eds. Tobias Faix et al. (Bonn: Verlag für Kultur und Wissenschaft, 1998), 31–37.

80 Understanding and Developing Theological Education

- The image of and expectations for a pastor have changed: from pastor to mentor/trainer, from shepherd to pedagogue.
- Educational programs must offer clear opportunities for continuing education and further study.
- Higher levels of flexibility and modularization will be required.
- More attention will have to be given to the social sciences.
- Instruction must become even more praxis oriented.
- Character formation must be given high priority.
- Partnership with the church for and during theological education must be strengthened.

Additional contributions to the analysis were:[111]

- The KBA schools in light of global changes in theological education (Bernhard Ott).
- The influence of the youth culture and its impact on students (Tobias Faix).
- Evangelical theological education in conflict with post-modernism: concrete alternatives for the future (Stephan Holthaus).
- The pedagogical qualifications of teaching personnel: expectations and challenges from today's young people (Wilhelm Faix).
- The challenge of character formation, the task of mentoring (Klaus W. Müller).
- How can we better represent the aims of Bible-based, Bible-believing theological education to the public? (Klaus Schmidt).

In conclusion, the substantial contribution to the reform of theological education from this 1997 document merits the following commentary:

1) The introduction includes the sentence, "The quest for a relevant education that is based on the Bible is a constant challenge for all evangelical schools."[112] Two poles are evident in this statement: (a) it's about education that is relevant to the times. This, in my opinion, is the main contribution of this study. It poses the question of how theological education can be (or again become) relevant in the context of post-modernism and the current youth

---

111. All were published in Faix et al., *Theologische Ausbildung*.
112. Faix et al., *Theologische Ausbildung*, 11.

culture. It was declining enrollment figures that prompted the study, and the study provided valuable suggestions for shaping the future. (b) It's also about a biblical base. This is assumed more than defined. At any rate the study contributes little to the concept of biblically based theological education. The general direction of the study is more about pragmatics than about principles.

2) The study has little to say about the scientific method. It would appear that the survey focused on praxis orientation, character development and the necessary role of the social sciences. An academic education was viewed as too theoretical and top heavy.

3) At about the same time, some schools began to energetically pursue academic recognition. Initially this happened by partnering with foreign universities. When the Bologna process gained traction, the desire for academic recognition through the German or Swiss university system became a more pressing part of the agenda of the KBA (see the 2004 conference).

4) Overall it would seem that questions related to the integration of the praxis-oriented Bible school ethos with the demand for academic training have not been sufficiently considered. The whole topic of the relationship between theory and practice will require additional reflection.[113]

5) Although the schools in the KBA may be seen as part of the missionary movement, the topic of missionary training receives only peripheral attention. One could wish that these missions schools would more explicitly discuss a kind of missionary training that would be address the needs of the future. It would be important in that process to consider questions from the field of the theology of missions,[114] but also the relationship between missions and theological education. This latter issue was considered by the Arbeitskreis für evangelikaler Missiologie [The German-language Evangelical Missiological Society] during its 1999 annual conference. The book that resulted, *Ausbildung als missionarischer Auftrag* [Education as a Task of Missions],[115]

---

113. Cf. chapter 5 of this Handbook.
114. Cf. Bernhard Ott, "Missionstheologie in evangelikaler theologischer Ausbildung," in *Gemeinsam im Auftrag des Herrn*, eds. Heinrich Löwen and Hans Kasdorf (Bornheim/Bonn: Puls Verlag, 1999), 123–139.
115. Klaus W. Müller and Thomas Schirrmacher, eds. *Ausbildung als missionarischer Auftrag* (Bonn: Verlag für Kultur und Wissenschaft, 2000).

constitutes an additional valuable evangelical contribution to the reform of theological education.

The Free-Church Seminaries

The free-church seminaries do not have a binding structure that could serve as the platform for a process of reflection. It's true that the presidents of these seminaries form the working group "Theological Education" within the Vereinigung Evangelischer Freikirchen in Germany and as such meet once a year for informal discussions. There is, however, no process for collective reflection about the basic issues of theological education within the free churches.

Internal discussions about theological education within the individual free-church denominations are published only occasionally. For example, the Baptists have published a few relevant articles in their *Zeitschrift für Theologie und Gemeinde* [Magazine for Theology and Church]. In the 2001 edition one can read thought-provoking ideas about the value (or lack thereof) of having an academically recognized educational path for the training of Baptist pastors,[116] as well as thoughts about the future of the theological seminary in Elstal.[117]

The majority of these free churches are connected to worldwide denominational networks. Discussions about theological education on the international level as well as other contacts with seminaries in other countries and on other continents provide additional inspiration for the developmental process of these seminaries.[118]

It would, however, enrich all of German-speaking Europe if the seminaries of the free-church denominations would formulate their own contribution to the future of theological education.

---

116. Hans-Harald Mallau, "Das Theologiestudium im BEFG und seine, akademische Anerkennung," *Zeitschrift für Theologie und Gemeinde* 6 (2001): 9–18.

117. Kim Strübind, "'Pastoren bilden Pastoren aus' – ein Entwurf für eine zeit- und sachgemäße theologische Ausbildung im Bund Evangelisch-Freikirchlicher Gemeinden in Elstal," *Zeitschrift für Theologie und Gemeinde* 6 (2001): 204–217.

118. See for example Nancy R. Heisey and Daniel S. Schipani, eds., *Theological Education on Five Continents* (Strasbourg: Mennonite World Conference, 1997).

Additional Literature
In recent years a growing number of works have been published that deal with the implementation of the Bologna process. By and large the Bologna process is critically received in these publications:

From the Protestant perspective
Reinhold Bernhard. "The Bolognanization of Theological Education in Germany and Switzerland." In *Handbook of Theological Education in World Christianity*, edited by Dietrich Werner et al., 584–593. Eugene, OR: Wipf and Stock Publishers, 2010.
Christian Grethlein and Lisa J. Krengel. "Auswirkungen des Bologna-Prozesses auf die Evangelische Theologie." [The Effects of the Bologna Process on Protestant Theology] *UNA SANCTA* 66, no. 2 (2011): 103–112.
The comprehensive dissertation by Lisa J. Krengel, *Die Evangelische Theologie und der Bologna-Prozess. Eine Rekonstruktion der ersten Dekade (1999–2009)*. [Protestant Theology and the Bologna Process. A Reconstruction of the First Decade (1999–2009)] Leipzig: Evangelische Verlagsanstalt, 2011.

From the Catholic perspective
Klaus Müller. "Wissenschaftliche Theologie an staatlichen Universitäten." [Scientific Theology at State Universities] *UNA SANCTA* 66, no. 2 (2011): 90–102.

From the free-church perspective
Bernhard Ott. "Fit für die Welt – Neuere Entwicklungen in freikirchlicher theologischer Ausbildung." [Fit for the World – Recent Developments in Free-church Theological Education] *UNA SANCTA* 66, no. 2 (2011): 113–122.

2.6 A New Agenda Leads to Paradigmatic Changes

We have now achieved an overview of recent reform and renewal efforts in theological education. Can the many-faceted discussion points and reform proposals be succinctly summarized? We have to try, although it will not be possible without a certain amount of over-simplification.

In the 1960s Walter Hollenweger introduced the phrase "The world sets the agenda" into the ecumenical dialogue. That is certainly true for theological education as well. All of the ideas, proposals, suggestions, and initiatives that have been discussed in this chapter can be seen as responses to a new agenda. The questions now being asked are of such a nature that they lead to reforms and upheavals of paradigm-shifting scope.

I see six great upheavals that present challenges to theological education and call for far-reaching, radical change:

1) The transition from the colonial to the post-colonial era, together with the fact that Christians in the Two-Thirds World are enriching global Christianity with their own voice and with great vitality, leads to serious questions directed at the Western church and its theological education in particular. The key points are: too much emphasis on the stability of the church, too little emphasis on missions; too institution-centered and therefore too elitist; too academic and distant and therefore not relevant for the church in its mission.

In the future, therefore, theological education will be fully geared toward the church and its mission. It will have a global, missiological, and ecumenical propensity and have a view toward the equipping of the whole people of God. It faces the challenge of integrating new upheavals and new movements with the treasure of tradition.

2) The paradigm shift in pedagogy, as seen, for example, in liberation theology and also in adult education, calls into question many traditional educational methods, especially those that are based on the top-down communication of knowledge. The relation between theory and praxis is being redefined and re-evaluated. Moreover, in the new educational paradigm, it is not the educational institution that is at the center. Rather the individual is at the center and shapes his or her own life story. Education must be person-centered, not institution-centered.

In the future, theological education will be person-centered and will integrate theory and practice, action and contemplation, thought and spirituality, experience and evaluation. At the same time It faces the challenge of determining educational requirements neither solely by the subjective desires of the individual nor solely by any short-sighted practical usefulness.

3) Today's pluralistic, post-modern culture has forever changed student demographics. There is no longer any such thing as a "typical" student. A variety of individuals with very different backgrounds and life stories are, at

their own initiative and at different times in their lives, looking for a variety of educational models. Homogeneous curricula will not survive for very long in today's competitive marketplace.

In the future, theological education will have to respond to the plurality of possibilities and needs with flexible, modular, and individually tailored educational offerings. At the same time, in the midst of all these centrifugal forces, it will face the enormous challenge of not falling victim to an arbitrary and senseless fragmentation but instead to develop integrated curricula.

4) The paradigm of the Enlightenment, that is, the Western way of thinking that is so tied to science and higher education, has created a further crisis. Western churches, which tend to follow this model of theological education, are not the churches that are growing and flourishing. If it is true that the quality of theological education can be seen by its fruit, that is, by the churches that it produces, then the Western academic model owes the Christians in the rest of the world an explanation.

In the future, theological education will not close its eyes to the weaknesses of the Western academic paradigm. It will open its eyes and widen its horizon. It faces the sizable challenge of fending off attacks against thinking and the scientific method, and of creating a theology that is thoughtful and intelligent and at the same time truly God-centered.

5) The fifth upheaval is found in the reality of a post-Christian Europe where confessing Christians are increasingly in the minority, where it can no longer be assumed that students have a thorough knowledge of the basics of the Christian faith, and where, because of disappearing Christian values, an ever larger number of students come from broken families.

In the future, theological education will have to offer, to a greater extent than ever before, a comprehensive introduction to the Christian faith, including practice in living a Christian life and living in community. That requires a holistic educational approach that addresses and develops the cognitive, spiritual, emotional, and social sides of the person. Theological education faces the challenge of not tackling this problem alone but rather in partnership with the church.

86 Understanding and Developing Theological Education

6) Finally, **globalization**, **liberalization**, and the **free market** are causing tremendous upheaval in the world of education. The Bologna reform is only a European version of this global phenomenon. Information technology and the free market dictate what is happening. Fascinating new opportunities result, while at the same time significant educational ideals are called into question. Evaluation, quality assurance, and accreditation are complex by-products of these developments.

In the future, theological education will have to succeed in the global market place as well as in a world that is shaped by information technology and by virtual communities. Schools will have to give an account of the output quality of their programs. In order to survive, they will have to become institutions of learning that are themselves learning. They will have to be continually changing and evolving, not simply administering traditions. At the same time they will face the challenge of preserving their identity and not chasing every new trend in a way that is unhealthy. In addition, they will have to discern what opportunities are offered by information technology and virtual worlds and at what pedagogical price these opportunities may be seized.

The theological education of the present and the future will inevitably take place in the context of all upheavals such as these. All of the contributions discussed in this capital seek to provide insights and solutions. They offer us ideas for the path ahead, into the future.

The following questions serve as a guide to the train of thought found in the rest of this handbook:

- Which theories of education and which models are available to us, and what traditions of theological education have influenced us (ch. 3)?
- A question directed toward the Bible and theology: Is it possible, is it essential, to give theological education a new foundation in the Bible and theology? Is it possible to articulate a theology of theological education (ch. 4)?

3

Foundations of Educational Theory: Traditions and Models of (Theological) Education

Anyone who works in the field of education, and particularly anyone who seeks to lead a theological training institution into a lasting future, must be familiar with the repertoire of educational models that have arisen historically and are being used today. Knowledge of educational theory is essential.

There is much talk today of innovative and alternative educational concepts. Such concepts are also needed in the field of theological education. Yet anyone who propagates innovations and alternatives without understanding what the new alternative is supposed to be replacing, and the nature of the traditional model to be renewed, will have little credibility. It is far too easy to propose new educational models that lack depth and that awaken feelings of déjà vu. Such models don't always deliver what they promise.[1]

This section provides a four-part introduction to the fundamentals of educational theory.

1) First, general categories of educational theory will be introduced (3.1).

---

[1]. I elaborate more on this point in "Mission Oriented Theological Education," *Transformation* 18, no. 2 (2001): 87–98.

2) The second subsection (3.2) deals with a number of typologies which have been used in recent literature about theological education to differentiate various models of theological education.

3) Third, the secular educational models currently available will be introduced (3.3).

4) Finally, an overview of the current models of theological education will be given (3.4).

Along the way a number of concrete questions arise:

1) Which educational traditions and models have influenced our school? What opportunities and limits does that present?

2) From which educational traditions and models would we like to draw our inspiration for shaping our school?

3) Or: To which educational traditions and models do we want to be a conscious and concrete alternative?

3.1 Foundational Categories of Educational Theory

3.1.1 Education and Training

The two terms "education" and "training" point to differing educational concepts.

Education refers to a more strongly academic path that leads to and includes university, graduate, and post-graduate studies. This model emphasizes the intellectual formation of the person through thoughtful engagement with human endeavors such as language, history and literature and with the realities of this world such as mathematics and natural sciences. This form of education happens without reference to or involvement in an occupation. Neither vocational training nor job certification is the primary goal.

Training, on the other hand, involves preparation for a vocation. It includes all programs and courses whose goal is to equip the student with skills needed for a specific occupation. Typical for this model are vocational schools.

In the realm of theological education, this means that at the theology schools of the universities, no training is done but rather, theological *education*. Only during the second phase of the education, the Vicariat (or apprenticeship), the first few weeks or months of a pastor's first ministry assignment, does actual practical (on the job) *training* happen.

Bible schools and theological seminaries, on the other hand, generally offer courses of *training*. Their programs are designed to qualify students for ministry in the church or missions or social services (diaconal ministries).

We have, therefore, both dimensions – education and training – in theological education.

3.1.2 Formal, Non-formal, or Informal Training?

Distinctions are made in educational theory between formal, non-formal and informal learning. The definitions are somewhat fluid and partially overlapping.[2] Some measure of clarity has been provided by the European Commission's definitions provided as part of the discussions of education within the European Union:[3]

Formal Learning

Learning that normally takes place in a school or training centre, is structured (in terms of the goals of learning, the timeframe of learning, or the furtherance of learning), and leads to certification. Formal learning is, from the viewpoint of the learner, goal-oriented.

Non-formal Learning

Learning that doesn't take place in schools or training centres and normally doesn't lead to certification. It is, however, systematic (in terms of goals, timeframe and materials). It is, from the viewpoint of the learner, goal-oriented.

---

2. For the background and the development of the terms see Bernd Overwien, "Informelles Lernen, eine Herausforderung an die internationale Bildungsforschung," in *Erfahrungslernen in der beruflichen Bildung – Beiträge zu einem kontroversen Konzept*, eds. Peter Dehnbostel, Werner Markert und Hermann Novak (Neusäss: Kieser, 1999), 295–314.

3. Quoted by Bernd Overwien, "Internationale Sichtweisen auf 'informelles Lernen' am Übergang zum 21. Jahrhundert," in *Grundbegriffe der Ganztagsbildung*, ed. Thomas Coelen (Wiesbaden: VS Verlag für Sozialwissenschaften, 2004), 56–57.

Informal Learning

Learning that takes place in everyday life, at work, in the family, or in free time. It is not structured (in terms of goals, time and support) and does not normally lead to certification. Informal learning can be goal-oriented but is, in most cases, not intentional but rather occurs incidentally, in passing.

The significance of informal learning has become apparent during the discussions of the past few decades. UNESCO's Faure Report (1972) says that approximately 70 percent of all learning occurs informally. It would be a huge mistake, therefore, for theological education to include only formal learning.

The various levels of learning and education can, however, be differentiated by their respective extent of institutionalization.[4] It seems good to me, therefore, to use the term theological education in reference to formal learning that is usually structured, offered by a school or training institution, and leads to a formal certificate, degree, or academic title.

The relationship to non-formal and informal learning can and should be ensured. Formal learning has no monopoly on learning and should never regard itself as sufficient in itself, a closed system. On the contrary, formal learning must remain aware of its own limitations and must intentionally include non-formal and informal learning in its overall pedagogical approach. To put it plainly: formal education must equip the student for lifelong learning of the non-formal and informal variety and never hinder the same.

3.1.3 Educational Levels

1) For some orientation in determining educational levels, we turn to the internationally recognized system developed by UNESCO, the International Standard Classification of Education.[5] The ISCED establishes the following levels of training or education:[6]

---

4. Cf. Overwien, "Informelles Lernen", 298.

5. In recent years the 1997 ISCED classification has been revised. The 2011 classification is current: http://www.uis.unesco.org/EDUCATION/Pages/international-standard-classification-of-education.aspx.

6. The summary which follows, originally written in German, follows the 1997 classification because a German text of the 2011 ISCED was not yet available at the time of writing (http://www.bfs.admin.ch/bfs/portal/de/index/infotek/nomenklaturen/blank/blank/isced/01.html).

ISCED 0 Pre-Primary Level

These programs are those from the very first stages of organized instruction up until the primary level. They are preparatory, take place in schools or centres, and are offered for children at least 3 years of age.

ISCED 1 Primary Level

These programs include the systematic learning of all three basic skills – reading, writing, and arithmetic – as well as an introduction into other subjects. Children begin the primary level between the ages of 5 and 7, and stay in this mandatory level for 6 years

ISCED 2 Secondary Level I

The courses of this level are subsequent to the primary level and complete the student's mandatory basic education. The courses are more heavily specialized. Classes are given in a variety of subjects taught by a number of specialized instructors.

ISCED 3 Secondary Level II

This level offer further learning after the basic (minimum) education. Level 3 (Secondary Level II) starts approximately 9 years after the beginning of primary school. The competencies which should be acquired during ISCED 2 (Secondary Level I) are minimum prerequisites for Secondary Level II.

Further distinctions are:

- The next kind of training or education which follows Secondary Level II and builds upon it. Programs are differentiated on the basis of whether they lead to (3A) further education at the university level, (3B) further vocational education, or (3C) entry into the work force.
- Program orientation and aims. General education courses are distinguished from vocational training programs.

- Cumulative theoretical length of the program (from the beginning of Secondary Level II). Those classified as Level 3A and 3B must last a minimum of 3 years.

ISCED 4 Post-Secondary, Non-Tertiary Level

These programs offer a post-secondary education without tertiary content. Prerequisite is the successful completion of an ISCED Level 3 program of at least three years in length. These programs are subdivided in the same way as those of ISCED Level 3.

The ISCED Level 4 is not required of all students who wish to pursue tertiary education. This level represents an optional supplemental course of study.

ISCED 5 Tertiary Level I

These programs offer an education with tertiary, that is, with markedly advanced content. Prerequisite is the successful completion of an ISCED Level 3A or 3B program, or 4A or 4B program respectively. The length of these programs (ISCED 5) is at least 2 years.

The programs are subdivided into 5A and 5B based upon the kind of further education which may follow upon completion of this level (that is, whether they lead to admission to a Level 6 program), or according to the content of the curricula (high-skill professions vs. practical vocational training), as well as the cumulative theoretical length of the program (at ISCED Level 5).

This level includes colleges, universities, technical schools and academies, and master's degree programs.

ISCED 6 Tertiary Level II

The programs at this level offer education for advanced study and research. Prerequisite is the successful completion of an ISCED 5A course of study. Students at this level write and defend a dissertation of publishable quality, based upon their own research.

This level is that of doctoral programs.

It is undoubtedly appropriate to reserve the term "theological education" for programs of the tertiary level. That means that the successful completion of Level 3 (Secondary Level II = minimum of 12 years prior education) is prerequisite. Along with the theological schools of the universities, seminaries as well as Bible schools and institutes belong to the tertiary level, provided they require successful completion of Secondary Level II (ISCED 3 or 4) for admission and offer a degree or certificate upon completion that qualifies the graduate to enter a profession or move on to advanced study (ISCED 6).

Borderline are those schools that offer adult education but do not meet the ISCED standards for tertiary level – neither in their entrance requirements nor in their graduation requirements. Such schools may be classified as ISCED 4 (post-secondary, non-tertiary). Some Bible institutes, short-term Bible schools, discipleship schools, including a large number of schools and training centres in the Majority World, belong to this category. It is a matter of debate whether such programs may be termed theological education.

2) The World Council of Churches, in its catalogue of theological training schools worldwide, suggests 6 levels which encompass these schools and which approximate the levels of the ISCED.

Level 1: Programs which do not lead to an academic degree and do not qualify participants for a specific vocation (pre-first degree). Normally such programs last one or two years and lead to a certificate (= ISCED 4/post-secondary, non-tertiary level).

Level 2: Programs which lead to vocational qualification or to an academic degree (first degree – BA, BTh, BRS). Normally these programs require 3–4 years after completion of the secondary level (= ICSED 5/tertiary I level).

Level 3: Programs which lead to a second vocational qualification or academic degree (second degree – MA, MTh, MRE, MAT). Normally such programs require two years after completion of the first degree (= ISCED 5/tertiary I level).

Level 4: Programs which lead to a second vocational qualification or academic degree (second degree – MA, MDiv, BD). Normally such programs require three years after completion of the first degree (= ISCED 5/tertiary I level).

Level 5: Doctoral programs with an advanced vocational goal (DPS, DMin) (= ISCED 6/tertiary II level).

Level 6: Doctoral programs with the highest advanced academic degree (PhD, ThD, DTheol) (= ISCED 6/tertiary III level).

An initial definition based on educational theory can now be ventured: By "theological education" we mean formal education at the tertiary level (in some cases also ISCED 4, post-secondary, non-tertiary). This may include elements of both *training* and *education*.

3.2 An Overview of Typologies

It is not easy to represent and compare the many-faceted historical developments and the multiplicity of educational theories that these developments have engendered. In order to achieve some sort of comparison, attempts have been made to group the many forms of education into models or types.

Models are intended to represent complex realities in simplified form, in order that these complex realities may be more readily understood and compared. There is, however, a danger with such models. Sometimes they are not drawn inductively from the complex reality. Sometimes the complex realities are forced to fit deductively designed models, predefined to correspond to a desired ideal. When this happens, reality is often so significantly simplified as to be distorted. Reality is altered to fit the model. Good models are derived inductively, observing what is. And good models include expressions of all the basic elements present in a complex reality.

If this is done, various complex realities can be explained and represented by models which more readily allow comparison. A typology of models can be constructed. Another potential problem which must be kept in mind is the nomenclature used for the models. It is tempting to assign the various model types a short, succinct designation, ideally a one-word moniker to characterize each model. But it is scarcely possible with one word to do justice to the diverse aspects of a model and to the complex realities it seeks to represent. Thus there is a real danger that the names themselves distort the reality further still. What is more, the single words chosen as names for the models may evoke associations and connotations that have little to do with the reality the models seek to represent. It is advisable to keep these pitfalls in mind as we introduce model typologies in the following section.[7]

3.2.1 Historical Models

Earlier we provided a thorough introduction to the historical paradigms that Edward Farley proposed in *Theologia* (1983). We can summarize them briefly here once more:

1. The *monastic* (pre-university) paradigm: Emphasis on pious learning.
2. The *scholastic* (university) paradigm: Emphasis on academic study.
3. The *clerical* (seminary) paradigm: Emphasis on professional/vocational training.

As has been previously stated, Farley castigates the *clerical-professional* paradigm especially. This paradigm destroys both the existential and the material unity of theology and of learning. Thus, according to Farley, the fundamental cause of the oft-lamented fragmentation of theological education can be found in the market orientation and vocational orientation of this paradigm.

Whether one agrees with Farley's assessment or not, his three-part typology is based upon thorough historical observation of Western educational traditions and reveals three fundamentally different emphases in and approaches to theological education. His model typology can be helpful in assessing an institution, identifying strengths and weaknesses, and determining effective plans for the future.

3.2.2 Philosophy of Education: Top Down or Bottom Up

Sidney Rooy[8] developed an additional typology. Working from a study by Charles Davis, Rooy compares four models:

---

7. Concerning the theory of models, see Herbert Stachowiak, *Allgemeine Modelltheorie* (Vienna/New York: Springer, 1973) and also "Der Modellbegriff in der Erkenntnistheorie," *Zeitschrift für allgemeine Wissenschaftstheorie* 21, no. 1 (1980): 53–68.
8. Sidney Rooy, "Historical Models of Theological Education," in *New Alternatives in Theological Education,* ed. René C. Padilla, (Oxford: Regnum, 1988), 51–72.

1) The *catechistic* model, whose roots Rooy identifies in the catechism of the early church. He describes this model as follows:

> We see that in this period the basic purpose of theological education was to prepare the members of the church for a life faithful to Christ and to be able to give reason for their faith in their testimony to others.[9]

2) The *monastic* model, which, according to Rooy, had its origins in the orders of the early cloisters and monasteries. He names Augustine and Benedict as representatives of a shift in emphasis from the training of all believers to a specialized training for the clergy. Thus this model advocates the formation of spiritual leaders in the context of communal living through the discipline of spiritual exercises, physical labor, and study.

3) The *scholastic* model began, according to Rooy, in the universities of the Middle Ages. The scholastic model stands for the shift away from the church (cathedral, monastery) and to the university as the place for (theological) education. Similarly, this model symbolizes the development of spiritual leaders as professors and teachers.

4) The *seminary* model, according to Rooy, was developed by Ignatius, Calvin, and other reformers. This model sees the primary purpose of theological education in the renewal of the church. This includes the comprehensive education of the church's elite as well as the training of pastors.

It will be left to church historians to determine to what extent this model typology accurately represents the realities of the early church, the Middle Ages and the Reformation. The leap from the Reformation into the present seems problematic to me. Can a typology that seeks to present the realities of the first 1500 years of church history devise categories that we can use today? Only within limits, I think. Pietism, the modern university (Schleiermacher!), the revivalist and missionary movements, and with them Bible schools and missionary training schools all receive only brief mention. Yet these are the sources of the models of theological education that are still effective today, as we shall see below.

---

9. Ibid., 56.

The contribution of Rooy's model typology, however, is to be found at a different level. The criticism I have just expressed does not do him justice. Rooy speaks in a Latin American context. His essay is based on a lecture he gave in 1987 at a consultation of the Fraternidad Teológica Latinoamericana on the topic of "New Alternatives in Theological Education." His work contains reflections of the dominant Catholic influence of the region, the concerns and objectives of liberation theology as well as ideas and initiatives from the TEE movement.

Rooy is interested in the social, political and cultural context that shapes theological education.[10] His thesis is that in all four of these models, a church with a top-down structure is assumed and indeed solidified. The spiritual elite receive training and education in order to rule over the church and its members and to guarantee that the status quo is maintained. The members of the church are disenfranchised and needed changes are prevented.[11] All of the models are about power in the church, and it is far from innocent. The church has often been allied with the state throughout history and helped to prop up a social structure that was often unjust. Theological education helped ensure the stabilization of a society desperately in need of change.

Knowing this background to Rooy's typology opens the way to new and promising applications. The question is not, which of these models is effective today. Instead Rooy's typology teaches us to distinguish two fundamentally different kinds of theological education.

1) Theological education that is *top down* (represented in all four of the historical models he presents). Theological education of this type has to do with power – the exercise of power and the maintaining of power. It is an expression of a hierarchical church. The elite receive training and education in order to guarantee stability and continuity. The emphasis is on ensuring proper church teaching and on maintaining order and control in the church. This comes at the price of the disenfranchisement and even oppression of the people in the church. It is not uncommon with these models for the church to be allied with those in political power, and the theologically educated church leadership thus props up – more or

---

10. Ibid., 51–52.
11. Ibid., 69.

less knowingly – unjust political and societal structures. After all, the church leaders themselves belong to the privileged beneficiaries of the system.

2) Rooy appeals for a kind of theological education that is *bottom up*. Inspired by liberation theology and consistent with the principles of TEE, this model advocates that theological education be made available to everyone, that the laity be given their rightful voice, equipped for ministry and empowered to serve. This brand of theological education views society and social structures with a critical eye. It has a subversive dimension and pushes for changes in the dominant structures in church and society.

Even though the social and ecclesiastical structures common in Latin America are not necessarily the same everywhere else in the world, and even though liberation theology is no longer *en vogue*, Rooy's analysis provides a valuable and lasting criterion. Top-down theological education is elitist and tends to create monopolies on spiritual ministry. It serves to maintain power structures in the church and support societal structures that may be unjust. Bottom up theological education takes the priesthood of all believers seriously and thus has as its goal the theological education of all believers, the ministry of all believers, and the empowerment of all believers. These two models are categorically different.

3.2.3 Dimensions of Theological Education Today

Graham Cheesman, who founded and led the Centre for Theological Education at Belfast Bible College until it closed in 2010, suggests the following paradigm typology:[12]

1) The *academic* paradigm of the classical university faculties and theological colleges that followed this model. The emphasis is on encouraging rigorous thought. The weakness lies in the lack of praxis. (Almost) everything happens in the world of ideas and theories.

---

12. Graham Cheesman, "Competing Paradigms in Theological Education," *Evangelical Review of Theology* 17, no. 4 (1993): 484–499.

2) The *monastic* paradigm that has its roots in monastic theological education and has found a present day iteration in the Bible school movement. Communal life and structured spirituality provide the framework for study. There is a tendency, however, for the atmosphere to become artificial and detached from reality.

3) The *training* paradigm, which Cheesman sees in the praxis-oriented education offered by evangelical Bible schools and seminaries. This paradigm focuses on the skills of vocational ministry and has a tendency therefore to concentrate on the pragmatic acquisition of these skills.

4) The *business* paradigm, which is evident in the strong emphasis on market principles and professionalism in many colleges and seminaries. Such educational institutions are led like companies that sell products (educational models) to the customers (students). Education is comparable to a supermarket. Curriculum development and the design of educational processes are of secondary importance.

5) The *discipleship* paradigm that emphasizes the relationship between the teacher and the student, and is based on Jesus' relationship with his disciples. It can be observed throughout the centuries in the form of the tutor or mentor.

Cheesman's intention is not to present five distinct types of education, but rather to identify five dimensions that are all present to a greater or lesser degree in every form of theological education. Each of these paradigms has strengths and weaknesses. That is why, according to Cheesman, all five dimensions should receive attention in theological education. Cheesman focuses his attention on the student rather than on the institution. Each person needs all five dimensions to arrive at maturity. Not every school will be able to offer all five dimensions with equal strength. No school should, therefore, claim to offer the *complete* theological education. Cheesman pleads for humility in this regard.

Based on his experience in theological education in Europe and Africa, Cheesman observes that Western educational models are strongly shaped by Western academic tradition and in recent years have developed further in the direction of professionalism (*training* paradigm) and market forces (*business* paradigm). The dimensions of communal life and discipleship are neglected.

Cheesman's paradigm typology can be of help in keeping various dimensions of theological education in balance. It can also help to identify weaknesses. At the same time, his typology frees educators from the need to be everything and do everything. From the student's point of view, it's important to keep all five dimensions in mind. A particular school may well be one-sided. That requires the student to be self-aware and self-directed. Mentoring and counselling for students becomes all the more important.

3.2.4 Athens – Berlin – Geneva – Jerusalem

We have already encountered David Kelsey's Athens-Berlin typology. Kelsey defined Athens as classical education and Berlin as modern scientific and professional training. Brian Edgar has recently taken up Kelsey's typologies[13] and added two further types which he calls Geneva and Jerusalem. Geneva designates a confessional or denominational model, as is often found in the seminaries of traditional churches and denominations. Jerusalem designates the model of the early church. Like Banks, Edgar considers this latter model to be missions oriented. Edgar compares the four models and shows the comparison in the following figure:

Athens	**Geneva**
Venue: Academy	Venue: Seminary
Characterization: Classical	Characterization: Confessional
Goal: Individual tranformation	Goal: Knowing God
Theology as "Theologia"	Theology as Doxology
Jerusalem	**Berlin**
Venue: Community	Venue: University
Characterization: Missional	Characterization: Professional/vocational
Goal: Evangelize the world	Goal: Strengthen the church
Theology as Missiology	Theology as Science

Figure 3

It is tempting to use Edgar's typology as a practical way of classifying theological education, but we shouldn't do so too quickly, without thinking

---

13. Brian Edgar, "The Theology of Theological Education."

it through. Two critical questions are certainly appropriate: (1) Do these categories reflect reality with enough accuracy to provide a meaningful, useful tool? Specifically, do the designations Edgar uses really reflect the basic characteristics of the four models? I am doubtful on several accounts. (2) Are these four models even comparable, or are we dealing with apples and oranges? It's worth considering the following:

- David Kelsey understood the *Athens-Berlin* typology in a way that attributed validity to both models and acknowledged that good theological education is happening today using both models. The *Athens-Berlin* typology seeks to show that theological education sought and found excellence in the university setting. A critical biblical-theological assessment of this typology, however, is lacking, as Kelsey himself says.
- Banks attempts to rectify this with his *Jerusalem* model. He proposes a "biblical" model for theological education. Whether he succeeds in convincingly and concretely contextualizing biblical input in today's university setting remains an open question (and will be considered further in the following chapter). Either way, *Jerusalem* is not a model that exists in the real world today but is rather a biblical-theological challenge to existing models.
- The *Geneva* model that Edgar adds to the mix is of another category altogether. It is neither a point of biblical-theological orientation (like the *Jerusalem* model) nor is it a further dimension of excellence in academic theological education. Rather, Edgar uses the *Geneva* model to point out that theological education takes place in a particular ecclesiological or theological tradition. His *Geneva* model is based in the reformed-Calvinistic tradition. It is this tradition which influences the terminology he chooses (Goal: Knowing God, Theology as Doxology). Other ecclesiological/denominational traditions would have their own specific emphases.

In conclusion I propose to use Brian Edgar's typology in the following way:
- Theological education as academic/university training exists in the tension between classical education (character formation – Athens), science and professionalism (academic work – Berlin).

- Such theological education will always be subject to challenges from biblical-theological criteria (→ Jerusalem).
- And finally, theological education will always have to answer the question of which ecclesiological or theological traditions it is shaped by, and in what ways it will serve these traditions.

These typologies can help us to assess specific programs and institutions of theological education and to keep various dimensions of theological education in proper balance. They are not sufficient, however, to allow us to assess and place theological education within the array of existing forms of education. Therefore the following two sections will introduce existing educational models.

3.3 Secular Educational Models: An Overview[14]

This section will seek to acquaint the reader with the various philosophies of education that are currently available in our society. My starting point is that of German-speaking Europe. For any who pursue theological education in Germany, Austria or Switzerland, this is the culture in which their training must be contextualized. For others, who are involved in theological education in other countries, these considerations may provide basic categories that are helpful in understanding education and training in other contexts. They may also enable a self-critical look at aspects of European educational philosophy that has been handed down to today's generation.

Specifically we will look at the following ideas: (1) the academic, university education model, (2) the dual model of vocational training, (3) the pedagogical paradigm shift of the 20th century, (4) the model of adult education, and (5) the praxis-oriented educational model common to post-secondary technical schools and academies.

The representation of various educational models leans heavily on the theory-praxis discussion, which will prove useful in the explicit treatment of this topic that will follow (ch. 5).

---

14. This section is a slightly revised version of my article, "Theologische Ausbildung im Spannungsfeld zwischen Theorie und Praxis," *Jahrbuch für evangelikale Theologie* (2003): 154–167.

3.3.1 The University-Based Educational Model

The educational system in our context (German-speaking Europe) is unique in comparison with other countries in having two educational tracks that are relatively distinct from one another: an academic education which includes sixth form and A levels followed by university, and a vocational track which includes vocational school and apprenticeship. This two-track model dates back to a conflict in the eighteenth century over the philosophy of education. One side of this conflict was represented by the neo-humanistic educational ideal that created the ethos of the modern university, thanks in large part to the work of Wilhelm v. Humboldt. The other side was represented by an emphasis on utilitarianism and the common good for all education. This emphasis grew out of the pedagogy of the Enlightenment and shaped the development of vocational education.[15]

On the one hand we have, therefore, the university-based educational model, which Jean Zumstein describes with three phrases: (1) commitment to finding the truth; (2) freedom in teaching and research, which leads to an independence from purpose; (3) responsibility to the public to serve human dignity.[16]

The ethos of the university is based on the neo-humanistic educational ideal, which assumes that the study of the classics of our cultural heritage prepares a person for life and work. Greek, Latin, and German are the basic tools needed to read the works of Greek, Latin, and German poets, philosophers, and historians. For this to happen, a young person must be given a sufficient number of years free from the obligation to work, so that h/she can devote those years to education. "To shield a young person from premature obligation to economic and political realities, Humboldt's educational philosophy asserts the fundamental freedom of human individuality and therefore gives priority to the comprehensive, all-round development of all

---

15. Cf. the short outline of this educational-political history by Kurt Sohm, *Praxisbezogene Ausbildung auf Hochschulniveau. Eine pädagogisch-praktische Herausforderung*, Vienna: facultas wuv universitätsverlag, 1999, 21-28.
16. Jean Zumstein, "Theologische Fakultäten an staatlichen Hochschulen," in *Kirche und Staat*, ed. Alfred Schindler, 84–89, (Zürich: TVZ, 1994); cf. Karl Jaspers, *Die Idee der Universität* (Berlin: Springer, 1980), 9–37 (Reprint from 1946).

human faculties, abilities and strengths."[17] The tools needed are to be found in secondary and tertiary (university) education.

This basic stance rests upon the assumptions of a worldview that Sohm describes as follows:

> The neo-humanistic philosophy of education arises from important assumptions about human (character) development. It is assumed that the ultimate development of an individual's formal powers to a unified harmony can only occur through the study of literary, aesthetic, and ethical content. It is further assumed that this development can only occur when the individual remains free from all obligation to the economic, political and technical dimensions of life. These factors are not conducive to education. They are tainted by the odor of utilitarianism and usefulness within a system of economic values.[18]

This educational ideal is, theoretically, still fundamental to the academic (secondary and university) educational path. In its pure form, however, it scarcely exists in today's world. The rise of the natural sciences in the nineteenth century coupled with the pedagogical revolution of the twentieth century (see point below) shook this ideal to its core.[19] Sohm concludes that the ideal goals were never reached.[20] Ropohl speaks of "a pseudo-humanistic program of encyclopedic punditry"[21] and criticizes this educational ideal in particular for being "classicistic" and "idealistic."[22] Classicistic in that it elevates the values of Greco-Roman antiquity as the ideal for perfect character, and idealistic in that it emphasizes the priority of the spirit over the world, and the priority of the internal over the external.

This last aspect is particularly meaningful for the current discussion of theory vs. praxis. Following Plato and Descartes, and particularly in the realm of the humanities, the superiority of thought, reflection, philosophy and

---

17. Sohm, *Praxisbezogene Ausbildung*, 23.
18. Ibid., 24.
19. Cf. Gerard Radnitzky, "Die Universität als ordnungspolitisches Problem," in *Die ungewisse Zukunft der Universität*, eds. Hardy Bouillon and Gerard Radnitzky (Berlin: Duncker & Humblot, 1991).
20. Sohm, *Praxisbezogene Ausbildung*, 24.
21. Günter Ropohl, *Technologische Aufklärung* (Frankfurt: Suhrkamp Verlag, 1991), 232.
22. Ibid., 217–218.

theory over action and praxis has won the day.²³ Thus today in the academic university world the relationship between theory and praxis is shaped by the Cartesian dualism of spirit vs. matter. This has created an ethos in which thought and theory are valued more than action and praxis.

3.3.2 *The Dual Educational Model (Vocational Training)*

An alternative to the humanistic university-based educational philosophy is to be found in learning a practical vocation. This educational tradition traces its roots back to the Enlightenment and the pedagogical emphasis on class and vocational training. In this tradition, in contrast to the neo-humanistic academic educational path, usefulness, the common good, work, and vocation are all emphases of education.²⁴

This path is familiar in our culture in the form of vocational schools (secondary level) and (tertiary level) training academies and master craftsman institutes. These courses of study are committed to a dual track approach, combining practical vocational training with schooling in theory.²⁵ Preparing the student to work in his or her chosen field is central to the educational philosophy of vocational training. The Swiss vocational education legislative code defines the requirements:

> This law establishes a vocational education system that allows individuals to develop personally and vocationally and to integrate into society, especially the work force, and equips them with the ability and the readiness to be vocationally flexible and to succeed in the work world.²⁶

The dual approach to education will remain important in German-speaking Europe in the future as well. A variety of efforts currently underway to reform and improve education demonstrate that there is an ongoing

---

23. Here in particular the Cartesian dualism of the superior *res cogitans* and the subordinate *res extensa*; cf. "Descartes" in *Philosopielexikon,* eds. Anton Hügli und Paul Lübcke (Reinbek: Rowohlt Taschenbuch, 2000), 143–144. Werner Brandl, "Descartes und seine Kritiker," in *Descartes und das neuzeitliche Denken,* Porta Studien 13, eds. Edith Gutsche and Hermann Hafner (Marburg: SMD, 1993). Adolf Köberle, *Descartes und die Folgen. Ein Weltbild in der Krise,* EZW-Informationen 92/IX. (Stuttgart: Evangelische Zentralstelle für Weltanschauungsfragen, 1984).
24. Sohm, *Praxisbezogene Ausbildung,* 22.
25. Cf. Article 13 in the Swiss federal legislation governing vocational education.
26. Ibid.

commitment to the value of praxis. An example in Germany is the project group "Innovation im Bildungswesen" [Innovation in the Educational System], which is part of the German Federal and State Commission for Educational Planning and Research Development. This project group has developed a program entitled New Concepts of Learning in Dual Vocational Education. This program has articulated the following goals:[27]

> The lasting goal of the innovations is to establish a new method of instruction and professionalism. The program seeks to promote the following goals for the students:
> - Orientation to the process of work (the relationship between study and work)
> - Independent and self-organized study (autonomous form of study)
> - Practical skills and vocational competence (occupational master craftsmanship and the ability to shape the work environment)
> - Holistic learning (the relationship between knowledge and experience, learning in teams, and holistic technical understanding)

An integration of study and praxis is essential for this educational model. This is a decidedly different relationship between study and praxis than is present in the academic university model.

Preliminary Observations: It's not difficult to see that the first educational model can be labeled theoretical while the second can be labeled practical. A closer look, however, will show that these designations do not tell the whole story. Both the university as well as an academic secondary education endeavor to be practical, to aim at equipping students for life. And vocational training seeks to include theory in its curriculum.

Nevertheless I believe that the terms practical and theoretical, as they often used to describe these two models, are appropriate. A university education has been historically – as described above – shaped by idealism and emphasizes the preeminence of spirit, idea, abstraction and theory over material, reality, concretion and practice. Despite claims to praxis-relevance, the academic educational model remains for the most part in "autonomy of spirit, abstinent from praxis and vocation."[28] Vocational education stands

---
27. See http://www.itb.uni-bremen.de/projekte/blk/programmtraeger.htm
28. Sohm, *Praxisbezogene Ausbildung*, 24.

in marked contrast. It is completely dedicated to occupational skills and thus to praxis. Perhaps Sohm is right in his diagnosis that, because of the (until recently) almost complete separation of these two educational paths, vocational education "—cut off from humanistic influence – has succumbed without reflection to the values of praxis and utilitarianism."[29]

3.3.3 The Paradigm Shift in the Pedagogy of the Twentieth Century

In outlining these two educational models we started with the conflict around educational philosophy in the eighteenth century and drew the lines of Humboldt's ideal of the modern university right up to the present day. That, of course, is not reality. Today's situation cannot be properly understood without considering the pedagogical paradigm shift that occurred in the twentieth century. This shift is associated with the names K. Marx, J. Dewey, M. Horkheimer, T. W. Adorno, J. Habermas, E. Bloch and P. Bourdieu, among others.[30]

It is commonly assumed that this revolution in pedagogy and the theory of knowledge began with Marx's Feuerbach theses.[31] There we read, among other things:

> (Thesis 2) The question whether objective truth can be attributed to human thinking is not a question of theory but is a practical question. Man must prove the truth – i.e. the reality and power, the this-sidedness of his thinking in practice. The dispute over the reality or non-reality of thinking that is isolated from practice is a purely scholastic question.[32]

---

29. Ibid., 24–25.
30. http://www.praxisphilosophie.de/ offers access to a broad network of today's praxis-based philosophical thought.
31. Cf. Bertrand Russell, *Philosophie des Abendlandes* (Zürich: Europaverlag, 1979), 792; Pierre Bourdieu, *Entwurf einer Theorie der Praxis* (Frankfurt: Suhrkamp Verlag, 1979), 228; Ernst Bloch according to Horst Müller: "Praxis als Schlüsselbegriff von Ernst Blochs Philosophie" http://www.praxisphilosophie.de/praxis.pdf.
32. Karl Marx and Frederick Engels, *The German Ideology, Part 1* (New York: International Publishers, 1970), 121.

> (Thesis 11) Philosophers have only *interpreted* the world, in various ways. The point, however, is to *change* it.[33]

This turns the theory of knowledge on its head. The preeminence of thought and theory as asserted by Plato and Descartes is now challenged by the quality and value of praxis. Praxis steps out of its shadow existence (as merely the application of pre-existing objective theoretical truth) and now claims to contribute to the discovery of truth. It is not possible here to discuss in detail how this paradigm shift in the theory of knowledge affected twentieth-century thought.[34] One thing must be said with regard to the current debate in theological education: Russell is right when he says that Marx's philosophy has much in common with what we today call instrumentalism. Instrumentalism coupled with pragmatism finds its primary outworking in the pedagogy of John Dewey. Instrumentalism and pragmatism are driven by the criteria of usefulness, functionality and expediency. Truth is not what is found in a timeless construction of thought and theory, preeminent over all action. Rather, truth is what works in practice. Truth is what is expedient and useful. Thus the criterion of truth is its effect not its cause.[35]

This paradigm shift in the theory of knowledge led to a variety of new pedagogical and didactical proposals in the twentieth century, all of which were marked by a radical praxis orientation. "Action-oriented didactic," "emancipation didactic," and "critical-constructive didactic" are just a few of the terms that arose in this context.[36] Many of these concepts merge together, according to Peterßen, in the 1990s in what became known as "systemic-

---

33. Ibid., 123.
34. Cf. Norbert Schneider, *Erkenntnistheorie im 20. Jahrhundert. Klassische Positionen* (Leipzig: Reclam, 1998). The brief discussion of criticism of Decartes by Husserl and Adorno in *Descartes und das neuzeitliche Denken*, eds. Edith Gutsche and Hermann Hafner, 28–37, is also insightful. Karl Lehmann offers a helpful overview of the philosophical debate about practical theology in: "Das Theorie-Praxis-Problem," in *Praktische Theologie heute*, eds. Ferdinand Klostermann and Rolf Zerfaß (Munich: Kaiser, 1974).
35. Russell, *Philosophie*, 792. Cf. Dewey, 828–835. See also the articles "Instrumenalismus" and "Pragmatismus" in *Philosophielexikon*, 319–320, 515, respectively.
36. Cf. Wilhelm H. Peterßen, *Lehrbuch Allgemeine Didaktik* (Munich: Oldenbourg, 2001). Because of his influence on liberation theology, the Brazilian pedagogue Paulo Freire is also important: *Pedagogy of the Oppressed*, trans. Myra Bergman Ramos (New York: Bloomsbury, 2015).

constructive" pedagogy. Peterßen summarizes the foundations of systemic-constructive pedagogy with the following three phrases:[37]

1) "Context instead of dualism": The Cartesian dualism of knowing subject and known object is done away with. A person is no longer seen as a "mere observer," separate from the object observed. Instead, the person and the object are in relationship with one another and together form a system. Every observation a person may make does not simply affect the object alone, but instead affects the relationships in the system, which includes both the observer and the thing observed.

2) "Construction instead of portrayal": Because of the systemic relationship between the knowing subject and the known object, a neutral and objective portrayal of the object by the observer is not possible. All knowledge is constructed by the observer, and the observer cannot avoid bringing something of his or own self into the process of observation and knowing.[38]

3) "Viability instead of truth": Peterßen concludes: "*The* truth, the one truth, cannot therefore exist. Any search for truth which apparently everyone appropriates for himself or herself and which supposedly is the foundation of all science must, therefore, remain fruitless. Reality as a construction is always the construction of the one who is doing or has done the constructing."[39]

To counter the resulting problem of an endless and crippling conflict in the construction of truth, constructivism asserts the principle of viability. That means, "The constructions are not ultimately 'true' but are nevertheless maintained, so long as they prove useful and do not conflict with experience or with other constructions."[40] Peterßen is right, therefore, when he accuses constructivism of utilitarian thinking.

---

37. Peterßen, *Lehrbuch Allgemeine Didaktik*, 95–135. Explanation of the three terms p. 98–101.
38. On constructivism, see Horst Siebert, *Pädagogischer Konstruktivismus* (Landsberg: Beltz, 2005), 3rd edition; Horst Siebert, *Der Konstruktivismus als pädagogische Weltanschauung* (Frankfurt/Main: VAS, 2002).
39. Peterßen, *Lehrbuch Allgemeine Didaktik*, 101.
40. Diesbergen quoted by Peterßen, *Lehrbuch Allgemeine Didaktik*, 101.

Preliminary Observations: The paradigm shift in pedagogy and theory of knowledge that has been briefly outlined here may be summarized with the assertion that the *Primacy of Theory* has been replaced by the *Primacy of Praxis*. Many philosophers and pedagogues would not agree with a formulation this radical and would instead prefer to speak more moderately of a dialectic between or combination of theory and practice. However the systemic-constructive concept makes clear that instrumentalism and pragmatism insist that every truth, every teaching, must be measured by its usefulness and functionality.

Theology, particularly orthodox-reformed and evangelical theology, strongly contradicts these developments of the twentieth century.[41] If this new theory of knowledge has the final word, argue its critics, every normative statement of the Scriptures and faith would be vulnerable to criticism based on said norm's usefulness and functionality. No longer is that true which has been given through the divine revelation of the Scriptures. Rather that is true which in current practice is conducive to freedom and human nature. How the terms "freedom" and "human nature" are defined is no longer determined by given norms (the Bible and statements of faith). Instead the content of these terms is now "constructed" in the here and now in the current context and situation. We cannot agree with this theological criticism. (Evangelical) theologians have not yet done their homework. Contributions from the field of the theory of knowledge must be taken into consideration. We will say more about this in section 4.3.[42]

3.3.4 The Adult Education Model

The paradigm shift described above not only led to changes in traditional educational models (vocational training and university education). Nurtured in the soil of the new understanding of the relationship between theory and

---

41. Among others, Horst W. Beck, *Marxistischer Materialismus im Schafspelz* (Wuppertal: Aussaat-Verlag, 1975). Klaus Bockmühl, *The Challenge of Marxism* (Colorado Springs: Helmers & Howard, 1986).

42. Cf. my own critique of (German) evangelical theological education in: *Beyond Fragmentation*, especially p. 188–197, 271–275, 294–315.

praxis, completely new educational models sprang up. One of these can be captured in the term *adult education*.[43]

Titmus outlined the basic pedagogical philosophy of adult education as follows:

> Fundamental to it is the idea that any adult is a free agent, responsible for his or her own action, who is therefore at liberty to participate or not in any educational experience as he or she chooses and who should determine the content and nature of that experience.[44]

M. S. Knowles, a pioneer of andragogy, sees four basic assumptions underlying the concept of adult education:

> As a person matures, (a) his self-concept moves from one of being a dependent personality toward one of being a self-directed human being; (b) he accumulates a growing reservoir of experience that becomes an increasing resource for learning; (c) his readiness to learn becomes oriented increasingly to the development tasks of his social roles; and (d) his time perspective changes from one of postponed application of knowledge to immediacy of application, and accordingly his orientation toward learning shifts from one of subject-centredness to one of problem-centredness.[45]

From this can be derived five characteristics of adult education:

---

43. Adult education as an independent pedagogical discipline began in the 1930s. Cf. Colin J. Titmus, ed., *Lifelong Education for Adults: An International Handbook* (Oxford: Pergamon Press, 1989), xxiii. In this context the term andragogy was introduced (used initially by E. Rosenstock in 1924) as distinct from pedagogy (education of children and young people). The term, however, did not catch on, in part because of the problematic of its fixation on the masculine. Cf. A. Krajny, "Andragogy," in *Lifelong Education for Adults*, ed. Colin J. Titmus (Oxford: Pergamon Press, 1989), 19. Also Henirich Hanselmann, *Andragogik. Wesen, Möglichkeiten und Grenzen der Erwachsenenbildung* (Zürich: Rotapfel Verlag, 1951).

44. Titmus, *Lifelong Education for Adults*, xxviii.

45. Foundational text by Malcolm S. Knowles: *The Adult Learner: The Definitive Classic in Adult Education and Human Resource Development*, 8th edition (New York: Routledge, 2015). Quotation taken from Krajny, "Andragogy," 21. Knowles' theory of andragogy did not remain without its detractors. In particular his sharp distinction between childhood education (pedagogy) and adult education (andragogy) drew criticism from those who preferred to emphasize a continuum between the two. In 1980 Knowles changed the subtitle of his book called *The Modern Practice of Adult Education*. Originally the subtitle was *Andragogy versus Pedagogy*. He changed it to *From Pedagogy to Andragogy*.

1) Adults want to be taken seriously as mature, autonomous, responsible persons within the educational process. That requires that (adult) education must be clearly leaner-oriented and learner-centred. Prokop and Geissler identify *self-active*, *self-responsible*, and *self-determining* learning as marks of adult education, along with lifelong learning.[46] This leads to the conclusion that the instruction process must be in large measure a partnership in which the learners are actively involved in the process. This requires that the learners assume a high level of responsibility for the success of the learning process.

2) Adults come into the educational process with both life experience and vocational experience and do not wish to be treated as empty containers that must be filled up with knowledge, but rather as competent people who contribute their life and work experience to learning process.

3) An adult's readiness to learn is strongly biased toward acquiring competencies to accomplish concrete tasks in life and work.

4) Thus adults are not looking to amass great amounts of theory to be kept in reserve. Instead they want to be able to quickly apply what they learn. Adult education is therefore not *initial education* but rather *continuing education*.

5) This leads finally to the conclusion that the content of adult education is less determined by the subject matter of classic courses and more structured around problems and challenges relevant to the (adult) learner's life and work.

Preliminary Observations: The field of adult education expands our palette of theory-praxis models. Adult education definitely no longer gives primacy to theory over praxis. Instead theory is input that aids a person in interpreting his experience, in order to increase his or her ability to handle current and future challenges. It can be assumed that adults enter the educational process with considerable life and work experience. And they enter educational processes that they themselves have chosen because they believe them to be helpful, based on their own needs.

Yet we dare not forget that surveys of participants in adult education have shown that people who have a solid *initial education* are more apt to

---

46. Ernst Prokop and Karlheinz A. Geissler, *Erwachsenenbildung. Modelle und Methoden* (Basel: E. Reinhardt, 1974).

take advantage of *continuing education* later in life.[47] That means that the two concepts of initial education and continuing education should not be played off against one another as mutually exclusive. Adult education should not be seen as a more praxis-based alternative to primary or basic education. Research indicates instead that a thorough basic education serves to develop a person's self-determination which later takes advantage of the benefits of adult education.

In relation to theological education, two thoughts deserve consideration:

1) To the extent that theological education is understood as basic/initial education, that is, as education which prepares the student for life in general and for a vocation in the church or missions, the pedagogy of adult education will have only limited significance. For one thing, most (still young) students lack the life and work experience that makes inductive learning (praxis reflection) possible. In addition, most students do not have enough experience to enable them to accurately assess their own educational needs. And finally, many young students may lack the personal maturity which includes the self-motivation and self-direction necessary for adult education. Theological education (as basic education) will, of necessity, have to rely on a higher level of outside direction, predetermined curricula and courses of study, longer phases of theory, and greater amounts of deductive learning.

2) Second, it must be kept in mind – and this will generate a healthy tension – that a growing number of students are beginning their theological education in preparation for a second career. Such students are typically between twenty-five and forty years of age and already have a basic education (in other fields) as well as work experience and/or (volunteer) ministry experience in the church. Moreover many of these students have already taken part in adult education as part of their ongoing vocational training and thus begin their theological education expecting a democratic, participatory, goal-oriented educational process. Such students will be bitterly disappointed if they find the culture of their theological seminary is hierarchical and heavily weighted toward deductive learning. Faculty members at institutions of theological education will thus be well advised to be familiar with and masters of the principles of adult education.

---

47. Titmus, *Lifelong Education for Adults*, xxix.

Theological education is thus faced with the challenge of blending two educational concepts, namely *initial education* and *adult education* (or *continuing education*). That is a sizable task.

3.3.5 The Technical University Model

This challenge brings with it a potential solution in the form of an additional educational model. Universities of applied sciences, or technical universities, which have arisen in recent years, seek to combine *education* and *training*. They offer, as Sohm says in the title of his book, praxis-oriented training at a university (tertiary) level.

In order for this to happen, these institutions provide technical *training* that is highly practical, vocationally specific, equipping the students with expert specialized knowledge and occupational skills. At the same time these schools also provide *education* by continuing to follow relevant aspects of the Humboldt model in order to equip students to be fully human. That can only happen when students learn to think and not only acquire expert specialized knowledge but also broader knowledge and perspective that provides orientation and life navigation skills. Such knowledge is achieved as students grapple with "ahistorical" and context-transcendent life questions that have been pondered by sages, philosophers, and pedagogues throughout the centuries.[48] Critically essential here are the fields of anthropology, psychology, history, sociology, ethics and values. Sohm insists that the pursuit of specialized knowledge and a broader education must not be allowed to occur as separate tracks that remain unconnected. Rather students must be taught to exercise their specialized skills within the larger framework of the great questions of human existence.[49]

If technical university *training* is to be (equivalent to) university *education,* if it is to be conducive to scientific thought and work, two things must be kept in mind:

---

48. Sohm's writing reflects a discourse that is ongoing within Western thought. In a broader, inter-cultural context, the question might arise whether terms such as "ahistorical" and "context-transcendent" are even appropriate. Cf. the writings of Marlene Enns in the bibliography.

49. Cf. Sohm, *Praxisbezogene Ausbildung*, 26–27.

1) First, teachers and students must both be given the freedom to grapple with science, with methods and with theories and their scientific implications, regardless of outcomes or conclusions.[50] It will be impossible within this model to complete a technical university education on the side while working full-time in one's profession. Even with a strong emphasis on praxis, the educational philosophy of the technical university is built on the principle of appropriate distance from praxis for the success of the scientific work.

2) A second consideration must be this: "To work scientifically requires a high level of theory." Where this is lacking, there exists "an inadequately trained theoretical problem consciousness" which in turn "limits the horizon of practical problems which can be identified and solved." When it comes to the possibility of solving problems, it is true that "the problem-solving capacity is determined by the theoretical level available to the problem solver."[51] This line of thinking makes it clear that it would be illusory to believe that any education could have maximum practical relevance if it simply gave practical instruction without an accompanying high level of theory. Quite the opposite: Practical instruction devoid of theoretical background has a narrow, limited perspective and can only serve shortsighted pragmatism. On the other hand, the teaching of theory can prove to be quite relevant to practice if it is geared toward the students' field of work.

The praxis orientation of the technical university differs fundamentally from the emphasis on praxis found in continuing (vocational) education that follows the model of adult education. An education at a technical university aims explicitly at more than "routine application of practiced skills and classroom knowledge."[52] Sohm sees the goal of a technical university education as "training students in such a way that afterwards in their vocational life they are able to work on practical problems with a high level of theoretical

---

50. Ibid., 32–33.
51. Ibid., 33.
52. Altrichter and Posch, quoted Sohm, *Praxisbezogene Ausbildung*, 36.

foundation."⁵³ The goal is "the ability to assess, evaluate, transform, develop, and expand knowledge in a technically complex social structure".⁵⁴

It is a "pedagogical-didactical challenge" – as Sohm puts it in the subtitle of his book – to achieve the integration of praxis and theory which this educational model intends. Sohm rejects a "technical-functional praxis orientation." One cannot give priority to the communication of theoretical knowledge apart from any practical context, in the hope that practical problems will be able to be identified as easily derived applications of the knowledge so recently acquired. Years of amassing exclusively theoretical knowledge will not necessarily enable a student to adequately apply that knowledge in later vocational life. It cannot be assumed that the study of general theoretical knowledge will automatically result in thoughtful judgment and the ability to exercise practical skills.⁵⁵

Sohm pleads instead for a "dynamic-reciprocal praxis orientation," the core of which he describes as one's own "personal representative praxis experience." Learning happens in a "permanent oscillation between theoretical knowledge and practical activity." On the one hand there is the fact that "the level of a person's theoretical knowledge limits that person's level of perception, insight and discernment when handling practical problems." This means that theoretical knowledge "is absolutely essential for the expansion of one's ability to solve practical problems." On the other hand, "encountering and dealing with practical problems is a core prerequisite for acquiring and using theoretical knowledge." This model of a dynamic-reciprocal relationship between theory and praxis seeks to give theory its appropriate place of primacy when it comes to the ability to recognizing and solving problems. At the same time it seeks to give praxis its appropriate place of primacy when it comes to the practical relevance of theory.⁵⁶

---

53. Sohm, *Praxisbezogene Ausbildung*, 35. The "independent thought and action" mentioned in this text must not be interpreted individualistically. The independent thought required stands in contrast to a mindless repetition of classroom content. In Western educational tradition, however, this call for independence is strongly individualistic. The thinking of an isolated individual can then easily be placed on a pedestal. From a biblical perspective, and also in view of other cultures, the element of community will need to receive greater emphasis.
54. Altrichter and Posch, quoted Sohm, *Praxisbezogene Ausbildung*, 36.
55. Sohm, *Praxisbezogene Ausbildung*, 36.
56. Ibid., 37–38.

Preliminary Observations: The technical university model provides us with further insights into the problematic of the relationship between theory and praxis. This model is somewhere in between the traditional concept of the academic university and the praxis-integrating vocational training. It seeks to create a synthesis that goes beyond the polarization between these two educational models. It maintains the freedom of scientific thought and work, independent of results, agenda, or application, and yet provides vocational certification for specific occupational paths, and thus elevates praxis to an integral component of its educational philosophy. It is an innovative educational model of the present day, fuelled by the pedagogical paradigm shift of the twentieth century. It moves beyond the one-sided primacy of theory and thought and makes praxis a full partner in the educational process. The key pedagogical principles, according to Sohm, are a high level of theoretical knowledge and a dynamic-reciprocal relationship of theory to practice. In this, the technical university model differentiates itself from the more pragmatic and less time-intensive model of adult education.

Having looked at the technical university model, we have arrived at the end of our overview of the educational models available in our society today, each with its own view of the relationship between theory and practice. In the paragraphs entitled *preliminary observations* we have taken a first look at the relevance and implications of each model for theological education. The next section will show concretely which models of theological education have developed and are available for evangelical theological education.

3.4 Traditions and Models of Theological Education: An Overview

Theological education occurs not only within the context of secular educational models but also within various traditions and models of theological education. These have, of course, connections to secular educational models, but must be considered separately. In view of the educational institutions which will receive our primary attention, the following models and traditions will be discussed: (1) the Bible school movement, (2) academic, university-based theological education, (3) the model of the American seminaries, and finally (4) newer, alternative models which can be placed under the heading Theological Education by Extension.

3.4.1 The Bible School Movement

Most evangelical educational institutions trace their roots to the tradition of the Bible and missions schools. These must be seen as closely connected to the modern missionary movement. The schools that were associated with the missionary movement were originally vocational training schools for prospective missionaries.[57] The missions schools of the classical missions movement, like the Basler Mission, the Berliner Mission, and the Barmer Mission, were among the first institutions of this type. The Basler School of Missions in particular saw itself as a place of vocational training for missionaries, as an alternative to an academic university-based theological education, which was not an option for many potential missionaries because they were tradesmen (and women).[58] These original missions schools did not survive, but they can be seen as prototypes for the Bible school movement that arose later. The oldest of these Bible schools was the St Crischona Seminary for Preachers and Missionaries, founded in 1840. In the 1880s the first Bible and missions schools were founded in North America, among them Moody Bible Institute and Prairie Bible Institute, which are still well known today.[59]

These schools were strongly shaped by the spirit of the missionary movement and must be viewed as the place where missionaries were recruited and trained. The ethos of the early Bible school movement can be described with the words *spiritual life* and *missionary passion*. As Witmer so fittingly wrote:

> *Go ye into all the world and preach the gospel to every creature.*
> This parting command of the risen Lord is the *raison d'être* for
> Bible institutes and colleges. It is the base of reference for the
> direction, the purpose, and the subject matter of Bible college
> education. The founders and their successors were dominated by

---

57. Cf. Klaus Fiedler, *Ganz auf Vertrauen. Geschichte und Kirchenverständnis der Glaubensmissionen* (Giessen: Brunnen Verlag, 1992). For the history of the evangelical missionary movement see p. 12–35. For the significance of Bible schools see p. 426–435.
58. Cf. Wilhelm Schlatter, *Die Geschichte der Basler Mission*, Vol. 1 (Basel: Verlag der Basler Missionsbuchhandlung, 1916), 30–31.
59. Fiedler, *Ganz auf Vertrauen*, 426–428.

the conviction that the church is under compelling obligation to make the gospel of salvation known to all mankind.[60]

Cheesman observes the following common characteristics within the Bible school movement:[61] (1) training for the Christian church without the destructive influence of the liberal and critical theology of the universities; (2) training lay people for service in the church and in missions; (3) training for missionaries in the modern missionary movement; (4) emphasis on spiritual growth and practical skills.

Although the Bible school movement has its roots in Europe, it blossomed in North America, where more than 250 such schools were founded between 1882 and 1940.[62] The lasting impact of Bible schools should not be underestimated. For one thing, they provided mission societies with thousands of missionaries,[63] and for another, they had a profound and lasting influence on North American evangelicalism.[64]

After the First World War, as a result of missionary activity from Anglo-Saxon countries, the Bible school movement took hold in Europe as well, especially in German-speaking Europe, and joined forces with the already existing tradition of non-university (evangelical) education. Quite a few of the schools that are connected through the Konferenz Bibeltreuer Ausbildungsstätten (KBA) have direct North American roots (for example,

---

60. S. A. Witmer, *The Bible College Story: Education with Dimension* (New York: Channel Press, 1962), 103. For a thorough presentation and analysis of the British Bible school and Bible college movement, see Graham Cheesman: *The Bible College Movement in the UK: A History and Interpretation* (Saarbrücken: VDM Verlag, 2009).

61. Cheesman, "Competing Paradigms," 488.

62. Virginia L. Brereton, "Protestant Fundamentalist Bible Schools: 1882-1940" (Columbia University, unpublished doctoral dissertation, 1981). As late as 1960, Witmer speaks of approximately 250 Bible schools in North America with a total of ca. 25,000 students, in *The Bible College Story*, 15, 34–38.

63. Pierce R. Beaver observed in 1976 that about 70% of all North American missionaries active at that time had been trained in these schools. See "The American Protestant Theological Seminary and Mission: An Historical Survey," *Missiology* 6, no. 1 (1976): 85. When you consider that in 1969 there were 33,290 North American missionaries active worldwide, the significance of the Bible school movement cannot be over-stated. Cf. Richard V. Pierard, "'Pax Americana' and the Evangelical Missionary Advance," in *Earthen Vessels: American Evangelicals and Foreign Missions 1880-1980*, eds. Joel A. Carpenter and William R. Shenk (Grand Rapids: Eerdmans Publishing, 1990).

64. Brereton, "Protestant Fundamentalist Bible Schools", provided evidence that the present strength of evangelicalism in North America is undoubtedly linked to the impact of the Bible school movement.

Brake Bible School) or received renewed momentum from the American Bible school movement.

With regard to the question of theory vs. praxis, there is no doubt that Bible schools are praxis oriented in several ways: (1) For one thing, there is a clear orientation toward the practice of missionary activity. Through information, motivation, and training, young people are to be equipped to invest themselves, their whole lives, in the endeavor of worldwide missions.[65] (2) In addition, the Bible schools were and still are life training schools where students learn to live a committed Christian life in community with others through communal living and the practice of spiritual disciplines. (3) Finally, internships, short-term serving trips, and practical Christian service experiences were and are an essential part of the training.

At the same time it must be said that the pedagogy of the Bible schools assumes the primacy of theory and therefore imply a lesser importance for praxis. The theoretical instruction is not critical, academic and analytic in the same way that the scientific approach of the universities is. Rather it is affirming, synthetic and motivational. But it is theory nonetheless.

It is not without justification that Ferris and Enlow use the word *indoctrination* in characterizing Bible schools.[66] Indoctrination means that predefined knowledge is taught with the intent to lastingly anchor a valid tradition in the next generation. Training of this kind can certainly be justified biblically and was widespread up until the beginning of the twentieth century. Since the time of John Dewey, however, indoctrination is seen as the pedagogy of authoritarian societies and not appropriate in a democratic setting.[67] The

---

65. The lectures and publications of Otto Rieker are among the most impressive appeals for a practical, missions-oriented Bible school education (see Bibliography).

66. R. W. Ferris and Ralph E. Enlow, "Reassessing Bible College Distinctives" (American Association of Bible Colleges, unpublished lecture, 1995), 3. The characteristics suggested by Ferris and Enlow are: (1) commitment to under-graduate preparation for vocational Christian service, (2) commitment to the priority of biblical formation – both mastery of the Bible and mastery by the Bible, (3) commitment to spiritual and ministerial development through the requirement to engage in practical ministry during training, (4) emphasis on Christian character development through setting and enforcing standards, (5) emphasis on indoctrination in orthodoxy as a safeguard to doctrinal purity, (6) emphasis on teaching practical ministry techniques and (7) emphasis on a view of leadership which stresses the intrinsic authority which accompanies divine appointment and guidance.

67. Cf. Ross T. Bender article "Indoctrination," in *Harper's Encyclopedia of Religious Education*, ed. Iris V. Cully (New York: Harper, 1990); also in Ross T. Bender, *Education for Peoplehood: Essays on the Teaching Ministry of the Church* (Elkhart: Institute of Mennonite Studies, 1997), 173–175.

teaching of theory by indoctrination is diametrically opposed to the ideals of a university pedagogy which seeks to foster independent critical thinking.[68] In the case of Bible schools, indoctrination is an explicit measure to combat the critical thinking of the universities. It is, according to Ferris and Enlow, "indoctrination in orthodoxy as a safeguard to doctrinal purity."

Preliminary Observations: The Bible school model presents us with an ambiguous picture of the question of praxis vs. theory. On the one hand, it is characterized by a strong emphasis on praxis, expressed in the promotion of personal spirituality, communal life, and passion for missions. On the other hand, this model, because of the educational philosophy of indoctrination, stands in sharp contrast to the pedagogical paradigm shift described earlier, as well as to the tradition of critical-analytical reflection of the universities.

The neo-humanistic educational ideal assumed that the study of classical literature would automatically unleash the educational effects of that literature and thus equip students for life.[69] By comparison, the educational ideal of the Bible schools assumes that the study of the Bible and orthodox theology will automatically equip students to rightly live the Christian life. In both cases the primacy and superiority of theory is dominant. In the case of the neo-humanistic educational ideal this primacy is based in the primacy and superiority of spirit over matter as seen by Plato and Descartes. In the case of the Bible school tradition, what Norbert Greinacher says in general about theology certainly applies:

> In theology in general and in practical theology in particular the primacy of theory over praxis is firmly entrenched. Often what is behind this is Plato's alienation from Christian teaching. Theory is seen as a static reality. In theology especially, the unchangeableness and therefore the superiority of truth, which the theorist studies, is contrasted with the changeability and therefore the inferiority of reality.[70]

---

68. To what extent indoctrination occurs even in the scientific critical setting of a university education is another question.
69. Cf. Sohm, *Praxisbezogene Ausbildung*, 23.
70. Norbert Greinacher, "Das Theorie-Praxis-Problem in der Praktischen Theologie," in *Praktische Theologie Heute*, eds. Ferdinand Klostermann and Rolf Zerfaß (Munich: Kaiser, 1974), 108.

Greinacher makes an important point here, in my opinion, with regards to evangelical theological education. The theological concept of truth that is given by God and therefore normative and unchanging (unchangeable), together with the primacy and superiority of thought as advocated by Plato and Descartes, leads to a view of the primacy of theology as "given" or fixed theory which can and should lead to practical action.

This leads to the concluding remark that the Bible school tradition seems on the surface to be very praxis oriented. At its core, however, it is heavily theory driven.

3.4.2 Theological Education as Academic Course of Study

When we speak about theological education as an academic course of study, we are talking about schools of theology at universities, church and denominational seminaries, and independent, non-denominational seminaries as well, so long as those institutions in this latter group understand themselves to provide tertiary (post-secondary, university level) education.

The fact that theological faculties have a place within the context of state universities is not to be taken for granted. They had to fight for this right in the eighteenth century, and it is largely due to the efforts of Friedrich Schleiermacher that they succeeded. His proposal for a curriculum for theological study[71] had a lasting influence on the issue of theory and praxis that we have been discussing.

Schleiermacher succeeded in establishing theology as a scientific discipline within the context of the modern university by defining theology as a *positive*, that is, purpose-driven science. As such, theology must be "related to an external purpose, that is, to a purpose outside of knowledge itself." Schleiermacher argues: just as medicine has as its purpose "the restoration of the body to its normal condition," just as law has its purpose "the establishment of justice," so theology has as its purpose "the maintaining of the Christian faith in the community." All of these sciences are *positive*

---

71. The text referenced here was written in 1811 and bore the title *Kurze Darstellung des Theologischen Studiums* along with the later version of the lecture notes of the Theological Encyclopedia by David Friedrich Strauss from 1831/32: Friedrich Schleiermacher, *Theologische Enzyklopädie 1831/32* (Berlin: Walter de Gruyter, 1987), hereafter quoted as ThE. For an interpretation of the *Theologische Enzyklopädie*, see Martin Rössler, *Schleiermachers Programm der Philosophischen Theologie* (Berlin: Walter de Gruyter, 1994).

"because they do not merely seek to represent but rather to create a state of being."[72] Herewith the study of theology was given an explicit praxis orientation, specifically an orientation to the praxis of church leadership.[73] That gives the study of theology a forward-looking orientation as well, with an eye toward church praxis. At the same time, a positive science is defined by its historical ties to the past. All praxis is rooted in history, and therefore the theory for present-day praxis is developed from an awareness of and a reflection of history. Schleiermacher is concerned about "the activity of the few, who possess the historical awareness necessary to maintain the identity and the communication of the faith."[74]

The concept proposed by Schleiermacher has enormous implications for our discussion of the relationship between theory and praxis. I'd like to point out three aspects: (1) the fundamental praxis orientation of theology, (2) practical theology as theory from praxis, and (3) the emphasis (or better: limiting) of the praxis orientation toward church leadership.

Schleiermacher's proposal has become, however, problematic in its implementation. Theology in the context of the university is in a state of emergency in terms of its justification. The justification Schleiermacher used – that of church leadership – is no longer relevant. Schleiermacher wrote at a time when the importance of the church for society was assumed to be self-evident. In this context it was easy to justify the scientific education of church leaders along with that of doctors and solicitors. This reasoning is no longer credible in today's post-Christian society. Theology must now find a new and different justification for its place in the university. Jean Zumstein does this for the reformed Protestant faculties in Switzerland by offering the following arguments:[75]

- Theology makes a contribution to the scientific assessment of the Christian tradition that is a significant element of our culture.

---

72. ThE section 1.
73. ThE sections 1 and 20; cf. Rössler, *Schleiermachers Programm*, 53.
74. ThE section 3; cf. Rössler, *Schleiermachers Programm*, 50–51. That theology thereby lost its place as normative science and henceforth defined itself only as the historical outgrowth of the church had, of course, far-reaching consequences, especially for the biblical sciences and the normative position of the Bible.
75. Zumstein, "Theologische Fakultäten," 97–99.

- Along with other faculties, theology carries "responsibility for defending the ethical values that are foundational to our humanistic universities."
- Theology opposes, "based upon its own tradition, any deification of knowledge or science."
- In addition, according to Zumstein, theology is able to exercise an integrative function in society. It can be an advocate for people and for their humanity and keep the memory of Christian tradition alive in a secular society.

Theology can serve the church precisely by being free, that is, independent of the church. In an era in which sects and fundamentalism thrive, theology "can warn against religious folly by providing a sober and factual image of the church." Thus the study of theology can indeed be the place where future pastors can obtain valuable "specialized competency to interpret Christian tradition with independence and relevance" – not as practical training for ministry in the church, but rather as an academic education that can serve as the foundation for a second phase of training (apprenticeship) during which the church profession can be learned.[76]

The study of theology in the context of the university lives, therefore, in the tension between the ethos of the university, which insists on "purpose-free" instruction and research on the one hand, and the clear orientation toward professional ministry in the church on the other. If it abandons the one, it loses its validity as a university science. If it abandons the other, it loses its original identity and its functional core. The literature on this topic gives ample witness to this tension.[77]

---

76. The view represented here by Zumstein has been confirmed several times over in recent years: Ulrich Gäbler and Ekkehard Stegemann in an interview with the *Badischer Zeitung* (3 April 1995, 7); a discussion within the protestant theological faculty of the University of Bern that starts with the premise that the study of theology is not training to be a pastor but simply provides the academic foundation for such training (*Reformierte Presse* 46 [1999]: 7). On the other hand, the so-called Concordat (church commission for pastoral training) took the Bologna reform of tertiary education as an occasion for developing an integrated model for pastoral training that amounted to a "shift in the culture of education" (cf. *Annex, Magazin der Reformierten Presse* 11 [2006]).

77. Cf. standard introductions to the study of theology, such as Rudolf Bohren, ed. *Einführung in das Studium der evangelischen Theologie* (Munich: Kaiser, 1964), 10–15 esp.; Gerhad Ebeling, *The Study of Theology* (Philadelphia: Fortress, 1978); Friedrich Mildenberger, *Theorie der Theologie: Enzyklopädie als Methodenlehre* (Stuttgart: Calwer Verlag, 1972); Henning Schröer, ed., *Einführung in das Studium der evangelischen Theologie*

Preliminary Observations: Evangelical theological education is therefore caught in the tension between two educational traditions – the academic, university-based model on the one hand and praxis-oriented missional model on the other. At first glance one is inclined to say that the university model is theory-oriented and the Bible school model praxis oriented. This is indeed the widespread perception, and therefore the praxis-oriented model is often given preference because of the needs of the church and its mission.[78] But as we have seen, things are not quite that clear cut.

The academic university model does not seek to provide a praxis-oriented experience in the way vocational training does. The diploma or degree conferred upon completion (of the university) does not certify vocational skills for ministry in the church or in missions. Instead, in the light of the Western/Christian tradition (which is to be learned during the course of study), a university (theological) education seeks to equip students with the ability to think critically and independently for the present day. Thus the university curriculum is not intended to be less practical but starts from the premise that the most superior practical skills are intellectual.

The Bible school model, on the other hand, is not praxis oriented in the sense of being "on-the-job" training. Quite the contrary, a large part of the schooling is given to indoctrination, that is, to the communication of knowledge.

Nevertheless the transition from the educational philosophy of the Bible school to that of the university is a paradigm shift, one which evangelical theological education would do well to be aware of: (1) instead of the comfort and assurance of indoctrination, the university model fosters independent critical thinking, (2) instead of encouraging spiritual and missionary passion, the university model prefers a distanced, objective perspective, and (3) instead of practical training, the university model offers critical praxis reflection.

(Gütersloh: Gütersloher Verlagshaus Gerd Mohn, 1982), 13–46 and 180–192 esp. Practical theology especially experiences this tension, which is reflected in the literature. An example is Klostermann and Zerfaß, *Praktische Theologie Heute*. Specifically addressing the problem of the relationship between theory and praxis are four essays by Adolf Exeler and Norbert Mette, Norbert Greinacher and Gerhard Sautter, 65–131; also see Martin Nicol, *Grundwissen Praktische Theologie* (Stuttgart: Verlag W. Kohlhammer, 2000), 243–257.

78. Otto Riecker has vehemently defended this viewpoint again and again in *Bildung und Heiliger Geist* (Neuhausen-Stuttgart: Hänssler, 1974); also *Universitäts-Theologie und Gemeinde-Frömmigkeit* (Neuhausen-Stuttgart: Hänssler, 1984).

3.4.3 The American Seminary Model

In view of the tension between Bible school training and university education just described, European evangelical students and teachers alike have often seen a solution in the model of the American seminary. This model seeks to bring together both elements: spirituality, missionary motivation and praxis orientation, along with academic work.[79]

The history of American seminaries begins in the early eighteenth century with the founding of Andover Theological Seminary (1808) and Princeton Theological Seminary (1812). These were schools that were financed by churches or denominations and which offered "post-collegiate" training for pastors in a three-year course of study independent from the colleges they were associated with.[80] These are characteristics of American seminaries to this day.

The influence of American seminaries on German-speaking evangelical theological education occurred in the past forty years in multiple ways: (1) A large number of German-speaking theologians studied at American seminaries, (2) American mission societies founded (or encouraged) schools in Europe based on the model of American seminaries (e.g. the Freie Theologische Hochschule, Giessen – formerly Freie Theologische Akademie), (3) schools in German-speaking Europe received academic recognition (accreditation) through cooperation and partnership with American seminaries (e.g. the Akademie für Weltmission, Korntal).

In order to understand the scope of this influence on German-speaking evangelical theological education, it is instructive to review the historical

---

79. This same integration was and is strived for in the seminaries and preacher training institutions of the European (state) churches as well as in the seminaries of the free churches. Cf. Klaus Haacker, "Warum und wozu (noch) kirchliche Hochschulen?" *Theologische Beiträge* 2, no. 6 (2002): 362–365; and Erwin Brandt, "Akzente und Perspektiven der ökumenisch-missionarischen Ausbildung an einer freikirchlichen Ausbildungsstätte," in *Impulse für eine Kirche von morgen. Beiträge zur ökumenisch-theologischen Ausbildung*, ed. Evangelisches Missionswerk (Hamburg: Evangelisches Missionswerk, 1997); Hans-Harald Mallau, "Das Theologiestudium im BEFG und seine 'akademische Anerkennung,'" *Zeitschrift für Theologie und Gemeinde* 6 (2001); Kim Strubind, "'Pastoren bilden Pastoren aus' – Ein Entwurf für eine zeit- und sachgemäße theologische Ausbildung im Bund Evangelisch-Freikirchler Gemeinden in Elstal," *Zeitschrift für Theologie und Gemeinde* 6 (2001).

80. Robert W. Lynn, "Notes Toward a History: Theological Encyclopedia and the Evolution of Protestant Seminary Curriculum, 1808-1868," *Theological Education* 1 (2002): 118.

development of the American seminaries. Edward Farley divides this history into three phases:[81]

1) A first phase can be described with the phrase "*pious learning (divinity).*" Emphasis was placed on the study of the Bible (including the ancient languages), the reading of theological literature (primarily of British origin), and learning to preach (*sacred rhetoric*).[82] It was spiritual and intellectual education in the classical sense of the word, that is, character building lessons in tradition with a view toward pastoral ministry. In this phase the pastor was seen as a spiritual leader, a man of God, who achieved a deeper fear of God through his studies and was therefore equipped for ministry in the church.

2) A second phase was characterized by Farley with the word "*scholarship.*" Due to the influence of German university-based theological education, the curriculum of the American seminaries became more academic as early as the middle of the nineteenth century.[83] As a consequence, the four-fold disciplines of the German theological educational model were adopted (Bible, History, Theology, Praxis). This brought with it a growing fragmentation of the curriculum. In this phase the pastor is an academic who scientifically masters the various disciplines of theology.

3) In the past fifty years, according to Farley, a further development can be observed. The pastor is seen as a "*professional*," as a pro with specialized qualifications for a career in the church. This pushes practical theology into a central role, to equip pastors-in-training with the necessary vocational competencies. Farley stresses that these three phases do not simply follow consecutively one upon the other but rather that phases one and two still reach into the

---

81. Farley, *Theologia*, 6–12.
82. Cf. Lynn, "Notes Toward a History," 122.
83. Farley, *Theologia*, 111: "The modern, European ideal of specialized disciplines had to be applied to theology. This ideal took hold in the United States under the impact of the Germanization of American theological education." That the American universities lost their Christian-religious soul largely because of the influence of German idealism and liberalism is the persuasive thesis of George M. Marsden, *The Soul of the American University: From Protestant Establishment to Established Unbelief* (New York: Oxford University Press, 1994), 101–112.

present day. Dominant today, however, according to Farley, is the professional-practical dimension of the "clerical paradigm."

It is this third historical phase that many European evangelical theologians see as an attractive model. Its praxis orientation is obvious and has several dimensions: (1) theological education in the seminary model has an explicit vocational orientation. It is designed to meet the specific qualifications needed in various fields of employment in the church and in missions. (2) It is functional and pragmatic. Quality standards are defined by "output."[84] (3) It tends to be pragmatic and eclectic in the formulation of theory, that is, it derives its theory module from theological, philosophical, sociological and psychological theories that are helpful in the formulation of a theory of praxis for pastoral ministry. (4) It tends to evaluate theories based on their practicality. (5) It spends more time on the application and implementation of theory than on critical analysis of theory or on formulating new theory based on philosophical reflection.[85]

Edward Farley has harshly criticized the recent developments in American seminary education.[86] His main criticism is directed at the functionalistic praxis orientation of the "clerical paradigm." Three points are worth noting: (1) The functionalism of seminary education looks very praxis oriented on the surface but has in fact exacerbated the praxis-theory problem. It views the pastoral task as no more than a sociologically definable public role and places emphasis on preaching, management, organization, teaching and evangelism. The ecclesiological and spiritual elements that are fundamental to church and ministry are largely neglected. When a functionalistic interpretation of the pastoral role serves as criterion, content and goal of theological education, a couple of things happen. Theology becomes disconnected from praxis, and theological thought and work become secondary, because the only thing that counts is pastoral technique. (2) In a continuation – but also a one-

---

84. Cf. the critical questions of Tim Dearborn, "Preparing New Leaders for the Church of the Future," *Transformation* 12, no. 4 (1995): 7–12.

85. One example is missiology: As Edward Rommen shows in his study of American evangelical missions theory, the theological foundations of missions as formulated by G. W. Peters have been widely accepted. All the rest of the efforts of North American missions theory have been devoted to application. Cf. Edward Rommen, *Die Notwendigkeit der Umkehr* (Giessen: Brunnen Verlag, 1987), 128–129.

86. Farley, *Theologia*, esp. p. 127–149. Cf. Bruce C. Steward, "Tensions in North American Theological Education," *Evangelical Review of Theology* 14, no. 1 (1990): 43–49.

sided functionalizing – of Schleiermacher's paradigm, the term "praxis" is reduced to the professional activities of the pastor and church leader. That has fatal consequences in two ways: First, the job of the biblical, historical and theological disciplines is limited to laying a theoretical foundation for pastoral activities. Theology as a whole tends to be reduced to no more than pastoral theology. The full breadth of theology – which offers perspective and direction to human behavior in all areas of life – is largely lost. The implicit message is that Christian practice is pastoral practice. (3) At the same time, seminary education is not at its core pastoral praxis, because the student is studying and not carrying out pastoral functions. Even if the student is studying part-time and working part-time in a church, his studies remain study and are not church work. It is theory apart from praxis. In contrast to Schleiermacher's theory, it is not critical reflection on the basic questions of pastoral ministry. Rather it is the cognitive communication of principles, manuals, models and techniques that are to be applied in praxis.

Not everyone agrees with Farley's critique. The debate about reform efforts intended to overcome the functionalistic-pragmatic fixation on praxis has continued since the publication of *Theologia*. Yet his critique has served to expose the basic contours of American seminary education. What takes precedence is the emphasis on praxis for the sake of church and missions. This praxis orientation has obvious pragmatic elements: theological education is measured by results.

Connected to this pragmatism is the high value given to empirical studies. Time and again sociological studies of missions and church growth have been, and continue to be, the source of new strategies, new methods, and also new definitions of theology. Donald McGavran's research in the area of church growth serves as a prototype for this trend.

I believe that it is this pragmatism that has created a culture in American theological education in which alternative didactic models, such as those that have arisen out of the paradigm shift described above, are accepted and used for their own purposes. For example, the concept of *clinical pastoral education* has been familiar in the United States since the 1920s,[87] and TEE,

---

87. Hans-Christoph Piper, *Kommunizieren lernen in Seelsorge und Predigt* (Göttingen: Vandenhoeck & Ruprecht, 1981), 37.

shaped by liberation theology (Freire), has found favor and acceptance in American evangelical theological education.[88]

Preliminary Observations: This pragmatism that we find in American seminary education is for theologians in German-speaking Europe attractive and provocative at the same time. On the one hand, this pragmatic-practical approach to theological education has the advantage of providing a high degree of usability. That which is learned can be used in concrete situations in missions and church work. This contrasts sharply with the academic theology taught at universities in German-speaking Europe, which often remains at a level of abstraction far removed from praxis. On the other hand, German and European theologians tend to have deep-seated scepticism toward any theology that seems too concerned with utility, functionality, or success.

Can it be that this tension between American (or should we say Anglo-Saxon) and German-European theology has its roots in the differing spiritual-historical traditions, there empiricism, here idealism?[89] Perhaps the British military historian John Keegan was not far from the mark, when, asked about the difference between the Germans and the British, he said:

> The German spirit is incomprehensible to the British. There is nothing in Great Britain that can be compared with the magnetic attraction that abstract ideas have for the Germans. The British think very pragmatically and practically, and that is reflected in the philosophical debate. We are empiricists, whereas the Germans are idealists. There is no common ground between empiricists and idealists.[90]

Thus American seminary education can provide a (necessary) challenge to theological education in German-speaking Europe – not to be bound by a spirit shaped solely by idealism but rather to ask without hesitation what concrete results for missions and church work are provided by theological education. We should not shy away from this (American) challenge.

---

88. Convincing evidence of this is found in the volume *Theological Education by Extension*, published in 1969 and edited by Ralph D. Winter of the School of World Mission at Fuller Theological Seminary in Pasadena.

89. Cf. the chapter "American Practicality and Germanic Ideals: Two Visions for Reform," in *Soul of the American University*, ed. Georges M. Marsden, 101–113.

90. John Keegan, "Der Krieg ist keine Frage der Moral," *Die Weltwoche* 51, no. 52 (2002): 81.

Theological education in Europe can avoid falling victim to a one-sided pragmatism at the expense of serious academic work by not looking to the North American seminary model alone, but also to the model of the European technical university introduced earlier. This can be especially instructive for the master's degree programs introduced at many seminaries in recent years. In many ways the pedagogical goals of these master's degree curricula, which are designed with church and mission work in mind, correspond precisely to those of technical universities. The Theory-Praxis-Integration model proposed by Sohm deserves close attention. The current theory-praxis debate in evangelical theological education is rather stuck. Sohm's model has the potential to provide ideas and direction for the future.[91]

3.4.4 Alternative Models of Theological Education

Finally we turn to educational models which have been largely shaped by ideas stemming from the pedagogical paradigm shifts of the twentieth century. Two categories in particular are noteworthy: (1) those which follow the model of Clinical Pastoral Education (CPE) and (2) those which may be grouped under the heading Theological Education by Extension (TEE).

As mentioned earlier, the origins of CPE in North America can be traced to the 1920s. The core of this concept lies in on-the-job training. Actual work and ministry experience is discussed in the context of individual supervision and group settings, and the process of learning is thus led and enhanced.[92] Piper points out that Heinrich Philipp Sextro developed a similar concept as early as the end of the eighteenth century in the Göttingen "Pastoral Institute." However, because of pressure from educational idealism ("the mind runs ahead of praxis once again") this model did not survive.[93] Today "clinical education" is a recognized instrument of praxis-integrating training in the German-speaking world. It is used primarily in the training of preachers and pastors, counsellors and therapists, especially in the second phase of pastoral training (apprenticeship) and in specialized training (e.g.

---

91. Cf. Sohm, *Praxisbezogene Ausbildung*, esp. 81–89.
92. Cf. Dieter Stollberg, *Therapeutische Seelsorge: Die amerikanische Seelsorgebewegung* (Munich: Kaiser, 1969); also Paul M. Zehr and Jim Egli, *Alternative Models of Mennonite Pastoral Formation* (Elkhart: Institute of Mennonite Studies, 1992).
93. Piper, *Kommunizieren lernen*, 14–27, quotation p. 26.

hospital counselling). More recent concepts like mentoring, coaching, and supervision adopt some aspects of CPE.

Theological Education by Extension has its roots in a paradigm shift in missions that has been underway since the Second World War. The churches of the Majority World, maturing to ever greater independence, expressed with increasing clarity their reservations about the usefulness and appropriateness of Western educational models. The Theological Education Fund of the World Council of Churches invested millions of dollars between 1958 and 1978 to build Western-style theological schools in the Majority World. Yet as early as the 1960s questions were being raised as to whether the pastoral training being offered was the right kind, that is, helpful in these contexts.[94] In 1963 the Presbyterian Seminary of Guatemala took the initiative to offer training that was decentralized, at a simple academic level, and tailored specifically to meet the pastoral needs of the participants. This is generally seen as the birth of TEE.[95] As early as 1977 F. Ross Kinsler could point to approximately three hundred TEE programs in seventy-five countries, involving between 30,000 and 40,000 students.[96]

There was pressure from the educational needs within the arena of missions in the Majority World and encouragement from the American pragmatism of the School of World Missions at Fuller Theological Seminary (McGavran, Winter). There was also a new pedagogy which found application within liberation theology (Freire). All of these factors contributed to the birth and growth of a new approach to theological education that deserves respect as a separate, independent model. Kinsler, one of the pioneers of TEE, has described TEE in varying ways and defined it with a number of terms. Common to all of these definitions is the consistent *orientation around the context and the person*. The ultimate criterion is something like this: Christian ministry is undertaken by gifted people in the church, and theological education has the responsibility to provide these people with the training that they need. Traditional educational models don't work for a number of reasons. They are elitist. They limit work in the church to the professionals. They erect

---

94. Cf. Newbigin, "Theological Education," 3–10.
95. Cf. Kenneth B. Mulholland, "Presbyterian Seminary of Guatemala: A Modest Experiment Becomes a Model for Change," in *Ministry by the People: Theological Education by Extension*, ed. Ross F. Kinsler (Geneva: WCC, 1983).
96. Kinsler, *Extension Movement*, xii.

hurdles to training (distance, finances, formal acceptance requirements). And they remove students from their own context.⁹⁷

Originally TEE was designed for use in the Majority World. Later, TEE programs were utilized in North America and Europe as well. This led to the development of a variety of concepts that all contained elements of TEE but could only be classified as TEE with the broadest understanding of that term. Among these are concepts like Distance Learning (e.g. The International Correspondence Institute, now known as the Global University), church-based theological education, Open Access Education (e.g. The Open University in Great Britain), and more recently E-Learning (training via the internet).

These new educational concepts tend to offer real promise to today's students, in two specific areas: (1) Openness, that is, wider access for as many people who desire training as possible. Traditional barriers are to be overcome – inability to meet formal acceptance requirements, geographic limitations because of family obligations, the need to maintain a job and earn money, impossibility of finding a replacement in the church (e.g. in a church planting situation). (2) Integration of praxis, that is, education and training parallel to and concurrent with work in the church or in missions. As a supplement to *learning by doing* or *on-the-job training*, TEE provides the theoretical biblical and theological content.

In order for such programs to deliver what they promise, there must be sufficiently demanding conditions, which is not always guaranteed.⁹⁸ As early as the 1980s some of those who were initially strong supporters of TEE began to voice criticism of extension programs. The number of failed programs increased, and along with lists of the positive benefits of TEE, observers formulated a growing list of deficiencies.⁹⁹

Concluding Observations: In this chapter we outlined an overview of the educational landscape. First (Section 3.2) in the form of various model typologies. Section 3.3 presented the current usable secular educational

---

97. Ibid., 3–60.

98. In conjunction with the consultation Global Open Access Theological Education at the Oxford Centre for Mission Studies, 7–11 February 2000, I conducted a critical analysis of these educational concepts. Cf. Ott, "Mission Oriented Theological Education."

99. Kenneth B. Mulholland, "TEE Come of Age: A Candid Assessment after Two Decades," in *Cyprus: TEE Come of Age*, ed. Robert L. Youngblood (Exeter: Paternoster, 1986).

models, and section 3.4 concentrated on the models of theological education. In addition, sections 3.3 and 3.4 took a look at the relationship between theory and praxis.

Thus we have drawn something like an educational map on which we can locate our programs and institutions. This map will also help us identify and pursue new directions. So that we don't lose sight of this overview, we will summarize here the models described in sections 3.3 and 3.4:

The *academic-university model* is intentionally not vocational training but rather training in critical thinking and discerning perception in a setting that is free from linkage to any vocation. It seeks to provide *initial education* and falls within the tradition of the neo-humanistic educational ideal, which emphasizes the primacy and supremacy of thought over praxis. An academic university course of study certainly seeks to be praxis-relevant. It is assumed that the powers of observation and critical thinking that are learned will enable a student to succeed in life and in work.

The *dual vocational training model* seeks to equip the student with the skills needed in a specific field of employment. It does not teach praxis devoid of theory but rather seeks to provide students with both specialized knowledge and vocational skills.

The *adult education model* has proved useful for meeting personal and vocational continuing education needs (lifelong learning). It takes the demands of an emancipatory pedagogy seriously and seeks to take students seriously as well, as mature adults. It builds upon the insight that people learn most successfully when targeted theoretical input stimulates them to reflect upon their (life and work) experience in such a way that leads to "Aha" moments (inductive learning).

The *technical university model* (universities of applied sciences) has as its goal to offer praxis-based education at the university (tertiary) level. In contrast to vocational training, technical universities do not seek to teach specific vocational skills. These are assumed as prerequisites. In contrast to adult education, technical universities are not aiming simply at skills that can be acquired quickly and applied in praxis immediately. Instead, this model seeks to reflect upon praxis at an academic level and is indeed equivalent to a university (tertiary) course of study. In contrast to other universities, however, the curriculum at technical universities is consistently designed with vocational requirements in mind and seeks to certify students' proficiency in a high level of vocational competencies.

Theological education in the context of the university falls under the academic-university model described above. It is therefore not vocational training for pastors. At the same time this model is certainly, based on its self-definition (drawn from the work of Schleiermacher), slanted toward church leadership. That creates, especially in practical theology, an unresolvable conflict between theory and praxis.

The *Bible school model* is, because of its history, geared toward praxis in missions. It seeks to motivate and equip students for missionary service. That occurs not only through classroom instruction but also through the practice of spiritual disciplines, communal living, and through internships, short-term mission trips, and Christian service assignments. Shaped by an understanding of the supremacy of theory over praxis and part of a conservative evangelical tradition, this model has a tendency toward (apologetic) indoctrination. Although significantly praxis oriented, a Bible school education, in large measure, is made up of deductive instruction.

The *American seminary model* aims to combine pastoral training (praxis) and academic study (theory) within the North American academic system. In recent decades seminary education has become more strongly pragmatic and functional. Because the content and quality of the curriculum are largely determined by the results (output) required, the seminary model tends to give priority to praxis over theory.

Alternative educational models such as *Clinical Pastoral Education* and *Theological Education by Extension* (and other models of *Distance Learning*) have a consistent focus on the person and on the context (culture). The basic concept is on-the-job training. These models are influenced by the pedagogical paradigm shifts of the twentieth century and lean heavily on the principles of adult education. They are decidedly praxis oriented. Because the benefits of these models can only be realized under ideal circumstances, many programs of this type are unable to deliver what they promise.

The consulting and accrediting activity of the EEAA confirms the trend toward more flexible, modular, praxis-integrated, and decentralized educational concepts. It is also clear that internet-based learning is growing and will continue to grow. Thus theological education is following a trend that can be observed in other fields of education as well. This creates enormous challenges for seminaries, because there is (still) a significant lack of skilled personnel in the areas of E-Learning and Blended Learning, both in terms of professors/instructors as well as technicians (IT professionals). Nevertheless it is clear that these new forms of learning will have a growing impact on theological education.

4

Biblical-Theological Foundations: Toward a Theology of Theological Education

For years there have been voices calling for the reform of theological education to be guided by foundational theological reflection. Earlier we called attention to Richard Niebuhr's 1956 study, in which he established a theological foundation for the reform efforts in North America. Edward Farley's more historically based study *Theologia* had the same aim. Elsewhere he explicitly stated that the problems of theological education could only be solved on the basis of theology.[1] David Kelsey had the same goal when he gave one of his books the title *To Understand God Truly: What's Theological about a Theological School?*

In his work *Reenvisioning Theological Education*, Robert Banks observed a shift of emphasis in the entire discussion about theological education since the mid-1980s "from operational to theological concerns." He is of the opinion, however, that these insights have thus far had little effect in the North American context. "Unfortunately, it has not yet changed the way most theological institutions operate."[2] In his work he attempts to reframe

---

1. Edward Farley, "The Reform of Theological Education as a Theological Task," in *Theological Education* 1 (1981): 93–117.
2. Banks, *Reenvisioning Theological Education*, 10.

theological education on a foundation drawn directly from the Bible. More about this later.

In the evangelical world it is primarily ICETE that has called for and encouraged the development of a theology of theological education. In the so-called Manifesto we read:

> Evangelical theological education as a whole today needs earnestly to pursue and recover a thorough-going theology of education.... We must together take immediate and urgent steps to seek, elaborate and possess a biblically informed theological basis for our calling in theological education, and to allow every aspect of our service to become rooted and nurtured in this soil.[3]

In 1993, Dieumeme Noelliste developed this theme more concretely under the title *Toward a Theology of Theological Education*.[4] Noelliste's arguments follow the same lines as the earlier work of Niebuhr and Stackhouse for the most part.[5]

Such an undertaking is as difficult and filled with pitfalls as it is necessary. A look at the articles in the *Evangelical Review of Theology* 29, no. 3 (2005) proves the point. This issue is devoted entirely to the topic of "Theology in Theological Education." It is somewhat problematic that the title already speaks of The Theology of Theological Education. It is not realistic to talk about the theology of theological education, nor is it clear what such a theology should accomplish. That becomes completely clear only when one looks at the individual articles, most of which are thought provoking. Each article approaches the subject from a different angle and introduces an additional element into the discussion. It would have been more modest and more honest to call this "Contributions to a Theology of Theological Education." Nevertheless, the articles in this issue of the *Evangelical Review of Theology* provide helpful insights, some of which may indeed prove to be essential building blocks of a theology of theological education.

---

3. ICETE, Manifesto, section 4, "Theological Grounding," http://www.icete-edu.org/manifesto.html

4. Dieumeme Noelliste, *Toward a Theology of Theological Education* (Seoul: World Evangelical Fellowship Theological Commission, 1993).

5. Ibid., 7–8.

Based on the situation here described, two things appear clear: First, the current upheaval in theological education desperately needs to be accompanied by theological thought and reflection. It is in fact necessary to formulate something like a theology of theological education. And second, thus far this has happened only in meager beginnings if it all.

It would therefore be presumptuous to seek to present a full-orbed systematic theology of theological education in the following pages. What I present here must be seen as an attempt to identify and reflect upon various contributions to and facets of a possible theology of theological education.

I will approach the topic in two steps:

1) First will be to identify building blocks of a theology of theological education which are drawn from the biblical text.

2) Then the attempt can be made to propose a theology of theological education which addresses the current questions.

4.1 Biblical Building Blocks for a Theology of Theological Education

Any attempt to construct a biblical foundation for theological education must be aware of the hermeneutical problems associated with such a task. Even the question, "What did theological education look like in biblical times?" is insidious. The historical distance is enormous, and there are no easy analogies from situations in our day to the biblical contexts. Simply to say, "Let's just do things like Jesus did" is naïve and shortsighted. Nevertheless Robert Banks is right to fight for a biblical rationale for theological education.[6] This presupposes, however, sound hermeneutical thinking.

Isa Breitmaier reaches the conclusion in her significant work, *Lehren und lernen in der Spur des Ersten Testamentes* [Teaching and Learning on the Trail of the First Testament], "that no direct line can be drawn from the understanding of teaching and learning in the Old Testament to today."[7] Our pedagogy is influenced by the ancient Greeks and by the Enlightenment and

---

6. Banks, *Reenvisioning Theological Education*, 79–82.
7. Isa Breitmaier, *Lehren und Lernen in der Spur des Ersten Testaments* (Münster: LIT Verlag, 2004), 376.

thus the distance to the biblical texts is too great simply to make a "leap" from those texts into the present day. Breitmaier is convinced, nonetheless, that the Bible (and in her studies especially the Old Testament) presents "a kind of learning that is independent of Greek thought"[8] and that it is therefore both legitimate and necessary to "start with the Old Testament and its pedagogical insights."[9]

Breitmaier is writing with the questions of present-day religious pedagogy in mind. She does not draw any direct conclusions for theological education. Her methodology is nevertheless useful and meaningful for theological education, as is the content of her work. More about this later.

Unfortunately, as far as I know there are no studies which provide biblical rationale for theological education with comparable thoroughness. Probably the most thorough recent study that provides a biblical foundation for theological education is the already mentioned work by Robert Banks, *Reenvisioning Theological Education*. Here we find the most complete preparatory remarks for the task as a whole. Through no less than four pages Banks cites the primary reasons why many people have chosen not to even try to use the Bible as a foundational text for constructing theological education. It is, after all, difficult if not impossible to expect directives for theological education from the Bible. He then convincingly argues for undertaking just such a task, fully aware of the hermeneutical pitfalls.[10] Using Banks and a few select other sources we can identify the following areas of hermeneutical problems:

- It is a hermeneutical predecision to read the Bible as God's revelation and therefore a normative document, and this has implications for theological education as well. In what I write in these pages, I am operating from this assumption.
- Any analogy between what we call theological education and the biblical texts which speak of schooling is at best very limited. The cultural and sociological differences are enormous. In each case we must proceed with care and ask what if any relevance there is to our topic.

---

8. Ibid., 20.
9. Ibid., 377.
10. Banks, *Reenvisioning Theological Education*, 79–82.

- Some texts speak more implicitly than explicitly about processes of training and schooling. The implicit statements must be handled carefully to avoid reading more into the text than is actually there.
- In many cases it will be necessary to distinguish between *des*criptive and *pres*criptive statements. Not everything which is *des*criptive in the text has to be taken as *pres*criptive authority for us today.
- Statements in the text should also be considered in the light of the realities of the ethnic groups and the surrounding community around the people of Israel. We can derive no theological rationale from situations in which Israel acted, in terms of schooling and training, just like the other peoples of their time and region. Rationale can only be derived from texts where it can be proven that Israel acted independently, based on God's revelation and on Israel's identity as the people of God.
- With a high level of self-awareness and discipline, we must resist the temptation to project today's questions and categories into the biblical text deductively. Conversely, we must do careful inductive work with the biblical texts.
- In view of the large quantity of biblical texts and the differences between them, from a variety of time periods and cultural situations, we must be careful not to try to arrive prematurely at *the* theology of theological education. We must remain open to the possibility of a number of models and varying theological accents within the Bible.
- We must always take care to understand the difference between *copying* and *understanding*. We must be careful not to try to naively copy biblical statements and realities. What we desperately need, however, are axiomatic biblical-theological principles that can serve as an orientation grid or map for theological education.

4.1.1 Theological Education in Light of the Old Testament

General Education and Leadership Training

In his research Robert Banks concentrates on explicit references to the training of leaders within God's people in the Old Testament. There is not very much to be found. In seven pages under the title "Ministry Formation Before Christ" he writes about the following topics:[11]

- The family was the primary venue for education and schooling up to the point of vocational training. For the most part, training in the home occurred informally.
- There is no evidence of formal (i.e. structured and institutionalized) training of leaders. In the case of elders and leaders (e.g. Moses, Joshua), it must be assumed that training of such leaders did not take place through formal instruction. Rising leaders learned from the example of experienced leaders within the context of the community. In some cases we can say that there was something like an "apprenticeship" during which a rising leader was introduced to the task of leadership at the side of an experienced leader (e.g. Moses – Joshua).
- The story of Samuel and Elijah may indicate that there was a more formalized path for the training of priests. This most likely consisted of a kind of "internship" in the holy place or temple.
- Banks sees the training of prophets as somewhere between more formalized instruction and informal life experience. At any rate there were at times schools of prophets (Elisha) or at the very least rising prophets who completed a time of apprenticeship under an experienced prophet (Elijah – Elisha).
- Similar methods were used to train young sages or scholars. Training seems to have consisted of a combination of more formalized introduction into the traditions of the sages and a period of informal learning through an apprenticeship under an experienced scholar.

Despite the existence of only a few specific biblical references and the lack of concrete details, Banks draws the following conclusions about the training of future generations of leaders within the people of God:[12]

---

11. Ibid., 83–89. Further, regarding education and school training in the Old Testament see Roland de Vaux, *Ancient Israel*, Vol. 1: *Social Institutions* (New York: McGraw Hill, 1965), 48–50; and Rainer Riesner, *Jesus als Lehrer* (Tübingen: Mohr, 1981), 97–199.
12. Banks, *Reenvisioning Theological Education*, 92–93.

- The main reason why someone entered an apprenticeship under an experienced leader was the desire to be actively involved in ministry for God.
- Anyone who entered such a course of training spent a great deal of time with his teacher, sometimes lived with him, or at least in close proximity to him.
- This required leaving one's own life context and relationships.
- The process of learning involved various methods: observing, experiencing, working, informal discussion, reflection, and direct instruction.
- Under the tutelage of experienced leaders, new leaders arose. Sometimes when these teachers died, the younger leaders became their successors (Joshua, Elisha).

What Banks gleans from the Old Testament may at first glance seem rather meager. It is, however, commendable that he respects the fact that there are very few explicit indications of any formal leadership training.

When you consider the fact that over long periods of time in ancient Israel there was "no educational system with schools and academic institutions apart from everyday life,"[13] it becomes clear that we will search in vain for direct comparisons to our formalized and institutionalized educational system. *Theological education as we know it and practice it today did not exist in the Old Testament!* We must not conclude, however, that we are doing everything wrong and must therefore return to what the Bible says. As Banks rightly signals, there are principles that can be gleaned from the Old Testament texts which can provide direction for us today.

I suggest, however, that we expand the framework somewhat. Banks narrowed his search to look for observable forms of schooling for the training of coming generations of leaders. But the question can also be formulated like this: What Old Testament texts, terms and topics shed light on theological education? From this perspective, wider horizons are opened:

---

13. Waldemar Janzen, *Werden was wir sind. Biblische Menschenbilder und ihre Bedeutung für uns* (Weisenheim: Agape, 2001), 62. Cf. Breitmaier, *Lehren und Lernen*, 83–86 ("There can be no talk of a general/universal school education.") Riesner argues that evidence can be found of schooling outside the family as early as the time before the kings. He provides evidence for specialized schools for court officials and priests during the time of the monarchy. Not until the Hellenistic period does Riesner see a "democratization" of education, leading to a "people's education movement" (*Jesus als Lehrer*, 153–164).

- What does the Old Testament say in general about religious instruction (i.e. about the communication of faith traditions)?
- What are the functions and tasks of those in leadership, and what training needs can therefore be assumed?
- In what ways are the biblical texts themselves a part of the pedagogical process (i.e. documents of instruction within the church)? What implications does that have for the training of leaders?

With the perspective of these questions in mind, we will examine a number of Old Testament texts, terms and topics. It can be assumed that with regards to our topic we will find an abundant harvest in the triangle of Deuteronomy – Ezra/Nehemiah – Wisdom literature.[14]

Theological Education in Light of Deuteronomy

The pedagogical significance of Deuteronomy is uncontested. Both the primary context (Moses' speech prior to taking possession of the land) as well as the probable secondary contexts (occasions when the covenant was renewed in later times) are clearly pedagogical occasions. That becomes particularly clear if texts like Nehemiah 8 are understood to be new settings for presenting the content of Deuteronomy.[15]

But not only that: The content of Deuteronomy is itself an instruction manual for teaching and learning among the people of God. Karin Finsterbusch sees Deuteronomy as "the birth of Israel as a community of religious teaching and learning."[16]

An evaluation of Deuteronomy leads to the following insights related to theological education:

---

14. Those are also the three bodies of text that Breitmaier, in her earlier mentioned work *Lehren,* examines and links with one another.

15. Breitmaier connects Deuteronomy with the Ezra's reading of the Law in Nehemiah 8, which she sees as an "ideal-typical reading of the Law" (Breitmaier, *Lehren und Lernen*, 10–16). She defends this thesis primarily by connecting Deuteronomy 31:9–13 with Nehemiah 8:3, 11 (Ibid., 16).

16. Karin Finsterbusch, *Weisung für Israel. Studien zum religiösem Lehren und Lernen im Deuteronium und in seinem Umfeld* (Tübingen: Mohr, 2005). The references here to this study are limited to the final chapter of this work (306–316). The individual studies can be deduced here as well.

1) Karin Finsterbusch not only concludes that Deuteronomy is "the birth of Israel as a community of religious teaching and learning." She goes on to argue that Moses, as the great teacher of the law (Torah), is the starting point for the handing down of the teaching to future generations, and that as a consequence the people of Israel maintains its identity as a community of teaching and learning. It is not primarily "theologians" following in the footsteps of Moses who are the focal point of Deuteronomy, but rather the whole community who are teachers and learners. All of Deuteronomy has therefore a communal aim. If we understand this characteristic of the community as a place of teaching and learning to be essential, foundational for the people of God, including the church in the New Testament, then we have to say with regard to theological education that training for a teaching role must ultimately have as its goal the growth and success of a whole community of teaching and learning. Institutionalized theological education must never claim a monopoly on education within the church. It must never estrange the grass roots and serve only the elite. On the contrary, theological education must be judged by how successfully it encourages instruction for everyone within the church. Even more concretely: Old Testament scholar M. Daniel Carroll argues rightly that the texts of Deuteronomy aim at the renewal of the covenant relationship (i.e. at reverence and love for God and at obedience).[17] Therefore a pedagogy that is drawn from Deuteronomy will have the spiritual formation of the children of God in view – their identity, their character, their way of life. That must be normative for theological education as well.

2) In addition, the emphasis in Deuteronomy on *hearing* and *doing* is noteworthy. "The goal of teaching and learning is to understand God's commandments and to act accordingly."[18] A central text is Deuteronomy 6, especially the formulation "Hear, O Israel" (Deut 6:4–5). This hearing has as its goal acknowledging and loving God as the only God. This acknowledging and loving God is then expressed in doing his will. The pedagogy that is expressed here is oriented around hearing and doing. The community of teaching and learning described above is thus a hearing community. It listens to God by listening to the reading of Scripture – the law/Torah (as seen

---

17. Daniel M. Carroll, "Perspectives on Theological Education from the Old Testament," *Evangelical Review of Theology* 29, no. 3 (2005): 228–239, especially 236–239.
18. Breitmaier, *Lehren und Lernen*, 290.

later in Neh 8). The hearing is intended to grow into doing. Hearing has not reached its goal until obedient action has resulted. What implications does that have for theological education? Theological education is above all an *introduction to hearing and obeying*. It must concern itself with the practice of Deuteronomy 6:4–5 – "Hear, O Israel! The Lord our God, the Lord is one. Love the Lord your God with all your heart and with all your soul and with all your strength."

3) A central facet of the teaching of Deuteronomy is the motif "do not forget" (4:9–10, 23; 6:12; 8:11, 14, 19). Two things are worth noting here: (a) The remembering or not forgetting has to do with the saving work of God in the Exodus from Egypt and at Sinai (the giving of the law and the establishment of the covenant). Israel's faith is rooted in God's saving work and in God's revelation of himself in history. Every generation is to be reminded of this. This must never be forgotten. The pedagogy of Deuteronomy, therefore, is marked by recalling and retelling the stories of God's activity by the entire community. It is less about dogmatics and systematic content and more about telling what God had said and done. Finsterbuch concludes her study with the sentence: *"If the Israelites live as a community of teaching and learning as envisioned in Deuteronomy, they will never forget where they come from, who they are, and who they will be in the future."*[19] The "curriculum" of Deuteronomy is intended to create identity through the recounting of the history of God's saving activity among his people, and also through re-anchoring God's claims on and instructions for his people in each new generation. (b) All of this – what God has said and done – is to be captured in writing and thereby "secured" (31:9). Quite apart from any discussion about when the process began of putting these things in writing, it is beyond question "that Israel had an early, close bond with the medium of writing."[20] Remembering was linked to the written word. That leads to the following conclusion with regard to theological education: The people of God find their faith, renewal of covenant, identity and mission by keeping alive the memory of God's words and deeds

---

19. Finsterbusch, *Weisung für Israel*, 316, (emphasis in original).

20. Breitmaier, *Lehren und Lernen*, 84. The author ends her discussion of formal education (reading and writing) in ancient Israel with this observation. Riesner provides evidence that indicates we can assume that reading and writing were taught in schools as early as the 12th century BC (*Jesus als Lehrer*, 112–113). Without fixing any specific time, de Vaux also argues that "writing was in common use at an early date" (*Ancient Israel*, 49).

through the use of written tradition. Therefore, it must be a central task of theological education to train people to keep the memory of God's words and deeds alive in the church and community. Put another way: theological education is a bulwark against forgetfulness.

4) Deuteronomy makes it clear that family (everyday life) and festivals (communal gatherings) were the primary venues for learning. The central instructions of Deuteronomy were intended to communicate faith and wisdom for living in the context of home and family (Deut 6).[21] All of Deuteronomy was intended to be read aloud before the entire assembly (Deut 31:9–13). If theological education is aligned with this pattern, it will never forget that the primary place of learning for God's people is not a theological school but rather the church and the family. Theological institutions can only be viewed, therefore, as secondary and supplemental, intended to serve and strengthen the primary places of learning. The quality of theological education must therefore never be judged by the academic accomplishments of professors and students. The decisive mark of quality is the demonstration and acquiring of competency in areas of pedagogy within the church (preaching, teaching, religious instruction, worship services). When we are discussing Ezra a little later, we will have more to say on this.

5) Finally, it is worthwhile to examine more closely the learning processes described and prescribed in Deuteronomy. The following elements are noteworthy (all of which can be observed in a concentrated way in chapter 6):
- The significance of asking questions and of dialogue.
- The priority that story telling has over a system of theological instruction.
- The importance of informal teaching and learning that arise out of everyday life situations.
- Holistic learning which doesn't happen only cognitively but which affects all the senses through symbols, rituals, festivals, stories and activities.

---

21. Waldemar Janzen calls it a classical text for religious education: "Education in the Old Testament," in *Still in the Image: Essays in Biblical Theology and Anthropology*, ed. Waldemar Janzen (Newton: Faith and Life Press, 1982), 93.

- The importance of mnemonic devices, techniques that are designed to help the learner retain content (memorizing through memory aids, rhymes, and other forms of cribs).[22]

Even if it is impossible to simply carry over all these methods into theological education today, we must not underestimate the lasting significance of the learning processes observable in Deuteronomy. Teaching and learning was aimed at shaping behavior and included the whole person. Tradition was so firmly anchored in heart and mind that it became determinative for life and behavior.

Regarding theological education in our day we can say: Cognitive, intellectual and academic work is a prerequisite for a precise application of the faith traditions captured in the Scriptures – but it is not enough. The teachings of the Christian faith dare not be processed merely intellectually and cognitively. They must be understood and integrated in a person's core (heart), so that they shape thinking, being, and behavior. Nothing less is "knowledge" in the biblical sense.[23] The goal of theological education must not therefore be knowledge alone but rather the fear of God that finds expression in worship and obedience. And even more: the fear of God and worship are not only the goal of theological education. They are the starting point for a true knowledge of God, as we will see below in connection with Psalm 1.

---

22. "The term mnemonic device comes from the Greek (mnemon = attentive) and recalls the muse Mnemosyne, who was the goddess of memory" (Cf. article "mnemonic" http://www.wikipedia.org).

23. Regarding the wide spectrum of meaning for the word *jada* see W. Schottroff, "jd erkennen," *THAT* (*Theologisches Handwörterbuch zum Alten Testament*) I, 685.701. The particular definition of the word as a technical term to describe the people´s covenant relationship with God is recounted by Delbert R. Hillers, *Covenant: The History of a Biblical Idea* (Baltimore: Johns Hopkins Press, 1969), 120–124. Banks, *Reenvisioning Theological Education*, 73–74, summarizes the lexicographic information: "Although there is no static definition of the word *jada* in the OT, it generally refers to knowledge – of God, others, and the world – that comes through experience. It involves awareness of the subject or object experienced and manifests itself in action that does full justice to that comprehension. Therefore it springs from whole-hearted as well as whole-minded engagement with reality, leading to what we might call a whole-willed response to it. This stands in contrast to a detached, dispassionate, objective knowing that requires only cognitive response."

Theological Education in Light of Post-Exilic Writings

We commented earlier on the connection between Deuteronomy and Ezra/Nehemiah, especially Nehemiah 8.[24] In the following section we will examine the person of Ezra and reading of the Torah described in Nehemiah 8, coming from the perspective of Deuteronomy.

1) With the person of Ezra the biblical narrative enters a decisively new situation with regard to the topic at hand. In Nehemiah 8 the function of the scribes becomes visible for the first time. Ezra has the task of bringing the Torah before the assembled people – literally "men and women and all who were able to understand" (v. 2). Supported by his levitical helpers, Ezra read "from the Book of the Law of God, making it clear and giving the meaning so that the people could understand what was being read" (v. 8). As a result, the hearers became doers, that is, they applied (translated into action) what was read and explained to them from the Scriptures. They came back, wanting to hear more and do more. The narrative recounts the beginning of a revival because of this encounter with the Scripture. But in order for the Torah to be understood, the scribe Ezra had to do the work of translating and explaining what was written.

2) Earlier we followed Finsterbusch's thesis that the continuation of the Torah-tradition was not secured by means of an office or position to follow in the footsteps of Moses, but rather by creating a teaching and learning community. Ezra/Nehemiah can make this insight even more precise: The continuation of God's revelation to Moses at Sinai was secured primarily through putting the revelation in writing[25] and secondarily through the office of the scribe. It is important to note that while Ezra (as prototype of the scribe) stands in the tradition of Moses, he has an entirely different function. He is not the first proclaimer of a revelation God has given him. He is rather the teacher of content that has been handed down to him in written form. This fact sheds light on theological education as training at the hands of "scribes" in the mould of Ezra.

---

24. The rationale for this connection has been convincingly presented in Breitmaier, *Lehren und Lernen*, 13–16.
25. That is documented in Deuteronomy 31:9.

3) From the scene depicted in Nehemiah 8 we can derive a *functional* definition of theological education. The questions are: What function(s) must theology fulfill and what results are intended? Only when these questions are answered can we ask: What preparation, equipping, or training does a theologian need? Based on Nehemiah 8, we can approximate answers to these questions:

> *Results*: The work of the theologian must have as its goal that the people of God are exposed to what God said and did in the past in such a way that it (the message and activity of God in history) becomes a reality in the present. Only then will repentance, renewal and revival be possible. The church is to be a hearing, understanding, and obeying community.
>
> *Function:* In order for this to happen, people need to be appointed who are trained and gifted to translate and interpret the Scripture in such a way that these results (above) are possible.
>
> *Training:* Now we can return to the question of education. Following Nehemiah 8, theological education must be *functional*. People must be equipped to understand, interpret, and communicate the Scripture in such a way that the words and deeds of God come alive in the community of teaching and learning that is the church.

4) If we ask about the qualifications of a scribe, Ezra 7:10 gives us some indication: "Ezra had devoted himself to the study and observance of the Law of the Lord, and to teaching its decrees and laws in Israel." Drawing from this short description a sense of what theological education should accomplish, assertions can be made in terms of the content as well as the sequence. There is here, in effect, a *curriculum*, a course of study that must be followed. It looks like this:

- Studying the written documents (hearing)
- Responding in obedience with one's own life (doing)
- Becoming equipped as a teacher of God's Word

The connection to Deuteronomy is obvious. The student must first of all be introduced to the fear and worship of God. This grows out of remembering and meditating on God's words and deeds and leads to obedient action.

Building on this foundation, the "scribe" is then to be equipped to serve the church as translator and interpreter of the Scripture.

Theological Education in Light of the Psalms

The wisdom literature and the Psalms are an additional section of Scripture that can shed light on the topic of theological education.[26] However, I will limit my remarks here to a very small text, specifically to ideas that arise from the Psalms and in particular Psalm 1.[27]

Recent scholarly approaches to the Psalms have suggested that we view the whole of the Psalter in its canonical form as a book of meditation for a scribe or a sage, with Psalm 1 as "reading glasses," "keynote" or "entry way" into the Psalms.[28] From this perspective the question arises whether Psalm 1 may not also be seen as the entryway into theological education. What would that look like?

1) The sharply contrasting position of the righteous and the wicked that we find in Psalm 1 presents a clear choice to anyone who enters the Psalms through this doorway, and thus submits to the pedagogy of the Psalter. In reality it is a two-fold choice: (a) First is the decision to live one's life in relationship with God (i.e. in meditating on his commandments).[29] (b) In contrast to this first decision are the negative expressions in verses 1–2. It's about not walking in the counsel of the wicked, not standing the way of sinners, and not sitting in

---

26. With regards to Proverbs see Breitmaier, *Lehren und Lernen*, 298–382, and Finsterbusch, *Weisungen für Israel*, 82–116. Regarding the significance of the wisdom literature for theological education, see Marlene Enns, "Recovering the Wisdom Tradition for Intercultural Theological Education," *Journal of European Baptist Studies* 5, no. 3 (2005): 5–23.

27. For these thoughts I am indebted to work done together with the board of the Arbeitsgemeinschaft für biblisch erneute Theologie (AfbeT) in Switzerland. Over the course of several years we were on a search for new (old!) ways of accessing theology. The path we chose was surprisingly simple: Under the guidance of two biblical scholars (Beat Weber, OT, and Peter Wick, NT), we tried to glean new insights through inductive study of the biblical texts. Psalms, and in particular Psalm 1, as an introduction to a biblically renewed theology, provided us critical orientation (cf. Beat Weber, "Psalm 1 und seine Funktion der Einweisung," in *Der Erneuerung von Kirche und Theologie verpflichtet*, ed. Philipp Nanz [Riehen: ArteMedia, 2005], 175–212). On the occasion of the 2002 annual conference of the AfbeT, I presented a paper which was an extended version of what we had drafted, including the implications for theological education. My presentation was entitled "Von einer biblisch erneuten Theologie zu einer biblisch erneuten theologischen Ausbildung." The text that follows is a revised and condensed version of that presentation.

28. Beat Weber, *Werkbuch Psalmen I* (Stuttgart: Kohlhammer, 2001), 45, 50.

29. Verse 2; chiastic center of the first stanza; cf. Weber, *Werkbuch Psalmen I*, 48–49.

the seat of scoffers. Ultimately anyone who enters into the study of theology through the doorway of this Psalm is given the promise to be planted like a tree by streams of water that will yield its fruit in season. The reader is given God's promise and affirmation from the very beginning.

Right at the entry point the student is asked to take stock of his own personal, existential faith. Success is only ensured if the response (to faith and to God) is the right one. Applied to our topic, this means that the study of theology cannot succeed without faith, without hearing from God, without the decision to live one's life with God. This raises questions about the viability of a purely academic course of study. It is not at all inconceivable that the texts of the Judeo-Christian tradition can be studied purely academically, without personal faith. Such an approach to study may provide many benefits. Psalm 1, however, indicates that there are limits. A study of theology intended to engage the wisdom of Scripture and provide thoughtful reflection of faith is only possible when faith is present to begin with.

2) Psalm 1 opens the book of Psalms by indicating that meditation on the law of God is the source of a successful life (v. 2). This introduction is programmatic. Recent studies of the Psalms and of the Old Testament canon show that the book of Psalms, in its canonical conception and its placement in the third section of the Hebrew Bible, establishes connections with the Torah. Psalm 1 and 2 play the role of introducing the book of Psalms, and this introduction includes references back to the Torah.[30]

We can therefore mark it down: The teaching of the Psalms takes the student of Scripture on a journey of theologizing that is based on the primacy of the Torah. The contextual and situational dimension of doing theology, as reflected in the individual Psalms but also in the post-exilic editing of the Psalter, is guided by this relationship to what already existed in the Torah. The ones who have committed to meditating on the Torah at the very beginning of their study are the ones who are pronounced blessed in Psalm 1. Therefore we can conclude that the study of the Bible is the first and most important of all disciplines.

---

30. Cf. Erich Zenger et al., *Einleitung in das Alte Testament* (Stuttgart: Kohlhammer, 2001), 26–27. (Notice in particular the connection between Psalm 1 and the end of Deuteronomy.) See also Weber, *Werkbuch Psalmen I*, 42–46.

3) The beginning and the ending of the book of Psalms prompt us to think about what *skills* a study of theology should produce. We have noted that the book of Psalms, in its canonical conception, can be seen as the book of meditation for the biblical scholar which guides the scholar on a path that starts with instruction in wisdom and culminates in worship. If this is true, it can suggest a pathway for theological education. In the words of Beat Weber:

> The Psalms conclude with the "Hallelujah-Finale" (Psalm 146–150) which provides the culmination of the Psalter in the form of universal worship of God. This spans an arc from the introduction to the path of obeying God (Psalm 1) all the way to the triumphal worship by the whole of creation (Psalm 150).[31]

And Erich Zenger says:

> Psalm 1 and Psalm 2 welcome the reader and Psalm 149 and Psalm 150 bid the reader farewell. Both are intentional, programmatic. These "pillar" Psalms are like two doors, two thresholds, which the reader is intended to cross, in order to pray the Psalms correctly *and* to go forth from them correctly, into a life of righteousness.[32]

Against this background, a two-fold path is laid out for the study of theology:

a) As the front door, Psalm 1 signals the introduction to a path of obedience to God. From the perspective of the wisdom literature, this provides a way to view the whole of life. The pedagogy of the wisdom literature as we know it in the Old Testament has the whole of God's creation in view, sees a person's life in an all-encompassing, holistic way, and makes no distinction between general education and religious training. It is not aimed at mere cognitive understanding nor at inward piety alone. Its aim is a holistic way of life aligned fully with the law of God. The pedagogy of the wisdom literature is oriented toward ethics and toward action. It is deeply praxis oriented, for every aspect of life. Therefore

---

31. Weber, *Werkbuch Psalmen I*, 44, with an acknowledgement of W. A. Brueggemann, "Bounded by Obedience and Praise: The Psalms as Canon," *Journal for the Study of the Old Testament* 50 (1991): 63–92.
32. Quoted in Weber, *Werkbuch Psalmen I*, 51.

the desire for a fundamentally life-oriented and action-oriented theology and theological education makes sense. But it's even more than this: If this is true, then it leads to the conclusion that theological education that is too narrow, geared only for pastoral tasks, is clearly insufficient. If practical theology has only pastoral and ecclesiological tasks in view, that is too meager. The horizon of the so-called pastoral paradigm is too narrow, its functionality too limited. It encourages a clergy-laity distinction that is unhealthy and implies that theology is only for those who will become pastors.

b) Theological education which takes its direction from the book of Psalms receives further orientation through the doxology with which the Psalter concludes. In addition to the orientation toward life and action through the wisdom of the Psalms, the doxology ensures an orientation toward God. If Psalm 149 and 150 bid farewell to the praying reader, as Erich Zenger suggests, then the study of theology must take leave of its students by equipping them to join in the "triumphal worship by all of creation."[33]

In conclusion I draw upon the words of Zenger: theological education should equip students to pray rightly and to live righteously.

Summary and Preview

We have examined the Old Testament with two questions in mind:

1) First, we were looking for explicit references to training of leaders within the people of God. We found relatively little. There was little evidence of formalized training, at least not as we know it today. The most obvious evidence was of an apprenticeship model in the relationship between master and student. This can serve as a model for mentoring relationships. Other than that, there is little textual material that is relevant for our study of theological education. The cultural distance is too great to draw any direct situational analogies.

2) Beyond this, we looked for texts that were broader and contained implicit references to pedagogical themes and which could therefore shed light on

---

33. Ibid., 44.

theological education. In the triangle formed from Deuteronomy to Ezra/Nehemiah to the Psalms we found significant material:

- Theological education in the form of leadership training must be viewed within the framework of the general "church pedagogy" of the people of God. To be a community of teaching and learning is intrinsic to the nature of God's people. Specialized theological education must never claim a monopoly on teaching and learning but instead must take place with a view toward encouraging general/universal "church training." We concur, therefore, with Daniel Schipani who says: "We see theological education as a special dimension of the broader teaching ministry of the church."[34]
- Theological education is first and foremost an act of hearing. It's about listening to what God says, and the theologian's primary source for this is what has been written down in the Scriptures. The core task of those in leadership is to call to remembrance what God has said and done in such a way that it leads to words and deeds in the present. A thorough knowledge of the Scripture is the first essential preparation for this task.
- It was clear at every turn that a "church pedagogy" rooted in the Old Testament – and theological education derived from the same source – should result in the fear of God, covenant faithfulness, and obedience. It is therefore a pedagogy that is deeply relational and profoundly active. Consequently, theological education must not remain stuck at the cognitive and intellectual level, concerned only with understanding and defining. It must lead to love for God and a wise way of life that is lived according to God's instructions. Theological education must lead to "right" praying and "righteous" living. It is instruction in worship (Psalter) and in how to live according to God's commandments. In other words (according to Ezra 7:10) theologians are to be taught to apply to their life whatever they find in their study of the Scripture, and to respond in obedience to God's Word.
- Finally, theological education should equip the student to teach God's Word to God's people (Ezra 7:10; Neh 8). Deuteronomy

---

34. Schipani, "The Church," 3.

makes it clear that what God has said and done is to be called to remembrance with such relevance and application that the community of God's people are challenged and equipped to live lives faithful to God's covenant. The primary venues for this instruction are not institutions of learning which are isolated from life, but rather they are the family, everyday life, and church. We also observed that a variety of methods can be drawn from Deuteronomy (story telling, question-answer-discussion, dramatic presentations, various mnemonic devices, symbols, and other memory aids).

In the New Testament we will learn whether these observations are confirmed, whether corrections must be undertaken, and where we find expansions and additions.

4.1.2 Theological Education in Light of the New Testament

In our consideration of the New Testament, we will proceed just as we did with the Old Testament. The first two sections will ask to what extent we can find anything in the life of Jesus and Paul that has directly and explicitly to do with leadership training. Then we will look more broadly to learn whether the New Testament church was also a teaching and learning community and what implications that may have for theological education.

Learning from Jesus' School of Discipleship

It has been tried many times to derive a model for theological education from the life of Jesus. It is beyond doubt that Jesus was a rabbinical teacher and that in a sense he founded a school. The thorough study by Rainer Riesner, *Jesus als Lehrer* [Jesus as Teacher], gives us ample details. It is inviting, therefore, to draw conclusions for theological education from Jesus' school of discipleship. The results of a number of studies will be introduced below:

1) On the occasion of the 1999 annual conference of the AfeM,[35] which had as its theme "Training as a Missionary Task," Thomas Schirrmacher delivered

---

35. AfeM = Arbeitskreis für evangelikaler Mission [Working Committee for Evangelical Missions]

a lecture entitled "Train Like Jesus and Paul" in which he pointed to four characteristics of Jesus' school of discipleship:[36]

   a) Jesus limited himself to a small group of disciples, *so that they could be with him* . . ., in the same way that a father can only care for a small number of children.

   b) Jesus chose the disciples "so that they could be with him *and so that he could send them out.*" The intensive interaction with and dependence on Jesus had as its goal that he would send them out.

   c) The disciples' training to be missionaries – living and working together for several years with *the* missionary Jesus Christ – did not happen arbitrarily or by accident. It happened according to Jesus' intentional plan that aimed at the disciples' independence.

   d) The training of Jesus' disciples included the entire spectrum of instruction and life, theory and practice, individual and group counselling, internal and external work, activity and rest, professional and private life. Teaching and counselling were one and the same.

Schirrmacher is well aware that we cannot simply apply lessons from Jesus and Paul to our lives today in a 1:1 ratio.[37] He assumes that it is not possible to "derive a training system for full-time workers" from the Bible.[38] He nonetheless sees "basic spiritual principles" that we should use as guidelines. Drawing upon patterns he observes in Jesus' discipleship methods (and a few others that he observes in Paul), Schirrmacher believes his own contribution lies in providing a "Plea for an Alternative Training Model for Missionaries and Pastors" (Plädoyer für eine alternative Ausbildung von Missionaren und

---

36. Published in Klaus W. Müller and Thomas Schirrmacher, eds., *Ausbildung als Missionarischer Auftrag* (Bonn: Verlag für Kultur und Wissenschaft, 2000), 7–45, the following points pages 11–15. Schirrmacher calls attention to two further studies: A. B. Bruce, *The Training of the Twelve* (Grand Rapids: Christian Classics Ethereal Library 1971), reprint of the 1894 volume; Hermann Harrell Horne, *Teaching Techniques of Jesus* (Grand Rapids: Kregel Publications, 1982), reprint of the 1920 volume; prior to 1970 under the title *Jesus: The Master Teacher*.

37. Thomas Schirrmacher, "Ausbilden wie Jesus und Paulus," in *Ausbildung als Missionarischer Auftrag,* eds. Klaus W. Müller and Thomas Schirrmacher (Bonn: Verlag für Kultur und Wissenschaft, 2000), 26.

38. Ibid., 27.

Pastoren), the subtitle of his lecture. He details in twenty-one theses what that might look like specifically in the context of today's educational models. In a very abbreviated form, it goes something like this: "Jesus and Paul trained their disciples by weaving together (1) the communication of content, (2) individual counselling, (3) group counselling, (4) encouragement toward independence, and (5) on-the-job training."[39]

2) Robert Banks also finds it extremely valuable to start with Jesus in developing a reform program for theological education.[40] He made the following observations which he applies to the current state of theological education:[41]

- a) Jesus' role as teacher was in many ways comparable to that of a Jewish rabbi, but there were also marked differences. Especially worth mentioning is the element of *friendship* and *love* between Jesus and his disciples/students. Jesus' discipleship training happens in the context of a community of friendship and love.

- b) Although there were different groups of disciples, comparable to concentric circles, there was no qualitative difference between the Twelve and the wider circle of disciples. The Jesus model suggests no differentiation between clergy and laity. Jesus' discipleship training is for everyone, and in principle each individual disciple can assume responsibility for any and all tasks.

- c) Jesus' discipleship training was purposeful, focused and holistic. He used not only verbal instruction (e.g. Sermon on the Mount, parables) but also the sharing of and participation in experiences such as forgiving of sins, healing, and driving out demons. All of that must be viewed as a purposeful training program that included "training sessions" and "immersion experiences." Overall, however, it was never about *"preparation for* mission" but rather about *"engagement in* mission."

---

39. Ibid., 26.
40. Banks, *Reenvisioning Theological Education*, 94–111.
41. Ibid., 108–111.

d) The training did not consist of entirely of activity, however, but included retreat, informal (teaching) conversations, and rest.

3) In the issue of *Evangelical Review of Theology* mentioned earlier, Sylvia Wilkey Collinson presents the results of her doctoral dissertation that was published under the title *Making Disciples: The Significance of Jesus' Educational Methods for Today's Church*.[42] Her study compares the discipling model with the traditional schooling model. She reaches the conclusion "the discipling model of teaching in its focus and methods shares a high degree of correspondence with the core values and beliefs of the Christian faith." While the schooling model is well suited for the communication of content from generation to generation, it fails when it comes to communicating a holistic way of life lived in a personal relationship with God marked by trust and commitment. Exactly that, however, is what the discipling model can and does deliver.

Wilkey Collinson makes a number of fundamentally correct statements about the relational and emotional aspects of educational and training processes. We can only agree with her in this, and especially that this can be observed in the life of Jesus in an exemplary way. Beyond that, however, her study is marked by significant deficiencies. If we take, for example, the work of Rainer Riesner,[43] it is not hard to determine that Jesus' teaching role included more formal school elements than Wilkey Collinson recognizes. On the other hand every recent textbook on school pedagogy contains many of the elements that Wilkey Collinson ascribes to the discipling model. This shows a lack of hermeneutical and methodological sensibility. Especially when applications for theological education are to be drawn from Jesus' role as teacher, careful hermeneutics are essential.

4) Of interest is also the provocative study by Peter Wick, who on certain points reaches markedly different conclusions.[44] Based on his exegesis of

---

42. Sylvia Wilkey Collinson, *Making Disciples: The Significance of Jesus' Educational Methods for Today's Church* (Carlisle: Paternoster, 2004).
43. Riesner, *Jesus als Lehrer*, esp. 408–499.
44. Lecture on the occasion of the 2002 annual conference of the AfbeT, published under the title "Verborgenes und Befohlenes: Schriftgelehrsamkeit und Jüngerschaft bei Matthäus. Exegetische Beobachtungen zum Verhältnis von Theorie und Praxis und Perspektiven für

Matthew 10:1–15 and Matthew 28:18–20, Wick puts forward the following theses:[45]

a) The strategy for teaching and learning is not always built upon the lesson of following Jesus' example. The disciples are not intended to always copy Jesus' behavior 1:1.

b) There is little praxis involved in the teaching/learning strategy. The only practicum is not a partial anticipation of the praxis that would come later. The context of this apprenticeship is too unlike the mission to the Gentiles.

c) There was an important part of their mission that they neither learned in theory from Jesus nor observed him doing: baptism with the Trinitarian formula.

d) Only the content that they were to teach to the nations was given to them by Jesus 1:1, as, for example, in the Sermon on the Mount.

e) In the Great Commission, Jesus commands his disciples to do something that he only partially taught them, something that he never demonstrated concretely, and something that they had never been able to practice directly.

Wick's observations suggest that we must be careful not to read back into the biblical text our present-day ideas about praxis-oriented education, on-the-job training, and learning by doing. That becomes especially clear when Wick demonstrates that the call to discipleship meant a call to a departure from one's customary way of life. It is everything other than the model (called for by representatives of TEE, for example) which envisions education in the life context of the students. Quite the opposite. Leaving one's previous context was essential to Jesus' training model.

The Gospels prove to be fertile soil for discovering building blocks for a theology of theological education. The studies mentioned above call attention to a number of noteworthy details. What is still lacking today, however, is

---

die Ausbildung in den kirchlichen Dienst im heutigen (hoch-) schulpolotischen Umfeld," in *Der Erneuerung von Kirche und Theologie verpflichtet*, ed. Philipp Nanz (Riehen: ArteMedia, 2005), 259–271.

45. Ibid., 263.

a comprehensive study that demonstrates with hermeneutical sensitivity to what degree a model for theological education can be derived from Jesus' school of discipleship.

Learning from Paul

The training and encouragement given by Paul to his co-workers has also been cited repeatedly as a basis for theological education. The studies by Schirrmacher and Banks referenced earlier provide a good summary of the insights that can be gleaned from Paul:[46]

1) In his essay "Ausbildung wie Jesus und Paulus" [Training Like Jesus and Paul], Thomas Schirrmacher concentrates on the fact that Paul makes exemplary use of Jesus' model of discipleship training. This is characterized by the integration of teaching and life, teaching and counselling, as well as modeling and imitating.[47]

Schirrmacher emphasizes the importance of the so-called "model chains." It has to do with the principle of multiplication, that is, that a person who is a leader and teacher trains a relatively small number of people, who in turn are to be equipped to train others. Schirrmacher finds this principle in operation as far back as the Old Testament (Moses – Joshua – elders). He sees it at work in the New Testament as well (Jesus – the Twelve – the sending of the Twelve).

Paul elevates this method to a principle in 2 Timothy 2:2: "And the things you have heard me say in the presence of many witnesses entrust to reliable people who will also be qualified to teach others."[48] Schirrmacher sees this principle operating more than once in Paul's life. This training model has several characteristics:

- The concentration upon a small number. A person who is teaching or leading does not have to train everyone or even a large number of people. Rather, he or she trains a hand-selected group of multipliers.

---

46. Cf. the comprehensive presentation of all of Paul's co-workers by Eckhard Schnabel, *Urchristliche Mission* (Wuppertal: Brockhaus, 2002), 1365–1384. Schnabel makes only passing reference to training.
47. Schirrmacher, "Ausbilden wie Jesus und Paulus," 16.
48. As quoted by Schirrmacher, "Ausbilden wie Jesus und Paulus," 20.

- The training process pays special attention to the relationship between a role model and imitators/followers. This requires that teachers and learners work together in ministry teams.[49]
- Training occurs primarily informally (Schirrmacher says "automatically"). Such informal learning is complemented by formal teaching sessions.
- This kind of training is fundamentally mission oriented. Learners are drawn into the mission of the instructors.
- The goal of the training is independence,[50] that is, the ability to multiply/reproduce oneself.

Based upon these observations, Schirrmacher criticizes formal, institution-bound theological education and calls for a return to the principles we observe in Jesus and Paul.

2) Robert Banks[51] also begins with the observation that Paul worked in teams and concludes that the traveling missionary teams were in fact schools.[52] Elsewhere Banks states explicitly that some people served an "apprenticeship" under Paul.[53] Learning in community is foundational, as are the relationships within the group as well as between teachers and learners. Banks places equal emphasis on the importance of the role model.

Based upon his study of the Scriptures (Old Testament, Jesus, Paul), Banks concludes that the training of future church leaders is best done "in-service," incorporating intellectual, spiritual and practical aspects.[54]

Banks, too, criticizes current institutionalized theological education based upon his study of the New Testament. In his conclusion he pleads

---

49. Ibid., 16: "Paul didn't work alone. Rather, he was always accompanied by co-workers (cr. Acts 17:15) who automatically received from him spiritual training at the same time."

50. Schirrmacher, "Ausbilden wie Jesus und Paulus," 15.

51. Banks, *Reenvisioning Theological Education*, 112–124.

52. Banks quotes Joseph Grassi's *A World to Win: The Missionary Methods of St. Paul the Apostle* (Maryknoll: Orbis 1965). Later (p. 117) Banks refers to Grassi's book *The Teacher in the Primitive Church*, Santa Clara 1973.

53. Banks, *Reenvisioning Theological Education*, 116: "Some have described these associates as 'apprentices' who were being prepared for further ministry through present practical learning."

54. Ibid., 126. Theological education "should orient itself primarily around 'in-service' ministry activities, within which intellectual, spiritual and practical concerns form a seamless whole."

for alternatives that are missional and wholly or partly field based, which "involves some measure of doing what is being studied."[55]

3) The picture which presents itself thus far is a challenge for theological education as most of us know it today. Jesus, Paul, and the Old Testament show a model that is more like what we call an "apprenticeship" (dual model) than like an academic course of study. This provides an answer to today's pressing call for an integration of theory and praxis. If we follow the pattern of Jesus and Paul (as described by Schirrmacher and Banks), the answer is "praxis-integrated" training. Whether that is the correct answer or the only answer is a question we will for now leave open.

In my opinion the picture must be expanded. There are a number of New Testament texts which say nothing explicitly about theological education but which nonetheless provide important building blocks for a theology of theological education. We will talk about a few of these. I propose the following methodological approach: We will ask what skills leaders in the church should possess and ask our way back from there to the question of how they should be trained.

Knowing and Adhering to What Has Been Handed Down

1) What is known as the "Great Commission" in Matthew 28:18–20 contains an explicit command to teach: "Make disciples of all nations, baptizing them . . . and teaching them . . ." We know from the grammar of the text that this is actually a command to make disciples that is to be accomplished by going, baptizing and teaching. We see here that the Great Commission is not merely about leading people to faith in Christ (that is, into a life of discipleship). It is much more than that. It is aimed at the whole life of all Christians. It is aimed at making the church a reality. "Teach them to obey everything I have commanded you." Thus we have before us a community of teaching and learning, exactly as we found in the Old Testament. This community is to be taught to obey everything Jesus taught his disciples.

When we read this from the perspective of the later church, it becomes apparent that this is about preserving the Jesus tradition in order that it can serve as the basis for the teaching of disciples. This is how we must imagine

---

55. Ibid. 142.

the origins of the Gospels. Matthew taught what Jesus had said and done, and little by little, he wrote it down. And thus it became the established tradition.

When we read the command to teach at the end of Matthew within the context of Matthew's whole gospel account, we don't have to wonder what is meant by "everything I have commanded you." It's the Gospel of Matthew in its entirety. And because we know that Matthew structured his gospel around five great teaching segments, we have to assume that these most certainly were to be included in the instruction of disciples commanded in 28:19.

Naturally this teaching was to aim at a way of life (teach them to *obey*), as was evident in the Sermon on the Mount (Matt 7:21–27) and as we learned in the Old Testament as well.

What might this mean for theological education? Anyone who teaches in the church must know the content that has been handed down to us in the Scriptures – *all* of it, because *all* of it is to be taught. Anyone who wishes to teach in the church must acquire a solid understanding of all the teachings handed down in the Scripture. And thus we have arrived back to where we were when we looked at the scribe Ezra. The term "scribe" carries a negative connotation, and it is true that scribes and their like can be legalistic literalists who are more likely to turn people away from following God and living according to his commandments. That's why Jesus speaks about scribes who have become disciples (Matt 13:52). That doesn't seem to have been the norm. But that's only one side of the question. Doesn't the end of Matthew's Gospel say implicitly that disciples are to become scribes, scholars and teachers of the Scripture? How else could they go into all the world and teach all nations *everything* that Jesus had commanded?

2) These thoughts can be expanded by the following observations: In the New Testament we repeatedly find the call to hold fast to the teaching or to that which has been handed down (tradition). Holding fast to the teaching of the apostles was among the four basic characteristics of the church in Jerusalem (Acts 2:42). Paul commanded the newly established churches to "hold fast to the teachings we passed on to you" (2 Thess 2:15). It is a central concern in the book of Hebrews as well (4:14; 6:18). Holding fast to the teaching of the apostles, to the confession, and to the traditions is only possible for the one who knows them in the first place. And only those who have studied them can know them.

3) At this juncture we should return to Rainer Riesner's *Jesus als Lehrer* [Jesus as Teacher]. Earlier I referenced this work in connection with Jesus' school of discipleship. But we must not overlook the fact that Riesner was not primarily interested in making a direct application of Jesus' teaching activity to the form of theological education in the present. Instead, his work is proof that with his "school" Jesus founded a tradition. The disciples were schooled in such a way that they were able to hand down in historically reliable form what Jesus said and did. Thus the oral tradition of the disciples became the historically trustworthy foundation of the Gospels.

What should be emphasized in connection with our topic is this: Jesus' school of discipleship should not only be taken in its formal structure as a model for today's (theological) education. We must also realize that Jesus founded a tradition to be handed down, and that every subsequent teacher in the church must not only be a disciple but also a scholar/scribe.

4) Now we can look at 2 Timothy 3:16–17. This classical text about the doctrine of inspiration is embedded in a context of church pedagogy. The section 3:10–17 is about Timothy's training. Verses 10–13 point to Paul's function as role model and Timothy's role as follower/imitator. In the face of threatening persecutions and deceptions, verse 14 issues a call to hold fast to what Timothy had been taught. What should be held onto is that which Timothy had learned from childhood on (primary place of learning = the family) – and that is the tradition handed down in the Holy Scriptures (v. 15). Then verse 16 goes on to affirm that these Scriptures are inspired by God (God-breathed) for the purpose of teaching, rebuking, correcting, and instructing in righteousness, so that the man of God may be thoroughly equipped for every good work.

With regard to our topic we see four things which are already familiar from the Old and New Testament texts previously cited: (a) The family and discipling relationships are the primary venues for learning. (b) Informal means of learning (seeing, observing, experiencing) are the most significant. (c) What has been handed down in written form is the normative point of orientation for training and education. (d) Training and education are aimed at right living.

This text is fully in line with the tradition of Deuteronomy, the Psalms, Ezra, and Jesus' school of discipleship. In our search for a theology of theological education, we must note that in the New Testament as well it all begins with an act of hearing – listening to what has been handed down and has been written down in the "god-breathed" Scriptures. That is perhaps not obvious at first glance if we simply observe Paul "at work," as Schirrmacher and Banks do.

But we must go one step further:

Doing Theology in the Context of Mission

The idea that the New Testament originated in a missionary context in which the writers were repeatedly faced with new cultures and new situations is not new, and is, in my opinion, accurate. The assertion can be traced back to Martin Kähler, who at least twice employed wording that was later famously expressed as follows: "Mission is the mother of theology."[56] More recently this idea has often been endorsed by David Bosch.[57]

What does this mean? While I argued in the previous section that holding fast to the tradition handed down in written form must remain an integral part of theology and of theological education, this must not be understood to mean that "old" formulations are to be memorized and reproduced with strict literalism. The task which the leaders of the first century faced was to communicate the old message in a new day and a new situation in such a way that the old message remained and yet touched the new day.[58] This is what we now call contextualization. It would be more precise to speak of contextual

---

56. Martin Kähler, "Die Bedeutung der Mission für Leben und Lehre der Kirche" (lecture held in Stuttgart, September 25, 1899), in *Schriften zu Christologie und Mission*, ed. Martin Kähler (Munich: Kaiser, 1971), 69. Exact quote: "Apologetics is the mother of all theology, and it [apologetics] arose to serve missions to the Greeks and Romans. If theology is a daughter of mission, then mission must be considered an essential part of the discussion." Kähler, "Die Mission – ist sie ein unentbehrlicher Zug am Christentum?" (extracted from *Angewandte Dogmen* 1908, 340–486) in *Schriften zu Christologie und Mission*, ed. Martin Kähler (Munich: Kaiser, 1971), 190. Exact quote: "It would not be an exaggeration to assert: The first [oldest] mission [missionary endeavor] became the mother of theology because it attacked the existing culture."

57. Cf. the chapter heading "Reflexionen über das Neue Testament als missionarisches Dokument," in *Mission im Wandel: Paradigmenwechsel in der Missionstheologie*, ed. David Bosch (Giessen: Brunnen-Verlag, 2012), 17. And most recently Christoph Stenschke, "Das Neue Testament als Dokumentsammlung urchristlicher Mission: Alter Hut oder neue Perspektive?" *Jahrbuch Evangelikale Theologie* (2005): 167–190.

58. For this formulation I am indebted to Arnold Bittlinger, *Gemeinde im Kraftfeld des Heiligen Geistes* (Marburg, 1971), 171.

theology. That demands special hermeneutical competence from those in leadership. Here are a few examples from the New Testament:

1) I begin with the story of the disciples on the road to Emmaus (Luke 24:13–35). At first glance this does not appear to be a missionary situation. But this story at the end of Luke's Gospel gives an indication of what awaits the community of disciples. The road to Emmaus is presented as a communal learning experience, as *meta-hodos* (with-way) in the original sense of the word *method*. Along the way the disciples talk about life's happenings (the "new"), and these events are interpreted in the light of the Scripture (the "old"). What is critical is the hermeneutical paradigm shift that the resurrected Christ provides (cf. *hermeneuo* in v. 27), that is, a new view of the Scripture, which makes possible a new interpretation of events. In other words, the traditional understanding of the normative Scriptures is no longer sufficient to interpret the new situation. What is required is a re-thinking, a new interpretation of the old text in a new context. Of course the situation described in this passage was unique because the interpretive perspective underwent a fundamental shift because of the death and resurrection of Jesus. Yet it remains true that the disciples were being prepared by what happened here for that which would become the norm in the course of the missional expansion of Christianity in the decades and centuries which followed. The tradition [the Scriptures] must be constantly re-interpreted in the face of missionary challenges in ever-changing contexts.

2) That becomes clear when we get to Paul. The majority of his writings are in essence new interpretations of Old Testament texts. In light of the fact that Jesus of Nazareth is the promised Messiah and that new challenges were arising almost daily in the mission to the Gentiles (non-Jews), an enormous amount of theological work was necessary. The book of Romans is probably the most significant demonstration of Paul's theological accomplishments.[59] If we attempt to observe Paul doing theology (theologizing), we quickly

---

59. Cf. Schnabel, "Der Römerbrief als Missionsdokument," in *Urchristliche Mission*, ed. Eckhard Schnabel (Wuppertal: Brockhaus, 2002), 1411–1414.

recognize that two things are not allowed: first, an interpretation of Scripture that is strictly traditional, and second, a complete break with tradition.[60]

3) What we observe in Paul can be just as easily seen in Hebrews, Peter, or John. How are we to understand the ancient texts about sacrifices, priesthood, and temple, now that Jesus has become *the* sacrifice, once for all (Hebrews)? How can a theology of the people of God be articulated that is consistent with the tradition (the Scriptures of the Old Testament) now that the diaspora is the norm that God has chosen for the church (1 Peter)? In the conflict with Gnostics, how can an understanding of "knowing" be articulated that is consistent with the tradition of the Scriptures but at the same time addresses the new questions (1 John)? How can the theology of the book of Daniel be formulated in such a way that it addresses the situation in the Roman Empire (Revelation)?

4) The work that leaders must do in all these instances is what I call "theologizing." It is not about changing the content of true theology. It is about mastering the art of contextual theologizing. The task of theology and also of theological education is not simply to reproduce the "old." It is to produce the "new" in the midst of wrestling with the challenges of mission.[61]

This occurs in a complex and dynamic process of dialogue in the church, engaging both the normative tradition [Scripture] as well as the contemporary challenges, under the leadership of the Holy Spirit. (All of that can be observed in Acts 15.)[62]

Summary and Preview
With reference to theological education the following conclusions must be drawn from what has been said:

---

60. On Paul's exegesis see E. Earle Ellis, *Prophecy and Hermeneutics in Early Christianity* (Grand Rapids: Eerdmans Publishing, 1978), 147–253; and Richard Longenecker, *Biblical Exegesis in the Apostolic Period* (Grand Rapids: Eerdmans Publishing, 1975), 104–157.
61. Cf. Horst Georg Pöhlmann, who speaks about the reproducing and producing functions of dogmatics: *Abriss der Dogmatik* (Gütersloh: Gütersloher Verlagshaus Mohn, 1973), 34.
62. I elaborated more thoroughly on this topic in a workshop on the occasion of the 2009 ICETE conference in Sopron, Hungary: "Doing Theology in Community: Reflections on Quality in Theological Education," later published in *History and Mission in Europe: Continuing the Conversation*, eds. Mary Raber and Peter F. Penner (Schwarzenfeld: Neufeld Verlag, 2011), 281–302.

- If the texts of the New Testament were written in the context of mission (as Kähler, Bosch and others have correctly argued), and if these texts represent exemplary and normative theology (which is the traditional Christian consensus), then theology and thereby also theological education can only be properly undertaken in close contact with mission. Theology and theological education that are isolated from the realities and challenges of mission become traditionalistic.[63] They end up doing theology for the sake of theology, and tend to float off into abstract theorizing. In short, they become meaningless for the church and its mission.
- Moreover, theological education has to be about more than simply learning the content of the tradition that has been handed down (Scripture). The art of theologizing must be learned. Doing theology is a skill. In a sense it is a craft, a trade, an art that must be learned. Familiarity with and skills in hermeneutics and in the theory of knowledge are needed. We concur with Heinzpeter Hempelmann who begins the forward to his book *Wie wir denken können* (How we can think) with the sentence: "Scientific theory, the philosophy of language, and hermeneutics are the key disciplines of every prolegomena reflection of evangelical theology."[64]
- On the other hand, missionary praxis must be conscious of the fact that theologizing is a part of the missionary task. Therefore theological education is also part of the missionary task. And not just in the sense of producing a steady stream of missionaries, but rather by assisting the church in its mission by fostering the craft of theologizing and by ensuring that leaders learn this "trade" as part of their education.[65] Missionary praxis that does not keep this in mind succumbs readily to pragmatism and in the long run loses its theological orientation.

---

63. Cf. Pöhlmann, *Abriss der Dogmatik*, 34: Theology that one-sidedly emphasizes the reproducing function becomes traditionalism.

64. Heinzpeter Hempelmann, *Wie wir denken können* (Wuppertal: Brockhaus, 2000), 7. Paul Hiebert is also foundational: *Missiological Implications of Epistemological Shifts* (Harrisburg: Trinity Press International, 1999). More about the theory of knowledge in chapter 5.

65. See Clemens Sedmak, *Theologie als "Handwerk": Eine kleine Gebrauchsanweisung* (Regensburg: Pustet, 1999).

- From this perspective, it must be said to Banks and others, who searched Jesus and Paul solely for missionary practice and discipleship training, that this is insufficient. It's true that the New Testament teaches us that theology and theological education can only be healthy when breathing the air of mission. But we also see that theologizing belongs to the missionary task and must be taught and learned as part of theological education.[66] If there is a missional paradigm for theological education (as Banks asserts), then this must be understood in its whole scope. Andrew Kirk makes an impressive presentation of this in *The Mission of Theology and Theology as Mission*.

With that we conclude the examination of the Bible and turn to the question, what implications this has for theological education today.

4.2 On the Way to a Theology of Theological Education

We will now attempt to take the next step and formulate a theology of theological education. It is important to practice what I just wrote about: It must be about more than simply *reproducing* – and even systematically arranging – the statements and observations of the Bible. Rather, we must succeed in *producing* the "old message" in "new times" in such a way that the "old message" remains but the "new times" are relevantly addressed. To put it another way, a theology of theological education must speak to the questions that theological education is asking today and shed light on them based on insights gained from study of the biblical texts.

4.2.1 From the Bible to Present-Day Challenges

At the beginning of this chapter I mentioned the hermeneutical difficulties involved in applying the content of the Bible to teaching and learning in our day. The comments I made at that point need to be expanded upon now, in order to construct a bridge from biblical times to the present.

---

66. In the current literature on church leadership the ability to theologize well is rarely mentioned as a desirable quality. Christoph Morgner is a noteworthy exception: *Geistliche Leitung als theologische Aufgabe*, (Stuttgart: Calwer Verlag, 2000).

1) I've already used the term "situational analogy." A situational analogy exists when the situation back then is comparable with the situation today in the sense that the message formulated then is relevant today. In the case of education, such a situational analogy is hardly possible. We already saw that the Old Testament had little in the way of a structured "educational system with schools and academic education separate from the rest of life." What little we do see in the Old Testament of formal education is not comparable to the extensive educational system of modern society.

We must exercise great care, therefore, when applying statements in the Bible about training, education, and schooling. This doesn't mean, however, that because education today is so different from education in biblical times, we should question the validity of our educational system and instead yearn for a return to biblical times. That is not only foolish, it is also impossible. It is therefore not appropriate to try to copy how Moses trained Joshua, how Ezra became a scribe, how Jesus trained his disciples, or how Paul became a theologian and a missionary. Even if we *wanted* to copy such historical models, we would fail, because our culture is so very different, and we will always remain the product of our culture and our context.

2) There is yet another reason why we should not attempt that kind of direct application: The educational training systems in biblical times were an expression of those historical and cultural contexts. Not everything that is said in the Bible about training and education is to be read as God's revelation. If we simply duplicate biblical conditions and apply them to educational situations today, we are simply copying the culture of the ancient Orient, Babylon, Greece, or Rome.[67]

3) We also recognize that there is no single uniform system of education found throughout the long biblical narrative that we can systematize and apply as God's plan for our day. The culture in Abraham's time had different ideas about education and training than what Joseph and Moses learned about in Egypt. The concept of education that led Hannah to send Samuel to Eli for an "apprenticeship" is not the same that made Ezra a scribe (biblical scholar)

---

67. Consider what Riesner says (*Jesus*) about how education in the Old Testament and in Jesus' day is to be seen in the context of the surrounding nations and peoples. There may be individual aspects in which Israel and the Jews acted independently, but on the whole education in Israel reflected that of the surrounding region.

in Babylon. And the rabbinical school system that forms the background for Jesus' school of discipleship is to be differentiated from the school system that was typical in the diaspora of the Greek/Roman era.

4) How then shall we proceed? The Bible itself gives us instruction in this regard. Because the people of God, as they moved through history, were subjected to constant cultural change, they had to contextualize the basic principles of the divine revelation in ever-changing situations. Leadership models and organizational forms are a good example. The transition from a wandering half-nomadic people, traveling from Sinai to Canaan, to the settled nation we encounter in the books of Samuel and Kings was a dramatic cultural and social change. That required a new organizational form that was found in the monarchy. This did not fall from heaven. It was copied from the surrounding cultures. The story is found at the beginning of 1 Samuel and is well known. Israel was not required to continue to live as a half-nomadic people, which would no longer have been appropriate in its new situation. However, the new organizational from was not to be adopted uncritically. It had to be "sanctified" so that it was compatible with the nature of the people of God. What we know as the law-governing kings (Deut 17:14–20) reflects the struggle to create a monarchy according to God's will.

This same method can be instructive for other areas as well. I suggest we do the same when it comes to theological education. Just because we are able to identify biblical educational models, we cannot demand that theological education never take the form of today's educational models. Just as Daniel, Ezra, and others had to live out their faith within the Babylonian educational system, and just as Jesus conducted his discipleship training in the context of rabbinical education, so we too are called to avail ourselves of a theological education consistent with the basic values of the kingdom of God within the educational models operating today.

5) This is why I presented the current educational models in chapter 3. I do not call for us now to abandon all these models and to create *the* biblical alternative, based on our insights from the Scripture. That alternative, too, would be a child of our times. Instead we must:
- Understand our educational models (ch. 3).
- Formulate theological criteria for theological education (we are about to do this).

- "Sanctify" contemporary educational philosophies and educational forms as we apply them in concrete situations (this will be the subject of chapters 6–8.)

What we need therefore are theological criteria that can guide us as we seek to shape theological education in our context. That is what we will now discuss. I will name four areas that should set the agenda for theology and theological education.[68]

4.2.2 God

Theology and theological education are about God. They must be about God. The term *theology* says as much. Yet what sounds so self-evident is neither obvious nor simple.

1) Helmut Thielicke's words to those entering upon the study of theology in his book *A Little Exercise for Young Theologians* are striking.[69] We read under the heading "The Study of Dogmatics with Prayer":

> The man who studies theology, and especially he who studies dogmatics, might watch carefully whether he increasingly does not think in the third rather than in the second person. You know what I mean by that. This transition from one to the other level of thought, from a personal relationship with God to a merely technical reference, usually is exactly synchronized with the moment that I no longer can read the word of Holy Scripture as a word to me, but only as the object of exegetical endeavors. [. . .]
>
> We might remember that Anselm begins his demonstration of God in his *Prologue* with a prayer, and that his dogmatics were therefore prayed dogmatics. This extraordinary fact would be understood altogether wrongly if seen as only an edifying preamble and therefore a sign of a special kind of piety. Anselm is here looking for nothing else than the expression of something

---

68. In some ways I am setting the same accents as Noelliste, *Theology of Theological Education*, who develops the following three basic principles of theology: 1. Training in the knowledge of God. 2. Training for the entire people of God. 3. Training for participation in God's project.
69. Helmut Thielicke, *A Little Exercise for Young Theologians*, trans. Charles L. Taylor (Grand Rapids: Eerdmans, 1962).

> that theologically is strongly relevant: a theological thought can breathe only in the atmosphere of dialogue with God.
>
> Essentially, theological method is characterized by the fact that it takes into account that God has spoken, and that now what God has spoken is to be understood and answered. But it can only be understood when I (1) recognize that what has been said is directed to *me*, and (2) become involved in formulating a reply. . . . Consider that the first time someone spoke of God in the third person and therefore no longer with God but about God was that very moment when the question resounded, "Did God really say?" (cf. Genesis 3:1). This fact ought to make us think.
>
> In contrast with this, the crucified Jesus, out of the uttermost darkness of abandonment by God, does not speak to men, does not complain *about* this God who has abandoned Him. He speaks *to* Him at this very moment – in the second person. He addresses Him as *My God* and even expresses His complaint in a word of God. [. . .]
>
> This observation, too, should make us think.[70]

2) What Thielicke presents to young students here is not a new topic in the discourse about systematic theology. A distinction has been made for quite a long time between *fides qua* and *fides quae;* faith expressed in life and faith expressed in words; believing "in" and believing "that"; personal faith and objective faith; I-you relationship and I-it relationship; confidence and insight; security and content.[71] It is well known that it is a particular problem of school life to integrate reflection *about* faith and the living out *of* faith. Klaus Mertes, who comes from the perspective of an Ignatian pedagogy, has spoken about how difficult it can be in an academic setting to keep the "primary discourse" (prayer, speaking with God) and the "secondary discourse" (reflection, speaking about God) in a healthy relationship of both

---

70. Ibid., 33–35 (italics in original).
71. Cf. Pöhlmann, *Abriss der Dogmatik*, 81; also Otto Weber, *Grundlagen der Dogmatik* II (Neukirchen-Vluyn: Neukirchener Verl. d. Erziehungsvereins, 1977), 296–303.

integration and distinction.⁷² It is not a case of either-or but rather of finding the right balance.

3) This is precisely one of the fundamental problems concerning the present-day models of theological education. Can theological education foster a student's relationship *with* God as well as deepen his or her academic reflection *about* God and about questions of salvation? Are both the personal *and* intellectual pursuit of God during theological education desirable and possible? The truth is that things often develop in two opposite directions:

    a) The academic study of theology in the educational model of the modern university has devoted itself primarily to the pursuit of intellectual thought *about* God. This is what this educational model at its core requires: not faith and subjectivity but a purely intellectual pursuit of the object being studied. The result is the objectification of God. Otto Riecker, in his work *Bildung und Heiliger Geist* [Education and the Holy Spirit], calls this "theologism," an exaggerated and one-sided objectification of all aspects of faith.⁷³

    To what extent the existential (personal) aspect is perceived as a deficit by students is evident in a recently published article by Christoph Ammann, "Die Flucht vor dem 'Ich'. Kristische Bemerkungen zur theologische Ausbildung" [The Flight from Self: Critical Observations about Theological Education].⁷⁴ Ammann is a (teaching) assistant and a doctoral candidate at the University of Zürich. His article highlights a problem of the highest urgency. Ammann speaks about the "needle's eye of the self" through which the content of theology must pass, but which unfortunately can do so only with great difficulty. He writes (p. 9):

> He (the theologian) has to know a great deal, but so long as he has not yet learned to handle this knowledge sensitively, independently, and appropriately to the situation, he has not yet learned the most decisive thing. It is this which makes him

---

72. Klaus Mertes, *Verantwortung lernen. Schule im Geist der Exerzitian* (Würzburg: Echter, 2004), 38–40.

73. Riecker, *Bildung und Heiliger Geist*, beginning with page 78.

74. Christoph Ammann, "Die Flucht vor dem 'Ich'. Kristische Bemerkungen zur theologische Ausbildung," *Facultativ* (magazine insert of the theological faculty of the University of Zurich, Reformed Press 01), (2004): 8–11.

to a theologian. Adopting a clear and at the same time open theological identity is an essentially subjective process.

Ammann calls for a theological education that prepares students for pastoral ministry and says, "This competency cannot be acquired without engaging one's very personal, individual self."

It would be a mistake, however, to think that this "theologism" is only to be found within the faculties of the state universities, which those from a pietistic-evangelical perspective like to label as liberal, modernistic, and critical. "Theologism" can also be clothed in evangelical, bible-based, even fundamentalist dress. Especially within rationalistic fundamentalism, horrendous objectification of God can sometimes be observed.

b) Contrasted with this objectification of God we find in many pietistic, evangelical circles an underlying scepticism toward all intellectual theological work. It is not uncommon to find this attitude at Bible schools and charismatic discipleship training institutes. Years ago Klaus Bockmühl diagnosed a "fear of thinking" in modern pietism and convincingly presented its drawbacks: a lack of theological corrective in preaching, silence in the face of the intellectual challenges of the day, damage done to the next generation, which is left without adequate orientation. Bockmühl draws the conclusion that "the abstinence of modern pietism in regards to theology is life-threatening."[75]

4) Miroslav Volf provided an answer to these burning questions in his lecture "Dancing for God: Challenges Facing Theological Education Today."[76] In a focused way, Volf looks for God in theological education. His thesis is that "God belongs in the very centre of theological education." The main thing, he says, is that the main thing remains the main thing in theological education. Theology means speech about God. That's what should happen in theological education – that listening to God becomes speaking about God. It is not enough to think about and to talk about what texts say about God. Theology

---

75. Klaus Bockmühl "Der Dienst der Theologie," in *Theologie und Lebensführung*, ed. Klaus Bockmühl (Giessen and Basel: Brunnen, 1982), 5–7.

76. Lecture on the occasion of the ICETE Consultation for Theological Educators, 18 August 2003, High Wycombe, UK, Miroslav Volf, "Dancing for God: Challenges Facing Theological Education Today," *Evangelical Review of Theology* 29, no. 3 (2005): 197–207. Also available at http://www.icete-edu.org.

is not speech about speech about God. It is speech about God. That, says Volf, differentiates theology from religious studies (the science of religion).

Volf elaborates on this subject matter by looking at the two terms "love" and "trust." He's interested in much more than just definitions. He asks, personally and provocatively, those who are engaged in providing theological education: Who or what do we trust *ultimately*? Who or what do we love *ultimately*? What makes theological education *theological* is, ultimately, God – not in some distant, dispassionate way ("What do we *say* that we trust?") but real trust in God and real love for God.

From Volf's standpoint we can conclude that theological education is something personal. Listening to God leads to trust and love. And listening can lead to action and to speaking about God. That, and ultimately nothing else, must be learned through theological education. This one central thing can best be taught in a multiplicity of courses and disciplines. But when this personal centre is missing, then the thing that makes theology *theology* is missing, and the thing that makes theological education theological is missing as well.

5) A theological answer can also be gleaned from one of the central texts of the Bible – a text we encountered earlier in this chapter: the "Hear, O Israel" text in Deuteronomy 6:4–5. Jesus later took this text of the Torah and, combining it with Leviticus 19:18, made the Great Commandment (Matt 22:34–40; Mark 12:28–31; Luke 10:25–28): "You shall love the Lord your God with all your heart, with all your soul, and with all your mind. This is the greatest and first commandment. The second is like it: You shall love your neighbor as yourself" (NRSV).

This text is explicitly about education. It is about boiling down biblical faith to what is absolutely essential. That's what theology and theological education must also be about. Focusing down to the essential leads us to love (Matt 22:37). Love is relationship. Love flows out of me to another. Love is turning toward another. In the two-fold Great Commandment it is turning to God and turning to our neighbor. This provides us with an axiom of theology and theological education: It's not about the inward focused, distanced, dispassionate intellectual reflection of the individual. It is about love. That means relationship, fellowship, community, devotion, and being personally moved. You cannot do theology in any biblical sense that is intellectually distant, dispassionate, uninvolved, and objectified.

Love for God in this text is described holistically, which, with regard to theological education, has to make us stop and pay attention:[77]

a) Love God *with all your heart*. "The Bible sees the heart as the seat of the will." Loving *with the heart* emphasizes the dimension of decision. It's about the decision to allow God in, to want to love him, to want to trust him, and ultimately to want to serve him. With regard to education, this can be expressed pedagogically as follows: Based on the Great Commandment, the appellative dimension, the call to decision certainly has an essential place in the teaching and learning of theological education. Of course, lectures on theology are not evangelistic or revival meetings. But if we study God in our theological education – and not merely from a dispassionate distance – it will not be out of the ordinary for us to expect God to speak to us and to call us to decisions.

In formulating the goals of theological education today we ask about the desired "output" competencies (At the end of this course the student will be able to . . .). Based on the Great Commandment, one of the desired output competencies must be that graduates love God, trust God and want to serve God with greater decisiveness and intensity.

b) Love God *with all your soul*. Here the emotions are in view. This is expressed in joy, according to Bockmühl. Some may want to use expressions like enthusiasm or passion. And here the dispassionate, sober-minded academic world grows quickly sceptical. There are, of course, passionate researchers, who learn ancient languages, analyze ancient texts, erect philosophical towers of thought and engage in energetic discussions with great enthusiasm and emotional dedication. And this is desirable. I prefer students who are excited by the material over those who are dispassionate and disinterested. But this is about more than fascination with the object to be studied. The heart should beat faster not (only) because of the doctrine of the Trinity, but at the thought that the God who created the world knows me personally and loves me.

---

77. For the thoughts which follow I am indebted to Klaus Bockmühl, *Das größte Gebot* (Giessen and Basel: Brunnen, 1980), 25–43. All quotes are taken from this text.

As an educational goal, this can be formulated as follows: At the end of this course of study students will love God and invest themselves in God's work with greater passion (joy, enthusiasm).

c) Love God *with all your mind*. That may seem foreign to us at first glance. Bockmühl writes that "for pious believers, the mind is the most distant region of the disposition." We could add, "for the academic, the personal is the most distant region." Yet in the Great Commandment all of these are combined in loving God. Theological education must, therefore, be about integrating thinking into what it means to love God. This can serve as a corrective to two errors:

- The first error is the attitude that thinking is the opposite of believing and poses a threat to vital spirituality. That usually results in not wanting to engage in thinking at all and viewing it as harmful. Or, doing intellectual work as a requirement (for example, as part of theological education) but holding it at as great a distance as possible from one's inner self, one's real being, which can lead to a split personality.
- On the other side, there is the danger of viewing autonomous thinking, independent of one's relationship to God, as having ultimate significance. That can make us into rationalists who can turn science and our own intellectual power into idols.

Again, the educational goal may be this: At the end of this course of study, students shall be able to think more deeply and thoroughly, in such a way that their thinking has become part of what it means to love God.

d) Finally, Jesus' two-fold Great Commandment says ". . . and your neighbor as yourself." Thus love has an additional direction – away from me to my fellow human beings, to the world. This second dimension must become an additional foundational element of theological education. I will have more to say about this in the following section 4.2.3. But first a few concluding remarks on this point.

6) We can summarize this first round of arguments as follows: Because by definition theology is about God (and not just about what others say or have said about God, and not merely from the dispassionate distance of the third person), in the final analysis theology lives from the encounter with God.

But theology is more than encountering God in mindless faith. Theology is a reflected and reflective understanding of God.[78]

Thus the task of theological education lies in what David Kelsey calls "truly knowing God," holistically through contemplation, argumentative discussion, commitment to God, and one's way of life.[79]

Chapter 5 will elaborate on how this speaking *with* God and speaking *about* God can be successfully integrated in practical theological education.

4.2.3 The Word of God

The first principle, "Theology and theological education are about God," must be followed by a second statement: ". . . this God has spoken and speaks." This leads to the assertion that listening to God's voice must be a second essential element of theological education. It will not be possible for us to develop a full-orbed theology of the Word of God here, nor can we handle the complex area of a doctrine of the Bible. We will concern ourselves with two simple matters. Based on the biblical texts there is a given, and that is: the preeminence, priority of the Scriptures in all theological work.[80] And there are a number of problems in the carrying out of theological education today. We will talk about both of these things now.

1) In all of the biblical texts that we referenced in the previous section, there is one thing that cannot be overlooked: It all starts with the voice of God and the activity of God. And God's voice and activity are woven into the tradition and captured in the Scripture as a binding guideline (canon). The Psalms, Ezra, the Gospel writers, Paul – all of them are clear: Theological work begins with listening to what has been handed down in the Scriptures. Theological education dare not ignore this fact.

---

78. Farley, *Fragility of Knowledge*, ix.

79. "This wisdom concerning God embraces contemplation, discursive reasoning, the affections, and the actions that comprise a Christian's life." David Kelsey: *To Understand God Truly: What's Theological about a Theological School?* (Louisville: Westminster/John Knox Press, 1992), also available at http://www.religion-online.org/showbook.asp?title=379. The quote is from the internet text, chapter 2 "Crossroads Hamlets."

80. Peter Wick both emphasized and provided evidence for the fact that the priority of the Scripture was of great importance in the biblical texts, for example in "Ein Text, viele Auslegungen," in *Das Christentum an der Schwelle zum 3. Jahrtausend*, eds. Albrecht Grözinger and Ekkehard Stegemann (Stuttgart: Kohlhammer, 2002), 77–90.

Biblical-Theological Foundations 181

Many things may be added to supplement this fact – for example, about God's direct voice through the spirit (the prophetic dimension), about the significance of community, or about many basic questions of exegesis and hermeneutics. Some of these questions must be handled later. But none of these questions should divert our attention away from this one thing, that theological education means becoming a biblical scholar. As self-evident as this may seem, the realization of this goal in today's models of theological education is fraught with obstacles.

2) One problem that confronts us in contemporary theological education may be illustrated with a brief story that pastor Wilhelm Busch recounted from his time as a student after the war:

> The little train rattled through the night into the mountains. I sat scrunched next to my mother in the fearfully overcrowded compartment and thought about whether I should tell her what was bothering me. She had picked me up in Tübingen where I was studying theology. And now we were traveling together in the direction of the Swabian Alb. Finally I gathered my courage and said, "You know, Mama, the Bible no longer gives me any joy. I'm finding so many things that are hard and difficult to understand. There are so many contradictions and things that are simply incomprehensible, and they make this book unbearable."
>
> My mother laughed out loud and said, "That's because you are reading the Bible in the wrong way."
>
> Somewhat offended, I flared up in such a way that a man sitting next to us let his newspaper fall to his lap and looked astonished. "Well, how should I read it? I'm reading it in the original Hebrew and Greek. I read commentaries. I attend class lectures . . ."
>
> Mother placed a hand on my arm soothingly. "I'll give you an example. Do you remember how, during the war, you were in the field for almost two years without any leave? I wrote you regularly during that time, telling you what was going on at home. And then one day a letter came from you that I will never forget. You wrote: 'I'm hearing in your letters about ration cards, about hording, about standing in line. Has everything changed?'

And then came the sentence that touched me so: 'How long have I been away, and how far away am I, that I can no longer understand letters from home?'"

I nodded. "Yes, yes. I remember. But what's that got to do with the Bible?"

"Well, you see," Mother continued, "you didn't say, 'My mother's letters are unbearable for me as a modern man.' You also didn't say, 'My mother's letters contain contradictions and senseless things.' You simply said, 'How long have I been away, and how far away am I, that I can no longer understand letters from home?'"

I began to understand. I listened attentively to my mother.

"The Bible is a letter like that, my son. It is a letter from the living God sent from the eternal home, written to you. If you can't understand the letter, you can't blame the letter. You are the cause. You must say, 'How terribly far away from my heavenly Father must I be that I can no longer understand his letter.'"[81]

We can laugh at this story. A pietist has "landed in the world" as he studies theology, and his pious mother seeks to rescue his faith. But we dare not simply dismiss this story. It takes us into the centre of another burning problem of theological education in the modern paradigm. Just as we observed two ways of interacting with God in the previous section (speaking *with* God and speaking *about* God), in the same way we see here two ways of interacting with the Bible: reading the Bible as *God's Word to me* and analyzing the Bible as a *historical-literary* document.

Johannes H. Schmid presents the unsatisfying situation and reaches the conclusion that many students struggle

> to make any positive connection between the scientific work at the university and their own personal faith. A kind of "double bookkeeping" occurs. On the one hand, one is held to a fundamentally critical approach to the Bible, and on the other hand, there is the personal spiritual encounter with the Word

---

81. In Heinz Schäfer, *Hört ein Gleichnis* (Stuttgart: Christliches Verlagshaus, 1971), 32–33.

and through sermons and the student's faith in the validity of the Word.[82]

Particularly disturbing is what Schmid calls "a kind of 'double bookkeeping.'" First of all, there is a lack of integration. Academic work and personal faith and life stand widely apart from one another. And that may be the lesser of evils. All too often personal spirituality is completely lost in the wake of the overwhelming force of methodological scepticism.

Yet the damage is not contained to the level of personal faith and individual spirituality. Rudolf Bohren laments that students come from their homiletics class to his lectures on exegesis and complain that they are now supposed to learn how to preach, but that after a critical analysis of the text, they now find that they have no content left to preach about. That ought to be alarming for the church.[83]

Here again I would like to emphasize that this is not a problem that is limited to "critical" theology at the universities. Students at evangelical and free-church seminaries often have similar experiences.[84] Intellectual, analytic interaction with the biblical text apparently tends to undermine the student's joy in the Bible as God's Word. Instead of being good news, the Bible becomes a problem.

But theological education has to be able to accomplish this: Students should be able to examine biblical texts with a high level of exegetical and hermeneutical competence without losing their ability to hear God's Word speak to them personally and spiritually. They should indeed be able to read and value the Bible as God's Word with even greater enthusiasm.

3) In some evangelical circles there is yet another problem in relation to the Bible. The motto here is: Hands off methodical-analytical exegesis! No scientific effort to arrive at linguistic, literary, or historical understanding! The result is a naïve view of the Bible that claims to be faithful to the Bible but has succumbed to a literalism that makes no effort to really understand

---

82. Johannes H. Schmid, "Was heisst biblisch erneuerte Theologie?," in *Unterwegs zu biblisch erneuerter Theologie*, ed. Johannes H. Schmid (Giessen and Basel: Brunnen, 1984), 7.

83. Rudolf Bohren, "Die Krise der Predigt als Anfrage an die Exegese," in *Dem Wort folgen. Predigt und Gemeinde*, ed. Rudolf Bohren (Munich and Hamburg: Siebenstern Taschenbuch Verlag, 1969), 65–96.

84. Cf. Raymond P. Prigodich, "Geistliches Leben und Hochschulbildung," *Evangelikale Missiologie* 18, no. 3 (2002): 106–111.

the text linguistically or historically. The problem here is self-deception. A person claims to be faithful to the Bible but refuses to truly understand the Bible and take it seriously in its linguistic-historical form.

Helge Stadelmann is right when he says that there is no "special access to the Bible for lay people."[85]

The primacy of the Scripture of which I speak is not to be attained by introducing stiff dogmatic statements about the inspiration and infallibility of the Bible, nor by "proving" all theological statements with verses from the Bible. The primacy of the Scripture which must be maintained in theology and theological education is characterized by a rejection of all dogmatic preconditions and by a precise and open "listening" to the biblical texts.

That is why, with regard to theological education, an inductive study of the Bible that is prepared to listen to the biblical text over any possible pre-formed opinions or biases, must have highest priority.

4) It becomes even more problematic when the Bible takes a back seat to direct prophecy. This tendency can be observed in a recent emphasis on prophecy in Pentecostal and charismatic circles.

To be clear, we must acknowledge that prophetic utterances (saying what has been heard directly from God) have an important function in the life of the church and that we in the evangelical tradition have often neglected this element. Klaus Bockmühl has pointed this out effectively in *Hören auf den Gott der redet* [Listening to the God Who Speaks].[86] He talks about "the exclusive embodiment of the Spirit in the Scriptures and his dependence upon the interpretation of an ordained pastor."[87] Bockmühl follows these observations with a balanced presentation of the Spirit and the Word which deserves our attention today. Peter Zimmerling also points out the fact that

---

85. Helge Stadelmann, *Grundlinien eines bibeltreuen Schriftverständnisses* (Wuppertal: Brockhaus, 1985), 89–90.
86. Klaus Bockmühl, *Hören auf den Gott der redet* (Giessen and Basel: Brunnen, 1991). Newly published in the Bockmühl-Works-edition: Klaus Bockmühl (Horst-Klaus Hofmann, ed.), *Leben mit dem Gott, der redet* (Giessen and Basel: Brunnen, 1998), 77–180. On the critique of the reformed restrictions on hearing directly from God cf. pages 154–164.
87. Bockmühl, *Leben mit dem Gott*, 162.

essential aspects of the New Testament message have been "neglected in reformed theology simply by equating preaching or exegesis with prophecy."[88]

It must be said furthermore that a growing number of Pentecostal theologians have acknowledged the potential for a one-sided view among Pentecostals and charismatics. They have offered a perspective on prophetic utterances that is theologically well thought out and thoroughly biblical. A noteworthy example is to be found in Matthias Wenk's dissertation *Community-Forming Power: The Socio-Ethical Role of the Spirit in Luke-Acts.*[89] Wenk shows that prophecy is essential in Luke and must be understood as a process that is anchored in the Scripture and integrated into the church.

With these critical and positive assessments of prophecy as a background, we must now return to theological education. Bockmühl is probably right when he speaks about a dilemma that we now face.[90] On the one hand we do theology in the shadow of the Reformation and orthodoxy with the two dangers of objectifying the Holy Spirit's voice and despising subjectivity. On the other hand within evangelical circles we are shaped by the subjectivity of the Enlightenment, especially in the form of pietistic spirituality.

The task of theological education must therefore have two elements: (a) The voice of God must not be reduced to the words of the Bible and certainly not to the interpretation of the Bible authorized by the church or by scientific/academic study. The practice of listening directly to God is an essential element of theology. Miroslav Volf said it well: "We theologians are either like Moses: We meet God on the mountain and are therefore able to say something about God and his plan for the world, or we are not theologians at all."[91] (b) On the other hand, we have seen through biblical research the central significance of God's revelation being committed to writing, as well as the basic primacy of the Scripture. That is why theological education must be dedicated, with great care and highest priority, to an accurate interpretation of the Bible.[92]

---

88. Peter Zimmerling, *Die charismatischen Bewegungen* (Göttingen: Vandenhoeck & Ruprecht, 2002), 169.
89. Matthias Wenk, *Community-Forming Power: The Socio-Ethical Role of the Spirit in Luke-Acts* (Sheffield: Sheffield Academic Press, 2000).
90. Bockmühl, *Leben mit dem Gott*, 164–166.
91. Volf, "Dancing for God," 201.
92. This goal is the subject of the articles in Helge Stadelmann, *Den Sinn biblischer Texte verstehen* (Giessen: Brunnen, 2006).

4.2.4 God's Project

We have already formulated two theological guiding principles for theological education:

1) Theology is about God. We must learn both to talk *with* God and to talk *about* God in an integrated way in all theological education.

2) Theology is about God's Word. In all theological education we must learn to read the Scriptures both as *God's Word to me* and as an *analytical-literary document*, in an integrated way.

This leads to a third guiding principle: This same God has revealed, through his activity and through his voice that we hear in the Scriptures, what he wants to do in and through this world, and what role we are meant to play. Therefore, theology is about God's project, God's work. In all theological education we must learn to be co-workers in God's projects. This concept is what we will now develop.

1) Let us begin with the problematic situation of theological education today. Earlier I referred to the striking opening of Gerhard Ebeling's *The Study of Theology*:

> The study of theology is beset by a crisis in orientation. Because our access to the unity and totality that constitutes the subject matter of theology is disrupted, the main domain of its subject matter and task has broken apart and crumbled into a bewildering conglomeration of individual items.[93]

Students who pick up this introductory book are confronted in the very first sentence with a problem: crisis in orientation. That phrase means that we have lost our way. We no longer know where we are or where we should go. That is not an encouraging perspective. Now of course, that is Ebeling's first word and not his last word in his book on the study of theology. But his diagnosis is symptomatic: Theological education is stuck in a crisis of orientation and therefore in a crisis of meaning.

---

93. Ebeling, *The Study of Theology*, 1.

2) The technical vocabulary for this problem is the *functional* direction of theological education. What should theological education prepare students for? What is its goal? What is its task? What should it accomplish? For whom and to what end?

When Schleiermacher founded the (first) theological faculty at a modern university, he gave it a clear *functional* direction: education/training for leadership in the church. This same functional direction has been largely adopted by theological seminaries that are not a part of the university system. This is especially true in the North American seminary movement.

3) On the one hand the functional direction of theological education today is largely undisputed, yet on the other hand in its concrete application it is controversial. Schleiermacher's paradigm has been questioned in North America (Niebuhr, Farley) and in the international and ecumenical discourse. Criticism is directed at narrowing the focus to the role of pastor within the realm of church leadership. Functional direction that is limited to the office – clerical, pastoral, professional – is definitely too narrow. Ever since Niebuhr's study in the 1950's, the language used in ecumenical circles is that theological education must be functionally directed toward *the ministries* of the church and not solely toward *the ministry* (the office).[94]

Dietrich Werner has called attention to the fact that in the German context the term *theological education* is used only in reference to the training of pastors, whereas the English term *theological education,* commonly used in the international discussion, comprises theological training of a much broader scope. Werner points out that a narrow understanding may result in (German) ecumenical circles when the term *theological education* is always translated as *theologische Ausbildung.*[95]

Matthias von Kriegstein takes the argument even further:

> The (English) term "theological education" signifies a claim to comprehensive theological education. The international discussion talks about a kind of training that includes emotions and behaviours along with the intellect. The relationship to praxis, to the church, to societal problems, to questions of spirituality

---

94. Cf. Banks, *Reenvisioning Theological Education*, 34–45, on the term "vocational model"
95. Werner, *Theologie zum Leben bringen*, 13.

and character development with claims to commitment all play a greater role than in the first phase of Protestant theological education (theologische Ausbildung) in Germany.[96]

4) This brings into view not just the office of pastor but the whole life of the church. That is why some refer to this as an ecclesiological paradigm, a functionality directed toward the church. Richard Niebuhr's study, which we have mentioned several times earlier, *The Purpose of the Church and Its Ministry: Reflections on the Aims of Theological Education*, will provide helpful orientation here. The core propositions are discernible in the title. A "doctrine of theological education" is shaped by the "doctrine of ministry (office)," and this in turn is shaped by the "doctrine of the church." If we seek to reclarify the function of theological education, we must begin with our understanding of the church (ecclesiology) and of the office of (pastoral) ministry. The logic of a theology-based functionality of theological education that is arrived at in this way looks like this:

- What kind of church should be produced (ecclesiology)?
- What kind of leadership/ministry is necessary to foster this kind of church (understanding of office and leadership)?
- What kind of training is necessary to produce this kind of leader/ministry (the task of theological education)?

What sounds almost like a method of curriculum development is in fact at the deepest level a theological question. Then, starting with ecclesiology, a second step can clarify our understanding of the leadership office and ministry. In other words, the question is, what ministries will be needed in the church of the future? That too is a theological, ecclesiological question. Only then can we ask the question, what curricula and structures are needed to train the leadership of these churches? The question of the goal and the content of theological education is thereby placed on a theological foundation.

Daniel Schipani follows this process in an exemplary way in "The Church and Its Theological Education: A Vision."[97] Schipani assumes a three-fold identity for the church: the people of God, the body of Christ, and the temple

---

96. Matthias von Kriegstein, "Theologische Ausbildung als 'Theological Education,'" in *Theologische Bildungsprozessen gestalten. Schritte zur Ausbildungsreform*, eds. Hans-Günter and Matthias von Kriegstein (Frankfurt: Spener, 2002), 61.
97. Schipani, "The Church," 5–35.

of the Holy Spirit. He sees here a reflection of God's essence and character as creator, redeemer and life-giver. From there, Schipani derives a three-fold reason for the existence of the church: worship, community, and mission. In summary, he formulates three tasks for the church:[98]

- Recognize and celebrate God's dominion (authority) – worship
- Embody God's dominion in history – community
- Take part in, proclaim, and represent God's dominion – mission[99]

From this Schipani develops a theology of ministries.[100] They are God's gifts to the church to equip the church for worship, community and mission. He is careful to emphasize the multiplicity of ministries and not to limit ministry to an office held by a professional.

On this theological foundation, Schipani can now develop a "theory" of theological education. His basic premise is: "We engage in theological education for the church in the world in the light of God's dominion." Specifically there are three levels of equipping:

- Equipping to lead the church in worship.
- Equipping to lead the church in building community.
- Equipping to lead the church in mission.

Moreover Schipani formulates the broader horizon of theological education which carries out the three-fold equipping for ministry in a three-dimensional conversation (three-fold agenda):

- The agenda of the Word and the Spirit (orientation toward the voice of God).
- The agenda of the past and the present history and tradition of the church.
- The agenda of the world (society, culture, politics).[101]

It is not my purpose here to defend the content of Schipani's theory of theological education. Other formulations will express other ecclesiological traditions. What's important here is the exemplary process: The functional

---

98. Ibid., 20–21.

99. The three-fold terminology common in ecumenical theology *leitourgia*, *koinonia* and *martyria* is obvious here, even though Schipani does mention it.

100. Schipani, "The Church," 24–27.

101. Cf. Bernhard Ott, "Eine Tagesordnung für Theologie und theologische Ausbildung in Westeuropa an der Schwelle zum 21. Jahrhundert," in *Gemeinde mit Zukunft: Herausforderungen und Perspektiven an der Schwelle zum 21. Jahrhundert* (Bienenberg Studienheft 3), (Liestal: Ausbildungs- und Tagungszentrum Bienenberg, 1999), 8–30.

direction of theological education is derived from theology, ecclesiology, and an understanding of ministry and not simply drawn from the pragmatics of the day.

5) It is true that the ecclesial functional direction for theological education that I have just outlined has not remained without criticism. In the course of twentieth-century discussions about the theology of missions, there was often talk of an ecclesio-centric narrowness. Focusing on the church can easily lead to a posture that is inward looking and concerned with maintenance, more interested in preserving the status quo than with missionary advancement. There was therefore a call for the same thought process to be applied to theological education that was introduced to the ecumenical discussion after the conference on world missions in Willingen in 1952. This way of thinking can be summarized along the lines of the following slogans: Let the church be the church → The missionary obligation of the church → The church is missionary by its very nature → The church participates in the *missio Dei*.[102] This calls for a mission oriented or missional paradigm of theological education.[103] The ecclesio-centric model thus receives the corrective that it must always be about the church's mission to the world. The basic emphasis is not *maintenance* but *mission*.[104]

Although there has been theological consensus for centuries about the fact that the church should not only be engaged in missionary activity but rather is in its very essence "sent," this insight has not yet fully convinced the world of theological research and education. A look at the discipline mission/missiology within theological education paints a sobering picture. According to David Bosch the picture looks like this: Far too often the subject of mission is still marginalized. The theology of mission has become a recognized discipline. Here and there we may find a chair of mission or even institutes of missionary science or mission departments. But it is rare that the

---

102. Cf. Bosch, *Transforming Mission*, 368–393. See also J. Dudley Woodberry, Charles van Engen and Edgar J. Elliston, eds., *Missiological Education for the 21ˢᵗ Century* (Maryknoll: Orbis Books, 1996); also Hans Kasdorf: *Missiologie und theologische Ausbildung* (Giessen: Freie Theologische Akademie, 1995).

103. See Banks, *Reenvisioning Theological Education*, who resolutely calls for a missional paradigm.

104. Schipani does this, although he prefers to keep the term *ecclesial paradigm*. The basic question is whether ecclesiology should be derived from mission, or the other way around.

Biblical-Theological Foundations 191

step is taken to a missional theology.[105] If we are to take seriously the biblical insights worked out earlier, theology and theological education must have a basic orientation toward the *missio Dei*. The theological reasoning can then be pictured as in figure 4:

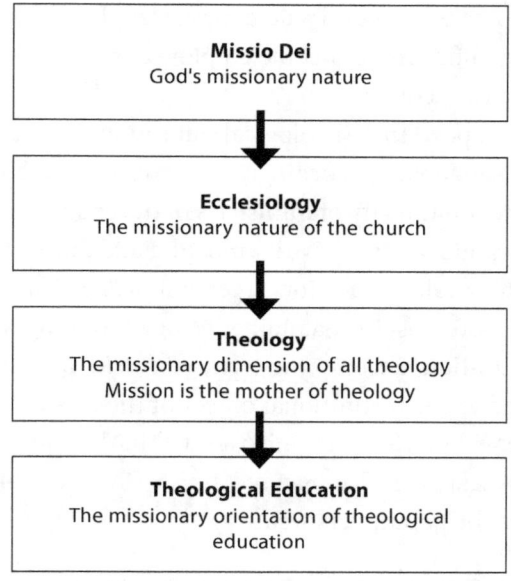

Figure 4[106]

6) Recent discussions have raised an additional question: Is our understanding of ministry limited to ministries carried out within the structures of the Christian church, such as church growth, preaching, pastoral counselling, teaching, and possibly diaconal ministries and mission as well? Since the 1960s, voices within ecumenical circles have emphasized that the potential of *lay* people, those who are employed in occupations *outside* the structures of the church, is of great significance for the mission of the church. To capture this potential the term "the apostolate of the laity" has

---

105. Bosch, *Transforming Mission*, 489–498.
106. I have provided comprehensive rationale for this approach in *Beyond Fragmentation*. Cf. Bernhard Ott, "Mission Oriented Theological Education" and "Mission and Theological Education," *Transformation* 18, no. 2 (2001): 68–86 and p. 87–98.

been introduced.[107] This way of thinking has only slowly gained a foothold in the world of theological education. When some theological schools today advertise with the slogan that they train for *Ministry, Mission and Marketplace*, they are acknowledging this reality. When theological education is defined as *ministerial formation*, the ministries cannot be limited to the classic functions normally assigned to pastors and paid church staff. It must also keep in mind the theological qualification of people employed in all walks of life, all areas of the society and the economy.

Therefore I propose that theological education be defined in principle as *ministerial formation*. Accordingly its goal is to equip people for accomplishing the multiplicity of ministries of the church and its mission. To avoid misunderstandings, two caveats must be added: First, the distinction between church adult education (general *Christian education*) and theological education must be maintained. Not all training within the church is theological education. Second, the term *ministries* must not be narrowed so as to be limited to the institutional offices of the church. Rather, the term must include the wide variety of ministries within the church and beyond, in society and the workplace. *Training for Ministry, Mission and Marketplace* – this phrase draws the parameters well.

7) We can thus summarize: Theological education must be built on a *functional* foundation. That is a theological statement. Theological education is a task within the framework and in service of the church, which is sent into the world to take part in God's project (*missio Dei*). It is the responsibility of theological education to equip people for this mission, not only for the traditional ministries of church and mission, but also for the wider horizon that can be included in the phrase *ministry, mission and marketplace*.

4.2.5 The Power of God

After these three theological guiding principles, each derived from the one before,
- it's about God,
- it's about God's Word,
- it's about God's project,

---

107. Cf. Bosch, *Transforming Mission*, 467–474.

we can now speak about the fourth guiding principle of theological education that must not be overlooked.

1) Training and education as we know them today aim at equipping! Take any textbook of practical theology and look through the table of contents:[108]
- Leading a church (Oikodomics and Cybernetics / Church Development and Communication)
- Planning worship (liturgy)
- Preaching (homiletics)
- Pastoral counselling (pastoral psychology)
- Teaching and instruction (Christian education and religious instruction)
- Loving your neighbor (diaconal ministries)
- Being present in the media (publicity)
- Being missional and evangelistic

In addition to equipping people in these classic areas of pastoral activity, there is an increasing demand for key competencies in the areas of personal and social skills. Theological education must equip people in these areas as well.[109]

The emphasis on a competency-driven education is being encouraged by the accreditation and quality control process which requires that output goals be identified. What counts is what students are able to *do* – what tasks they are equipped for – at the completion of their studies.

2) This emphasis on equipping and skills is, on the whole, welcome. It does, however, conflict with the fact that the most essential things in church growth and mission cannot be accomplished by human effort. Transformation that breaks into this world and brings wholeness and salvation – to an individual, a community, a society – is by its very nature a work of the Holy Spirit. It is grace, which is beyond the reach of human accomplishment. That is the nature of charisma.

---

108. The bullets are adapted from Nicol, *Grundwissen Praktische Theologie*. The last bullet has been added.

109. Cf. William Faix, "Die Bedeutung von Schlüsselqualifikationen für die theologische Ausbildung," *Jahrbuch für evangelikale Theologie* (2005): 191–210.

It is not my purpose here to enter into a discussion about the degree to which God or people contribute to the work of church growth. In the parable of the growing seed (Mark 4:26–29) as well as in 1 Corinthians 3:5–11 we can see that both divine activity and human effort are necessary for a church to grow. Certainly the secret of growth is the gracious activity of God beyond any human work or effort.

3) In this regard theological education is a special case. Unlike many other fields of endeavor, the theologian works in an area which by its very nature demands that the worker must rely upon the activity of God. Work in the church and its mission dare not rely on what people are able to build by their own effort. It must rely on what is humanly *im*possible. As important as the training and equipping in theological education is – of that there is no doubt – theological education must also be training in powerlessness and dependence on God. Especially in an era in which equipping in skills tends to stand in the forefront in educational circles, there are theological reasons that make a "sanctification" of current educational concepts necessary for theological education.[110] This is necessary not least of all for the protection of the graduates, because it inevitably leads to overwork and thus to burnout if one's training leads one to believe that the work can be "done," when the truth is that what really counts cannot be "done" by human effort.[111] That means specifically that the doctrine of grace as well as pneumatology must have a high value, not only in dispassionate dogmatic reflection but in a personal, existential way.

4.2.6 The Church as the Primary Place of Learning

A further facet of a theology of theological education arises when we ask *where* theological education occurs. Theological considerations have shown that theological education is a particular task of the church as a community of teaching and learning. It is fundamentally the job of the church which should happen in the church and for the church. What does that mean?

---

110. Cf. above regarding the law governing kings in Deuteronomy 17.
111. On the integration of ability, powerlessness and spirituality in church leadership and church growth see Daniel Zindel: *Geistesgegenwärtig führen – Spiritualität und Management* (Schwarzenfeld: Neufeld, 2003); and Hans-Jürgen Abromeit, et al., eds., *Spirituelles Gemeindemanagement* (Göttingen: Vandehoeck & Rupprecht, 2001).

1) The primary *place* for theological education, therefore, is the church. Only secondarily may it be located in other contexts, for example in the university. This differentiates theological education from a study of the science of religion. By way of example, this principle is expressed in a text from the Associated Mennonite Biblical Seminary:

> Thus the framework for theological education is not primarily established by the university but by the fellowship of believers. Certainly the theological faculty is a part of both the academic and the church tradition. Nevertheless it is more the Judeo-Christian tradition . . . than Western culture (that shapes the milieu of the university) that is the true home of theological education. In short, we look more to Jerusalem than to Athens to find criteria for determining the form, the essential content, and the style of our plans.
>
> It is self-evident that the theological faculty is responsible both to the university and to the church for its form and its nature. From the university, it gets its severity, integrity and objectivity. It learns how to handle the tools of modern critical science, and it reaps the fruits of this work in the attempt to understand the social and cultural environment in which the church carries out its mission.
>
> Theological education is also responsible to the church, not only because the church is the reason for its existence and provides ongoing support, but also for a more profound reason. The Judeo-Christian tradition, of which the church is a part, provides a reminder of the subtle temptation to pride inherent in every human endeavor, especially those of an intellectual nature. In the attempt to objectify the content of Christian faith and to express it in comprehensible categories that are useful for our purposes, we encounter a serious danger. The truth of the gospel lies there where it *confronts* us and makes us *responsible*.[112]

---

112. Associated Mennonite Biblical Seminary, "Theological Education in the Free Church Tradition," in *The People of God*, ed. Ross T. Bender (Scottdale: Herald Press, 1971), 166–207; quote from p. 166.

I propose, therefore, that we understand theological education to be those courses of study that define themselves as the task of the church and that are done to serve the church. The primary venue for theological education is the church. The secondary venue is the world of science.

2) Closely connected with the question of the venue for theological education is the question whether theological education should occur locally in the context of the church or in separate institutions. This topic will have to be developed more thoroughly later. For now it must be said that my plea for the church as the home (primary place) for theological education is not the same as a plea for theological education that is integrated into the church. Concepts like *home-grown leadership* and *in-ministry training* sound alluring, but they overlook how important distance is for the training process.[113]

3) Finally, the thesis of the church as the primary place of learning implies the pedagogical significance of relationships and community. Biblical research has consistently revealed a pedagogy that is dependent upon life in community.[114] Elements such as the relationship between instructors and students, role models, mentor relationships, as well as living and working in teams, are essential for theological education.

4.3 Midway Point: What Is Theological Education?

After all the prior discussions about the educational theory and theological principles underlying theological education, we are now in a position to undertake a more precise definition of terms. What do we mean by theological education?

1) For theological reasons:

---

113. This was mentioned in chapter 3 in connection with educational models, and the concept of distance will come up again in chapter 5 in connection with the integration of theory and praxis.

114. See the biblical study by Markus Printz, *Grundlinien einer bibelorientierte Gemeindepädagogik* (Wuppertal: Brockhaus, 1996), especially the chapter "Das Erziehungsfeld" [The Training Ground] beginning with p. 231. Even though theological education is to be differentiated from church pedagogy (Christian education), these biblical observations are foundational.

Biblical-Theological Foundations   197

- Theological education is the study of God, both academically and existentially, involving both thorough thought *about* God and personal conversation *with* God, both thoughtful *theology* and worshipful *doxology*.
- Theological education is the study of the Bible, which, as the word and activity of God handed down to us, has primacy over all other sources. Theological education approaches the Bible through expert linguistic, historic, literary and hermeneutical analysis as well as through spiritually listening to God's Word.
- Theological education is undertaken with the whole horizon of God's project (*missio Dei*) in view. Theological education serves the church in its mission. It equips people for the various ministries in (and of) the church, which is sent into the world.
- Theological education understands equipping to be about more than abilities and accomplishments. It will train people in powerlessness and dependency upon the activity of the Spirit of God.
- The church is the home of theological education. There are good reasons for providing theological education in institutions geographically separated from the local church. Such institutions provide appropriate distance from church praxis and make possible a dialogue that goes beyond the boundaries of the church (for example in the context of higher education). Nonetheless the church remains the primary place of responsibility and relationship.
- Theological education is impossible without relationships and community. Communal life, relationships between instructors and students, role models and mentoring are essential elements of theological education.

2) Within categories of educational theory, we understand theological education to be:
- Training, that is, equipping for a task (vocational training), although an essential aspect is that part of the training that is not (yet) aimed at preparation for a specific vocation or profession.
- Formal training in structured programs that normally lead to some form of certification or degree.

- Curricula and courses of study at the post-secondary, usually tertiary level.

Now we are equipped with the background in theology and educational theory we need in order to turn our attention in the next chapters to the various aspects involved in making theological education a reality.

5

Integrating Theory and Practice in Theological Education

Throughout chapters 3 (Foundations of Educational Theory) and 4 (Biblical-Theological Foundations) the struggle for integration was apparent as an overall theme. This struggle must remain in the forefront with regard to praxis in theological education as well. Chapter 6 will be about developing curriculum in such a way that integration will be fostered at every level. For that to succeed, "instruments" in the form of categories, definitions, and contexts are necessary, and these are the subject of this chapter.

The two terms "theory" and "practice" continue to be dominant in this discussion. Virtually every aspect of fragmentation and of the desired integration that we have spoken about can be assigned to one or the other of these almost magical terms. In this chapter it is our intention to provide concrete analysis of these terms and in particular to examine our own thinking with regard to theory and practice and where necessary to expand or correct that thinking.

The first thing we need to do is to shed light on the theory-practice debate. Section 5.1 will do that by taking another look at the Greek categories *Theoria*, *Praxis* and *Poiesis*.[1] The next three sections will then examine the holistic nature of education using the framework of these three concepts.

---

1. Cf. Stackhouse, *Apologia*, 84–135, who makes his presentation using the framework of these three terms. Although I do not follow Stackhouse in detail, I am indebted to his work for many ideas.

5.1 Shedding Light on the Theory-Praxis Debate[2]

5.1.1 The Problem and Suggestions for a Solution

The ICETE Manifesto will serve as our starting point and introduction. In paragraph 7 it states:

> **Integrated Programme**
>
> Our programmes of theological education must combine spiritual and practical with academic objectives in one holistic integrated educational approach. We are at fault that we so often focus educational requirements narrowly on cognitive attainments, while we hope for student growth in other dimensions but leave it largely to chance. Our programmes must be designed to attend to the growth and equipping of the whole man of God. This means, firstly, that our educational programmes must deliberately foster the spiritual formation of the student. We must look for a spiritual development centred in total commitment to the lordship of Christ, progressively worked outward by the power of the Spirit into every department of life. We must devote as much time and care and structural designing to facilitate this type of growth as we readily and rightly provide for cognitive growth. This also means, secondly, that our programmes must foster achievement in the practical skills of Christian leadership. We must no longer introduce these skills only within a classroom setting. We must incorporate into our educational arrangements and requirements a guided practical field experience in precisely those skills which the student will need to employ in service after completion of the programme. We must provide adequately supervised and monitored opportunities for practical vocational field experience. We must blend practical and spiritual with academic in our educational programmes, and thus equip the

---

2. This chapter is a revised version of two workshops, thus far unpublished, which I conducted at the ICETE Consultation for Theological Educators on 18–22 August 2003, in High Wycombe, UK. The titles were: "From Theory to Practice: A Critical Assessment of Some Recent Developments" and "Beyond Theory and Practice: Steps Toward Integration."

whole man of God for service. This we must accomplish, by God's grace.

The integration of the spiritual, the practical and the academic aspects of theological education is called for here. That integration is what this chapter is about.

We encountered a holistic understanding of education in the previous chapter when dealing with biblical-theological foundations. Whether we think of Ezra's life motto "study-obey-teach God's Word" or of the greatest commandment "love God with all your heart, mind, and soul"; whether we consider the term "knowledge" or the relationship between "hearing/listening" and "belonging/obeying," the biblical texts constantly present us with a holistic picture which includes at least three of the components suggested in the Manifesto.

A closer examination of the section cited above, however, gives us pause:
- It calls for the integration of the three elements of *spirituality*, *practice*, and *academics*. I do not know whether the sequence is intentional or accidental. It is clearly indicative of the relative weight assigned to these elements within the text of the article.
- We observe two "places": Academics are placed within the classroom. Practice is placed within vocational field experience. Interestingly, spirituality is assigned no specific place.
- Most of the section is devoted to spirituality and practice. Academics are only mentioned three times in this section.
- The section is a strong plea for spirituality and practice. These two components are described in exclusively positive terms. Academic work, by way of contrast, is judged critically. There seems to be little value placed on academics in the section.
- Practice is more specifically defined by the term "skills" three times.
- Integration is defined by the verbs "combine" and "blend."

The emphasis of the article is clear: it opposes an overly academic, overly theoretical approach and pleads for more spiritual equipping and practical training. Although the section calls for integration and holism, it is reactionary and anti-intellectual. Theory and academic work are more nearly tolerated as a necessary evil than they are valued, honored and integrated. That may be understandable in light of an over emphasis on theory and academics, but it does not lead us to the integration that we need. Despite its good intentions, this section remains stuck in clichés: there (too much) theory, offered in the classroom, here (too little) practice, in vocational field experience.

In what follows we will have to get beyond such clichés if we want to achieve real integration. But first let's take a brief look at these clichés, which look something like this:

- Practice means *doing* something. Theories are *ideas about* something.
- Practice is *active*. Theory is *passive*.
- Practice is *dynamic*. Theory is *static*.
- Practice is done with the *hands*, theory with the *head*.
- Practice means *proximity*. Theory means *distance*.
- Theory *comes first*. Practice is the *application* which follows.

Assumptions such as these prove to be of little use when examined more closely, because they are vague and misleading. Our study of biblical texts has revealed a large degree of holism and integration. The terms theory and practice are not found in the Scripture. They have seeped into our culture from Greek thought. That is not to say that the terms are not useful. On the contrary, a clarification of terms that have their roots in Greek thought can provide direction along the path toward a greater measure of integration.

In what follows we will arrive at a deeper understanding of theory and practice based on the writings of Aristotle. I am not at all suggesting that we adopt Aristotelian philosophy completely and uncritically as our foundation for theological education.[3] However the concepts of *theoria*, *poiesis* and *praxis* have the potential to shine significant light on our discussion of theory and practice.

5.1.2 Praxis, Theoria and Poiesis

Aristotle delineates *theoria*, *praxis* and *poiesis* as three basic disciplines of human thought and action. Figure 5 serves as an introduction to the basic categories:[4]

---

[3]. On the significance of Aristotle for theology, especially for scholastics, see Diogenes Allen and Eric O. Springsted, *Philosophy for Understanding Theology* (Louisville: Westminster John Knox Press, 2007), 77–101.

[4]. The table is drawn from Friedrich Rost http://friedrichrost.de/wt/theorien.pdf (with acknowledgement of Dieter Lenzen, *Orientierung Erziehungswissenschaft*, Vol. 3 (Reinbek: Rowohlt-Taschenbuch-Verlag, 1999), 32.

Reflection Knowledge	**Theoria** Competency: Reason Direction: Truth
Action Responsibility	**Praxis** Competency: Virtue Direction: Goal
Production Ability	**Poiesis (Doing, Making)** Competency: Ability Direction: Purpose

Figure 5

Let us examine the three concepts more closely:

Theoria

It is not the Aristotelian understanding of the concept of *theoria* that is most helpful for our topic, but rather the concepts of *praxis* and *poiesis*. Nevertheless we will briefly outline Aristotle's concept of *theoria* here. *Theoria* is reflection – thinking, meditation. Its aim is to arrive at truth. The skill needed is reason. In contrast to Plato, Aristotle places more emphasis on the perception of things. Truth is arrived at inductively through abstract thinking. For this reason some have called him an empiricist.[5] *Theoria* leads to knowledge, that is, to the knowledge of the truth.

According to Aristotle, theory deals with metaphysics, specifically with theology and ontology, that is, with the being of all things.[6] Aristotle derives his metaphysical principles from physics, however. Thus metaphysics comes sequentially, in the process of knowledge, after physics, although metaphysics is ultimately ranked above physics.

Aristotle ascribed "a higher rank to purely theoretical thought . . . than to the practical." Thus he solidified the supremacy of thought over action.[7] His thinking is also shaped by the idea that the human soul is above the body, and that the mind is above the soul. That is why mental work, contemplation, philosophy, and theory are assigned the highest significance. Not until the

---

5. Which is controversial, cf. Wolfgang Röd, *Kleine Geschichte der antiken Philosophie* (Munich: C. H. Beck, 1998), 186–192.
6. On Aristotle's concept of theory cf: ibid., 193–235.
7. Ibid., 194–195.

pedagogical paradigm shift described in chapter 2 was the supremacy of thought seriously questioned.

The relationship of practice to theory is, according to Aristotle, two-fold: For one thing, *theoria* is not directed to *poiesis*. Philosophy is purpose free. It is not concerned with producing anything. Its value is not measured by its productivity. Because in metaphysics, the highest goal of man is knowledge, philosophy is inherently mankind's highest aim. On the other hand, philosophy, which finds truth in *theoria*, certainly has its effects on *praxis* in the form of good and wise ways of life in society.[8] This leads us to two *praxis* terms which we will explain in the section that follows.

I will not further elaborate here on Aristotle's understanding of *theoria*, nor will I seek to draw applications for theological education. The real contribution of his thinking seems to me to be found in his concepts of *poiesis* and *praxis*.

Poiesis

With regards to our understanding of *praxis*, it is helpful to realize that Aristotle uses two terms to describe what we call *praxis*.

The term *poiesis* he uses to describe the making and producing of things. Ability (in the sense of skills) is required (*techne*). The meaning of *poiesis* lies in its purpose. It is productive. We can speak, therefore, of a *making* or *producing praxis*. *Poieme* intends to produce "something."

Making or *producing praxis* is a means to an end. The meaning is not in the *making* itself but rather in the *product* that is made. The value of practical skills is measured by the resultant output. Skills are as valuable as the things they able to produce.

In addition, *poieme* is limited to the production of a specific object. When the project is completed, *poieme* is no longer active. The production of a sermon requires *making praxis*, that is, *poieme*. When I prepare a sermon, I need certain skills to accomplish this task. If I interrupt the process of sermon preparation in order to do something else, then I cease to be, in terms of sermon preparation, *practical*. I am no longer practicing the skills of sermon preparation. Once the sermon is finished and preached, the exercise of

---

8. Ibid., 195, 198.

Integrating Theory and Practice in Theological Education

poieme-praxis, that is, the skill of producing a sermon is done with – until the next time.

It seems to me that our current understanding of *praxis* – or should I say, the call for more emphasis on practice – is fixated strongly on *poieme*. Practice then means making, producing, manufacturing. As a result, when we talk about practice it comes down to skills and techniques (how to… know how). How limited this understanding of *praxis* is becomes apparent when we take a look at the Greek term.

Praxis

For Aristotle, *praxis* means not only the production of things but also one's way of life. What is required is not (merely) ability, in the sense of skills and techniques, but rather the art, the intelligence, to live life wisely and virtuously – *all* of life, not just specific acts of doing and producing. This understanding of *praxis* encompasses all of life and can be described with the words wisdom, intelligence, and ethics.

If we take this concept of *praxis* seriously, then there is not a moment in life when I am not *practical*. For as long as I live, I am practicing life. Whether I am thinking, reflecting, studying, doing, making, or producing, I am always *practical*. I live wisely or less wisely. I live an ethically responsible life, or less so. But I am always *practicing* life. And I am not doing so as an isolated individual, but rather in a social and political context, which was important to Aristotle. *Praxis* has as its goal the creation of a good society.

5.1.3 Implications

The implications of such a perspective are significant (see figure 6 on the following page). The entire theory-practice debate appears in a new light:
- Activities we often consider to be unrelated to *praxis* – studying, thinking, reflecting – are now part of our life practice. Studying thus acquires an ethically valid practical dimension. Studying is a part of living and can be done in an ethically responsible way, virtuously, wisely – or not. Some are quick to call for more emphasis on *praxis* but are not prepared to carry out the *practice* of studying in a virtuous, wise and ethically responsible manner.
- We now avoid the mistake of thinking (and saying) that time spent in study is merely preparation for life, unrelated to anything

practical. Time spent in study is time spent living, and in this sense it is life *practice*.
- Some may note that an understanding of *praxis* that is limited to *poieme-praxis* is too narrow and is only interested in doing and in skills. This narrow understanding of the term *praxis* must be expanded to include life practice. Then it is no longer about merely products and techniques but about way of life, virtues, wisdom, and ethics – embedded in a societal context.
- Both – *theoria* and *poiesis* – are encompassed within the term *praxis*. Reflection and action, thought and activity, standing at a distance and getting involved – all of these belong to life practice, a way of life that is wise, virtuous, and ethically responsible.

This means that theological education must have as its goal the training of practitioners, not merely theoreticians. Thought and action are both required. Both *theoria* and *poiesis* are to be seen as responsible life practice. Such practitioners know that there is no *theoria* without the corresponding *poiesis*, and that there is no *poiesis* without the *theoria* behind it. They will, therefore, keep thought and action in relationship with one another, so that each informs, stimulates, and corrects the other. In this way *theoria* as well as *poiesis-praxis* will be understood within the context of a wise and responsible way of life within society.

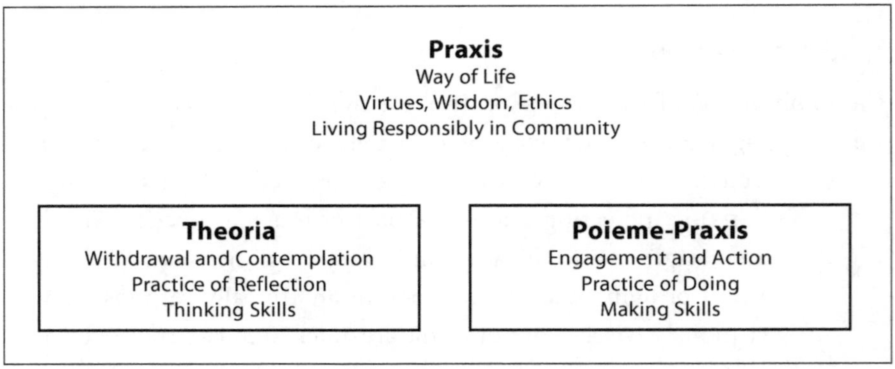

Praxis
Way of Life
Virtues, Wisdom, Ethics
Living Responsibly in Community

Theoria
Withdrawal and Contemplation
Practice of Reflection
Thinking Skills

Poieme-Praxis
Engagement and Action
Practice of Doing
Making Skills

Figure 6

In what follows I will attempt to outline a holistic approach to theological education using the framework of the three terms *praxis*, *theoria* and *poiesis*.

I will use Aristotle's terms as a starting point and an outline structure in the next three sections, but I will not remain within Aristotelian thought patterns.

5.2 Spirituality and Character Development

I am intentionally placing education in *praxis* (that is, for an intelligent, wise and responsible way of life that encompasses all of life) at the beginning. This seems to me to be the highest educational goal. Only when we start with *praxis* can we truly proceed with *theoria* (the intellectual work) and *poiesis* (productive skills) wisely, intelligently and responsibly. Moreover, *praxis* has the most enduring long-term effects. Many points of knowledge acquired through education must later be revised. And new skills must constantly be learned, so an education that provides only a certain skill set will prove inadequate.

We are seeking to convey the concept of *praxis* education with the two concepts of spirituality and character development, well aware that such an approach can at best be one of those helpful constructs that sometimes slice up the truth in unhelpful ways and are ultimately unable to encompass the whole truth.

5.2.1 Theological Education and Spiritual Formation

I suggest the use of the term spiritual formation. It combines the concept of spirituality with that of education (formation) in a way that no other comparable term does.

Thoughts from the German translator of Dallas Willard's *Renovation of the Heart* may be helpful in an effort to understand multi-faceted dimensions of the term spiritual formation:

> The term "spiritual formation" used here in the English original includes both the life change accomplished by the Spirit of God as well as the process of reorientation of one's life that a person actively undertakes. In this German translation we will use various terms, depending on the context: spiritual growth,

spiritual restructuring, spiritual shaping, spiritual transformation, spiritual character formation, and spiritual reorientation of life.⁹

I would also like to note that I do not intend to position spiritual formation as yet another element of theological education. This is not about introducing spiritual formation as an additional component of theological education, giving it more attention or integrating it more closely with other disciplines. Put another way: This is not about introducing a new department of "spirituality," promoting it, and weaving it together with other departments or disciplines. Rather, this is about understanding the whole of theological education as spirituality.

That is why spirituality is purposely not placed under *poiesis* but rather under *praxis*. Thus spirituality is not to be understood as yet another discipline to be integrated with the others but rather as an integrative force. We may well speak of a paradigmatic shift of emphasis here which is foundational for all that follows.

In what follows in this chapter and also in the corresponding section of chapter 6 (6.5.4) I will make frequent reference to the documents of the Programme on Theological Education (PTE) of the World Council of Churches. These were authored in a two-year study process from 1987–1989 and are still today among the most fruitful resources for the integration of theological education and spirituality. The process began in 1987 with a workshop in the Iona Abbey in Scotland, where a position paper was published intended to stimulate further discussion. Six thousand copies of this paper, with the title *Iona Document*, were distributed worldwide.¹⁰ This workshop was followed by a meeting of the leadership commission in Prague in 1988 and then a larger consultation in Indonesia. The lectures and statements from this closing consultation have been published in Samuel Amirtham and Robin Pryor's *Resources for Spiritual Formation in Theological Education*.¹¹ The *Iona Document* is also included in this volume.

---

9. Dallas Willard, *Aus dem Herzen leben* (Giessen: Brunnen-Verlag, 2004), 6, footnote.
10. World Council of Churches, ed., *Spiritual Formation in Theological Education* (Geneva: WCC, 1987); here quoted as *Iona Document*.
11. Samuel Amirtham and Robin Pryor, *Resources for Spiritual Formation in Theological Education* (Geneva: World Council of Churches, 1989).

What Is Spirituality?

What exactly are we talking about when we use the word "spirituality"? Spirituality has become a popular buzzword, which, because of its wide spectrum of possible meanings, is hardly useful without some clarification and definition.[12] Yet Peter Zimmerling argues convincingly that the word can and should be used in Christian theology in spite of all reservations.[13] However, a working definition of (Christian) spirituality is needed in order for us to speak meaningfully about this term.

1) In general terms, spirituality may be defined as "openness and permeability for the mystery of the reality that surrounds us."[14] In a very broad definition like this one, the word spirituality is to be understood in the context of critical response to a materialistic and mechanistic worldview. It's about having the whole of reality in view – whatever that may mean in detail – and developing a holistic way of thinking and living. Somewhat more narrowly, and more explicitly related to religiosity, Alister McGrath defines spirituality as follows:[15]

> Spirituality concerns the quest for a fulfilled and authentic religious life, involving the bringing together of the ideas distinctive of that religion and the whole experience of living on the basis of and within the scope of that religion.

General definitions such as these are important for open dialogue. Yet a specifically Christian definition is equally important.

2) Gerhard Ruhbach asserts that any definition of spirituality must start with the work of the Holy Spirit.[16] It's about an attitude or way of life that is the result of the work of God's Spirit, is founded in Christ, is directed toward

---

12. Ariane Martin's *Sehnsucht – der Anfang von allem. Dimensionen zeitgenössischer Spiritualität* (Ostfelden: Schwabenverlag, 2005), provides an excellent religious-sociological overview of dimensions contemporary spirituality in Europe. From a theological perspective, foundational works are: Alister McGrath, *Christian Spirituality* (Oxford: Blackwell Publishers, 1999); Christian Möller, *Der heilsame Riss. Impulse reformatorischer Spiritualität* (Stuttgart: Calwer, 2003); Peter Zimmerling, *Evangelische Spiritualität. Wurzeln und Zugänge* (Göttingen: Vandenhoeck & Ruprecht, 2003).
13. Zimmerling, *Evangelische Spiritualität*, 15.
14. Möller, *Der heilsame Riss*, 44.
15. McGrath, *Christian Spirituality*, 2.
16. Gerhard Ruhbach, article "Spiritualität," *ELThG*, 1880–1883.

God, and encompasses all of life. In the light of Galatians 5:25 ("Since we live by the Spirit, let us keep in step with the Spirit"), the whole of life must be in view. Spirituality must not be reduced to prayer, Scripture reading, and church attendance.

3) Some have defined spirituality based on the Great Commandment (Matt 22:37–40). Thus spirituality involves emotion, mind, and will (deed), all bound together in love – love of God and love of one's neighbor. Augustine's *ordo amoris* (order of love) is worth noting here. The working committee of the ecumenical Programme on Theological Education articulates this as follows:

> Our spirituality is not what we explicitly express, nor what we profess to believe, but how we order our loves. That ordering may be unarticulated, even quite unconscious, but the resultant spirituality pervades our whole life and involves our whole person. Our stewardship of time, energy, and substance reflects the way we live out and express the ordering of our loves.[17]

The central question of spirituality is, therefore, who receives my first love? The question is not, as Miroslav Volf says, what or whom I *profess* to love most, nor what or whom I *should* love most. The question is what or whom I *actually* love most.[18] This definition has universal applicability. A person's spirituality can be measured by the *ordo amoris*.[19] We can speak of Christian or biblical spirituality when a person's love is directed toward God and neighbor.

4) Peter Zimmerling takes a different tack when he says, "Under spirituality . . . I understand . . . faith that is lived out and finds outward expression and which has its basis in Paul's appeal for 'spiritual worship' (Rom 12:1–2)."[20] Thus he defines spirituality as a worshipful way of life. If we get even more precise, based on Romans 12:1–2, then it is about the dedication of one's life (sacrifice) motivated by God's mercy, and about a God-enabled transformation of one's thinking that leads to new (renewed) discernment and behavior.

---

17. WCC, *Iona Document*, 8.
18. Volf, "Dancing for God," 202.
19. Cf. WCC, *Iona Document*, 8.
20. Zimmerling, *Evangelische Spiritualität*, 16.

5) In the face of many calls for a "new" spirituality, Manfred Seitz points to an "old" text which basically says everything that is needed – Micah 6:8:

> He has shown you, O man, what is good, and what the Lord requires of you – to act justly and to love mercy, and to walk humbly with your God.

For Seitz this text leads to a simple conclusion: "... it's as easy as that: live from God's Word, encounter other people with gratitude, and pay attention to your relationship to God. That's it. Nothing more!"[21]

6) Heinzpeter Hempelmann bases his definition of spirituality on 1 Corinthians 12.[22] In contrast to current trends, he pleads for "more life from God" instead of "more experiences."[23] "Spiritual experiences" are "a thing of the church," according to Hempelmann. From 1 Corinthians 12 he articulates a church-based spirituality with the following components: Christ-spirituality, Logos-spirituality, Bible-spirituality, worship-spirituality, and ministry-spirituality.

7) Christian definitions of the word spirituality often make use of the old word "piety." Opinions differ as to whether spirituality is simply a new expression of piety or whether the two terms must be differentiated and held in relation to one another.[24] Markus Printz uses New Testament texts to demonstrate that *eusebeia* can only be understood as "a life of faith in relationship to Christ." And he reaches the conclusion: "That's why piety emphasizes strengthening and developing one's relationship to God in Christ and in this way leads to growth in faith."[25]

8) Alister McGrath makes it convincingly clear that Christian spirituality cannot be separated from Christian theology, that is, from dogma. To name

---

21. Manfred Seitz, *Erneuerung der Gemeinde. Gemeindeaufbau und Spiritualität* (Göttingen: Vandenhoeck & Ruprecht, 1985), 63–64.
22. Heinzpeter Hempelmann, *Gott erleben in der Gemeinde. Kernsätze zum Wesen evangelischer Spiritualität nach 1. Kor 12* (Birsfelden: ArteMedia, 2004).
23. Ibid., 14.
24. Cf. the article "Frömmigkeit" in *RGG*, Vol. 4, 388; the article "Spiritualität" in *RGG*, Vol 7, 1590; Möller, *Der heilsame Riss*, 40–41; Seitz, *Erneuerung der Gemeinde*, 55–60; Zimmerling, *Evangelische Spiritualität*, 15.
25. Printz, *Grundlinien einer bibelorientierten Gemeindepädagogik*, 105–116. Key texts are: 1 Timothy 3:16; 6:3; 2 Timothy 3:12; Titus 2:11–12; 2 Peter 1:3.

just one example, using the doctrine of creation, McGrath shows that two entirely different kinds of spirituality arise if a person sees the world as created by God on the one hand, or, on the other hand, by an evil, demonic power opposed to God. In the first case, it leads to a spirituality that sees the world (and the body) positively and thus is open to the world. In the second case, it leads to a spirituality that sees the world negatively and thus turns its back on the world. McGrath calls the former biblical faith, and the second Gnosticism.[26] This points to the significance of the relationship between theology and spirituality, a topic we will take up shortly.

9) Based on these theological, dogmatic reflections, it becomes clear that within the realm of Christian spirituality, it is appropriate to speak of spiritualities in the plural. Each of the differing traditions and denominations within Christianity has developed, consistent with its own theology, its own brand of spirituality, each with its unique accents. McGrath speaks about the "theological variables" of spirituality and cites the varying views of Mary in different churches, confessions and denominations.[27]

More recent publications from the perspective of a reformed or evangelical spirituality (Hempelmann, Möller, Seitz, Zimmerling) emphasize the centrality of the Word, grace, and justification. These are an attempt to defend against the (Catholic) danger of seeing saving power in the strivings of pietism. They also seek to counter both a pietistic spirituality that is too narrowly internal and a Pentecostal/charismatic spirituality that is too strongly identified with experience. Thus we see here, too, that denominational theologies are determinative for the particular form spirituality may take.

Several things have become clear through this journey through the current struggles to arrive at a definition for Christian spirituality:

- The term "spirituality" has become established in the German context as well as in the wider discussion in the church and theological circles. It is generally preferred to the older term "piety."

---

26. McGrath, *Christian Spirituality*, introductory examples p. 28–31; a thorough treatment of the theological foundations of Christian spirituality p. 35–81.
27. Ibid., 10. Richard Foster also gives a good overview of a variety of traditions of Christian spirituality in *Streams of Living Water: Celebrating the Great Traditions of Christian Faith* (San Francisco: HarperSanFrancisco, 1998).

- Christian spirituality must be precisely defined in light of the esoteric and neo-religious "spiritualities" afoot today. Without clear definition, reasonable dialogue both within the church and outside the church is hardly possible.
- Christian spirituality will be consistently directed toward the God of the Trinity. It's about relationship with the Creator-God of the Bible. It's about faith in Christ the Redeemer. And it's about the life-giving, life-renewing Spirit of God.
- All of the definitions have made it clear that spirituality is about the whole of life and all of its relationships. It is about nothing less than a way of life based on faith in God and encompassing all facets of life. Christian spirituality is not something that one does along with other things (practices, exercises, rituals). Rather, it is about being and doing everything one is and does out of a vital relationship to God.

As it relates to theological education this means: spirituality is not something that can be cultivated alongside of and complementary to an academic course of study in order to achieve a healthy balance. Spirituality determines the way one studies. But what does that mean for spiritual formation – for learning spirituality? That is what we will consider next.

Spirituality in Theological Education

1) A look at the literature on this topic will quickly show that spirituality (piety) and theology (theological education) do not mix well. They seem to mix (or not) like oil and water. They seem to fight like cats and dogs.[28] McGrath and Zimmerling agree with this assessment but quickly add that it hasn't always been like this and need not be this way. Not until the Enlightenment and the development of theology and theological studies as an academic discipline within the context of modern universities did the tension arise, which we bemoan today, between faith and thought, between piety and academic study. Why did this happen? Based on McGrath and Zimmerling, we can cite two reasons:

---

28. Cf. McGrath, *Christian Spirituality*, 27–28; Zimmerling, *Evangelische Spiritualität*, 16–18.

- The shift in emphasis from theology as "loving God with your mind," that is, as the intellectual pursuit of the God one believed in, to a distanced, objective treatment of the subjects "God" and "faith."
- A reductionist understanding of reality that engages in science "as if God didn't exist" and therefore dismisses all "spirituality" as unscientific and unfit for academic pursuits.

2) Today, however, there is consensus: theology and spirituality belong together – and that must be applied in theological education as well. Thus the PTE working committee stated:

> Because theologies and spiritualities are intimately interwoven, it is impossible to say which comes first. Is it a theology (i.e. reflection about God and understanding the tradition of faith) which generates a corresponding spirituality (i.e. the living, praying, acting and suffering according to that faith)? Or is it rather the spirituality of a worshipping and serving faith community which gives rise to a particular theology?
>
> However these questions are answered, in no case must theology and spirituality be separated. While spirituality is more than applied theology, and theology is more than reflected spirituality, they are interdependent.
>
> Special attention may have to be given to the spiritual formation in particular situations. But in principle the true and proper study of theology is already a beginning of spiritual formation, and spiritual formation happens wherever the study of theology is pursued.[29]

Such an integration of spirituality and theology is a goal yet to be reached. The reality is that much of theological education still has a long way to go. That is true not only for university-based theological studies. It is true as well for denominational and evangelical seminaries. How can we succeed in integrating theology and spirituality in theological education?

3) To begin with we can hold on to the fact that the need for such integration has been recognized in recent years in the world of tertiary theological

---

29. WCC, *Iona Document*, 11–12.

education in Europe. For many years now the importance of ascetics in theological education has been emphasized in introductions to theological education.[30] More than forty years ago Rudolf Bohren began his introduction of the field of practical theology with ascetics, specifically with these words:

> For the old reformers *theologia practica* was to a large extent the teaching of the *vita spiritualis* (spiritual life) of the church. Just this area, which is criminally neglected today, is what the student should give his attention to as soon as possible. This is about the theological foundation of the ecclesiological and secular existence of Christians and is therefore a prerequisite for all other fields of study. Ascetics make clear that theology cannot be studied without personal engagement.[31]

Three things are said here, implicitly or explicitly:

a) Theology cannot be studied from the objective distance of science. Theology, by its nature, cannot be studied without personal engagement. Said another way, one cannot study the Christian faith without personal faith.

b) Ascetics are the prerequisite for all other fields of study because ascetics are ultimately about the existence of Christians in the church and world.

c) It is the student's task to give attention to ascetics right from the start.

But what does Bohren mean specifically? Borrowing from tradition, he articulates the following dimensions:

- *Meditatio*: Engaging the Scriptures
- *Oratio*: Prayer
- *Tentatio*: Trials and temptation

Bohren deems it important not only to articulate these spiritual disciplines but also to practice them. Spirituality must be supported theologically and engaged in practically.

---

30. Cf. Bohren, *Einführung*, 25–26; Schrör, *Einführung*, 67–75; Nicol, *Grundwissen*, 209–218.
31. Bohren, *Einführung*, 25.

4) Despite Bohren's emphasis on practice, it's impossible to overlook the fact that virtually all the talk about spirituality in the introductions to theological studies that we've named has to do with reflection far more than practice. Consistent with the definition of practical theology as theory derived from practice, spirituality is dealt with "theoretically." This thought process is important, but it cannot replace action (practice). Klaus Mertes is right when he emphasizes:

> Praising God is not the same as speaking about God. It is the exercise of the "primary" religious discourse. This discourse happens in worship, in confession, in the singing of hymns, in prayer, and also in deeds, in helping the poor, the suffering, the small and the weak. The "secondary" discourse is speaking from a distance – about worship, about faith, about God . . .
>
> It is foundational for the school to distinguish between these two discourses. The primary discourse, for example, cannot be graded . . .
>
> Classroom instruction is, for the most part, secondary discourse – and should be. But care must be taken not to overload the secondary discourse with goals that it cannot achieve. Religious instruction does not replace prayer. Quite the opposite. It can become an activity which substitutes for a primary discourse that is lacking.
>
> That may sound trivial, but it is not, in view of the fact that the secondary discourse so easily falls into the trap of thinking it can lead to faith and piety. Where the primary discourse is lacking, it can never be replaced by the secondary.
>
> The primary discourse can be "practiced" . . . In this sense it belongs in school. Practice is not the same as "talking about." Practice is exercise.[32]

What Mertes writes here about Christian schools and Ignatian pedagogy should be noted as well when it comes to theological education. It is not enough to talk about spirituality within the framework of practical theology. Lectures on spiritual formation are not the same as spiritual formation.

---

32. Mertes, *Verantwortung lernen*, 38–39.

Karl Barth's *Evangelical Theology: An Introduction*[33] or Helmut Thielicke's *A Little Exercise for Young Theologians*[34] are examples of an introduction to (theological) studies that integrates theology and spirituality. They are classics. And yet they remain "secondary discourse." They talk "about" and "speak from a distance." As important as such textbooks and lectures are, they must not be allowed to "become an activity which substitutes for a primary discourse that is lacking." And so the question is: How can theological education include not only theoretical reflection about spirituality but the actual exercise of spirituality? The key word is "*exerzitium*" (= practice, exercise).[35]

5) Before we think about potential "exercises" in the context of theological education, we have to be clear about what theological education should aim to accomplish in this regard. One could argue, of course, that spiritual exercises are certainly important but do not belong within the scope of theological education. The practice of spiritual disciplines, for example, could be seen to fall within the purview of the church. Are such arguments acceptable? Yes and no.

a) It is certainly true that we cannot expect theological education to provide a comprehensive practice of Christian spirituality. When churches or students themselves demand this of theological education, they are over-estimating the capacity of formal schooling. Spiritual formation must be seen as part of the broader horizon of church pedagogy. If we talk about the pedagogical terms of *fields of learning* or *places of learning*, where spirituality can be learned in practical ways, then we must look first to the family and the church, as we saw in chapter 4.[36] These primary venues for church instruction cannot be replaced by a theological school. Primary responsibility for *education for discipleship* cannot be delegated to a theological seminary.

b) On the hand theological education cannot assume that everyone practices spiritual formation, nor can spiritual formation simply be delegated to the church. There are many reasons for this: (i) Because theological

---

33. Karl Barth, *Evangelical Theology: An Introduction* (Grand Rapids: Eerdmans, 1992).
34. Helmut Thielicke, *A Little Exercise for Young Theologians*, trans. Charles L. Taylor (Grand Rapids: Eerdmans, 1962).
35. Cf. Printz on the "practice" of piety (1 Timothy 4:7 – *gymnaze de seauton pros eusebeian*), *Grundlinien einer bibelorientierte Gemeindepädagogik*, 110.
36. Cf. Printz, *Grundlinien einer bibelorientierte Gemeindepädagogik*, 231–292.

education, as described earlier, creates a problem by objectifying faith, making it an object of study, it is also the duty of theological education to contribute something directly toward a solution for this problem. Said another way: There are a number of challenges for the life of faith that are directly caused by a person beginning to think about faith in an objective, methodical, academic way. Theological education must offer help for these problems. (ii) If it is true that "believing in" and "believing that," faith and thought, spirituality and theology, should be integrated, then that integration must be lived out in an institution of theological education. Where else, if not there, can students see, experience, and practice this kind of integration? Any theoretical and classroom talk about integration loses all credibility if students cannot see and experience it. (iii) Finally, theological education has to make allowance for the fact that an ever-increasing number of students come from a background without any basic Christian influence from their family or church. Thus Malcolm L. Warford comes to the conclusion:[37]

> The seminary is now required to be in itself a place of basic formation in the gospel as well as a community that equips men and women for the church's ministries . . . Seminaries, therefore, are increasingly responsible for an even larger proportion of students' spiritual formation.

One may dispute Warford's conclusion and argue that this job cannot be done by theological education. But churches and schools cannot deny the truth of his assessment.

6) What are the consequences? In chapter 6 we will talk about implications for curricula, and I will be operating on the basis of two basic premises: (a) The whole of spiritual formation must be considered when planning theological education. But spiritual formation cannot be the responsibility of theological education alone. (b) Spiritual formation can only become a reality through a network of connections and partnerships and through the involvement of a variety of players.

Prior to undertaking any changes in curriculum at a theological school, however, it can be helpful to discuss a number of questions. In seminars on

---

37. Warford, *Practical Wisdom*, 3–4.

this topic I often present the following theses to stimulate thought and to serve as a basis for discussion:

> 1) Studying theology often creates challenges for the student's faith. It's not unusual for students to experience a crisis of faith during their time of study. (Thielicke says students' faith-voice changes.) Spiritual formation can help students during this phase. Two questions should be in view: (a) Why do these crises arise? That is, what are the specific challenges? (b) How can students constructively work through (not suppress) these crises and challenges?
>
> 2) The message of the Bible and of faith can be handled in different ways: (a) Like a *consumer*, who digests the message as a meal, to receive strength and nourishment. (b) Like a *chef*, who prepares the meal in order to serve it to others. (c) Like a *nutritionist*, who analyzes the meal in order to identify its contents and understand its nutritional value. The majority of students have experienced (a) in the church. During their time of study, they experience (b) and (c). That can lead to tension and disappointments.
>
> 3) Students also experience multiple shifts of emphasis in this regard: (a) From the simple gospel to complex theology. (b) From personal faith (believing *in*) to thoughtful consideration of the content of faith (believing *that*). (c) From a predominantly well-ordered and affirmative proclamation of the message to a strongly analytical and problem-seeking interaction with the Scripture.
>
> 4) These challenges must be viewed positively as steps of maturation moving the student to an adult faith. It's about leaving behind the faith of childhood without losing childlike faith. This process involves a number of dimensions, including (a) Overcoming a "stop-gap" view of God, in which God is only there for the things we haven't yet been able to understand or explain. (b) Differentiating between truth and understanding, and recognizing the relative nature of the broad spectrum of all understanding (see 1 Cor 13:12). (c) Realizing the subjective nature of every experience with God.

5) Spiritual formation within theological education must aim to encourage a holistic and integrative spirituality. Matthew 22:37–39 can provide helpful guidance: (a) A spirituality of *love*; (b) toward *God* and *neighbor*; (3) with *heart, mind* and *soul*.

6) This captures the particular challenge of integration. Whereas for many people it is nothing new to love with heart and with soul, it is often a new experience (that must be discovered and affirmed) to see study as an act of spirituality (loving God with the mind). The old saying is true: True theology is doxology.

7) When seeking to include spiritual formation in theological education, there are various factors to consider: (a) Spiritual formation cannot be relegated to a few specific "boxes." The integration of faith and thought must be woven into every subject matter (how we teach, how discussions are conducted, what homework assignments are given). (b) A separation between spiritual life and academic work (here lectures and classroom, there devotionals) must be avoided. (c) Spiritual formation cannot be separated from people and relationships. That means the example (modeling) of instructors and professors is of great significance. (d) Appropriate vehicles must be created where questions of holistic growth can be asked and where there is space and freedom for the wide-ranging discussions that arise.

8) The task of spiritual formation within theological education must have goals in view that go beyond the course of study and endure long past graduation. Students must be prepared for ministry in church and mission: (a) The self-motivated practice of spiritual disciplines that is suitable for ordinary, everyday life and not just for the conditions found in the community of a seminary or Bible school. (b) Preparation for the particular spiritual challenges in Christian ministry (powerlessness and divinely given authority, giving and receiving, the danger of burnout, preparation for future phases of life).

7) In addition, specific pedagogical questions can be dealt with in regards to possible changes in curriculum. Printz demonstrated how the practice of spiritual formation can be concretely integrated in church pedagogy. Using the example of the single topic of "Living with the Word of God," he suggests the following didactic learning goals:[38]

Knowledge about:
- The structure of the Bible as an aid to independent Bible study
- A clearer grasp of the relationship between the multi-faceted content areas of the Bible
- An understanding of the historical and cultural setting of the Scriptural writings
- The potential for living out of and with the Word of God

Attitudes and commitments such as:
- Being convinced that the Word of God is essential as a source of strength and authority for everyday life.
- A willingness to study God's Word.
- The faith to believe that God will speak personally to those who read his Word.
- A willingness to receive correction from the Scriptures in our view of God and in our behavior.
- The conviction that it is essential to make room for silence so that we can hear from God.
- And closely related, the willingness to rearrange our priorities.
- A willingness to obey God's voice.

---

38. Printz, *Grundlinien einer bibelorientierte Gemeindepädagogik*, 113–114.

> Skills such as:
> - The ability to organize one's time and to plan time for the tasks at hand. Every relationship lives from the investment made in it, and that includes making time for intensive personal interaction with God.
> - As prerequisite for this: the ability to set priorities. This in turn requires the ability to make decisions and to distinguish the important from the urgent.
> - The ability to be in silence.
> - And the ability to see silence as more than just the absence of noise but rather to see silence positively as an opportunity for listening for and hearing God's voice in a special way.
> - The ability to concentrate on one thing alone, without distraction.

I am not suggesting that we mindlessly follow Printz's suggestion. What I want to draw attention to is the process. If we can manage to take the broad and somewhat intangible topic of spiritual formation and break it down into concrete, practical, understandable attitudes, skills, and bits of knowledge, then we will have an instrument in our hands with which we can identify precise, well-reasoned measures to be used in curriculum development.

Preliminary Observations: We have been considering the area of *praxis*, in its original meaning of a comprehensive way of life. We have a concept of spirituality and spiritual formation that has a solid foundation in the Bible and theology and that, in a comprehensive way, points to a relationship with God and a way of life that is directed and shaped by God. Whenever we talk about *praxis* in theological education, we should do so primarily in this way. What is meant here is not the range of skills needed for pastoral or missionary service, not the maker-praxis (*poiesis*). But rather what is meant here is the praxis that affects our being. That includes what we understand as character development. What impact that should have on curriculum development will be considered in chapter 6.

Additional Literature

In recent years there has been a growing awareness of the spiritual deficits of theological education. There have been renewed efforts to address these deficits and recent publications seek new ways to more effectively integrate spirituality into theological studies.

Stefan Altmeyer et al., eds. *Christliche Spiritualität lehren, lernen, leben* [Teaching, Learning and Living Christian Spirituality]. Göttingen: V und R Unipress, Bonn Univ. Press, 2006. Regarding theological education in particular see the following chapter in this book, Rolf Zerfass, "Gott denken lernen. Theologiestudium als spirituelle Praxis" [Learning to Think God Thoughts: The Study of Theology as Spiritual Practice], 193–204.

Eberhard Hahn. "Theologische Ausbildung zwischen Wissenschaft und Glaube." [Theological Education between Science and Faith], *Jahrbuch für evangelikale Theologie* [Journal of Evangelical Theology] 22 (2008): 7–14.

Ralph Kunz and Claudia Kohli Reichenbach, eds. *Spiritualität im Diskurs: Spiritualitätsforschung in theologischer Perspektive* [Spirituality in Discourse: Spirituality Research in Theological Perspective]. Zürich: Theologischer Verlag Zürich, 2012.

> Brigitte Enzner-Probst, "Spiritualität lehren und lernen. Aspekte einer systemisch konzipierten theologischen Didaktik von Spiritualität im Theologiestudium" [Teaching and Learning Spirituality: Aspects of a Systemic Concept of Theological Didactic of Spirituality in Theological Studies], 113–124.
>
> Sabine Hermission, "Modelle zur Förderung von Spiritualität in Vikariat und kirchlicher Studienbegleitung" [Models for Encouraging Spirituality during Church Internships and Mentoring Programmes], 143–157.
>
> Peter Zimmerling, "Integration der Spiritualität in das Studium der evangelischen Theologie" [Integration of Spirituality into the Study of Protestant Theology], 125–142.

Contributions on theological literature

Jens Martin Sautter. *Spiritualität lernen* [Learning Spirituality]. Neukirchen-Vluyn: Neukirchener, 2007, 21–109 (not explicitly about theological education but foundational nonetheless on the learnability of spirituality).

Simon Peng-Keller. *Einführung in die Theologie der Spiritualität* [Introduction to the Theology of Spirituality]. Darmstadt: WBG, 2010.

Ian M. Randall. "Der geistlichen Leidenschaft den ersten Platz einräumen: Prioritäten in der Seminarausbildung" [Giving Spiritual Passion First Place: Priorities in Seminary Education]. *Theologisches Gespräch* [Theological Conversation] 31, no. 3 (2007): 107–124.

C. John Weborg. "Mit Gott Leben" [Living with God]. *Theologisches Gespräch* [Theological Conversation] 31, no. 3 (2007): 125–147.

Articles in "Zeitschrift für ökumenische Begegnung" [Magazine for Ecumenical Encounter] **UNA SANCTA 66, no. 2 (2011)**

Athanasios Vletsis. "Charismatische oder akademische Theologie? Das Ringen der orthodoxen Theologie um ihren Platz an einer staatlichen Universität am Beispiel der griechisch-orthodoxen Kirche" [Charismatic or Academic Theology? The Battle of Orthodox Theology for its Place at a State University based on the Example of the Greek Orthodox Church], 123–132.

Michael Bollig. "Der überdiözesane Seminar St. Lambert in Lantershofen. Modell einer außeruniversitären Form der Priesterausbildung" [The Trans-Diocesan Seminar St. Lambert in Lantershofen: A Model of a Non-University Form of Education for Priests], 147–154.

Massimo Faggioli. "Die neuen geistlichen Bewegungen in der katholischen Kirche und die Priesterausbildung in den Seminaren" [The New Spiritual Movements in the Catholic Church and the Seminary Education of Priests], 155–163.

5.2.2 Encouraging Character Development

1) It was more than fifty years ago that Romano Guardini uttered the sentence that became something of an adage: You get the impression today that the world is ruled by children who may possess knowledge, power, and technology, but who are utterly lacking in character. The title is "The Adult Human":

> Now emerges what we call "the man," "the woman." The male and female personality, full of character, that life can rely upon, because they have gotten past the immediacy of impulses and the flood of emotions and have arrived at what counts and what lasts. It can be counted among the more dangerous symptoms of our times that their image has become weaker . . . Among their qualities are inner strength, the quiet power of organizing, holding on, moving forward, which forms the basis for all that we call home and family [. . .] The absence of these qualities leads to the strange impression that you so often get these days: that our existence, with the unforeseen nature of all knowledge, the

monstrous nature of power, and the precision of technology, is actually governed by children.³⁹

In the terminology we are using in this chapter, that means that *theoria* and *poiesis* – knowledge and technology – are present and confer power. But what is dangerously lacking is *praxis* – maturity, wisdom and character.⁴⁰

2) At first glance it may seem that character development is a part of spirituality, as we have described it. One can certainly see it that way. In some sense character development and spirituality are flip sides of the same coin. Whereas we looked at spirituality from the theological and spiritual perspective, we will now attempt to express ourselves in the language of psychology and pedagogy.

We must, however, add what Paul Tournier once remarked, that especially among pious people there would seem to be only a few who have a fully developed character.⁴¹ It is not a given, apparently, that pious people are also mature people. One can, of course, pose the question whether such people are truly pious in the biblical sense. Whatever the case, when we seek to get a grasp of praxis in theological education – full-orbed maturity and a wise way of life – then it's appropriate to think in terms of character development.

3) A couple of thoughts about this term: Sometimes one speaks of character growth or character shaping. The terms may seem to have identical meaning, but not if we look more closely. Even our choice of terms will reveal a pedagogical bias. On a continuum, personality development and character shaping are the outermost points left and right.⁴²

---

39. Romano Guardini, *Die Lebensalter. Ihre ethische und pädagogische Bedeutung* (Wurzburg: Werkbund Verlag, 1967), 39–40.
40. Likewise we must reference Martin Buber here. His contributions to pedagogy give significant insights into character formation that is rooted in the Christian faith. That is particularly true of three lectures published in Martin Buber, *Reden über Erziehung* (Gütersloh: Gütersloher Verlagshaus, 2005), 11th edition. On the more recent assessment of Buber as pedagogue cf. Birgit Ventur, *Martin Bubers pädagogisches Denken und Handeln*, (Neukirchen: Neukirchener, 2003), and Martha Friedenthal-Haase and Ralf Koerrenz, eds., *Martin Buber: Bildung, Menschenbild, und Hebräischer Humanismus* (Paderborn: Schöningh, 2005).
41. Paul Tournier, *The Seasons of Life* (Eugene, OR: Wipf and Stock Publishers, 2012), 32.
42. Cf. Felix Studer, "Christliche Erziehung als Erziehungshandeln," *Was geht bei uns? Informationsblatt des TDS-Aarau* Nr. 197 (1997): 4–14.

Character *growth* emphasizes the inner strengths that unfold and take shape. The idea is "endogenic," that is, it can be assumed that the developmental processes are determined by the predisposition of the individual. Upbringing is then understood to be "allowing to grow." The term "pedagogical pessimism" is used, meaning that parental (and educational) influence is scarcely possible and hardly desirable. Such pedagogical approaches rely upon the innate goodness of the individual. The task of parents (and educators) consists primarily, then, of enabling, and not hindering, this positive and natural growth process. Such a pedagogical perspective tends to overestimate the innate goodness of the individual. Expressed in theological language, the fallenness of humanity is underestimated.

By way of contrast, character *shaping* emphasizes external influences exerted upon the individual. This is termed "exogenic." Crassly put, the individual is seen as a pliable mass of clay that must be shaped and formed. This leads to "pedagogical optimism," the idea that parental (and educational) influence is possible and desirable. Such a view underestimates the individual. In biblical terms, the presence of the image of God is given too little consideration.

The term character development is more neutral and is at the centre of the continuum. This seems to me to be the appropriate perspective of a biblical anthropology. It's about both things: helping the inborn gifts and potential of an individual to unfold to their full potential, and also establishing boundaries and applying correction. These two things are perhaps more closely aligned than we might think. Human dignity and the capacity for guilt are two sides of the same coin.[43]

These pedagogical considerations are foundational for establishing educational processes. If we fail to identify the correct "centre," if we don't set out from the right starting point, then seminaries, schools, and faculties will become biotopes or unruly workshops. And now of course we must ask what and why.

4) What do we mean by a "mature person"? Over and beyond what we have already said about spirituality, we must think about three areas:

---

43. Cf. Mertes, *Verantwortung lernen*, 52.

- Awareness of one's own character and intentional effort to change in those areas that are deficient.[44]
- Recognition of one's own gifts and potential.
- Mastery of the growth steps necessary in each phase of life.[45]

5) When it comes to the "how," how growth, development, steps toward maturity and change can be encouraged, there are various levels that must be kept in mind:[46]

    a) The cognitive level. Topics of character development and steps toward maturity are handled thematically. That can lead to a greater awareness of the problem and of the work to be accomplished. Such insights alone often trigger certain developmental steps.

> *Example*: A course each semester that specifically encourages spirituality and character development:
> - Introduction to discipleship (e.g. Foster's *Celebration of Discipline*)
> - Life and family history (family systems)
> - Forms of spirituality throughout history
> - Discovering and developing spiritual gifts
> - Deepening spiritual life in each stage of life
> - Preparation for pastoral ministry

    b) Formal diagnostic. Recognized tests and assessments offer significantly more specific information about personality, character, strengths and gifts. Such assessments should be a required part of the educational process. Whether it is a gifts assessment, the DiSC

---

44. Cf. Michael Dieterich, *Persönlichkeitsdiagnostik* (Witten: Brockhaus Verlag, 1996).

45. Cf. Rudolf Seiss, *Dynamik der geistlichen Entwicklung. Schritte und typische Verlaufsformen geistlichen Wachstums* (Giessen and Basel: Brunnen-Verlag, 1994); Bernhard Ott, *Wurzeln und Flügel. Schritte zu ganzheitlichem Wachstum* (Birsfelden: arteMedia, 2004). Also the works by Romano Guardini and Paul Tournier cited previously.

46. Cf. Faix, *Schlüsselqualifikationen*; Klaus W. Müller, "Persönlichkeitsprägung als Herausforderung: Mentoring als Aufgabe," in *Theologische Ausbildung zu Beginn des 21. Jahrhunderts,* eds. Tobias Faix, Wilhelm Faix, Klaus W. Müller, and Klaus Schmidt (Bonn: Verlag für Kultur und Wissenschaft, 1998), 123–152; Tobias Faix, *Mentoring. Chance für geistliches Leben und Persönlichkeitsprägung* (Neukirchen-Vluyn: Neukirchener, 2000).

profile, or the Myers-Briggs type indicator assessment – testing should be conducted in a careful and professional manner.[47] That includes ensuring that the assessment is accompanied by appropriate feedback and counselling, so that more than just a "freeze-frame" result is captured but rather real support and guidance is offered.[48] This brings us to a third level:

c) Counselling – Mentoring – Therapy. These terms include a wide palette of measures that all seek to offer students appropriate levels of individual assistance in their own personal and character development.

d) Team experiences – Small groups. Significant steps toward maturity are often encouraged through informal learning. This occurs often in teams and small groups. That is why teamwork experiences and small group discussions are measures which must be incorporated into theological education.

6) Finally, the character development of the teaching faculty will be a factor in the character development of students that should not be underestimated. That means that everything we have said thus far must be applied to professors and instructors as well as students. Those who are teaching about spiritual formation will only be able to do so credibly if they themselves are living out the practices and values they are communicating. Specifically: do they themselves have sufficient knowledge about character development, maturation processes, and life stages? Have they themselves undergone regular evaluation and assessment? Are they themselves still learners in this area? Are they themselves in an ongoing mentoring, coaching, or counselling relationship? Are they themselves involved in some kind of team or small group?

Using concepts from transactional analysis, Bernd Weidenmann has shown how much the character development of professors and teachers influences instruction and therefore also the character development of students:[49]

---

47. For an evaluation of various assessments see Dieterich, *Persönlichkeitsdiagnostik*, 78–126.
48. Ibid., 65–67.
49. Bernd Weidenmann, *Erfolgreiche Kurse und Seminare* (Weinheim and Basel: Beltz, 1998), 42–44.

- Teachers whose *critical parent self* is dominant will not take students seriously as adults. They will be strict with students, make petty rules, be very controlling, and implicitly communicate: you are lazy, ill-bred children who need correction and discipline. Such teachers will experience open or covert resistance. Their approach will keep students from developing into responsible, self-directed people.
- Teachers whose *nurturing parent self* is dominant will spoil students and not offer them sufficient challenge – and thus also, in the end, not take them seriously as adults. Such teachers try to please everyone, so that everybody feels good. In such cases, students are likely to become passive or dissatisfied. Students will fail to develop a sense of responsibility for their own actions.
- Teachers whose *helpless child self* is dominant will hide behind their weaknesses and inabilities and ask for understanding. They will not challenge their students because they fear possible resistance. Because such teachers demand nothing of students, students' growth and development is not encouraged.
- Teachers whose *clever child self* is dominant always manage to keep everyone in a good mood with their humor and artfulness. Such teachers entertain their students in order to be well liked. Success in the classroom is limited because students are entertained but not stretched or challenged.
- Teachers whose *adult self* is dominant assume their responsibilities in a professional and mature manner. They respect students as adults who, in the final analysis, will have to do their own work and learning. Such teachers know that people can only grow and mature when they are appropriately challenged.

In what ways can these insights, which have something to say about character development, affect curriculum planning? We will say more about this in chapter 6.

5.3 *Theoria*: Thought, Understanding, and Science

In considering the whole field of theory, thought, the intellectual and academic dimensions of theological education, there are several things to keep in mind:

1) Within the revivalist tradition (neo-pietism, evangelicalism) thinking has gotten a bad rap. Klaus Bockmühl, taking his lead from Adolf Schlatter, speaks about the "fear of thought."[50] He shows why and with what damaging results evangelicalism has often neglected theology and the intellectual effort involved.

Scepticism on the part of many evangelicals about intellectualism and academic theology is related to the fact that the study of theology at modern state universities has fallen under the spell of reason and higher criticism and has suffered as a result.[51] Misguided theology is often responded to by an avoidance of theology instead of intellectual work under God's leadership.[52] Thought is not foreign to all evangelicals, however. The fundamentalist wing of evangelicalism in particular has distinguished itself by a highly rationalistic apologetic.[53]

Based on the Great Commandment (Matt 22:37), it cannot be stressed enough that holistic spirituality includes loving God with *all my mind*. This provides a corrective in two directions: for one thing, it shows that the intellect is not foreign to faith but rather is an essential part of what it means to love God. And for another, it shows that the intellect is not autonomous but should be engaged in love for God.[54]

Anyone who is responsibly involved with theological education will have to pay serious attention to questions of knowledge, truth, understanding and intellect. Heinzpeter Hempelmann writes, "Scientific theory, philosophy of language, and hermeneutics are the key disciplines of every prolegomena-reflection of Protestant theology."[55] It is from this perspective that we will discuss a few basic questions of the theory of knowledge and scientific theory.

---

50. Here and in what follows I am referencing Bockmühl, *Theologie und Lebensführung*, 5–11.
51. On the conflict between theology and critical science see Heinzpeter Hempelmann, *Kritischer Rationalismus und Theologie als Wissenschaft* (Wuppertal: Brockhaus, 1980).
52. Reihard Frische gives a positive answer: *Theologie unter der Herrschaft Gottes* (Giessen: Brunnen, 1979).
53. Cf. Paul G. Hiebert, *The Missiological Implications of Epistemological Shifts: Affirming Truth in a Modern/Postmodern World* (Harrisburg: Trinity Press International, 1999), especially the chapter "Positivism and Theology," 18–22.
54. See Bockmühl, *Das größte Gebot*, 31–33.
55. Hempelmann, *Wie wir denken können*, 7.

2) Earlier I introduced the Aristotelian terms *theoria*, *praxis* and *poiesis*. It will be helpful to keep those ideas in mind now. However, I will use the term *theory* in a non-Aristotelian way. Questions of knowledge, intellect, and understanding should be approached from a much broader perspective. Aristotle will remind us, however, that *praxis*, as discussed earlier together along with spirituality and character development, is not opposed to *theory*, but rather includes it. Study is not a retreat from life. When we are doing intellectual and academic work, when we are studying and thinking, we are still living. From this perspective, study is life practice.

Henri Nouwen said again and again that one of the great evils among students is that fact that students often consider that while they are engaged in their studies they are waiting for "real" life, which will follow. In his South American diaries he recorded his observations as a student in language school in Latin America and his experience as professor at Yale Divinity School in the USA, and he concludes: "The tendency is always there to live, to behave, to think as if life is not here but there, as if it isn't happening now, but will happen later." Yet Nouwen found that life happens now, studying with other students, in community, in sharing various life experiences. Nouwen's plea to live life now, even while studying, goes so far that he writes, "If we all were to die on the last day of our language school course, none of us should say, 'I wasted my time.' Language school should have such inherent significance that its usefulness is secondary." That is *praxis*, as described above. This view of life is characterized by the insight that life has more passive phases, marked by receiving and reflecting, but also more active phases, marked by activity and productivity, and that *both* are *life*. Both are life *praxis*. Both are authentic living. The fact that this perspective is so seldom found at schools and universities is, for Nouwen, "the irony and the tragedy of almost all theological and pastoral education." He concludes further: "It's not surprising, therefore, that so few find 'out there' what they couldn't find 'right here.'"[56]

Drawing from Henri Nouwen, I want to formulate here a strong plea, not to see time spent in training and education as separate from life and praxis that must be gotten through somehow, but rather to see them as real life. To fill those times (of study) well, with quality and care, is an ethical responsibility.

---

56. Henri J. M. Nouwen, *Wohin willst du mich führen? Notizen aus Lateinamerika* (Freiburg: Herder, 1983), 99–101.

Nouwen is right: Those who don't live their lives as students carefully and purposefully will probably not succeed in doing so after the completion of their studies either. They will perhaps become life technicians but not automatically life *practitioners*, those who are mature, spiritual individuals.

3) Finally it is important to note that the relationship between theory and practice (or *theoria*, *praxis* and *poiesis*) can be defined in various ways. In what follows we will become acquainted with differing definitions and ideas about theory, and it will be crucial to note the relationship of each to action. We will not attempt to determine in any dogmatic way the *right* relationship of theory to practice. Rather we hope to learn a repertoire of thought and theory models, each with its own relationship to practice and each of which comes into play, sometimes separately, sometimes together with others. The good teacher is not the one who thinks s/he has found the "right" model of theory and practice. The good teacher is the one who can draw from a repertoire of models and employ various models effectively, constructively for the educational process.

Specifically, we will now consider the following questions:
- What do we mean by thought?
- What do we mean by theory?
- What do we mean by understanding?
- What do we mean by science?

5.3.1 Two Ways of Thinking

First it may be helpful to distinguish two different ways of thinking. Of course we can only do so in a simplified and abbreviated manner. The ways of thinking that I'm talking about have occasionally been represented in a comparison between Descartes and Blaise Pascal. The one may be called *thinking under the sole authority of reason*, and the other *thinking with the heart*.[57]

---

[57]. In what follows I am drawing upon Köberle, *Descartes und die Folgen*; as well as Hanswalter Giesekus, *Glaubenswagnis. Leben und Erkennen aus der Sicht des Blaise Pascal* (Wuppertal: Brockhaus, 1997); also Hemplemann, *Kritischer Rationalismus*; and the comparison between Kant and Hamann in Hempelmann, *Wie wir denken können*. Lesslie Newbigin's *Foolishness to the Greeks: the Gospel and Western Culture* (Grand Rapids: Eerdmans, 1986), is particularly helpful in providing a critique of modernity's view of science, especially the two chapters "Profile of a Culture" and "What Can We Know? The Dialog with Science."

Thinking Under the Sole Authority of Reason

Descartes was disillusioned by all of the theories that had been developed up until his day and did not trust traditional wisdom. He wanted to start fresh and establish a solid foundation for epistemology. He intended to do this by questioning everything until he hit upon something that he was not in a position to question. He believed he had found this foundation when he formulated the famous sentence: *cogito ergo sum* – I think, therefore I am. Critical reasoning became for him the foundation for all understanding. The only thing that has validity as truth is that which can stand up to critical human reasoning and which can be arrived at by intellectual conclusions. Everything else is to be classified as "opinions" or "faith."

Thus the search for truth became subject to the dictates of radical criticism and the sole authority of human reasoning. Descartes applied this path to knowledge to every area of reality. Nothing was deemed to be true unless it withstood the judgment of critical reasoning.

Descartes' thinking held sway in the "philosophical ego-isolation" as well.[58] The process of intellectual search for truth could be undertaken by an individual in isolation, far from the reality of life. Truth would be found where a person was entirely "head." The isolated thinker, shut off in his study, became the ideal picture of a seeker of truth.

A further result of Descartes' philosophy is the complete division between matter and spirit.[59] As we saw earlier, the distinction between, yes, the absolute separation of *res cognitas* from *res extensa*, resulted in the spiritual/intellectual and the material existing side by side. God has nothing (more) to do with nature. In one fell swoop, theory (thought) and practice (action) were separated qualitatively from one another.

Yet despite all that, Descartes should not be misunderstood as a critic of God or as an atheist. Quite the opposite. For him, reason was the only trustworthy instrument that would lead to certain knowledge of God. He formulated a proof of God's existence based solely on rational logic. He was thus able to prevent faith and religion from being becoming marginalized by human reasoning. One can say that he recaptured faith and religion by means of thought and reason. But God and religion were thereby reduced to

---

58. Köberle, *Descartes und die Folgen*, 10–13.
59. Ibid., 13–15.

the "imaginable." Köberle is right when he concludes that "Descartes' God is a purely rational construct."[60].

Thinking with the Heart

From Blaise Pascal, a contemporary of Descartes, came a sentence that is often quoted as a key to understanding his thinking: *"C'est le coeur, qui sent Dieu, et non la raison."* And that sentence does indeed capture the core of his epistemology. Yet it would be a mistake to suspect Pascal of an emotional, anti-intellectual piety. He too was convinced that the whole dignity of man is found in his intellect and that members of the human race are distinguished from all other creatures by their ability to think. Köberle writes, "Even the raison de coeur is an act of understanding born of the passion for thought. And it brings to light insights that far exceed the logical and geometric intellect."[61]

One characteristic of reason, as encountered in Pascal, is the awareness of the helplessness and limitations of human beings, including their power of thought. Pascal is unwilling, therefore, to place ultimate trust in human reasoning. Humans and human intellect are much too much like reeds shaking in the wind and therefore not the final determinants of truth. Thinking with the heart is thus modest and humble.

This kind of thought does not seek and find final certainty in trust in its own reason but rather by turning to the God who has revealed himself in history and to whom the Bible gives witness. Pascal himself had experienced this personally, and that experience gave rise to his statement: "The God of Abraham, Isaac and Jacob, not the God of philosophers and scholars."[62]

"Thinking with the heart is a loving way of thinking," writes Köberle, and thereby places Pascal's epistemology in proximity to the Great Commandment (Matt 22:37). When we are borne along by the assurance that God loves us, even disciplined intellectual work is shaped by love for God and for others.

In comparing Descartes and Pascal, there is no effort to play off reason against non-reason. Both were enormous intellects, and both viewed the ability to think as that which makes humans human. Yet Descartes and Pascal present us with two ways of thinking. The one is a view of reason that places

---

60. Ibid., 5.
61. Ibid., 7.
62. The entire text may be found in Giesekus, *Glaubenswagnis*, 39–40.

complete trust in the intellectual capacity of the individual, places everything in subjection to the intellect, and expects to find final truth through human critical thinking. Whenever theology and theological education have adopted this view of reason, they have gone astray. The greatest error is in reducing reality to that which can be imagined by human reason. The historical-critical method, in its classical definition by Ernst Troeltsch, is only one result of this way of thinking.[63]

The modest and humble thinking with the heart stands in contrast. By trusting in God, who has revealed himself in history in the person of Jesus Christ, to whom the Bible gives reliable witness, intellectual work can be done in the service of God and with a posture of love. That is the kind of reason that must shape theological work.[64]

5.3.2 Cultural Differences in Thinking

Our thoughts thus far have moved within the framework of Western traditions of thought. Other ways of thought, however, can be found when we compare other cultures. That becomes apparent in every arena and on every level in our world that is increasingly globalized. International companies have long been aware of the difficulties that can arise within multicultural work teams.[65] Geert Hofstede's study, *Interkulturelle Zusammenarbeit. Kulturen – Organization – Management* [Intercultural Teamwork: Cultures, Organization, Management], has become a standard text for anyone whose work involves intercultural teams. Significant differences in how we think occur not just between Western societies and those of the Majority World. Members of North American and European management teams face difficulties arising from different ways of thinking, and management consultants offer help and seek to create understanding through appropriate training classes.[66]

---

63. Cf. Peter Stuhlmacher, *Vom Verstehen des Neuen Testaments* (Göttingen: Vandenhoeck und Ruprecht, 1986), 24–25.
64. See Reinhard Frische, *Theologie*, for a theology in the school of the pietist Spener.
65. Geert Hofstede, *Interkulturelle Zusammenarbeit: Kulturen – Organisationen – Management* (Wiesbaden: Gabler, 1993).
66. One example about North American-European teamwork: Sylvia Schroll-Machl, "Kulturbedingte Unterschiede im Problemlöseprozess," *Organisationsentwicklung* 1 (2000): 76–91.

Theology and theological education do not operate outside these realities either. Those engaged in international, intercultural theological dialogue have long been aware that different cultures think differently when it comes to theology as well. Western theology can no longer assume that it has a monopoly on theological thought.

One study that has tackled this problem thoroughly is Marlene Enns' dissertation.[67] Enns compares what is known as *analytical thinking* with *holistic thinking*. In table 1 she draws comparisons in four areas.[68]

Holistic Systems of Thought	Analytical Systems of Thought
High regard for the object being studied and its context, and an effort to understand the object in its relationships.	Concentration upon a selected object for study, and an effort to understand the object in isolation.
Complex, multi-causal descriptions of realities that tend to have the character of attempts at explanation and from which no certain prognosis can be derived.	Linear, mono-causal descriptions of realities that tend to have the character of valid explanations and from which prognoses can be derived.
Arguments are based largely upon experience.	Arguments are based largely upon logic.
Logical contradictions in argumentation pose no problem and indeed are to be expected.	Logical contradictions in argumentation pose a problem and are not expected.

Table 1

Enns applies these insights to theological education. She points out strengths and weaknesses of each way of thinking and emphasizes that the two approaches complement each other and thus can lead to fuller understanding. It is worth asking, however, whether it is appropriate to call non-Western

---

67. Marlene Enns, *Towards a Theoretical Model of Mutuality and its Implications for Intercultural Theological Education: Holistic and Analytical Cognition* (PhD dissertation Trinity International University, 2003). See also Marlene Enns, "Now I Know in Part: Holistic and Analytical Reasoning and Their Contribution to Fuller Knowing in Theological Education," *Evangelical Review of Theology* 29, no. 3 (2005): 251–267; "Theological Education in Light of Cultural Variations of Reasoning: Some Educational Issues," in *Theological Education as Mission*, ed. Peter Penner (Schwarzenfeld: Neufeld Verlag, 2005), 137–151; "Recovering the Wisdom Tradition for Intercultural Theological Education," *Journal of European Baptist Studies* 5, no. 3 (2005): 5–23.

68. This is a very simplified figure intended to show the general direction of Enns' argumentation. See Enns, "Now I Know in Part," 253–256; Enns, "Theological Education," 139–144.

thought "holistic." Wouldn't an integration of these two culturally different ways of thinking more appropriately deserve the name "holistic"?

Nevertheless, the insights which Enns presents are foundational for theology and theological education, which today certainly belong within the sphere of a global, multicultural church. Any culture which assumes its own way of thinking is absolute, is not only arrogant, it loses any chance of attaining "fuller knowledge."

5.3.3 Various Types of Theories

The terms "theory" and "theoretical" are often used in connection with training and education, in more recent times often disparagingly, by those who bemoan too much theory and desire more practice. Yet "theory" and "theoretical" are not sharply delineated concepts. We will only achieve a greater degree of clarity in the theory-practice debate if we define theory more precisely. Several questions and thoughts are worth noting:

- The *(implicit) interest* behind a theory: What primary interests lie behind the formation of a theory? Who seeks to say what to whom with a theory? Who seeks to accomplish what with a theory, and where?
- The *methodological dependence* of a theory: What methods have led to this theory and what can (or cannot) be expected from these methods?
- And finally the *performance capacity* of a theory: What is this theory capable of clarifying? What claims can it make (normativity, scope, universal applicability)? What prognoses does it allow?

In the wake of Wilhelm Dilthey, a distinction has been made between *explanatory* and *comprehensive* theories. Hans Gruber provides this definition:

> Whereas the natural sciences seek an "explanation" for the object under study based on conformity to (universally valid) natural laws, the humanities seek to grasp the object under study by understanding it ("in time"). The methodology of "explanation" and "comprehension" differ significantly. The "explanatory" sciences control their hypotheses through reproducible

observation and experiments. The "comprehensive" sciences interpret a single "deed," "text," "occurrence."[69]

This distinction is useful for theology because the current discussion about theory and methodology in theology mirrors this differentiation exactly. We must now consider this further.

Comprehensive Theories

Theology has traditionally been assigned to the humanities or social sciences. It deals with intellectual realities (ideas, language) that are accessible in writing (texts) and seeks to understand and interpret these texts through the use of hermeneutical methods. What results are primarily comprehensive and representative theories. Using the methods of exegesis and hermeneutics, we try to understand what Paul understood by "the righteousness of God," and we generate a corresponding theory of "the righteousness of God" in Paul's writings. Christian theology, however, goes a step further. Based on its view of Scripture (revelation), it is not content to leave the study of Paul's writings with a *comprehensive* or *representative* theory. It wants rather to speak of a *normative* theory. This evaluation is based on the axiom that the Bible is God's normative revelation.

Viewed through the grid of the questions posed above, this means:

Interest: The *interest* of theological research traditionally lies in defining truth, in the sense of normative statements about the whole of reality (God and the world). The church, as the subject of theological work, thereby seeks to tell its members and indeed all people what is true and what they ought thus to believe.

Methodology: Christian theology bases the formation of its theories *methodologically* on the interpretation of texts – primarily the text of the Bible (*norma nomans*) and secondarily on the confessional texts of history (*norma nomata*). Using the methods of textual analysis and interpretation (exegesis and hermeneutics), texts are studied and theories are formulated.

Performance Capacity: These theories are first and foremost *comprehensive* and *representative* theories, which capture in the form of a theory what certain

---

69. Hans Gruber, "Hinführung zum wissenschaftlichen Arbeiten. Ein Leitfaden," 8, Available at https://www.uni-frankfurt.de/48891434/Hinfuehrung-zum-wiss-Arbeiten.pdf.

writers have formulated and intended. Such theories are limited in range since comprehensive and representative theories can only interpret isolated facts, texts or occurrences (Gruber). The explanation of Paul's understanding of the righteousness of God is only able, at this first level, to suggest what Paul in his time and context understood by "the righteousness of God." Based on traditional Christian doctrine of the Scripture (revelation), a doctrine of the righteousness of God based on Paul's writings in the Bible demands a broader scope. It claims to be normative in a way that transcends time, culture, and religion.

This first group of theories has been described using words like *fundamental, philosophical, speculative, idealistic, deductive,* or *propositional*. These terms don't necessarily all mean the same thing, but they have something in common. They describe theories as a system of thoughts and definitions which claim "objectivity" independent of history and context. Such theories claim to be based in an extra-historical reality and thus to exist outside the constantly changing realities of history. Praxis, by way of contrast, belongs to the ever-changing realities of history. This understanding of theory derives from Plato's understanding of the immaterial, eternal, and unchanging quality of ideas, as well as from Descartes' distinction between "*res cognitans*" (mind, soul) and "*res extensa*" (matter, body). According to Plato, such theories are recognized through rational perception, through thinking (*dianoia*) and insight (*noesis*).

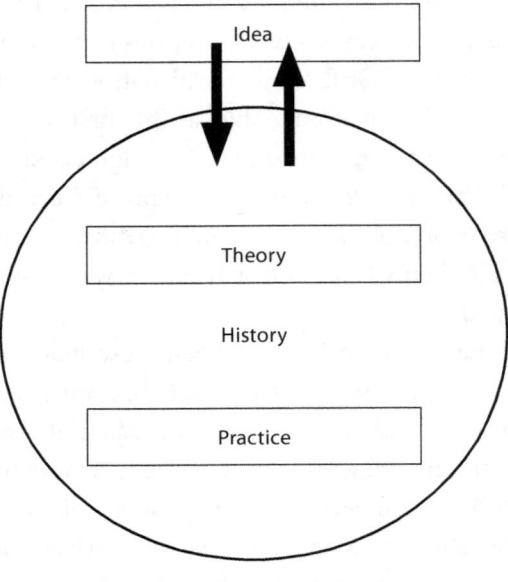

Figure 7

Such theories are characterized by two features in terms of their relationship to praxis:

1) They are unrelated to praxis in their origins because they are derived from "ideas" that are independent of praxis rather than from inner-historical realities.

2) They claim priority over praxis, a priority which is two-fold:
   a) First, theory is more valuable than praxis and is thus qualitatively superior. It is not subject to historical relativity and changeability but is of intellectual, eternal, other-worldly quality. Theory is objective and universal. It deals with truth, with reality.
   b) Therefore theory also has chronological priority over praxis. The movement is from "correct" theory to application (praxis).

The implications of such an understanding of theory for education are obvious:

1) The *qualitative* primacy of theory leads to a higher valuation of thought, reflection, definition, and argumentation. Mental and

intellectual work, decoupled from praxis, is considered more valuable activity than praxis. An academic education is more highly esteemed than practical training. Academicians and scholars outrank mechanics and technicians.

2) The *chronological* primacy of theory results in educational processes that start with instruction in theory. Chronological primacy leads to *pedagogical* primacy. Anyone who wants to learn something must *first* learn the theory, and only then comes the application.

This two-fold primacy of theory over practice is justified by the fact that basic theories are generally understood to be normative. When it comes to theological education, the question must be asked whether and to what extent theological teaching (dogmatics) corresponds to this category of theory.

The type of theory just described has been under attack, however, on two fronts: (a) In the world of modern science (enlightenment paradigm) the appeal to revelation that is not methodologically demonstrable or reproducible is unacceptable. The science of theology is, therefore, not able to formulate *normative* theories, in the sense of "transcendent normativity."[70] It can only generate *comprehensive* or *representative* theories, which may then be *believed* to be normative theories within a faith community.[71] (b) In addition the humanities and social sciences in general have been criticized as providing one-sidedly deductive access to reality. In order to compensate for this, there are calls for the exploration of "experiential religion." And that brings us to the next type of theory.

Explanatory Theories

Recently theology has shifted more in the direction of social sciences. That is particularly true when it comes to practical theology, missiology, and the science of religion.[72] The social sciences study the tangible realities of life today. They are not so much interested in ideas *about* the world and humanity

---

70. According to Jaco S. Dreyer, "Theological Normativity: Ideology or Utopia," in *Normativity and Empirical Research in Theology*, eds. Johannes A. van der Ven and Michael Scherer-Rath (Leiden: Brill, 2004), 4.

71. Cf. Astrid Dinter, Hans-Günther Heimbrock, and Kerstin Söderblom, eds., *Einführung in die empirische Theologie*, (Göttingen: Vandenhoeck & Ruprecht, 2007), 46–51, on the phrase "methodischer Atheismus in der Theologie."

72. For a thorough discussion of the methods of practical theology, see Stephanie Klein, *Erkenntnis und Methode in der praktischen Theologie* (Stuttgart: Kohlhammer, 2005).

but rather in the real-life existence of people in the world.[73] The social sciences employ empirical methods of research. But two schools of empirical research have formed within the social sciences, which are commonly called *quantitative* and *qualitative*.

- *Qualitative research* is modeled after the humanities. It examines language (e.g. interviews) and employs the methods of hermeneutics. Qualitative research seeks to delineate, understand, interpret. The quality and kind of its interpretations reflect this. In the world of practical theology today, the research approach of *grounded theory* is widely used.[74]
- *Quantitative research* is modeled more after the natural sciences and makes *explanatory theories* possible. Through precise (statistical) scrutiny, mechanisms of human behavior can be identified. Generative theory may be able to explain how a thing functions. Based on such functional theories prognoses and steps toward optimization can be derived. Such theories are therefore called *functional, pragmatic,* or *how-to* theories.

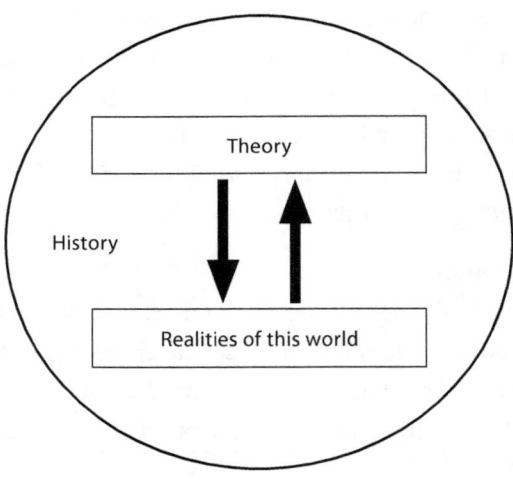

Figure 8

---

73. It is telling that the subtitle of the book cited earlier by Dinter, Heimbrock and Söderblom is "Exploring Real Life Religion."
74. Cf. Klein, *Erkenntnis und Methode*, 239–265. On the validity of generative theory see p. 257–260.

Let's examine this type of theory for interest, methods, and performance capacity:

Interest: The *interest* of quantitative research is of a *functional* and *pragmatic* nature. One seeks to discover how a thing functions, in order to optimize its performance. The classic question of the church growth movement (McGavran) was: Under what observable conditions do churches grow? From there, it can be predicted that if this or that condition is optimized, churches will grow.

Methods: Qualitative empirical research bases the formation of its theories *methodologically* on measurable expressions of real-life faith. Mathematical, statistical methods are used to generate explanatory or functional theories.

Performance Capacity: These theories can be seen as pragmatic truths.[75] These are theories which say how something functions (or not) under certain conditions. Such theories allow for prognoses, since it may be assumed that under the same conditions, a system will function in the same way. Based on such predictions, optimization of a system is possible. Thus practitioners in the church and in missions ask pragmatically: What can we do so that it works better?

Critical Theories

The term "critical theory" arose out of the epistemological paradigm shift of the twentieth century (see above, section 3.3.3), is rooted in Marxist philosophy, and associated with the names Max Horkheimer, Theodor Adorno, and Jürgen Habermas (the Frankfurt School). Critical theory represents a radical break with all previous understandings of theory.

The basic idea is that all theories are constructions of human thought, conditioned by the respective contexts, formulated in the interest of specific sociological or ideological powers. Theories are, accordingly, a part of praxis. In fact, they are justification for praxis.

---

75. On the definition of "pragmatic truth": "At its roots, pragmatism holds that intelligent organisms, in trying to survive the environments in which they find themselves, develop ideas, beliefs, and theories that are 'true.' These are not 'true' in some absolute sense, but true in the sense that they work for those organisms. They work amidst the conditions in which the organisms find themselves" (David C. Berliner in the foreword to Arnold B. Danzig et al., eds., *Learner-Centred Leadership: Research, Policy, and Practice* [Mahwah: Lawrence Erlbaum Associates, 2007], xi).

Critical theory is about exposing theories that justify praxis and calling them into question, especially in those instances where praxis oppresses, disenfranchises, or wields power. Critical theory is an intellectual instrument of liberation (see figure 9). It is not surprising, therefore, that critical theory took hold within liberation theology, in large part through the work of the pedagogue Paulo Freire.

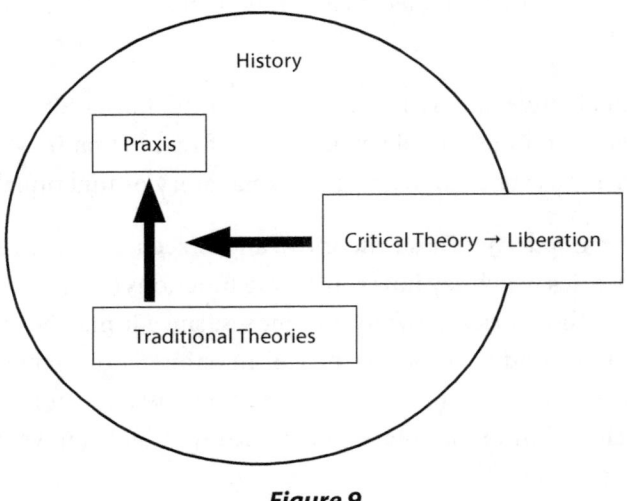

Figure 9

It is true, of course, that a Christian perspective raises significant objections to Marxist thinking and the philosophy of the Frankfurt School. Yet it must not be overlooked that critical theory points out a mechanism that does indeed require critical reflection. It is certainly true that theories are often postulated simply to justify certain (otherwise objectionable) practices. That is why it is appropriate to see the theories as part of praxis. Moreover it is justifiable, indeed it is necessary, to call such mechanisms into question, to expose them, and to demand liberation from said mechanisms.

Summary and a Look Ahead

While reflecting on theories in connection with theological education, we must remember that our task is to recognize that there are various types of theories. They may differentiated based on *interest, methods,* and *performance capacity*. A competent treatment of theories within theological education requires us to be familiar with and know how to apply a variety of types of theories.

That, however, is only possible through an introduction to an overview of theory application and theory formulation, consistent with the academic level of higher (tertiary) education. This will deal with the three basic questions previously raised:

Knowledge-driven Interest: According to J. Habermas, three basic interests may be identified:[76]

> a) *Technical interests*, that are interested in the facts about the functionality of systems for the purpose of predicting and implementing processes of optimization (= explanatory or functional theories; pragmatic truths).
>
> b) *Comprehensive interests*, which seek to interpret historical realities in their contexts in order to grasp their meaning and significance (= comprehensive theories; normative theories).
>
> c) *Emancipatory interests*, that call into question the closed and self-confirming circles between theory and praxis in order to enable freedom from these strictures (= critical theories).

Methods: Knowledge about the performance capacity of methods:

> a) *Hermeneutical methods* can produce descriptive or comprehensive theories. They analyze language and seek to understand their meaning in context.
>
> b) The same is true of *qualitative empirical methods* (e.g. Grounded Theory). The kinds of data and the means of gathering data may differ, but here too it is about the hermeneutical interpretation of language.
>
> c) *Quantitative empirical methods* produce functional theories. They provide data that help us to explain how systems function.

---

76. Cf. Klein, *Erkenntnis und Methode*, 106–108; Dinter, Heimbrock, and Söderblom, *Empirische Theologie*, 51–54.

Performance Capacity: The various types of theories differ in their performance capacity in terms of normativity, scope, and ability to form generalizations.

> a) *Comprehensive theories* deal with specific, concrete situations and have limited scope. The possibility for prognoses and functional applications is limited. If transcendent (normative) theories are derived from them, this is done based on axioms that are not subject to scientific control (e.g. authoritative Scriptures).
>
> b) *Explanatory theories* claim to make universally valid assertions about functionalities under identical conditions. Such theories allow prognoses and functional applications.

All these considerations lead to the question, when it comes to theology, of the normativity of its assertions. That is what we will deal with in the following section.

5.3.4 Truth and Understanding

As has already been stated, the question of truth is especially crucial in theological education and deserves special attention. A number of fundamental clarifications are necessary.

Pre-Modern, Modern, Postmodern

The problem of truth and understanding is most readily apparent when we take a stroll through the three eras that are now often called pre-modern, modern, and postmodern. The philosophical questions raised are complex and go beyond the scope of this treatment. Two studies may be helpful for the topic at hand: Heinzpeter Hempelmann's article "Streiten für den Streit um die Wahrheit?" [Arguing the Battle for the Truth?][77] and for a trans-cultural perspective, Paul G. Hiebert, *Missiological Implications of Epistemological Shifts: Affirming Truth in a Modern/Postmodern World*.[78] Drawing from

---

77. Heinzpeter Hempelmann, "Streiten für den Streit um die Wahrheit?," in *Glauben wir alle an denselben Gott? Christlicher Glaube in einer nachchristlichen Gesellschaft*, ed. Heinzpeter Hempelmann (Bad Liebenzell: VLM, Verl. der Liebenzeller Mission, 2005), 52–78.

78. Paul G. Hiebert, *Missiological Implications of Epistemological Shifts: Affirming Truth in a Modern/Postmodern World* (Harrisburg: Trinity Press International, 1999).

both of these texts, I will venture a concise summary of the problem and a possible solution:

1) Hempelmann characterizes the pre-modern era using three theses:
   - There is truth.
   - There is only one truth.
   - It is possible to say exactly what the truth is.

Within this framework, truth and understanding of the truth are one and the same. One can assume that what one perceives is identical with perceived truth. When Hiebert uses the terms "positivism," "photographic view of knowledge," or "naïve realism," he is pointing out just this view of perception. Truth and understanding of the truth are here equated in a way that is uncritical and unthinking. Hiebert calls attention to the fatal consequences of this way of thinking from a missiological perspective, pointing to the colonial era of missions: Western theology was exported worldwide as "the truth." The assumption that one's own understanding of the truth *was* the truth became an instrument of power – power which was used to force a particular understanding of the truth upon others and indoctrinate them with it as universally valid.

2) The situation changed in the modern era, which Hempelmann describes as follows:
   - There is truth.
   - Of course there is only one truth, but
   - What that truth is must remain a subject of debate.

And there will be debate, because truth and understanding of the truth are no longer seen as one and the same. It can still be said that there is only one truth – to which no one has final and complete access – but there are many differing perceptions or understandings of the truth. Terms such as contextual understanding or perspective understanding make clear that there is now seen to be a pluralism of understanding(s). It is now necessary to fight in order to arrive at an understanding that is as close to the truth as possible. That is, in the final analysis, what we have come to know as the search for truth within modern science.

3) Over the course of the modern era, however, there arose an ever-increasing scepticism whether understanding and truth could ever possibly be identical. This led to the postmodern era, which Hempelmann characterizes as:
- There is truth, but
- There is not just one truth, but rather many truths – based on subjective, contextual understandings and perspectives,
- Therefore there is no longer, nor should there be, any battle for the truth.

A pluralism of understanding(s) thus led to a pluralism of truth(s). An understanding that is subjective, limited by context and perspective, is now declared to be a possible truth.

Truth is no longer something that reaches me from the outside, and is recognized as truth. Truth is constructed by individuals, hence the term constructivism. If we add to this mix the criterion of functionality – what is true is what works – we have arrived at instrumentalism or pragmatism.[79]

What might a Christian response look like?

Contours of a Christian Theory of Understanding in a Postmodern World

Hempelmann and Hiebert suggest similar paths. Hempelmann pleads for an ongoing, never-ending fight for the truth. He rejects postmodern pluralism when it comes to an understanding of the nature of truth. He does not suggest, however, a return to pre-modern times. That would not only be impossible. It would also be wrong, because Paul's statement that "we know in part" (1 Cor 13:12) makes clear that truth and understanding are not one and the same.

Hiebert's proposal, from a Christian perspective, to choose a path of "critical realism" is similar. Neither the naïve realism of the pre-modern world, nor the constructivism, relativism and pragmatism of the postmodern world can do justice to the Christian faith. Only the careful and critical differentiation between truth and understanding will do, according to Hiebert.

Both Hempelmann and Hiebert make use of a modified form of Kuhn's paradigm theory to create a place for theology in the world of science.[80]

---

79. Cf. the overview that Hiebert gives by means of a table showing the step-by-step development of the theory of understanding. Hiebert, *Missiological Implications*, 38, 70.
80. Cf. Hemplemann, *Kritischer Rationalismus*, 269–288; Hiebert, *Missiological Implications*, 42–45, 68–116.

Integrating Theory and Practice in Theological Education

Hiebert prefers to speak of a configuration of understanding rather than of a paradigmatic theory of understanding.[81] His thesis is that we use real and objective data to configure theories that go beyond the data. Thus a connection to truth and reality is established. The "facts" are external to the person and are not constructs of his thinking. On the other hand, our theories are not photographic images of these truths and realities but are (human) configurations, which are always culturally and contextually conditioned. Hiebert sees value in these insights in view of the global nature of today's church and cross-cultural missions, as the title of his book indicates.

Implications for Theological Education[82]

What does this mean for theological education? The challenge to theological education, based on Hiebert's input, can be illustrated in three figures:

A first model of the theory of understanding depicts how theology has been taught traditionally, particularly in evangelical schools (figure 10):

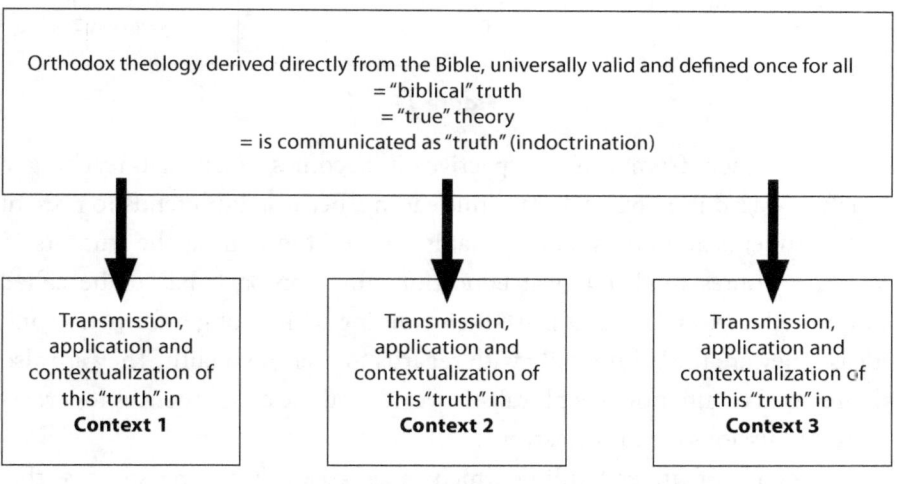

Figure 10

This epistemological model reflects naïve pre-modern realism. There is not enough differentiation between truth (and its revelation in the Bible) and

---

81. Ibid., 78.

82. For what follows, see the concluding chapter of my dissertation, *Beyond Fragmentation*, 294–316. Further reasoning and sources can be found there.

understanding (as articulated in theology). It is assumed that we are able to formulate a universally valid orthodox theology that can serve as objective truth alongside the Bible.

This view of the theory of understanding falls victim to an illusion. In reality, what happens looks like this:

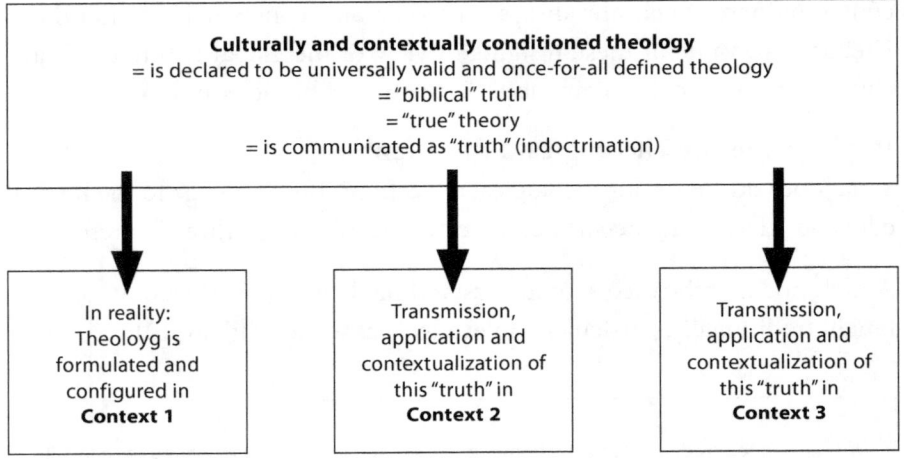

Figure 11

When seen from this perspective, it becomes clear that teaching a theology based in naïve realism is misleading, because it pretends to present to the students an understanding that is one and the same as the truth itself. When it comes to theological education, this approach has to be called inferior education. Students leave their training with wrong information and ideas. They are misled not only with regards to their own faith. They are also ill prepared to function in a pluralistic world, and the consequences for cross-cultural missions can be disastrous.

A theory of understanding which takes seriously the perspective that Hiebert proposes is seen in figure 12.[83]

---

83. Cf. Hiebert, *Missiological Implications*, 70, 113.

Integrating Theory and Practice in Theological Education

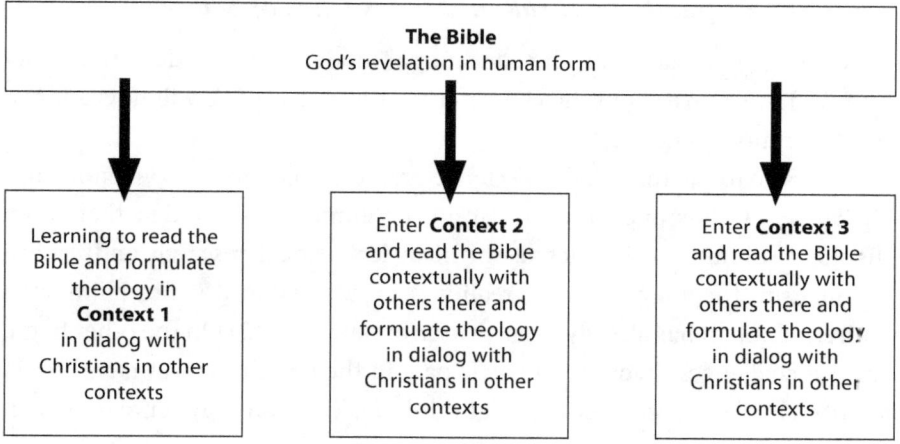

Figure 12

In summary, the implications for theological education are:[84]

1) Students must learn to distinguish between understanding and truth.

2) The primary task of theological education is not simply to teach theology as truth, but rather to teach the skill of theologizing. Hermeneutics and the contextual formulation of theology are therefore crucial.

3) Students must become aware of the context of their own theology and of the theological traditions by which they are influenced.

4) Contextualization must not be limited to the contextual application of a pre-defined theology. It must also include the contextual formulation of theology itself.

5) The Bible, as *norma normans*, remains the only standard by which theology must be measured.

6) Theology should be taught positively, in a way that places criticism in proper relation to the whole, with the sensitivity of a counsellor and with a view toward advancing the students' progress.

---

84. Cf. also Sedmak, *Theologie als "Handwerk"*.

5.3.5 The Capacity to Think and the Nature of Science

When we first spoke about the educational model of the modern university (at 3.3.1), we spoke about the characteristics of science. We will now address this topic more concretely.

It is safe to say that modern science presents theology with an enormous challenge. (1) For one thing, it cannot be emphasized enough that when theology submits to the dictates of historical-critical research and critical rationalism, theology's span of reality is greatly reduced if not eliminated entirely. Enough has already been written about this.[85] (2) On the other hand, science challenges theology to participate in the search for truth, and to do so with clear and precise conceptual thinking. That can only serve to benefit theology.

This challenge is not lessened by the insights of intercultural studies (cf. Enns). On the one hand, the contribution of Western thought lies in its logic and conceptual-linguistic precision. On the other hand, Western thought must acknowledge that traditional analytical thinking is often rather reductionist. Other cultures of thought can serve to broaden the horizon.[86]

At whatever level theological education is offered, the following elements of the scientific method should be practiced.

Linguistic Precision and Clarity of Thought

Here we must first deal with the basic elements of thought. In higher education it is normally assumed that students have acquired these intellectual skills during their secondary education. But that is not always the case. Many independent seminaries (those not within state universities) often admit students who have not completed a standard secondary-level education but who have instead learned a trade in a dual track system. In this case, it is less likely that such students have acquired the basic skills of analytical thinking.

Current instructions for scientific work typically do not touch on these basic skills. They simply describe the methodological process involved in researching and writing scientific works. I am therefore citing a somewhat older yet still valuable text, the chapter by Ulrich Beer entitled "Denken –

---

85. Outstanding in this regard, Hempelmann, *Kritischer Rationalismus*.
86. Cf. Enns, "Now I Know in Part," 256–265.

(k)eine Kunst" [The Art of Thinking].[87] It will suffice here to briefly mention the individual elements (those who are want a more detailed description can refer to the source):

Terms:
- Differentiation between the *thing*, the *term*, and the *word*.
- Understanding of levels of abstraction.
- Clarifying terms according to *content* (consisting of characteristics) and *scope* (consisting of subterms).
- Mastering principles of *definition* (a. Identifying within a category. b. Naming specifics.)

Clear and precise terminology and definitions serve to clarify communication.

The typical mistakes made in the area of definitions and terminology are:
- The same terms used differently within the same work or project.
- Using terms that are filled with different meaning in other contexts.
- Erroneous and imprecise use of terms.
- Using the term that is to be defined in the definition itself.

Opinions and Conclusions:
- Understanding terms as packaged opinions – and vice versa, opinions as unpackaged terms.
- Correctly using conclusions as associations (networks) of terms.

Clarity of thought is crucial. Those who do not master this skill will form erroneous opinions and reach false conclusions. Their thinking will be misguided.

Common mistakes with regard to findings and conclusions are:
- False generalizations.
- Over-simplification (simplifying in a way that distorts the truth instead of simplifying by identifying key elements).
- Subjective and unfounded value judgments.
- Halo effect (non-factual attribution of characteristics based on invalid associations; a form of cognitive bias in which readily

---

87. In Ulrich Beer, *Methoden der geistigen Arbeit* (Tübingen: Katzmann, 1978), 84–96.

identified external characteristics lead to inaccurate assumptions about internal or less readily identified qualities).
- Using arguments and assumptions that first must be proven.
- Trap reasoning (e.g. presenting false alternatives, false comparisons, using straw men).

The (desired) precision in thought and language should not be confused with more complicated and less comprehensible scholarly language. Of course it is true that complex subject matter must often be handled with ambitious, exacting language. In the final analysis, however, clear and precise language that satisfies the demands of science can be simple and understandable.

Critical Thinking

A further dimension of scientific work is critical thinking. Despite the common perception to the contrary, this does not mean that a critical thinker questions everything, constantly complains, and is against everything. Drawing from its Greek roots, the term "critical" simply means that judgments must be formed and decisions made. Critical thinking means nothing more, therefore, than being mentally alert and forming judgments.

When engaging in critical thinking, several levels of criticism can be differentiated:
- Critical reception of information (teaching, lectures): I must decide what I do with the information I receive, how I organize it, what value I give to it, etc.
- Self-criticism: I question my own thinking, and I evaluate my previous opinions and way of thinking in light of new information, etc.
- Openness to criticism: I receive criticism directed toward me, evaluate it, weigh it, and make decisions.
- Evaluate, judge: I compare various positions and can make informed, reasoned judgments.

Intellectual Virtues

This "art of thinking" (Beer) is no luxury and is not something that is opposed to Christian faith. Quite the contrary: in view of the fact that God created human beings as thinking creatures, the perfection of our powers of thought should be seen as "loving God with all our minds" and ultimately as an act of worship. "Good" and "right" thinking has an ethical-moral dimension. It is

Integrating Theory and Practice in Theological Education 255

justifiable to speak of intellectual virtue. W. Jay Wood presents a compelling summary in his book *Epistemology: Becoming Intellectually Virtuous*.[88] Based on Wood's work, we can identify four areas of intellectual integrity:

- Virtues in terms of *acquiring knowledge*: a thirst for knowledge, curiosity, a willingness to learn, a love of the truth, intellectual integrity, perseverance, powers of observation, willingness to prudently consider all circumstances and consequences, endurance.
- Virtues in terms of *retaining knowledge*: precision and truth in remembering; the ability to retain knowledge through understanding and comprehension; the ability to articulate and defend.
- Virtues in terms of *communicating knowledge*: communication skills, precision and honesty in communicating knowledge, an awareness of the dangers of manipulation and deceit, an ethical approach to knowledge as power.
- Virtues in terms of *applying knowledge*: consistency in application; harmony between thought and action, words and deeds; integrity, wisdom, and appropriateness.

If we consider intellectual work from this perspective, it becomes perfectly clear that thinking is *practiced*. We have every right to expect exceptional ethical behavior and attitudes in the intellectual work involved in theological education (and from all Christian thinkers).

In summary, we can, at the end of this chapter, maintain three things:

- We can differentiate between reflection and action, between thinking and doing; but we cannot simply set theory and practice over against one another. Thinking is part of the practice of life. A good education will, therefore, teach students to *practice* intellectual work ethically and responsibly as part of their lives.
- Reflection and action, thinking and doing, must be held in relation to one another. Thinking just for the sake of thinking is bad practice. The relationship between reflection and action can, however, vary from situation to situation. It is not the task of the educational process to teach the one and only correct relationship

---

88. W. Jay Wood, *Epistemology: Becoming Intellectually Virtuous* (Downers Grove: InterVarsity Press, 1998).

between reflection and action. Good teachers have access to a whole repertoire of theories and forms of thought, each with its own relationship to life and living.
- Within this framework, various educational programs may have differing emphases in terms of the relationship between theory and practice. In a university setting, praxis will have a different status than in a discipleship training course or an adult education seminar. In any setting, however, good and ethically responsible intellectual work must be done, always with real-life application – practice, action – in mind.

We will now turn our attention to this practice/action, by considering the word *poiesis*.

5.4 *Poiesis*: Competencies and Skills

We are in the process of forming a holistic view of education using the three terms *Praxis*, *Theoria*, and *Poiesis*. We have come to understand *praxis* as a wise way of life which doesn't (yet) have individual productive acts as its aim, but rather includes the whole of existence. In this sense, both reflection and action, both thinking and doing, are a part of *praxis*. Second, we have understood *theoria* to encompass the intellectual, thinking, reflecting side of human life. Now we turn to the third area, to *poiesis*.

1) When we speak of *poiesis*, we most decidedly and concretely mean action, behavior. Not talking about or thinking about action, but action itself. In the introduction to this chapter we saw that *poiesis* can be understood as productive *praxis* which has as its goal the concrete making of something. The required competency is *ability*. The Greek term *techne* is used in this context. It's about technique, skills. *Poiesis* can be understood as a means to an end. The value is not in the *techne* itself, but rather in the product that is made.

It is not easy to find a suitable word in our language for *poiesis*. We often say praxis, but that is confusing, since the first of these three concepts carries the label *praxis*. I suggest that we use the term *skills* from now on.

2) Skills can *only* be acquired by the practical execution of activities, that is, by practice. We must be consistent here. An educational program or training

course cannot teach skills without practice. We may distinguish between (classroom) instruction and training. *Vocational skills cannot, for the most part, be learned in the classroom.*[89] That means specifically that when we formulate action-oriented instructional goals for course descriptions ("At the end of this course, students will be able to . . ."), those goals cannot realistically go beyond what will actually be *done* (practiced) in the course in question. In a course (or curriculum) in counselling, it cannot be an instructional goal that by the end of the course, participants will be able to lead a counselling session, unless students actually lead counselling sessions as part of the course. That doesn't mean this must be included. It simply means that instructional goals must be realistically formulated. Every educational program, every curriculum, must have clear expectations about what it can deliver in terms of *skills*. What can theological education deliver?

3) The question cannot be answered in a one-size-fits-all manner. It depends which educational model is being used for a particular course of theological training. Theological training institutions must be very clear about what they are, and what they are not; about what they can and cannot deliver. In chapter 3 we learned about the university (academic) model and the vocational education (dual track) model. These two models differ significantly in what they can deliver in the way of vocational skills.

4) Higher (tertiary) education by definition is not primarily seeking to impart vocational skills. Ute Woschnack and Peter M. Frischknecht from ETH Zürich write:

> Although the marketplace is demanding more and more graduates from universities, the primary goal of the universities is not a practical education like that offered by vocational schools. The strength of the universities is to teach specialized subject matter and equip students for scientific work.[90]

Two things are thus paramount in a university education: 1. Specialized knowledge – that belongs in the arena of *theoria*. 2. Scientific work – that is

---

89. Cf. Klaus W. Döring and Bettina Ritter-Mamczek, *Lehren und Trainieren in der Weiterbildung* (Weinheim: Beltz, 1999), 21–22.
90. Ute Woschnak and Peter M. Frischknecht, "Schüsselqualifikationen – Vom Arbeitsmarkt verlangt! Von der Hochschule gelehrt?," *Personal* 54, no. 10 (2002): 27.

the skill, the "trade" of creating a product (a scientific work or project) using appropriate means and techniques.

This educational philosophy was the norm for theology as a course of higher (tertiary) education through the end of the 20th century. An interview with Ekkehard Stegemann and Ulrich Gäbler, two professors in Basel, gives poignant expression to this fact:

> **Question:** "Is the generation of theological students that you are training capable of entering the pastorate at the conclusion of their studies?"
>
> **Stegemann:** "Of course they need the Vicariate (a period of time akin to a medical residency). And you must realize that the job of a pastor is an intellectual one, not a practical one. A student must therefore first of all acquire intellectual competencies."
>
> **Gäbler:** ". . . We train our students to recognize problems and then to overcome these problems theologically. This requires, however, additional training (Vicariate or apprenticeship or residency).
>
> **Question:** "What is the relationship between praxis and theory (doctrine) in their course of study?"
>
> **Stegemann:** "When students pose this question, my response is: 'Your praxis now is to make yourselves theologically competent.'"
>
> **Gäbler:** "What is praxis? The pastorate in a church? We can't keep transmitting romanticized ideas. For me, praxis is the recognition of societal problems and the ability to find language for them."[91]

It's clear in this classic understanding of higher education that *training* in pastoral skills is not intended to be part of a university theological education. That doesn't mean, of course, that no vocationally relevant skills at all are learned or practiced. It means that such skills are those that involve intellectual work, use of the scientific method, and reflection.

---

91. Ekkehard Stegemann and Ulrich Gäbler, "Früh Kontakt mit den Kirchen suchen," *Basler Zeitung*, April 3 (1995): 7.

The acquiring of (or training in) pastoral skills is not forgotten entirely. It is relegated to the period which follows graduation – the Vicariate (= residency or apprenticeship).

This classic university model of theological education is not without its critics. When the Protestant theological faculty of the University of Bern issued new regulations for exams in 1999 and stated that "the study of theology provides only the academic foundation for pastors" and does not provide "pastoral training," considerable opposition ensued.[92]

New trends are developing in Switzerland as well. The Bologna reform of higher education affected the churches as well. The Reformed Churches of Switzerland, associated with one another in the Concordat, proposed an integrated model of pastoral training which would create a link between university education and the training of pastors from the very beginning. Thus the vocational training of pastors is understood to be a partnership between the church and the university. Therefore it is not an exaggeration to say that there has been a cultural shift in terms of pastoral training.[93]

5) Unlike a university education, the dual track model aims to teach specific practical skills. In order for this to happen, sufficient time has to be allotted for such training and practice to occur in a vocational real-world setting during the course of study. This normally happens through an apprenticeship in the desired vocational field, through an extended practicum (or internship), or in specialized apprentice shops. Regardless of the specific format, vocational skills are acquired *on the job, learning by doing, praxis-integrated.*

6) Theological training institutions must clarify therefore what they want to accomplish, and what they don't intend to accomplish. Whatever model is decided upon, that which is done should be done well. False hopes should not be raised. A school that decides on a university (or university-like) model

---

92. Cornelia Nussberger, "Keine Pfarrerausbilding," *Reformierte Presse* 46 (1999): 7. How great a struggle there is to include practical training within the framework of an academic theological education is evident in two conversations published in the journal *Pastoraltheologie* 89 (2000). One is a dialog between Peter Bukowski and Eberhard Hauschildt ("Rückfragen an die akademische theologische Ausbildung," 474–482). The other consists of correspondence between Isolde Karle and Dietrich Stollberg ("Über den Pfarrberuf. Ein Briefwechsel zwischen Dieter Stollberg und Isolde Karle," 524–528).

93. Cf. *Annex*, magazine of the Reformed Press, 11, 2006. The text of the educational guidelines of the concordat can be found at http://www.konkordat.ch.

will, if it does its job well, be praxis-relevant, but it will not offer vocational training. And a school that decides to focus on practical training for tasks in the church and missions will not be able, in the same amount of time, to transmit intellectual competencies at a university level. It is not a university or university equivalent.

A clear declaration of purpose is particularly problematic for those schools that operate somewhere in between these two models. I am thinking here of certain Bible schools and missionary training institutions that do not offer an academic (university level) course of study, but rather seek to provide practical training. What that looks like exactly often remains unclear. If the training provided is based primarily on classroom instruction, then the practical skills are often neglected. Real vocational training is lacking. The instructional content may be praxis oriented, but it still remains *theoria*. Often such institutions offer a high level of *functional theory*, which we earlier called *how-to* theory. Students are told how something is to be done, but they don't actually do it. That is not wrong, but it must be explicitly declared to be what it is: It is the theory of praxis.

Even for evangelical and denominational seminaries that are striving for university-level recognition, there is often the need to clarify purpose. Even if training for pastoral ministry or missions is the clearly stated educational goal, and even if praxis orientation is strived for in the pattern of the best universities of applied sciences (technical academies),[94] false hopes should not be raised in terms of practical training. It is only training aimed at *poieme* if practical training occurs in a real-world vocational setting. Evangelical and denominational seminaries are often confronted with churches that are not prepared to offer graduates a vicariate (residency / extended internship). Therefore any real practical vocational training must happen while the students are enrolled in the seminary. At the same time, these schools are striving for an academic level equivalent to the university. To actually make both things happen simultaneously is extremely challenging, and I confess to harboring serious doubts as to whether this has ever been successfully achieved.[95]

---

94. On the educational philosophy of such technical academies/universities of applied sciences, see section 3.3.5.

95. Cf. the discussion related to the theological seminary of the Bundes Evangelisch-Freikirchlicher Gemeinden in Elstal: Mallau, *Theologiestudium*, and Strübind, *Pastoren*.

Integrating Theory and Practice in Theological Education 261

7) This plea for a clear definition of what will be accomplished (and what won't) in terms of practical vocational training for pastors and missionaries during their course of study is also directed to the study of "practical theology." It is not uncommon to encounter unrealistic expectations for the study of practical theology which are based on misunderstandings. Practical theology, as introduced into the curriculum of theological studies by Schleiermacher, is certainly praxis oriented and should be relevant to real-life praxis. Practice in exercising intellectual competencies is provided – skills that will be used in pastoral ministry. But practical theology does not aim to be vocational training for all of pastoral *poiesis*. In current definitions, two benefits of practical theology are often emphasized: (a) For one thing, practical theology is *applied science* in the sense that it attempts to think theologically about praxis. (b) For another thing, practical theology is *observational science* which observes the realities and phenomena of religious life and then develops these observations into articulated theories.[96] But for all of that, it remains theory.

North American seminaries, like the evangelical and denominational seminaries in Europe, tend to view practical theology more in terms of the old (= prior to Schleiermacher) *pastoral theology*, that is, as an instructional manual for pastoral ministry.[97] Yet even there, practical theology is mostly theory. It is *functional theory*, which teaches how a thing ought to be done, but which usually does not include actual real-life practice.[98]

8) What do these rather lengthy introductory thoughts mean in terms of *poiesis*, which is the subject of this section? When we talk about *poiesis* (= skills), we cannot hide behind terms like *praxis oriented, praxis relevant*, or *practical theology*. Of course all these things are important and have their place. But here we must go beyond all forms of *theoria* and move into the realm of execution, practice, action, training. In the terminology that is currently used in certified vocational training, we have to speak now about *key qualifications, key competencies,* and *vocational-specific qualifications*.

---

96. Cf. Nicol, *Grundwissen Praktische Theologie*, 243–257.
97. Cf. Schröer, *Einführung*, 151.
98. As we saw earlier, Edward Farley's criticism is directed to just this point. The study of theology becomes a pastoral *how-to theory*. That may produce technical specialists, according to Farley, but it produces neither theologians nor wise and mature personalities.

5.4.1 Key Qualifications, Key Competencies

1) Key qualifications are about competencies that go "beyond specialized, vocational knowledge."[99] Dieter Mertens, who introduced the term into the conversation within the world of vocational instruction, understood key qualifications to be,

> such knowledge, skills, and abilities that don't necessarily show direct relationship to specific practical activities but rather which (a) comprise the aptitude to hold a number of positions and accomplish multiple functions simultaneously and (b) the aptitude to master a series of (usually unforeseen) changes and challenges throughout life.[100]

This reveals the insight that in order to succeed in work and in life, a person needs not only work-specific skills but also a variety of life skills that go beyond any particular vocation. Moreover, in an era marked by increasing mobility and a rapid rate of change, no one will be able to rely for a lifetime on vocational skills learned during their initial education. Changes in the employment market and in workplace practices demand high levels of mobility and flexibility from everyone. What counts are the skills and competencies that enable people to succeed beyond their specialized vocational knowledge, that is, to adjust quickly and reliably to new situations that were not necessarily part of their original vocational training, and to acquire the knowledge and skills which the new situation demands.

By now the concept of "key qualifications" has become an essential topic in vocational training. The literature on this topic is abundant. It is not my intention to reference the whole scope of this literature.[101] However

---

99. Woschnak and Frischknecht, *Schlüsselqualifikationen*, 26.

100. Dieter Mertens, "Schlüsselqualifikationen. Thesen zur Schulung für eine moderne Gesellschaft," in *Wirtschaft – Arbeit – Beruf – Bildung: Dieter Mertens: Schriften und Vorträge 1968 – 1987*, eds. Friedrich Buttler and Lutz Reyher (Nürnberg: Institut für Arbeitsmarkt- und Berufsforschung, 1991), 566.

101. Foundational to the current discussion in the field of education are the definitions of competencies in the OECD Program for International Student Assessment (PISA): The German document bears the title "Definitionen und Auswahl von Schlüsselkompetenzen" at http://www.oecd.org/pisa/35693281.pdf. Equally valuable are the definitions of the national qualifications guidelines in the educational sector, e.g. "Deutscher Qualifikationsrahmen für lebenslanges Lernen" (DQR) at http://www.deutscherqualifikationsrahmen.de/

some clarification with regards to theological education may be helpful and important.

2) The terms "competencies" and "qualifications" are often used interchangeably and without distinction. Actually competency is the newer term, which has begun to replace "qualifications" in recent years.

> The term "qualifications" had become problematic because it sought to combine the handling of situational demands (a specific activity) and the personal qualities needed to do so. Competencies are less about vocational demands or activities and more about the general disposition of people which enables them to meet the demands of life and the world.[102]

The term competency goes beyond the transmission and replication of knowledge and skills to "meeting the demands of life and the world." It is about the capacity to integrate. The now classic definition by Franz E. Weinert puts it this way:

> Competencies mean "the cognitive skills and abilities that an individual possesses or can acquire in order to solve problems, as well as the motivational, volitional and social willingness and ability to apply these solutions successfully and responsibly in a variety of situations."[103]

3) Over the past thirty years a number of lists of key qualifications have been compiled. The following four-fold classification is widely used:
- Technical competencies
- Methodological competencies
- Social competencies
- Personal competencies

Although this framework can readily be called "classic," it is not without its critics. Opponents have noted that technical competencies don't really belong to key competencies; that it is difficult to distinguish between technical and methodological competencies; and that methodological competencies

---

102. http://de.wikipedia.org/wiki/Kompetenz(Pädagogik). Cf. Philipp Gonon, "Neue Studien zum Thema Schlüsselqualifikationen," *Panorama* 6 (2002): 11.
103. Franz E. Weinert, *Leistungsmessungen in Schulen* (Weinheim and Basel: Beltz, 2002), 27.

belong to a lower, more detailed level of classification.[104] One of the most compelling newer frameworks comes from Dieter Euler, who starts with three basic relational spheres people face:[105]

Objective Competencies: Skill in dealing with materials or symbolic objects, objects in nature, in culture, resources, tools, machines, computers, texts, formulas, etc.

Social Competencies: Skill in dealing with other people in various constellations of relationships, e.g. families, groups, teams, communities.

Self Competencies: Skill in dealing with facets of one's self, e.g. emotions (anxiety, aggression) or behavioral patterns.

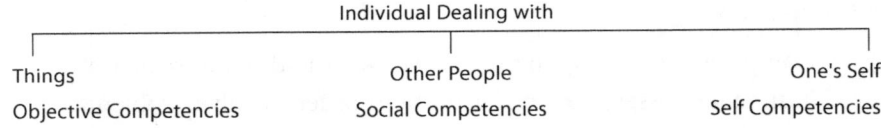

Figure 13

Although Euler's framework is logical and persuasive, in the real world of schools and businesses, lists of competencies are compiled that seem to be relevant to the particular situation.

4) Regarding theological education, William Faix, in a provocative study, demonstrated the relevance and potential for application.[106] Faix not only shows the need for theological education to adopt key qualifications. He also compiles a list of key qualifications that he compares to similar lists often appearing in job listings, demonstrating that the skills needed in other vocations are also relevant for employment in the church.

---

104. Dieter Euler, "Schlüsselqualifikationen zwischen Idee und Wirklichkeit," *Panorama* 6 (2002): 15.
105. Ibid., figure.
106. Faix, "Die Bedeutung von Schlüsselqualifikationen."

5) How can insights like these influence education? While there has been much high quality thought and discussion about key qualifications for years, "the impact on vocational training has not gone beyond rhetoric."[107] There is still a long way to go before there is a successful application in vocational training. It has only been very recently that schools have started consistently building key competencies into the teaching plans. Moreover we have only just begun the process of assessing key qualifications.[108] When we discuss possible applications in the sections that follow, it must be kept in mind that we are moving in largely unexplored territory.

Regarding theological education, the following is a list of helpful literature:
As part of its accreditation guidelines, the EEAA made available a list of key competencies for theological education (http://www.theologicaleducation.net/articles/view.htm?id=9).
The topic of "compentency-oriented theological education" is comprehensively treated in several volumes of "Theologie und Hochschuldidaktik" [Theology and the Didactics of Higher Education]:
Monika Scheidler and Oliver Reis, eds. *Vom Lehren zum Lernen. Didaktische Wende in der Theologie* [From Teaching to Learning: Didactic Turning Point in Theology]. Münster: LIT, 2008.
Florian Bruckmann, Oliver Reis, and Monika Scheidler, eds. *Kompetenzorientierte Lehre in der Theologie. Konkretionen-Reflexion-Perspektiven* [Competency-orientation in Theology: Concrete Steps, Reflections, Perspectives]. Münster: LIT, 2011.

6) When it comes to encouraging the use of core competencies and key qualifications in the classroom, we first have to think about the pedagogical and didactic (im-)possibilities, including the following:
- Experts are agreed that key qualifications are not learned by just talking about them but by creating situations in which these competencies and skills can be practiced. That does not rule out the possibility of teaching content about key competencies at

---

107. Euler, "Schlüsselqualifikationen," 15.
108. Cf. Günter Klein and Jürgen Ripper on early efforts to evaluate key qualifications in school settings: "Schlüsselqualifikationen im Blickpunkt," *Magazin Schule* 9 (2003): 10–11; also at http://www.kultusportal-bw.de/servlet/PB/menu/1190230/index.html.

the appropriate time. But the primary place of learning for key qualifications is surely not a classroom lecture on the topic.

- Moreover it must be remembered that an individual's core competencies and key qualifications are revealed in their life story as well as in their gifts and personality. It is therefore not possible to define one set of core competencies for everyone. Instead, each individual must be encouraged to develop core competencies based on his/her own personal history, gifts, and personality.[109]

- Experts define competency as knowledge + experience + attitude.[110] That means that formal schooling can have only a limited influence on the development of key qualifications. Especially in the early stages of vocational education it is true that: "Education cannot deliver competencies in this sense because the component 'experience' is lacking."[111] Even where a practicum or internship or other method aims to provide experience, we should be under no illusions as to their effectiveness. Essential core competencies can only be learned in real-life vocational situations, "by handling the real-world daily business of the job, by dealing with specific challenges like pursuing one's own project ideas or assuming responsibility for important tasks."[112] Real-life situations like these can only be partially and artificially replicated within the setting of an internship. Thus the entire responsibility for acquiring core competencies and key qualifications cannot be assigned to the educational process. One only acquires core competencies in life, and life is more than formal training and education.

- Educational institutions should, however, deliberately and professionally assume responsibility for their part in encouraging the development of key qualifications. In the school environment it is true that: "The development of key qualifications does not happen automatically. It is the result of an intentional structuring of the teaching-learning process." That is why the use of "specific

---

109. Cf. the intriguing attempt by Faix to link key qualifications to the personality assessment tool PST-R ("Die Bedeutung von Schlüsselqualifikationen," 205–206.)
110. Cf. http://www.olev.de/p/potenzial_v_mitarb.htm#DefinitionSQ.
111. Ibid.
112. Woschnak and Frischknecht, "Schlüsselqualifikationen," 30.

teaching methods" is essential.[113] We will discuss some of these more specifically in chapter 6 in conjunction with the development of teaching plans.

5.4.2 Vocational-Specific Skills

We turn now to the acquiring of vocational-specific skills.

1) First we will need to get an overview of the "ecclesiastical fields of operation," that is, of the vocational realities graduates will face. Martin Nicol, drawing on *Grundwissen Praktische Theologie* [Basic Knowledge of Practical Theology], lists the following arenas:

- Church planting, church growth, and church leadership
- Worship and liturgy
- Preaching
- Pastoral counselling
- Christian education (Sunday school, etc.), religious instruction
- Compassion and justice ministries; serving the poor, the ill, the needy, the marginalized

In addition to these classic pastoral ministries Nocol lists:

- Media, publicity, communications
- Talking about God (Bible – language)
- Celebrating life (spirituality – everyday life)
- Fashioning transitions (life history – church calendar)
- Observing form (art – religion)

Going beyond Nocol's list, I would like to add specifically:

- Missions, evangelism
- Interchurch (ecumenical) dialogue and cooperation
- Political involvement and work for peace

The aim here is not to propose a practical theology and to discuss all the possible arenas of activity. This overview is only intended to demonstrate areas in which specific competencies are needed. And then the question arises: How and where will these competencies be acquired?

---

113. Euler, "Schlüsselqualifikationen," 15.

2) The first, basic answer is: skills are only acquired *by doing*. It is important to be consistent here. Skills are not acquired by talking about them. We saw earlier that *theoria* is important and can and should be praxis-relevant. But no amount of thought or talk *about* church ministry can take the place of actually *doing* church ministry. Somewhere, somehow, during the course of theological education, there must be the chance to actually and actively *do* ministry tasks.

3) It is certainly true that teaching and learning vocational skills can only happen in a partnership between various actors. It cannot be the goal of educational institutions to teach or deliver every possible vocational skill within the structures of the school itself. Partnerships must be formed with churches, mission agencies, nonprofit organizations, and other potential employers, in order to work together to provide the necessary structures for supervision. Additional concrete steps in curriculum development will be discussed in chapter 6.

In this chapter we have attempted to form a holistic and integral view of education, using the three concepts *Praxis*, *Theoria*, and *Poiesis*. We have set the three terms alongside one another, and the inter-connection and interplay among them has become clear. In particular, I have suggested that we view *Praxis* (way of life, wisdom) as *Theoria* (thinking), and that we view *Poiesis* (action, behavior) as a comprehensive, integrating force. And now the question arises, how integral teaching and learning processes can be concretely applied. That is what the next chapter is about.

6

Curriculum Development in Theological Education

Equipped with all the knowledge we have gained thus far, we are now able to proceed with the task of developing training programs for theological education. I am talking about *proactive* program development. This means that we not simply offer predefined courses of study that have been developed over time, and that we do more than make changes in established curricula in *reaction* to new challenges. Instead, we look *ahead* and develop programs that anticipate the future. This is a challenging task requiring enormous foresight.

This chapter begins with a transitional section that leads us from where we have come thus far to the practical task of curriculum development (section 6.1). Section 6.2 presents the thesis that curriculum development must be done in partnership. Sections 6.3, 6.4, and 6.5 deal with the process of curriculum development following the classical steps: 1) starting point, 2) goal formulation, 3) from starting point to the goal.

6.1 Foundational Considerations[1]

6.1.1 WHO? The Question of Responsibility and Support

1) The question of "Who?" should not be answered hastily with "the theological schools and training institutions." If we take seriously everything

---

1. This section is based on a lecture I presented at the Congrès 2000 de l'Association d'Églises de Professeurs des Pays Francophones at the Institut Biblique et Missionaire Emmaüs, St.-Légier, 16–18 April 2000, entitled "Erneuerung der theologischen Ausbildung für die

we've heard thus far, we will realize that theological education must happen in partnership. In recent years Patrick Johnstone has called for churches, mission societies, and training institutions to work together to accomplish the work of Christian missions.[2] Such an appeal must be welcomed, even though it seems to me that what Johnstone calls partnership is merely an appeal for churches and schools to become better personnel recruiters for world missions.

2) Theological seminaries, churches, and mission/service organizations definitely belong together. They share a common task – to train the next generation of volunteers and leaders. But it's also understandable that churches and theological schools live with a certain level of constructive tension in their relationship to one another. Theological education must be close enough to the pulse of church and missions to understand the agenda and the mission of the church, and at the same time maintain enough distance to be able to have something to say from the perspective of the Bible, history, and broader reflection.

3) The *proximity* of theological education to the church, missions and service will mean that schools no longer formulate goals, define curricula, and develop teaching plans in the isolation of the ivory towers of academia, but rather in dialogue with alumni and with representatives from the church, missions, and service organizations. Relevance and proximity will also be enhanced if professors and instructors are themselves involved in ministry in the church, missions, and/or service organizations.

4) The requisite *distance* can be ensured if the church gives its training schools freedom and if the schools *use* this freedom and where necessary fight for it. Only then can the tasks of research, reflection, and instruction be done without being dominated solely by the current needs of the grass roots. These are important, but it is equally important that theological education, drawing from the reservoir of biblical and ecclesiological tradition, address topics

---

Erneuerung der Gemeinde." An earlier version was published as the closing chapter of the article "Theologische Ausbildung im Spannungsfeld von Theorie und Praxis," *Jahrbuch für Evangelikale Theologie* 17 (2003): 149–196.

2. Patrick Johnstone, *Viel größer als man denkt: Auftrag und Wachsen der Gemeinde Jesu* (Holzgerlingen: Hänssler, 1999), especially the diagram p. 340.

that no one wants to address but which need to be addressed thoughtfully and prophetically.

5) Theological education built on partnership also means that responsibility for training rests together upon leaders, staff, and volunteers – in full awareness of the fact that both the church (or mission agency) and the school play a role in a person's training. It's a mistaken belief (that is nonetheless widely held) that the training institution is solely responsible for the whole of a person's education, that a person's training can be completely delegated to the school, that students finish their schooling fully trained, and then begin their ministry in the church *complete*, ready to go. We could wish for a partnership between church, mission, school, and students in which each partner recognizes that they all shoulder responsibility together. This can even be formalized through a contract in which each partner assumes responsibility for his or her role. This can ensure that calling, practical experience, theoretical input, critical thinking, coaching, evaluation and vocational decisions are integrated and not played off one against the other. In the following section, we will examine in more detail what this kind of educational partnership can look like.

6.1.2 WHAT? *The Question of Goals and Content*

The orientation toward the church and its mission mentioned earlier must be consistently brought to bear when it comes to developing curriculum, formulating instructional goals, and determining content.

1) This means first of all that instructional goals will be formulated with the global responsibility of theological education in mind. Because the curricula of many theological schools are still strongly shaped by traditional theological education, the formulation of precise instructional goals is often lacking. To simply distribute the usual courses in Bible, history, systematic theology and practical theology in the usual proportions into the time available in the typical student calendar will not result in goal-oriented education that will satisfy the demands of today's pedagogy. The formulation of instructional goals must be precise, and it must be undertaken in partnership between school and church, as described above.

Well-formulated goals include cognitive, affective (emotional), and functional (behavioral) elements. Within these three broad categories there are more detailed sub-categories that make it possible to differentiate clearly between cognitive, affective and functional goals. For example, in the cognitive category, it is possible to distinguish between knowing, understanding, analyzing, synthesizing, and evaluating.[3] In this way, teachers and administrators, along with alumni and representatives from the church and mission, can best determine the appropriate requirements for graduation. These are best expressed through sentences which answer the question: What qualifications (skills) must students possess when they completes this program? A standard sentence that requires a concrete, behavioral answer may read something like this: "At the end of this course, students are able to..."

Processes like these are not an optional luxury. They are the norm in accredited institutions of learning. Often instructional goals are too heady, especially when they are formulated solely by teachers. Teachers concentrate too much on cognitive goals. Care must be given, therefore, to ensure that goals are formulated in all three areas. In view of the integration of theory and practice, goals which require synthesis and integration deserve special attention. This is where decisions are made that determine whether the integration of theory and practice will succeed or not.

2) A second step in developing curricula is to define content. It must be ensured that the individual courses constitute steps that lead to the educational goals. If the educational goals have been defined as described in step one above, this second step will often lead to a clash between the classical curriculum in its four-fold format and the goals that have been articulated. The question is: Who determines the priorities? If theological education is to remain faithful to the authority of the Scripture, then priorities cannot be determined simply by the situation of the current day. Rather, as custodian of the Christian faith, theological education has the responsibility of introducing an agenda into the current day. On the other hand, if theological education is to take seriously the questions of the church and its mission, then the agenda cannot be determined simply by the traditional list of course subject matter. The sentence attributed to Walter Hollenweger has its validity: "The world

---

3. For more on the classification of instructional goals see Nathaniel L. Gage and David C. Berliner, *Pädagogische Psychologie*, Volume 1 (Weinheim and Basel: Beltz, 1983), 45–53. Also in English under the title *Educational Psychology* (Boston: Houghton Mifflin, 1998), 6th revised edition.

sets the agenda."[4] Elsewhere I outlined the agenda that must be addressed by theological education today as follows:[5]

- Theology in the midst of changes and crises
- Theology in the tension between Bible and culture
- Theology in diversity and unity
- Farewell to one-sided rationalism
- Postmodern pluralistic view of truth
- Post-Christian pluralism of religions
- Ecclesiastical homework at the end of the Christian West
- Missions in a global context in the post-colonial era
- Taking a stand when ethical values are deteriorating

The more we succeed in bringing both of these agendas to bear in our curriculum development, the more convincing will be our integration of theory and practice. It will surely not suffice to encourage a few courses to build bridges into the present while most courses look to the past, following the agenda of tradition. Every course must face the questions of the present day and answer those questions in light of the wealth and perspective that tradition provides.

A more courageous and more integrative path is to design new courses which take up the challenges of the current day and seek to examine them in an interdisciplinary way, if possible using an interdisciplinary teaching team. The curriculum model developed by Andrew Kirk and introduced at the end of this chapter (6.6.1) goes even a step further and constructs a course of study that is missions-oriented and aims at integration from start to finish.

3) Finally there is a third step that involves the details of course descriptions, that is the formulation of course syllabi. Here too factors of integration can be considered. This starts with the definition of instructional goals, comparable to what was discussed earlier. And then it involves the detailed structure of the

---

4. Walter Hollenweger, "The World Is the Agenda," in *Die Kirche für andere*, ed. Walter Hollenweger (Geneva: World Council of Churches, 1967), 23–30.

5. Bernhard Ott, "Denken und Handeln im Kontext einer nachchristlichen Gesellschaft: eine Tagesordnung für Theologie und theologische Ausbildung in Westeuropa an der Schwelle zum 21.Jahrhundert," in *Gemeinde mit Zukunft: Herausforderungen und Perspektiven an der Schwelle zum 21. Jahrhundert: Symposium zur Eröffnung des Theologischen Seminars Bienenberg, 11-13 September 1998*, eds. Bernhard Ott et al. (Liestal: Ausbildungs- und Tagungszentrum Bienenberg, 1999), 8–30.

course. A course can simply follow the outline and structure of a textbook in its presentation of content, or it could, for example, follow the learning steps in Kirk's model, which very effectively incorporates principles of integration into all study assignments. If these are well formulated, they can lead students to think and work in an integrative manner from the very start. The terms *cognitive*, *affective* and *behavioral* can be useful categories when formulating study assignments. Sections 6.3 and 6.4 will deal even more specifically with curriculum development.

6.1.3 HOW? The Question of Processes and Methods

In the final analysis, integration has to be incorporated into the process and methods of education. It has to be reflected in how the learning process is structured as well as in the instructional methods of the classroom. Decisions made in these arenas will be foundational. To design an educational process that truly integrates theory and practice, it is essential to be familiar with the concepts of *deductive* and *inductive* learning introduced in section 5.3.3.[6]

1) We saw earlier that traditional educational models often function with a one-sided emphasis on deductive learning. Students learn theory from their teachers and from their textbooks, in the hopes that they will be able to apply the theory later in real-life situations. Piper diagrams the deductive learning approach in this way.

---

6. For what follows, see Piper, *Kommunizieren lernen*, especially the chapter "Erfahrung," 44–51.

Curriculum Development in Theological Education 275

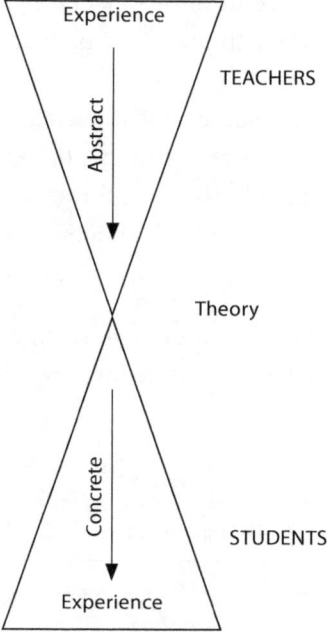

Figure 14

Deductive learning processes are those in which the teacher, as the knowing one, transmits that knowledge to the student, who is the unknowing one. The point of contact is the abstract theory. Deductive teaching has an important place but tends to be top down and heavily theoretical. The student has no direct access to the experiential reality that underlies the theory. It is left up to him to apply the abstract theory in his life in concrete ways. Unfortunately this happens only occasionally or with minimal success.

The deficiencies of this approach are well known:
- Education is seen as the transmission of theory and the acquiring of knowledge.
- Students have difficulty seeing the relevance of the theoretical learning, because they lack experiential application.
- Students lose motivation quickly if they see no connection to real-life experience. They feel overloaded with theory.
- There is a tendency to get stuck in the abstract and to see abstract reflection as an end in itself.

- Students have a surplus of theory upon graduation, a surplus that has to be balanced with practical application in vocational and life settings.
- Students tend to assume that knowledge can be communicated abstractly, that the "correct" theory can be learned and then applied.

Traditional courses of study that last for several years and are lacking in practical application tend to suffer from a one-sided, deductive approach to learning.

2) By way of contrast, there are inductive learning processes that seek to combine theory (reflection) and practice (action) in a dynamic and creative interaction (see figure 15).

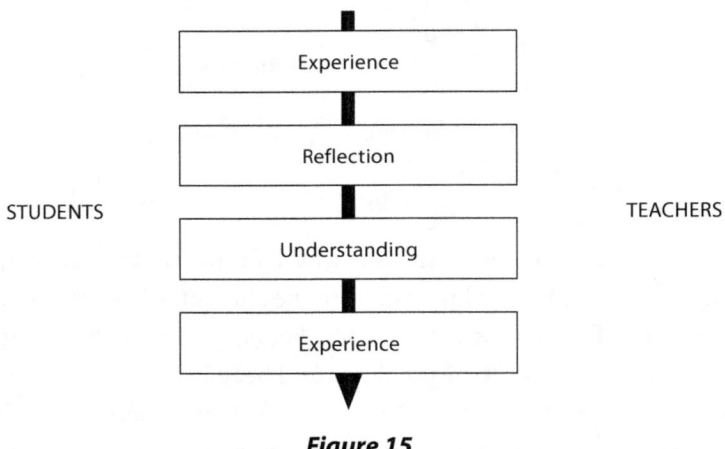

Figure 15

Inductive instruction is problem-oriented, relevant, and characterized by discovery. It is assumed that students will gain new insights through active observation and reasoning. The key experience is the "aha" moment, when the light bulb goes on, theory becomes real and is grasped in real-life practice. It is these "aha" moments that ultimately lead to experience, because "experience is . . . always understanding. To the extent to which I understand, I am able to integrate what has happened, so that it becomes part of my experience." Students who move from event to experience in this way are "ready to meet the challenges of similar events in the future."[7] The task of the instructor is to

---

7. Piper, *Kommunizieren lernen*, 46–47.

lead students from events to experience to readiness. There is, of course, also some deductive content to be communicated along the way.

Inductive learning includes the following characteristics:

- All theoretical content should be preceded by practical experience. The more practical experience is included, the higher the degree of learning.
- Theoretical content must help students to assess practical experience. What has been experienced must be included in classroom instruction.
- Theory that is learned through successful life experience results in "aha" moments (insights) instead of producing a sense of being oversaturated with theoretical head knowledge.
- Sufficient time must be allowed for theoretical reflection, so that it can be truly thoughtful and deep.
- Practical experience can be preceded by instruction in theory. The theory can then be tested in practice. Too much theory without practical application can demotivate students and lead to theory overload.
- Phases of theory and practice must be intentionally intertwined.

3) In summary, extremes are to be avoided in the structure of learning processes. Lengthy periods of theoretical study characterized mostly by deductive instruction without practical experience are definitely too heavily theoretical and cannot be considered to be integrative. However, long periods of practical experience with little or no theoretical input or time for reflection are equally unhelpful. It is difficult to determine what the ideal combination looks like. It will depend on a number of factors, including the student's own individual life story. Students who are at least thirty years old and have several years of ministry experience in the church or missions are likely to enjoy time spent on theory and reflection, so long as they result in "aha" moments. Young students confronted with the same amount of theory and reflection at the beginning of their course of study will likely find it too "heady" and theoretical because they will find it difficult to relate the theory to any practical life experience. Therefore it is desirable to offer different courses of study for different groups of students.

Equally important as alternating periods of theoretical and practical learning is the connection between the two. It is not uncommon for a course of study to alternate segments of theory with segments of practice, which have little or no relation to one another. Such a curriculum has only the illusion of integrating theory and practice. It is easy in such instances to fall prey to useless "additionalism" – constantly adding new practical or theoretical courses in order to restore balance, without ever achieving a real connection between theory and practice (more on this in 6.5).

4) This brings us to the arena of *methods*. It is clear from what has been said thus far that if there is to be true integration of theory and practice, it must happen in the area of instructional methods. In order to encourage the kind of connection between experience (e.g. internships) and classroom instruction that we've been discussing, measures like these may be necessary:[8]

- Study assignments during the semester refer directly to experience gained in internships done during the previous term and encourage thoughtful reflection about that practical experience.
- During an internship (or other practical/experiential phase of study), an academic assignment is given (reading, writing a paper), which is intended to help students reflect upon their practical experience.
- Integrative (interdisciplinary) courses.
- Integrative assignments in all courses.
- Work projects.
- Dissertations must show integrative treatment of their subject matter.
- Exams must test integration.

Moreover it is important for instructors to have sufficient teaching qualifications. They should be familiar with the concepts of the psychology of learning, such as Piaget's theory of the development of cognitive capacity.[9] Only then is it possible to design instruction that has the appropriate proportion of abstraction and concretion for the students.[10] It is also helpful to be familiar

---

8. Cf. Kurt Sohm, *Praxisbezogene Ausbildung auf Hochschulniveau*, 81–89.
9. Cf. Gage and Berliner, *Pädagogische Psychologie*, 348–358.
10. Cf. Michael Dieterich, *Auf dem Weg zum Beruf* (Hamburg: Handwerk und Technik, 1991), 101–109. Dieterich applied Piaget's theory of cognitive development to the vocational

with the concept of experiential instruction (to what degree instruction is praxis oriented). This is a useful tool in encouraging the integration of theory and practice.[11] In addition to such basic understanding, a teacher must be able to apply a variety of instructional approaches appropriately and draw upon a wide repertoire of methods which can be used goal- and situation-specifically in the classroom.[12] In this regard, every teacher needs continuing education (more on this in section 6.4).

6.1.4 WHERE? The Question of Context

1) Another basic decision related to the theory-practice debate has to do with the place or context in which education takes place. The classic education, following the neo-humanistic ideal, emphasized a classroom setting where students could be free from the burdens of vocation and every day life. Critics accused this model of being ivory-towered, too disconnected from the real world. These same critics call for a more praxis-integrated education, more akin to on-the-job training.[13]

---

training of tradesmen and tradeswomen. He discovered that not only can the gradual development of cognitive capacity be observed over the course of a lifetime, but that every learning process along the way is most successful when it takes this gradual cognitive development into consideration – beginning with a concrete action (practical experience), then formulating observations, then drawing conclusions about "laws of operation" and finally moving to constructing abstract theories. Dieterich adds an additional phase, which he calls "synoptic thought." In this phase people are not only able to grasp individual aspects in abstract thought; they are also able to see these insights in relation to other insights (synoptic = see together), that is, they are able to think in the realm of connections. Dieterich points out to educators – and this is noteworthy – that "it is possible that a large proportion of young people have not yet reached, or have only partially reached, the fourth phase of cognitive development" and that "a significant proportion of adults can only partially operate with this kind of thinking."

11. Cf. Jean-Pierre Crittin, *Erfolgreich unterrichten* (Bern: Haupt, 2003), 35–39.

12. This Handbook will not deal with the area of didactic any further. From a plethora of literature on the subject I reference here only the following: Döring and Ritter-Mamczek, *Lehren und Tranieren*; Karl-Heinz Flechsing, *Kleines Handbuch didaktischer Modelle* (Eichenzell: Neuland, Verlag für Lebendiges Lernen, 1996); Wilbur J. McKeachie, *Teaching Tips: Strategies, Research, and Theory for College and University Teachers* (Boston: Houghton Mifflin, 2002); Jörg Knoll, *Kurs- und Seminarmethoden* (Weinheim: Beltz, 2007); Weidenmann, *Erfolgreiche Kurse und Seminare*.

13. Cf. Dearborn, "Preparing New Leaders," 9. "Theological education is best provided to part-time students who are full-time Christian servants. Training for ministry should occur in ministry, rather than before ministry."

2) Before a decision of this nature is actually made, it is important to be clear about the meaning of *distance* and *proximity* (e.g. praxis or real life) when it comes to the educational process. *Proximity* in this sense means an actual in-practice or on-the-job situation. Concepts like "learning by doing," "on-the-job training," "contextual education," "grass roots education," "praxis-integrated learning," etc. are used to describe this proximity. Some current alternative models of theological education place great emphasis on proximity to practical experience. More traditional educational models tend to emphasize the distance to concrete practical activity. They seek to create a setting where students are not burdened by vocational demands so that there is freedom and time for thought, reflection, and mental effort.

3) A holistic didactic that integrates theory and practice places appropriate emphasis on both *proximity* and *distance*. Long periods of education in an academic environment that is removed from praxis, especially when students enter this phase when they are still quite young, can easily lead to top-heavy cognitive overload and to a student's being sick and tired of theory. Or in some cases, when a student is of an intellectual bent, such an education can yield an ivory tower academic, far removed from the realities of life, who is only interested in art for art's sake. On the other end of the spectrum, some whose education occurs in an alternative environment, fully praxis-integrated, may fall prey to the illusion that being constantly involved in ministry in the church or missions automatically improves the learning process. This is an illusion because this approach disregards the fact that thoughtful reflection, from a place removed from the pressures of ministry, supported by new and challenging theoretical input, enables a person to see their life and work with fresh eyes. Integrative theological education, therefore, will provide both practical experience (proximity) and space for theory and reflection without the burden of praxis (distance) in a productive balance.

6.1.5 WHO? *The Question of Instructors*

1) At the conclusion of this introductory overview, it is important to state that a great deal depends upon the qualifications of those who teach. A shift within educational institutions toward greater integration of theory and practice will never happen on the level of *hardware* (structures, programs, etc.) alone. Such a shift must be embodied in the *software* (people). It has

already been stated that instructors must have a good understanding of pedagogy and didactics. We'll delve here a little deeper.

2) It must be acknowledged that an instructor cannot effectively teach any content that he or she does not embrace and embody. The more an instructor personally integrates theory and practice, the more able s/he will be to transmit that integration in the classroom. Examples of things which are conducive to the integration of theory and practice in the life of the instructor are:
- A commitment to regular volunteer ministry in the church or in missions.
- Longer periods of full-time ministry in the church or missions.
- Exposure to a wide range of educational models in one's own educational background (classic academic education, alternative models, adult education at European or North American schools).
- Cross-cultural experience in missionary settings in the Majority World.
- Bi-vocational work as teacher and simultaneously in another vocation (ministry or secular environment).
- Close contact with students through small groups, coaching, counselling, or informal contacts.

3) The fact that teachers serve as role models can have unintended consequences. The fact that a professor has chosen an academic career path, whereas the majority of students are studying to prepare for ministry in the church or in missions, can create conflict in the mind of students – a conflict between where their education is intended to take them (praxis-oriented church or missions ministry) and the role models they find in their teachers. This tension can be exacerbated when teachers – intentionally or unintentionally – give the most praise and affirmation to the students who most closely mirror their own image, that is, to the students who excel academically. In such situations, the integration of theory and practice demands that teachers not only be academicians, but that they themselves embody the integration of theory and practice and are careful not to elevate their career path to the model for all students.

4) To encourage the integration of theory and practice, those who teach must themselves view their instruction and consciously structure the

classroom environment as a holistic experience. The principles of the "three modes of teaching and learning" can be an enormous help in this regard.[14] If communication in the classroom occurs exclusively through purely cognitive teaching methods that imply that the only thing that matters is the head, the intellect, thinking, and theory, then students will likely take to heart these implicit messages more than any lip service given to the importance of integrating theory and practice.

5) In order to be able to view instruction as a holistic experience, teachers must have a high level of self-awareness. They must understand their own *role* and be familiar with their own *screenplay*. The more explicitly teachers communicate that classroom instruction is an experience (i.e. praxis) in which they are completely involved with their whole beings, the more effectively they will embody the integration of theory and practice.

6) In our journey through these six concretizations, we keep encountering the concept of implicit messages. This should not be underestimated. Those in the field of pedagogy refer to the *hidden curriculum* of an institution of learning. This *paramessage* is not explicitly communicated in writing or orally but rather through what may be called the *institutional culture* (more on this in ch. 8). This is about the congruence between what is explicitly taught and written and what is actually lived out in the culture of the institution. This is what integration of theory and practice is all about, after all – that this congruence is evident in life. If an educational institution is not able to achieve a high level of congruence between educational theory and educational practice, between promises made and promises kept, between hearing and doing, between walk and talk – then all the rhetoric in the world about the integration of theory and practice will bear little fruit.

After this initial overview, we turn now to the individual steps in the process of curriculum development.

---

14. Crittin, *Erfolgreich Unterrichten*, 19–44.

6.2 Curriculum Development and Partnership[15]

6.2.1 What Is Curriculum?

The term curriculum has already been used many times in this book without having been explained. That explanation will now be offered.[16] The etymology of the word curriculum reveals that it is derived from the Latin *currere* (= run, hurry) and means run, race, cycle, rotation, lap. As early as the seventeenth century the term was used for lists of subject matter to be taught. In the German-speaking world, the term was replaced with "Lehrplan" (teaching plan). In the English-speaking world, "curriculum" is the common term for a course of study or for the list of courses to be taken during a period of study. S. B. Robinsohn's 1967 book *Bildungsreform als Revision des Curriculums* [Educational Reform as Revision of the Curriculum] brought the term back into use in the German-speaking world, and since then the term is again widely used as the technical term for teaching plan or course of study.

In its narrower definition, the term curriculum is used to designate a teaching plan, that is, a list of subject matter or courses. Used in a wider sense – and more in keeping with its etymology – it may refer to the structure of an entire course of study, an entire educational path. In this wider sense, curriculum refers not only to a list of courses offered, but to all the various components that go into making a structured educational experience. This includes: learning goals, content, methods, situations, strategies, and evaluation.[17] I am using the term here in this wider sense.[18] It includes all measures undertaken during the course of an educational experience to

---

15. The following sources offer helpful input on curriculum development: Crittin, *Erfolgreich Unterrichten*, chapter 4; Robert W. Ferris, ed., *Establishing Ministry Training: A Manual for Programme Developers* (Pasadena: William Carey Library, 1995); new, completely revised edition: Robert Brynjolfson and Jonathan Lewis, eds., *Integral Ministry Training: Design and Evaluation* (Pasadena: William Carey Library, 2006); Klaus Götz and Peter Häfner, *Didaktische Organisation von Lehr- und Lernprozessen* (Weinheim: Dt. Studien-Verl, 1999); Ross F. Kinsler and James F. Emery, eds., *Opting for Change: A Handbook on Evaluation and Planning for Theological Education* (Pasadena: William Carey Library, 1991).

16. For a discussion of the term curriculum in the German-speaking context, see Gunter Otto and Wolfgang Schulz, "Der Beitrag der Curriculumforschung," in *Enzyklopädie Erziehungswissenschaft*, Vol. 3, 49–62.

17. See the article "Curriculum (Curriculumtheorie)," in *Kleines Pädagogisches Wörterbuch*, eds. Josef A. Keller and Felix Novak (Freiburg: Herder, 1991), 58–60.

18. Cf. Ferris, *Establishing Ministry Training*, 66–67.

achieve the educational goals. In this sense, all the elements introduced in section 6.1 are a part of curriculum. These measures must be defined and applied.

6.2.2 Developing Curriculum in Partnership

As discussed earlier, education should happen in partnership between educational institutions and the church and mission societies. Each partner, drawing on its own unique situation, has an important contribution to make. This becomes clear as soon as the effort is made to articulate educational needs, that is, to define what education or training is actually needed.

The term "needs" here is ambiguous. Who knows the real needs? Who is competent to identify the true need for education?[19] In the wake of the paradigm shift described earlier, the idea was raised that professional theologians and educational specialists were certainly not suited (by themselves) to know and articulate the needs of the grass roots, ordinary people. Educational/training needs must be formulated – according to this perspective – by those who actually do the everyday work. The philosophy of adult education would generally suggest that the people who are seeking education are the ones who know best what their needs are.

Even without lengthy justification, it seems clear that this is only partially true. We must differentiate between subjectively perceived needs and objective needs. What potential students subjectively see as their educational needs is scarcely the same as what they really need. Even what a church or missions leader may formulate as needs is not the whole picture. Just as the professor at an educational institution has only a limited perspective, so too the people at the grass roots level have only a limited perspective.[20]

It is possible to identify four players in the definition of needs, each with his or her own contribution to make:

1) I'll begin with the person who is interested in pursuing additional training or education. He or she is most directly affected, is looking for the right course of study, and obviously has ideas, wishes, needs. It is fundamental that an educational institution recognize this. Schools and institutions that ignore

---

19. On "Bedarfsorientierung" see Götz and Häfner, *Didaktische Organisation*, 52–72.
20. Some seek to differentiate between subjective needs and more objective requirements.

the needs of potential students should not be surprised if they have declining enrollment figures. At the same time, interested persons are only partially able to identify their true educational/training needs. They often do not know the vocational tasks they want to prepare for, and they do not have years of experience working with people in the church or in missions. The needs expressed by potential students are quite subjective and are formulated from the perspective of those who do not have the breadth of experience needed to determine what kind of training and preparation a pastor or missionary really needs. Nevertheless it would be inappropriate to simply dismiss these subjective desires and to communicate condescendingly that these desires are naïve and unrealistic. Educational philosophy tells us that felt needs are one of the strongest motivational factors. To ignore the needs expressed by potential students is to undermine an effective motivational tool. Anyone beginning a course of study wants to be sure that he or she will receive what he or she is looking for. Naturally a student's perceived needs will expand during the course of study. That's why aspiring students cannot be the only voice that is heard.

2) People engaged in the vocation that the education or training is intended to prepare for (often they are graduates or alumni of the institution) can relate from their own experience what is needed in this particular field and to what extent their training has been helpful. These are voices that must be listened to. Pastors can tell us what they do every day in pastoral ministry and what qualifications are needed. Missionaries can tell us from first-hand experience what challenges they face in their specific situations and what competencies are needed to successfully meet these challenges. Yet even the perspective of these practitioners is limited. Quite often the training needs cited by such practitioners are restricted to the arena of skills (*poiesis*), because the day-to-day work demands specific skills. In some cases, practitioners are tempted to say that what they learned in their theological training is of little or no use to them. It is easy to forget that basic biblical-theological knowledge, including a solid grasp of the biblical languages, provides a foundation from which the pragmatic issues of everyday ministry can be securely addressed. This is not a plea for a one-sided education focusing only on Bible and theology. It is, however, a plea not to allow the call for practical skills to be the only voice heard when determining educational needs.

3) Leaders in the church, in denominational structures, and in missions often offer a somewhat different perspective. Whereas pastors and missionaries may speak from a perspective "on the ground," those with wider leadership responsibilities tend to speak from a birds-eye view. This perspective can lead them to a different assessment of educational needs. Their greater distance from everyday ministry and their view which goes beyond the local situation gives them an awareness of the bigger picture. That can lead to the identification of educational needs that a person involved in a specific ministry may not see. These voices from the leadership perspective need to be heard as well.

4) Lastly, there are those who are teaching at educational institutions. These are the people who tend to be the farthest removed from realities of ministry in the church or in missions. They have, however, the most extensive knowledge of church history. They have studied the texts of the Bible thoroughly. And hopefully they are the ones who are the most competent in the fields of pedagogy and education. Their voice alone would be too far removed from everyday practice in the church and in missions. A curriculum designed exclusively by theologians and educational professionals tends to be too focused on history and on traditional content. At the same time, a curriculum designed without input from this group will most likely be lacking in just these areas.

5) It's safe to say that those who are closest to praxis will demand a curriculum that focuses on vocational skills. Those who are further removed from praxis and who see the historical context will want foundational courses to be central to any curriculum. To use preaching as an example, those engaged in preaching will want to see communication skills at the top of the curriculum list. Those further removed from the task of preaching will insist on a curriculum that focuses on solid biblical and theological knowledge as a necessary foundation for preaching, including knowledge of the original languages, depending on the educational level. Both voices must be heard. Conclusion: The question of educational needs must be answered in consultation with the various groups concerned.[21]

---

21. Cf. Jonathan Lewis and Robert Ferris in Ferris, *Establishing Ministry Training*, 24–25. Lewis and Ferris talk about the importance of involving all the "stakeholders" in the process.

6.2.3 Forms of Partnership

Partnerships for curriculum development can take various forms. I'll briefly introduce three here:

Needs Analysis in Discussion with All Partners

By needs analysis we mean a thorough clarification of the educational needs by a competent authority. That can be a single person or a team. Ideally this authority is not aligned with any of the participating groups but is committed to consulting with all of them.

Producing a needs analysis is primarily a process of gathering data.[22] Data can be gathered in a number of ways:[23]

- Individual interviews (formal or informal) with people from the various groups mentioned above.
- Group interviews or observation of group discussions.
- Surveys using questionnaires (open questions, rating scales, or multiple-choice questions).
- Observation of real-life praxis.
- Evaluation of indirect sources such as job descriptions, performance reviews, etc.

The task of those responsible is to gather the data, evaluate the data, and arrive at the educational needs based on the data.

A study conducted in the 1990s among the schools in the Konferenz Bibeltreuer Ausbildungsstätten (KBA) followed this process for the most part.[24] School administrators, teachers, students and church leaders were all surveyed in a very thorough, comprehensive research project. The survey was not intended to provide data for the identification of educational needs. It did, however, provide the data necessary, with input from all parties, for outlining essential elements of educational needs.

They specifically reference the practitioners at the grass roots level, the teachers, the church and mission leaders, and the potential candidates for training/education.

22. Götz and Häfner, *Didaktische Organisation*, mention other methods of needs analysis used in the business world (p. 60–71). I restrict myself here to the method of data gathering.
23. Ibid., 62.
24. Cf. Faix, Faix, Müller, and Schmidt, *Theologische Ausbildung*.

Workshops with Various Partners

Another method brings various partners together in a workshop setting where specific curriculum needs and goals are worked out together.[25]

This approach was used in 2003 for a gathering in Switzerland involving a number of seminaries and theological training institutions. The invitation read:

> ***What are We Equipping Our Students For? Competency-Based Education***
>
> On the Day of Continuing Education observed by theological seminaries and Bible schools in Switzerland we want to consider the question of whether and to what extent we are successful in equipping people for ministry in the church, missions, and social service. We will start with the desired "output competencies" and work our way back to the goals and content of our curricula.
>
> Representatives of churches, denominations and mission societies are also being invited.
>
> Using the "open-space method," . . . will lead us through the day.
>
> The goal is to clarify our output expectations and to recognize the implications for our teaching plans and curricula.

As announced, the "open-space method" was used to jointly identify and articulate what students at these educational institutions are to be equipped for. The following three areas surfaced as the most important:

- Training for the church in a post-Christian Europe. Question: What ecclesiology drives our training program? What is the situation in the churches where our graduates will serve?
- Training a postmodern generation. What are the implications for our educational approach?
- Training in view of the danger of burnout. How can burnout prevention become part of our training?

---

25. Cf. Ferris, *Establishing Ministry Training*, 24–40. Ferris' suggestion has to do primarily with the development of new training courses for missionaries in a missions setting. His practical tips for conducting such workshops are valuable for other settings as well.

Workshops like these should become commonplace within individual schools and institutions as well, whenever new curricula are being developed, existing curricula are being revised, or it is time to ask whether the current programs are meeting the needs.

Standing Committee or Professional Commission

A further model is the standing committee (or professional commission). By this we mean a group of people, including representatives from all the demographics mentioned earlier, who meet regularly with the school administrators and teaching faculty to discuss questions related to the curriculum. When a school invests one day a year to discuss the curriculum with a standing committee of this sort, it opens itself to the judgment of those outside the institution. It hears the opinions of graduates and alumni who are now engaged in ministry, as well as the voices of those who are in a position to observe graduates and alumni as they carry out their ministry tasks. Schools should be keenly interested in such input. Such days may provide opportunity to examine individual aspects of the curriculum more closely, or they may yield observations and assessments of the curriculum as a whole that are helpful in determining future (new) directions. The following topics have proven useful:

- The goals that appear in catalogues and other printed material – do they coincide with the actual teaching/learning goals? Are they relevant from the perspective of outsiders?
- Individual instructors introduce courses, perhaps Old Testament one time and systematic theology or missiology another. The standing committee can offer its assessment. Is the course content in line with the overall learning goals? What have graduates who are now in ministry, or those who observe graduates in ministry, found to be especially helpful, or less so?
- Internship programs are evaluated and improvements sought.
- Measures taken by the school to encourage students' spiritual life and character development are presented. Any related materials are made available and discussed by the entire group. What expectations do outsiders have of schools in this regard? And what do school administrations expect from churches? Is the

partnership between church and school working? Or does it need to be improved?

All three methods have the same goal: It is not the job of the school alone or the church alone to design and carry out training. It is a responsibility to be carried out in partnership. In order to achieve this, nice-sounding words and declarations of intent are not enough. Partnership must get concrete, specific, practical. The three examples outlined above serve as encouraging examples.

6.3 Where Are We Now? Entrance Requirements

When it comes to curriculum development, in order to define the path from starting point to goal in any meaningful way, we have to first define the starting point. In the language of pedagogy, that means the entrance requirements. The following areas must be considered:

6.3.1 Formal Entrance Requirements and/or "Open Education"

In the course of our discussion of the paradigm shift, we already encountered the tension between traditional, formalized entrance qualifications and more recent admissions processes which are more open.

Traditionally the admissions process is based upon formal completion of the previous educational level, with the corresponding degree or diploma. Anyone who wishes to begin a course of higher (tertiary) education must first have successfully completed his or her secondary education. Specifically, anyone who wishes to study at the university must have completed his or her A levels. Anyone wishing to go to college, must have finished high school. Anyone wishing to study at a technical university (university of applied sciences or "poly") must have completed the appropriate vocational school. Anyone wishing to study at a Bible school or seminary must demonstrate that he or she has successfully completed at least twelve years of formal schooling of some sort.

These sorts of entrance requirements have the advantage of being simple. However, they also have significant disadvantages. (1) They only measure the academic qualifications required to complete the previous educational level. Other areas important in vocational life, such as gifting, character development, and spirituality, are not assessed. (2) There is limited guarantee that students really master the content represented by their diploma.²⁶ (3) The system is "closed" in that it offers little flexibility to accommodate "late bloomers" or "cross trainers" (those seeking to begin higher education later in life or coming from career or educational paths other than the traditional ones).

Efforts have been made to compensate for these disadvantages. (1) Most theology schools have added criteria related to personal and spiritual maturity to go along with the academic criteria. References and reports from the student's church supply the data. (2) Many courses of study now begin with foundational classes intended to bring a student's knowledge to the desired entry level. (3) Open access to higher education has become more common in the English-speaking world (especially in Great Britain) and is known as "open education." Open education handles the admissions process according to the principle that every candidate should receive the chance to prove himself or herself during his or her studies, relative to his or her potential, even in those cases where the preceding level of education has not been successfully completed.²⁷

As a result of the growing emphasis on lifelong learning, it has become more common in recent years for students to receive credit for any knowledge or skills they have acquired, regardless of the means – formal learning, non-formal learning, or informal learning. This is true for meeting admissions criteria and receiving credit for required studies. In most European countries comprehensive guidelines have been established for evaluating and recognizing competencies previously acquired. Terms and programs such as Recognition of Prior Learning, Accreditation of Prior Learning (APL), Accreditation of Prior Experiential Learning (APEL), Prior Learning Assessment (PLA), or Prior Learning Assessment and Recognition (PLAR) have become widespread.²⁸

---

26. Cf. Hans-Georg Herrlitz, "Geschichte der Gymnasiale Oberstufe," in *Enzyklopädie Erziehungswissenschaft* Vol. 9/1, 89–107.

27. Cf. F. Ross Kinsler, "Open Theological Education," in *The Extension Movement in Theological Education*, ed. Ross Kinsler (Pasadena: William Carey Library, 1981), 61–88.

28. Two relevant documents here: "Revised European Guidelines for the Validation of Non-formal and Informal Learning" (http://www.iconet-eu.net/index.php?option=com_remository&Itemid=11&func=fileinfo&id=75&lang=de) and the 2012 Accreditation Manual of the EEAA, Paragraph 3.3.3 "Evaluation and Recognition of (Prior) Informal and Non-formal Learning" (http://eeaa.eu/downloads-and-tools/the-eeaa-manual).

6.3.2 Open Access to Education: Possibilities and Limitations

Theological education which takes seriously the paradigm shift previously discussed will not remain rigidly bound to traditional formal admissions requirements. It will move toward more open access, which will target people who need training for service in the church and in missions. Open education does have its drawbacks, however, which we should be aware of. Open education cannot mean that anyone who wants to may come, regardless of qualifications. It is necessary, therefore, to take certain supportive measures. Open education faces two primary obstacles:

1) When students' basic educational levels are widely varied, it is difficult for a class to make progress together. If the instructor takes pains to bring along those who lack important aspects of background knowledge, students who entered meeting all necessary requirements will likely be under challenged. If, on the other hand, the instructor keeps a pace ideal for the best in the class, those who lack the necessary background knowledge will likely be left behind. If admissions requirements are relatively open, the learning pace in the classroom must not be adjusted to fit those who lack the necessary background. With open education, students must take responsibility for acquiring the knowledge they lack through self-instruction. To be fair, it must be said that it is not always the students who have benefited from open access who have difficulty keeping up in the classroom.

2) Open education assumes that students who lack the qualifications to meet formal entrance requirements will be able to do the work required and complete the education at the same level expected of every student. Someone must determine if a candidate possesses the necessary potential. That is not easy to do. It is possible, therefore, for students to be admitted who are not able to do the work required. If this is not recognized early in their studies, it is possible that such students continue through an entire program only to fail at the end. That is not fair to such students and is a burden to the institution.

These potential problems must be addressed with appropriate measures. If admissions requirements are rigid and formal (often heavily academic), exceptions may need to be made. The following criteria are often used:

1) Formal training in a different, usually related, subject. Sometimes candidates do indeed have schooling at the desired level but in a different field. For example, someone has completed a course of higher (tertiary) education but not in the field of theology and thus does not meet the criteria for admission to a master's degree progamme. In this case, the ability to study at the required level is clearly present, but basic knowledge in the field is lacking. That can be remedied as in point 4.

2) Ministry/work experience in a relevant field. It is not uncommon for persons to apply for theological training who more or less grew up in church or mission work. They may have served for years in the church, or missions, or social services, without ever completing the usual vocational training. Now they desire advanced theological education. However, the fact that they have never completed the kind of education usually required before admission to an advanced degree program, may mean that they are required to start (their education) all over. That hardly makes sense in view of the years of experience they have in ministry. Such persons may be admitted to some degree programs, often linked to the completion of a customized introductory course (see point 4).

3) Recognition of non-formal education in the field. People who have already worked for years in a vocation relevant to the field of study – whether as active lay people or professionally – have usually acquired significant knowledge through self-learning. This may occur through the reading of relevant literature, attendance at workshops and seminars, or adult education courses. This learning can be recognized when admissions criteria are being assessed. (See the comments and suggested literature in the earlier section on Recognition of Prior Learning.)

4) Preparatory studies in basic knowledge. The educational on-ramps outlined in points (1) to (3) must be seen as partial qualifications. The criteria needed for a successful completion of the anticipated course of study are only partially met. What is lacking may be compensated for by pre-entrance studies. A variety of measures may be implemented:
- All candidates who seek admission via the paths outlined in (1), (2), and (3) must complete a pre-entrance basic course of one or two semesters.

- A customized preparatory program is designed for such students, made up of classes and subjects they must complete before admission. The preparatory course may be completed at the seminary they wish to attend or at another school.
- The customized preparatory course may consist of a list of literature that must be read prior to admission.

5) Entrance exam. In some cases an entrance exam may be used to determine whether a student has mastery of the basic knowledge required.

6) Admission on probation. Occasionally in the context of open education, students may be admitted on probation for a semester. During this time, they must demonstrate that they are able to meet the demands of the program.

Preliminary conclusions: This clarifies the question of entrance requirements. It is worth thinking through exactly what students should face as criteria for admission. These can be summarized using the categories found in the following table:

Knowledge, Intellectual Competency and Skills:	Practical skills and competencies:	Attitudes:
We expect that newly admitted students . . .	We expect that newly admitted students . . .	We expect that newly admitted students . . .
(Here formulate the knowledge of the subject matter that will be expected of students first entering the program.)	(Here formulate the practical vocational and/or ministry experience expected of students first entering the program.)	(Here formulate the level of spiritual maturity expected of students first entering the program.)
(Here formulate the language and thought skills expected.)		(Here formulate the level of character development expected of students first entering the program.)

Table 2

Actually making a catalogue of expectations like this serves a number of purposes:
- It makes clear to candidates what the entrance requirements are.
- It aids in evaluating applications (references, CV, academic records) according to the entrance requirements.

- Finally, it helps in the formulation of educational goals, which go beyond the entrance requirements but are at the same time achievable (more on this shortly).

Beyond what has been said here, individual learning assessments are not uncommon. These can be useful when, for example, in adult education very diverse groups must be trained. I will not go into this process here, since it is not normally employed in theological education.[29]

6.4 Where Do We Want to Go? Graduation Requirements

The desired results – graduation requirements – are usually worked out in multiple steps. Differing processes are used. Robert Ferris proposes the following three-step process:[30]

- Developing a "graduate profile" (*outcome profile*)
- Derive from this the educational goals (*training goals*)
- Expand these to include specific learning objectives

It is important when employing a detailed process such as this that the differences between the steps be understandable. It is very easy for a group that has never been involved in a process like this and is unfamiliar with the terminology to quickly feel out of its depth. Robert Ferris and Lois Fuller, for example, define the difference between "outcome goals" and "training goals" with these words:

> Outcome goals focus specifically on those qualities which distinguish effective practitioners – who they are and what they are able to do. Training goals look more comprehensively at the training task. Training goals include outcome (i.e. character quality and skills) goals, but they add knowledge goals as well.[31]

It seems to me that the differentiation needs to be more precise.[32] I shall attempt this in the following section.

---

29. More on this in Götz and Häfner, *Didaktische Organisation*, 74–80.
30. Ferris, *Establishing Ministry Training*, 23–84. Cf. Crittin, *Erfolgreich Unterrichten*, 43–49. Crittin distinguishes simply between guiding goals (= educational goals) and directional goals (= course or subject goals). In my judgment there is an intermediate level that is lacking here.
31. Ferris, *Establishing Ministry Training*, 45.
32. I personally participated in a workshop for curriculum development led by Robert Ferris, and I found that most of the participants were confused by this differentiation, that is, they

6.4.1 *Developing a Graduate Profile*

Learning goals are defined first of all as global formulations, in sentences such as: "Upon conclusion of his/her training, the graduate will be able to . . ." These are general vocational goals. Crittin gives the following examples from vocational training and continuing education:[33]

- After completing training, the air traffic controller is able to direct air traffic in all situations in such a way that safety is guaranteed as first priority, and efficiency is guaranteed second.
- Manufacturing employees are trained in such a way that they can be placed in any role in any production process.
- Upon completion of their nurses' training, graduates have the necessary skills to be placed in medical and surgical departments according to their areas of specialty.

In all three examples the graduate profile is defined by the demonstration of vocational skills. The first concern has to do with practical occupational skills.

As an example from theological education, the goal of an MA program in Pastoral Ministries is defined as follows:

> Graduates of this program are able to serve the church in its mission by fulfiilling pastoral ministries. In the tension between Bible and society, they are able to communicate the Christian message in an understandable and relevant way, to offer pastoral counselling, to lead a church, and to foster its evangelistic and missional development.

The formulation of such a goal does not just happen, of course. The following phases may be worked through during a workshop:[34]

1st Phase: Compiling a list of competencies a graduate should have in vocational praxis. The list is compiled by asking the question: "What core competencies do you expect from a graduate of this program?" The answers are written individually on note paper and posted on the wall.

---

were unable to understand (or accurately articulate) the difference.

33. Crittin, *Erfolgreich Unterrichten*, 45.

34. Jonathan Lewis and Robert Ferris suggest a somewhat different approach in Ferris, *Establishing Ministry Training*, 23–41.

Curriculum Development in Theological Education 297

2nd Phase: Using the pieces of note paper, similar competencies are grouped together.

3rd Phase: Small groups of participants each take a set of similar competencies and seek to summarize each competency in a single sentence. These sentences are written down and posted on the wall.

4th Phase: The sentences (summary statements of core competencies) are ordered by importance or priority, in at least two groupings: Need to have (absolutely necessary) and nice to have (a valuable plus, but not absolutely essential). The nice to have competencies are then set aside.

5th Phase: The graduate profile is formulated using the remaining (need to have) statements of core competencies.

6.4.2 Defining Educational Goals

Learning goals are identified in a second step. Learning goals start with the graduate profile and ask what skills and capabilities the individual's education must instill in order for the graduate to possess the desired vocational competencies.

Referring to the vocational qualifications (guiding goals), Crittin formulated the directional goals (course or subject goals) that follow. Ferris calls these *training goals*.

For the air traffic controller, for example:
- The air traffic controller can correctly read weather maps and derive from them sensible measures for regulating air traffic.

For employees of the manufacturing company:
- Employees of the manufacturing company know the five different procedures used in our plant to process plastic.

For nurses:
- Nurses are able to help answer questions for both patients and employees.

Such educational goals can be defined with even more detail. To do so involves using what is called the "taxonomy of learning goals." In the field of pedagogy, it is common to identify three or four basic categories. The following three classic categories originated with the American Benjamin Bloom:[35]

1) Cognitive or intellectual goals (knowledge and reasoning)

2) Affective or emotional goals (attitudes and opinions)

3) Motor or functional goals (behaviors and skills)

Interestingly, these three basic categories correspond to a large degree with the concepts of *theoria*, *praxis* and *poiesis*, which we introduced earlier.

Other experts have subdivided the cognitive into "knowledge" and "understanding / recognition."[36] I believe this distinction is very useful when it comes to theological education, because there is a significant difference between acquiring knowledge and being able to think or reason. This leads to a four-part taxonomy, such as the one proposed by the Staatsinstitut für Schulpädagogik (ISP) [National Institute for School Pedagogy] in Munich:[37]

Goal Category	Level or Intensity
Knowledge (information)	Insight – Overview – Knowledge – Familiarity
Ability (operations)	Skills – Dexterity – Mastery
Recognition (problems)	Awareness – Discernment – Understanding
Values (attitudes)	Openness – Aptitude – Interest – Enthusiasm – Decisiveness

Table 3

The verbs used in formulating educational goals are important. They should be action and behavior oriented, observable, and measurable. That means that verbs that express a condition that is internal, not observable, are less suited for use in formulating educational goals. Verbs like "know," "understand" or "believe" should be replaced wherever possible with action-oriented, measurable verbs. Here are some examples:[38]

---

35. Extensively described in Gage and Berliner, *Pädagogische Psychologie*, 45–63.
36. Cf. Götz and Häfner, *Didaktische Organisation*, 110.
37. Cited in the article "Lernziele," in *Kleines Pädagogisches Wörterbuch*, 228.
38. See also suggestions by Ferris in *Establishing Ministry Training*, 76.

Original	Better Verb Usage
The graduate knows ...	The graduate is able to explain ...
	The graduate can interpret ...
	The graduate can connect ...
The graduate understands ...	The graduate can apply ...
	The graduate can compare ...
	The graduate can judge ...
The graduate is familiar with ...	The graduate can appropriately apply ...
	The graduate can argue/defend ...
	The graduate can express ...

Table 4

The reader can see the use of verbs in the following example, drawn from educational goals formulated as part of the MA program in Pastoral Ministries cited earlier:

Qualities/Attributes: Advanced Skills in Biblical Interpretation
- Be able to appropriately use various approaches and methods of critical exegesis.
- Be able to perform thematic biblical studies, implementing advanced skills of biblical theological studies.
- Be able to appropriately apply various approaches in hermeneutics and contextualization in the interpretation of the Bible in a chosen context.

Qualities/Attributes: Advanced Skills in Historical-Theological Reflection and Interaction
- Be able to undertake critical historical studies, especially in areas relevant to their own church tradition and their professional ministry.
- Be able to reflect critically on and come to conclusions about doctrinal and ethical issues, engaging with the Bible, the history of Christian theology, the contemporary church (globally and ecumenically) and society.
- Be able to dialogue meaningfully with the wider church and society from an evangelical- Anabaptist point of view, making available the rich spiritual, communal and socio-political heritage of the peace-church tradition.

> **Qualities/Attributes: Advanced Professional Skills**
> - Be able to communicate the Christian faith meaningfully, convincingly, and sensitively in the chosen context in various settings of pastoral ministry, such as preaching, teaching and evangelism.
> - Be able to give leadership to the church, implementing strategies for church development, so that the church may engage more fully in its mission to the world.
> - Be able to counsel people respectfully and sensitively, implementing the necessary psychological skills appropriately, and being aware of the potential and the limitations of pastoral counseling.

This second step – from Graduate Profile to Educational Goals – demands experience in education and understanding of pedagogy. Moreover it takes some time and concentrated thought to translate a graduate profile into educational goals such as these. Therefore it is scarcely possible to accomplish this during a workshop involving all the educational partners. However the partners should be engaged in the ongoing process. For example, the educational goals formulated by the rector or by a professor are communicated to all the partners for their reflection and input.

When formulating educational goals, the limitations of this process should not be overlooked. In recent times massive criticism has been leveled against educational goals that are too narrow. If educational goals merely serve to feed people into the manufacturing and consumer processes of a globalized economic system, in line with the *Fitness for Purpose* philosophy, then well-meaning education has devolved into something far less desirable. Such criticism has been voiced by constructivist pedagogues. They contend that a rigid, educational-goal-oriented didactic presumes to be able to control learning from the outside and fails to recognize the unpredictability of the learning process.[39]

It is certainly valuable, however, to formulate educational goals if they are understood to be directional goals which provide focus and orientation for learning. Taking these things into consideration, once these goals are articulated, curriculum planning can take the next step.

---

39. Cf. Siebert, *Pädagogischer Konstruktivismus*, especially chapter 6. See also John West-Burnham's "Understanding Quality," in *The Principles and Practices of Educational Management*, eds. Tony Bush and Les Bell (London: Sage Publications, 2002), 313–324, for a critique of a quantitative understanding of quality (focusing on measurable educational goals).

6.5 How Do We Get There? Developing Curriculum

As we have already said, we understand the term curriculum in its broad sense, including the entire educational process. It's not just about establishing a list of courses. It's about defining the process that will help a person from start (admission requirements) to finish (graduation requirements). This process happens in six steps:

- First, a list of all the available components must be compiled.
- Second, the study plan can be outlined.
- Then the individual courses can be defined more precisely.
- In addition to courses, other elements (organizational forms) must be built into the curriculum.
- Attention should once again be paid to integration.
- Finally, thought must be given to evaluation.

6.5.1 *The Components of the Curriculum*

A curriculum is more than just instructional events in the form of courses, classes, and subject matter. Experts speak of organizational forms which should be appropriately employed within the curriculum.[40]

The organizational forms that are available can be placed on a scale from classroom (students and teacher are together) to self-study (students are alone). Drawing upon Götz and Häfner, we can compose the following list of organizational forms:

In the Classroom (students and teachers present)
- Instruction (lecture, reading, lesson)
- Seminar, workshop
- Assignments done in conjunction with instruction

Transitional Forms (decentralized, some student-teacher contact)
- Tutorials, study groups with a teacher present
- Independent study groups (without a teacher)
- Independent internship/practicum (without a teacher, possibly with local supervision)

---

40. Cf. Götz and Häfner, *Didaktische Organisation*, 80–95. Crittin speaks of planning measures, *Erfolgreich Unterrichten*, 49.

Self-Study Forms (students normally left on their own)
- Unsupervised practical work
- The study of literature and the writing of papers
- Programmed instruction (=programmed material, correspondence courses)
- E-Learning

This list is certainly incomplete, and will need to be expanded or adapted, according to the situation. It is important, nevertheless, to compile such an inventory when developing a curriculum, in order to be able to make use of every possibility.

Two things must be clarified, however, before we can proceed with concrete planning and the use of the various organizational forms:

1) Every organization has potential and limitations. It is important to know these. Much has been written about on this subject.[41]

2) Which organizational forms may be employed depends on a variety of factors which must be taken into account:[42]
- Time
- Distance and availability of the students
- Distance and availability of the teachers
- Additional personnel needs (tutors, guidance counsellors, internship supervisors, etc.)
- Facilities/buildings and their infrastructure
- Availability of presentation and information technology
- Availability and accessibility of resources (libraries, internet, etc.)
- Finances

Once this inventory is known, along with the related possibilities and limitations, the educational process can be drafted.

---

41. Cf. Götz and Häfner, *Didaktische Organisation*, 84–92. Ferris, *Establishing Ministry Training*, 85–103.
42. See Klaus Götz and Peter Häfner, "Analyse der organisatorischen Voraussetzungen," in *Didaktische Organisation von Lehr- und Lernprozessen. Ein Lehrbuch für Schule und Erwachsenenbildung*, eds. Klaus Götz and Peter Häfner (Weinheim: Dt. Studien-Verl, 1999), 80–82.

6.5.2 The Course of Study

In most cases, the existing, proven models are used, with possible modifications to accommodate individual needs. In some cases, however, it is both possible and important to develop completely new structural models.

The Classical Structural Models

In what follows, I will present and comment upon several models.

1) The traditional structure at universities in the German-speaking world divides the academic year into two semesters – the winter semester from October to March, and the summer semester from April to September. During the first fifteen weeks or so of each semester there is classroom instruction (lectures, seminars, practice sessions, etc.). The rest of the semester (often temptingly called semester holidays) is intended to be used to complete assignments and write papers.

2) Bible schools and seminaries not connected with a university often have other semester schedules. The majority of these schools follow the American academic year, which – corresponding to the guidelines of the EEAA and adopting the American template – consists of two semesters of fifteen weeks each. Generally the first semester occurs before Christmas, from September to December, and the second falls somewhere between January and June, depending on when holidays, semester breaks, and internships may be scheduled. The summer months are most often devoted to holidays or internships.

Some schools follow the calendar of the local public schools (primary and secondary).

Naturally there are variations. Some schools offer a shortened semester in August, January and/or in June, similar to the Interterms or Interims common in some North American schools.

The majority of these classical structures assume that students are enrolled in full-time study and live relatively close to the schools.

Alternative Structural Models

In recent years, efforts to accommodate the needs of students (cf. paradigm shift) have led to the rise of new structures. In an age when more and more students are working in their jobs and studying part-time, more flexible, modular models are needed.

Example 1: A seminary conforms roughly to the semester structure described in paragraph (2) above, but introduces some innovations within this framework. As in the dual track model common in vocational training courses, students are often already working in a church (or elsewhere) and attend classes three days a week. Courses are structured in modules, so that students can complete courses cumulatively, one at a time (accumulating the corresponding credits) and thus adjust the pace of their studies to fit their needs. Courses are also offered regionally, so that students can study close to home. No additional infrastructures are needed for this model, since the facilities of local churches are used and local libraries are accessed.

Example 2: A seminary alters its complete course structure so that it is flexible, modular, and adapted to the needs of students. This makes sense when a majority of students are from cross-cultural settings (missionaries) and are completing their master's degree programs little by little during their periods of home assignment (furlough). Within the traditional timeframe of an academic year (from September to July), seven-week short semesters are offered, as well as two-week and one-week compact courses. By means of a modular curriculum built on a system of academic credits, students are able to complete their master's degree program a little at a time, as their schedule allows.

Example 3: Another seminary offers students who are already working in a church or other organization in German-speaking Europe a flexible approach for their studies. The semester structure adopted in this case is as follows: the semester begins at the end of August with a three-week course block that students must attend in person. Following this, there is a period of "free study," during which time students complete assignments and write papers for the courses they have enrolled in. In January there is another block of three and one-half weeks, which students must attend. This block begins with seminars, in which the assignments and papers completed in the previous semester are presented and discussed, followed by three weeks of classes which serve as introduction to the material for the new semester. The period given to self-study follows from February until the end of May. In June, students again attend a two or three-day seminar, which closes out the academic year.

Curriculum Development in Theological Education

These examples are not presented as ideals, but rather to demonstrate that an important first step in developing a curriculum involves defining or redefining the structural schedule of the academic year. Every system has advantages and disadvantages. There will almost certainly need to be compromises made between an academic ideal and the given realities. Any number of factors must be taken into consideration. Some of them will be discussed below.

6.5.3 Courses and Course Descriptions

"Historical" or "Contemporary" Curriculum?
In a second step we turn now to classes and their content. Earlier we indicated that a curriculum can be defined as "historical" or "contemporary." "Historical" means that the courses are more or less predetermined by what has developed historically and by the grouping of courses according to "majors" or "schools." "Contemporary" means that the courses in a curriculum are chosen in response to the needs that come to light in praxis (see figure 15).

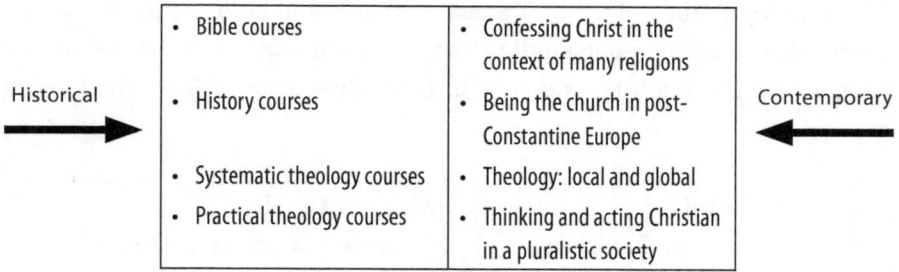

Figure 16

It would be presumptuous, however, to simply dismiss a historical curriculum as belonging to an old and outdated educational paradigm, while viewing a contemporary curriculum as one that satisfies the demands of a new paradigm.

It's important to distinguish here between a bachelor's level and a master's level program. A bachelor's program will place greater emphasis on the historical curriculum. A master's program is more likely to focus on current questions and address these questions in an integrative way.

Some of the more innovative, modular, and flexible programs leave it relatively open, which courses students take and when. That means that it is possible to take praxis-oriented courses in the early semesters, and foundational (historical) courses can be delayed until the later semesters. Such flexibility, however, can prove counter-productive. If a student enrolls in principles of church growth and homiletics in the first year of a bachelor's program – because these sound practical – but postpones taking Greek, church history, and introduction to dogmatics until later semesters, there is not much left of curriculum integration, and the quality of education received is seriously in jeopardy.

What I present here rests on the assumption that both are needed: "historical" and "contemporary" courses. A possible blend of two is represented in figure 16.

The historical model:

Advantage: Ensures a logical progression from mastery of the basics to integration with today's relevant questions.

Disadvantage: Study of the basics takes too long and has too little relevance. Follows the classical understanding that education must precede training and happens best through the study of history while isolated from the burden of praxis.

Bachelor's Level	Master's Level
Classical "historical" courses	Courses that are developed in response to present-day challenges and that address these challenges in an integrative way

Figure 17

The contemporary model (alternative, flexible, modular):

Advantage: The integration of tradition and present-day questions is possible from the very beginning. From the start, courses have relevance for praxis.

Curriculum Development in Theological Education

Disadvantage: Important foundational knowledge is lacking in the early semesters, knowledge necessary to meaningfully address present-day questions.

Courses that are developed in response to present-day challenges and that address these challenges in an integrative way
Basic foundational courses corresponding to the traditional curriculum model

Figure 18

I suggest, therefore, the following model:

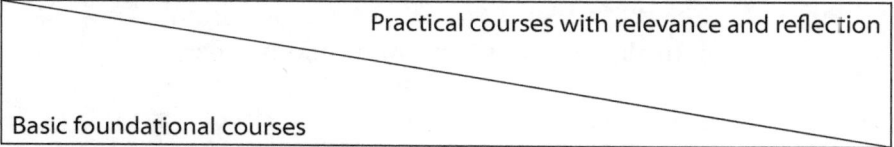

Figure 19

Foundational courses dominate in the early stages of study and decrease semester by semester, as more and more courses are added that deal with topics of practical relevance.

Developing Course Descriptions

Once the individual courses are identified, course goals and content must be articulated. That happens in the course description, or syllabus. A syllabus serves several purposes:

- It aids teachers in their planning. A carefully worded syllabus necessitates a thorough teaching plan. Teachers must hold themselves accountable for what is accomplished in the course.
- Second, it aids students by providing information about every aspect of the course. The syllabus is the teacher's vehicle for telling students the intentions, goals, and expectations of the course. A well-crafted syllabus is an expression of good communication on the part of the instructor.

- For the institution, the syllabus helps in the coordination and integration of the curriculum. Teachers should have access to the syllabi of their colleagues' courses in order to facilitate better coordination. By viewing all the syllabi, the academic dean is able to gain an overview of the entire program and make adjustments where necessary.
- Finally, course descriptions are a tool used in the accreditation process. Officials responsible for ensuring the quality of instruction use syllabi as one criterion in their assessment. In some accreditation systems, the syllabus is the primary component used to determine whether or not a school's program will be recognized. Schools are obligated to carry out the instruction as outlined in the syllabus.

A syllabus normally contains the following information:

Course Title (and numeric designation)

Professor(s)/Instructor(s)

Status in the curriculum
The syllabus defines for whom the course is designed and states any prerequisites. It may say, for example, "This course is required for all students in their first year" or "Students enrolling in this course must have previously completed the course Introduction to Exegetical Methods."

Short description (of goals and content)
The syllabus briefly describes what the course seeks to accomplish. It may read something like this: "This course provides an introduction to methods of Bible interpretation . . . The course will give students the knowledge and skills necessary to . . . The first section will be about . . . Followed by . . . Finally . . ."

Instructional goals
When formulating instructional goals, it is helpful to use the structure mentioned earlier (section 6.4.2):

- Holistic instruction is guaranteed when instructional goals include all four categories: knowledge, recognition/understanding, attitudes/values, and ability/skills.
- Good goals are action-oriented. The choice of verbs used is critical (see section 6.4.2 above.)
- Instructional goals should include observable desired behaviors.
- To be motivational, instructional goals must be appropriate to the students' starting knowledge and skill level and yet challenging as well as relevant in view of the students' vocational goals.
- Honest instructional goals do not promise what they cannot deliver.
- Effective instructional goals are formulated in coordination with the goals of other courses and the overall educational goals of the institution. Significant questions to be asked are: In what way does this course contribute to achieving the overall educational goal? How is this course coordinated with other courses? What foundation does it lay? What does it build upon? It is worthwhile to take the time to answer these questions very practically.
- Effective goals serve as criteria for measuring learning. (See the final bullet below under evaluation.)

Content overview

Here the course content is listed in detail, ideally linked with the corresponding dates in the classroom.

Student workload expected and evaluation

This point is often reduced to "homework" or "assignments." What is valuable here is to communicate that successful learning can only take place when the students study. Instructors can neither study nor learn for the students. Students must do that themselves. What level of effort is expected of the students is spelled out here. The following factors must be considered:

- It is important to give an account of the time required for this course. Usually there is a guideline for how much study time outside of class will be required for each hour in the classroom. It goes without saying that such guidelines cannot be interpreted legalistically. Students cannot be expected to time their studies with a stopwatch. Motivated students will always invest more time than the minimum expected. But in terms of the communication between the school and the students, it is important to state clearly the time requirements for a course. It is therefore helpful to establish a guideline which defines how much study time outside of class is expected for each hour spent in the classroom. In most cases the accrediting association suggests that students should expect to spend at least as much time in study outside the classroom as is spent in the classroom.

- It is important both for the instructors and the students that teachers communicate their expectations clearly. It has proven useful for teachers to attach an approximate time expectation to each homework assignment they give. This prevents teachers from giving unrealistic assignments and it lets students know exactly what is expected of them.
- Homework assignments can contribute significantly to the holistic learning process when the work required includes all of the categories mentioned earlier – knowledge, recognition/understanding, attitudes/values, and ability/skills. It is obvious that in the case of courses such as Hebrew, dogmatics, or pastoral counselling, that is not always possible. Nevertheless, in most cases, with a little creative thinking, assignments can provide a holistic learning experience.
- Important decisions related to the integration of theory and practice are made with each homework assignment. We mentioned earlier that it can easily happen that classroom and practical experience (such as internships) exist side by side, more or less unrelated to one another. This can be countered by including in homework assignments the task of reflecting on the learning gained from praxis.
- Finally, along with the description of the expectations placed on students, the means of evaluating learning must be defined. Students must know in advance what will be evaluated, what will be weighted more heavily, and what the evaluation criteria will be.

Literature:
Finally, every syllabus should include a reading list. This serves several purposes: Students see what the required reading is. In addition it lists

relevant texts "for further reading" that can serve as resources for advanced learning or for research papers. The reading list also establishes for teaching colleagues, the school administration, and even the accrediting institution what the foundational literature for this course consists of. It is not the purpose of the reading list to provide a comprehensive bibliography for the course subject matter. Literature that is neither accessible nor relevant for the student contributes little to the learning process.

6.5.4 Additional Organizational Structures and Measures

In addition to the courses, there are other organizational structures that belong to the curriculum. What are the things that will contribute to a successful study cycle from start to finish? The three basic categories examined in chapter 5 (*theoria, praxis, poiesis*) include supporting structures for the curriculum.

From Knowing to Understanding

What additional structures (beyond the classroom experience of lectures, discussion and other forms of instruction) are needed to reach the goals of "knowledge" and "reason" in the cognitive area? The potential that various organizational forms have for "knowing" and "understanding" can be seen in table 5, taken from Götz and Häfner:[43]

---

43. Götz and Häfner, *Didaktische Organisation*, 92.

Structure	Knowing	Under-standing	Pragmatic	Affective	Emphasis
Lecture	++	0	-	0 (indirect)	Communication of information by experts
Seminar, Exercises (subject specific)	++	++	-	+	Understanding and practice with supervision by experts
Internship, Workshop	0	+	++	+	Practical experience with supervision and instruction by experts
Tutorial (participant specific)	++	++	+	0	Self-directed practice with assistance when needed
Study Group (participant specific)	++	++	++	0	Self-directed learning and practice in community
Unsupervised internship (accidental)	+	++	++	+	Practical learning No control
Simulation (subject specific)	0	++	0		Practice with no risk
On-the-job training (situation specific)	-	0	++	+	Baptism by fire Potentially high-cost learning
Interactive study programs	++	+ (technology) otherwise –	(++)	0 (-) (indirect)	Efficient communication of information. Coverage of large audience.
Print media	++	0	-	0 (-)	Efficiency with large audience questionable (no feedback)

- = No potential   o = Some potential   + = A good deal of potential   ++ = Very high potential

Table 5

Curriculum Development in Theological Education

There are, accordingly, four organizational structures of teaching and learning that lead most efficiently from knowing to understanding and which, therefore, should be included in the curriculum to supplement classroom instruction:

- Seminars and exercises
- Tutorials
- Study groups
- Simulations/Case Studies

Spiritual Formation: Fostering Spiritual Growth

1) Traditionally the following measures have been used to foster spiritual life and character development:

- Devotionals
- Small groups
- Team serving events
- Retreats
- Solitude days
- Access to counselling/coaching/mentoring

2) This list can be expanded. The study mentioned earlier by the PTE of the World Council of Churches contains a catalogue of suggestions for fostering spiritual formation in theological education.[44] Under the title Means for Sustaining Christian Spirituality, the following seven factors are named as foundational in terms of spiritual formation:

- Spiritual formation has an individual, personal dimension but is lived out in community.
- Academic study and spiritual life must not be separated. They must be related to one another.
- Times of silence and solitude – alone and in community – are essential for cultivating and reviving spiritual vitality.
- Spiritual formation should always happen in relation to the local church. Participation in worship services and involvement in the life of the church are core elements of spiritual formation.
- Spiritual growth is enhanced when people are faced with the difficulties and challenges of life. Theological education should

---

44. Amirtham and Pryor, *Resources for Spiritual Formation*, 159–163.

not shelter students from the realities of life. Rather, a natural confrontation with real-life needs and problems should be fostered through involvement in the church, missions, and society.
- Exposure to a variety of liturgical traditions can expand our spiritual horizons and deepen our spiritual life.
- Ecumenical and cross-cultural experiences can help us to see beyond the familiarity and comfort of our own worship style and traditions, and to open ourselves to the possibility of integrating previously unfamiliar dimensions of spirituality into our own life.

Measures can be taken to address these factors during the process of developing the curriculum for theological education.

3) The PTE study suggests the following steps for fostering spiritual formation:
- When wanting to intentionally and methodically encourage spiritual growth, it is always good to keep in mind that there are no specific methods which are guaranteed to produce specific spiritual results which can then be observed and measured. Instead, it is about creating environments in which spiritual life can be stimulated, cultivated, and deepened.

  And the whole person must be kept in mind. People don't "learn" spirituality through intellectual reflection about it. People learn spirituality by practicing spirituality, although it must be said that intellectual reflection plays a part. The inner life of the person should not be isolated, however, but placed in relationship with other dimensions of his/her life, such as the academic and social.

  Spiritual life is in its essence voluntary. No one can be forced to be spiritual. That does not mean that there cannot be outside influences such as attendance at (required) events. The basic posture must remain, however, that true spirituality is something that comes from within and is practiced voluntarily.

  Spiritual formation should begin where the students are, not where the institution hopes they will be when they complete their studies.

  In the world of spiritual formation, everyone learns from everyone else. The distinction between teachers and students

is removed. Students and teachers are all on a common path of spiritual growth.
- Spiritual formation is the task of the entire faculty, of all teachers, professors, and instructors.

  Every person who teaches is part of the spiritual formation process by virtue of the example of his/her own spiritual life.

  Every teacher should (in the syllabus) account for the ways in which spirituality will be encouraged in each course. Moreover, dimensions of personal and spiritual growth should be explicitly integrated into every course.

  Spiritual formation cannot be delegated to specific courses, disciplines, or persons. That does not mean that specific courses, disciplines, or persons cannot specifically and explicitly focus on spirituality. However the entire faculty must maintain an awareness of its collective responsibility to foster personal and spiritual growth.

- Even if spiritual formation is not – and need not be – an explicit instructional goal in most courses, the significance of classroom instruction for encouraging spiritual life should not be underestimated. The relational climate in the classroom, the way theological topics are handled, as well as the persona of the teacher (as a whole person) including the spiritual dimension of his/her life is all part of the implicit learning process of spiritual formation, especially when seeking to integrate academic work and spiritual life.

- Beyond these more informal dimensions of spiritual formation in the classroom, however, formalized processes outside the classroom are needed. Among these are instruction in personal spiritual life, conversations in small groups, and the availability of pastoral counselling. It has often proven useful to have students write their spiritual autobiography. Other forms of reflection and self-evaluation in the area of spirituality can be helpful as well. There are, however, potential role conflicts to be aware of. A person who is an academic supervisor, who gives and grades exams, who gives evaluations, or who must enforce disciplinary measures, is often not the person students want to talk with about spiritual

formation. It can be helpful, therefore, to offer spiritual guidance through personnel other than the teaching faculty.
- And finally, spiritual (holistic) maturity is a lifelong process, for which a variety of people and factors share responsibility. Theological education, which seeks to prepare men and women for pastoral ministry in the church, must make the fostering of spiritual life a high priority aim of its curriculum. That is the responsibility of the educational institution. And this responsibility consists first of all in encouraging students to take responsibility for their own spiritual life. After all, life is much more than school and studying. Spiritual growth occurs primarily within the context of the church. From the perspective of the school, this means that the churches must be considered partners in the work of spiritual formation. And the churches must realize that they help bear responsibility for the spiritual development of "their" students. There must be an active partnership between school and church.

4) Appropriate measures for fostering spiritual (holistic) life must be incorporated during the process of curriculum development. It must be kept in mind that traditionally the classic courses will tend to dominate the curriculum, whereas measures aimed at personal development will tend to be seen as having secondary importance and therefore migrate to the margins. We must work against this tendency.

The measures and suggestions highlighted in this section should be incorporated into the curriculum as organizational structures that have equal value and equal rights. It is best to include in a syllabus all the measures aimed at encouraging spiritual formation and personal development and to distribute this syllabus to students, in order to give spiritual formation the formal weight it deserves.

Integrating Key Qualifications into the Curriculum
1) The first step is to **define a list of key qualifications** that should be supported by the curriculum: The project Evaluation von Schlüsselqualifikationen (ESQ) [Evaluation of Key Qualifications] sponsored by the state of Baden-

Wuerttemberg in southwest Germany defined the following key qualifications and developed corresponding evaluation methods:[45]
- Work methods
- Initiative and independence
- Communication skills
- Conflict resolution skills
- Ability to cooperate
- Presentation skills
- Problem-solving skills
- Capacity to take responsibility

For theological education, the following key qualifications could be defined:[46]
- Leadership skills
- Conceptual skills
- Social-cultural skills
- Communication skills
- Conflict resolution skills
- Capacity for teamwork
- Self-awareness and self-confidence
- Ability and willingness to learn

2) The second step is to **assign specific key qualifications to individual elements of the curriculum.** Normally teachers are asked to identify which key qualifications are fostered, and to what degree, in their courses. The University of Wales, for example, requires its teaching faculty to indicate, using the framework shown in table 6, which key qualifications are integrated into their classes and course work.[47]

3) The third step is to **introduce new and improved measures for fostering key qualifications.** What is possible here may depend on the type

---

45. Günter Klein and Jürgen Ripper, "Schlüsselqualifikationen im Blickpunkt," *Magazin Schule* 9 (2003): 10–11.
46. Faix, "Die Bedeutung von Schlüsselqualifikationen," 207.
47. Taken from the program management documents for the master's degree program offered in partnership by the Theological Seminary Bienenberg and Theological-Diaconal Seminary Aarau.

of school. Schools of higher education (tertiary level) will be able to create different emphases than vocational training schools (dual track model). Ute Woschnok and Peter M. Frischknecht at the ETH Zürich suggest three concrete measures schools of higher education can take to more effectively foster key qualifications:[48]

- Alternatives to classroom lectures: exercises, tutorials, term papers, seminar presentations, etc. Such measures foster: teamwork, oral presentation skills, report writing skills.
- Case studies. This encourages the use of knowledge beyond the scope of the immediate subject, the ability to deal with complex problems, and the application of what has been learned to real-life situations.
- External vocational internship. This creates a learning environment (outside of the classroom) which makes it possible for the student to learn by doing. Processing the experience enables the student to integrate the experience into his/her learning. Internships also foster personal growth and social skills.

Measures such as these can easily be integrated into theological education, to the advantage of all (see table 6).

4) In summary, schools can determine which key qualifications can be fostered throughout an entire curriculum. The Ludwig-Maximilian University in Munich, for example, has required all teaching faculty to demonstrate what key qualifications they are fostering in their classes. The faculty of Protestant theology reported:[49]

The scientific study of Protestant theology deals with the doctrine of God. The foundations are provided by the biblical texts and the creeds of the church, which are studied in accordance with the rules of science. Tradition, experience, and the contemporary environment are then held in relationship to one

---

48. Woschnok and Frischknecht, "Schlüsselqualifikationen," 28–30.
49. From a 2006 information brochure for students.

another in a continual process of thought and reflection. Church history and dogmatics (the doctrine of the Christian faith) are critically examined, particularly in their relation to philosophy and world religions. Questions of lifestyle and social-cultural norms are discussed in relation to theological ethics. Practical theology deals with the current practice of faith in the church and in society. The study of systematic theology together with other courses shapes a student's thought and behavior in his/her vocational life after graduation.

- Students have the opportunity to practice the skills of public speaking and to consider their target audiences in formulating their approach. Students have access to the school's media technology to support them in their work. Students learn to assess how their intended meaning (whether through written or oral communication) has been received. They learn to listen and to respond to the needs of their audience. Graduates of Protestant theology are experts in communication.
- The methodical study of Christian doctrine and tradition makes it necessary to establish a certain distance to one's own religiosity. This is a valuable prerequisite for developing the capacity for empathy.
- The study of Protestant theology equips students to take a stand on contemporary moral and political issues, which can often produce inner conflict. Students are skilled in handling conflict – both internal and interpersonal.

  The school's international contacts and participation in the cultural life of a large city lead students to expand their horizons beyond their own field of study and beyond their own country and culture.

Learning Vocationally Specific Skills

1) When it comes to learning vocationally specific skills, there are three phases during which such learning is possible:

- First, concrete vocational skills may be acquired *prior to* any formal theological education. Students always arrive with varying amounts and kinds of experience already under their belts. Good teachers will recognize this and incorporate this into their classroom instruction. Here, however, we are speaking not of general life and church experience that virtually all students possess, but rather of specific vocational ministry experience which some students may have had before they begin their theological education. This may have come through adult education classes, post-graduate courses, or technical universities (poly-technical institutes). For formal theological education, this means that concrete vocational experience does not need to be part of the curriculum. On the other hand, it also means that the curriculum can assume that (some) students already have vocational experience. Their previously acquired skills become part of the instructional environment, and students receive guidance in assessing the experience they have had. (See the following section 6.5 on inductive learning.)
- Second, concrete vocational skills are not acquired until *after* formal theological education has been completed. In such situations, the formal curriculum is freed from the responsibility of teaching vocationally specific skills.[50] In this case – and this must be emphasized here – the typical university-based theological education is followed by a second phase of training in and through the churches. This constitutes a pastor's *practical training*. In this second phase of training, the traditional classroom approach is no longer the focal point, but rather practical experience, coaching, and feedback. This approach can be problematic for theological seminaries who operate according to the university model but whose graduates serve in churches that are not prepared to provide this kind of practical training (extended apprenticeship). In such cases, there are bound to be serious deficits in practical training.
- Third, concrete vocational skills can be acquired *during* the time of formal theological education. Two models may be identified: (i)

---

50. We saw earlier that intellectual/academic work is itself, of course, a vocationally relevant skill.

Curriculum Development in Theological Education 321

IT Skills	Hireability	Study	Problem Solving	Communication	Cooperation
Students…					
…can oversee, assess, and learn the use of IT, as well as identify means of their own further development.	…can assess the level of their own competency and identify ways to develop competencies demanded by employers.	…can function autonomously in studying and using learning resources. They can intervene in a professional manner to assist others in the process of independent learning.	…are confident and autonomous in solving problems. They are able to isolate, clarify, assess, and handle the most significant problems, providing effective solutions.	…can confidently enter into the academic and professional discourse in their field.	…can clarify a group assignment, lead a group, and work with/in a group to achieve designated results. They make appropriate use of the strengths of group members. They are able to negotiate with confidence and successfully resolve conflict.
…can prepare and use IT to support the efficient assessment of the search, selection, and presentation of information. They are able to access alternative research avenues and find new data where appropriate.	…are able to thoughtfully assess the competencies they possess and to improve the strategy for acquiring said competencies.	…can, with minimal supervision, learn independently by making use of all available resources in their field. They are able to ask for and make effective use of feedback.	…evidence confidence and flexibility in identifying and defining complex problems as well as in applying appropriate knowledge and skills to achieve solutions.	…can enter a conversation effectively and professionally and can produce detailed and coherent project reports.	…can participate productively in the learning process of a professional group. They can both exercise and support leadership. They can negotiate in a learning environment as well as in a professional environment and can resolve conflict constructively.
…can plan how to gather information needed to achieve necessary results, and know how to use such information. They are able to make use of the appropriate structures and procedures to gather and develop information.	…can create and implement a strategy for developing competencies demanded by employers.	…use a broad spectrum of tools and a flexible approach for studying. They identify their own learning needs and actively improve their performance. When assignments are clear, they can study and learn autonomously.	…can identify core elements of problems and thoughtfully choose appropriate means of solution.	…can communicate effectively and appropriately within their field, and, employing a variety of methods, can produce clear and concise reports about practical procedures, including all relevant information.	…can constructively participate in the learning process of a group by giving and receiving information and ideas, as well as incorporating feedback. They are able to build professional work relationships within their field.

Table 6

Students study part-time while they are engaged in ministry part-time or full-time. (ii) The curriculum includes internships and/or other experiential components. In both cases the curriculum must include provision for the acquiring of practical vocational skills. Yet the two models are significantly different. (i) In the first case, practical involvement in vocational ministry is given and lies outside the direct responsibility of the school. (ii) In the second case (internships), the practical vocational situation is somewhat artificial. Students engage in ministry but do not bear full ministry responsibility. In this case, the school is responsible for the processes and instruments used to provide practical training.

It is not my intention here to evaluation these three models. Each has its advantages and disadvantages. What is important is that schools recognize what they must do in order to fulfill their educational and training mandate, and that they do so with excellence.

2) Based on the decisions made above, concrete measures must be undertaken in terms of curriculum development. The organizational structures available have already been outlined in the table based on the work of Götz and Häfner (section 6.5.4):

- Simulation and practice (practical experience with no risk from failure)
- Supervised internships/apprenticeships (practical experience under the tutelage of experts)
- Unsupervised internships (practical experience without correction or instruction)
- On-the-job training (baptism by fire)

3) Jean-Pierre Crittin's scale of "experiential proximity" goes a step further and can be useful in curriculum planning. As with concentric circles, various forms of learning can be closer to or farther from vocational reality. The centre represents the reality of vocational/ministry life. The outermost circle represents theoretical lectures about vocational experience – theory about praxis. The whole scale, with all the steps in between, is shown in figure 20.[51]

---

51. Crittin, *Erfolgreich Unterrichten*, 35–38.

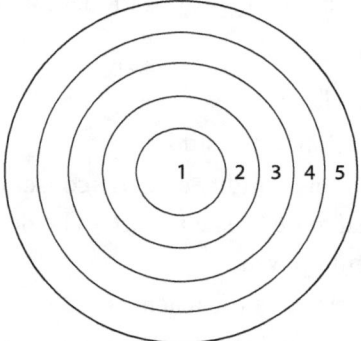

Figure 20

4) Crittin's scale can be used in the classroom (didactics) as well as in curriculum planning. We will limit ourselves here to the latter. The following are among the possibilities:

1. An internship (practicum) in a real-life vocational setting. It must be remembered, however, that an internship does not completely reflect reality, since it does not involve long-term vocational experience in which the participant carries full responsibility.

2. Practice within the protected environment of the school (for example, preaching in homiletics class).

3. Practical experience analogous to vocational life, yet within the educational institution (for example, team work, leading a group, project work, organization, making presentations, serving as a student representative on faculty or administration committees).

4. Role-play.

5. Case studies.

6. Observing through film/video or visits to churches.

7. Guest speakers who are engaged in pastoral ministry.

5) When it comes to acquiring concrete vocational skills, methods commonly used in vocational training are applicable. Skills can only truly be learned by doing. Basic didactic principles, which cannot be explained in

detail here, apply.⁵² The following proven model can serve as an example for vocational education:⁵³

The Four-Step Method

First Step
: Preparation of the students:
Dispel their timidity and self-consciousness. Describe material to be learned, work to be done. Awaken interest. Set them up well.

Second Step
: Presentation by the teachers:
First presentation: Explain and demonstrate: WHAT happens.
Second presentation: Explain and provide rationale: WHAT – HOW – WHY
Third presentation: Demonstrate, naming specific learning steps and emphasizing essential points. Demonstrate frequently, as needed.

Third Step
: Execution by the students:
First round: Open discussion and input. Correct serious errors.
Second round: Students explain and provide rationale: WHAT – HOW – WHY
Third round: Ensure students understand learning steps and essential points. Ask and answer questions. Repeat as needed.

Fourth Step
: Completion of instruction:
Allow students to practice on their own. Designate someone whom students can consult with questions or problems. Ask and answer questions. Initially provide frequent correction and help. Note and affirm progress. Provide correction as needed. Offer affirmation and recognition. Gradually decrease amount of instruction.

---

52. For my classroom work I have found the work of Hans Aebli helpful: *Zwölf Grundformen des Lehrens* (Stuttgart: Klett-Cotta, 1985).
53. Dieterich, *Auf dem Weg zum Beruf*, 98–101. Dieterich presents additional didactic methods useful in vocational education.

6.5.5 Curriculum Integration

Table 6 provides an overview of the elements of curriculum we have discussed thus far. Now the task is to form these elements into a curriculum, to a course that must be followed in order to reach the desired educational goal. Doing this is not without pitfalls. As has been stated before, curriculum planning is subject to forces that must be resisted:

- Additionalism without integration: A growing number of courses, events, and structural elements are added, in order to address weaknesses, but integration is lacking. The curriculum is expanded but not improved by this approach.
- Battles for territory and time: Certain courses, including those with classical content, traditionally belong to certain curricula. New, innovative courses and other elements that are intended to help students more fully reach their holistic educational goals, often face a daunting fight to find space and time in the already crowded curriculum.

It is the responsibility of the academic dean to take the measures necessary to ensure that a balanced curriculum is achieved. There are a number of tools available that can help to arrive at a desired level of integration. (See table 7).

The traditional elements of a curriculum	Curriculum cycle / Time allotments	Courses and course descriptions	Additional organizational structures
In the classroom: - Instruction - Lecture - Other teaching events	Traditional models: - Semesters - Continuous courses - Pre-defined course of study	Defining course content "historically," i.e. based on theological tradition	Moving from knowing to understanding: - Seminars and practice exercises - Tutorials - Work/study groups - Simulations
Group assignments	Alternative Models: - Modular - Flexible - Cumulative course of study	"Contemporary" definition of course content, i.e. based on current challenges	Encouraging spiritual formation and character development: - Devotionals - Small groups - Forming ministry teams - Retreats - Silence and solitude - Counselling
- Self-study - Homework assignments			Acquiring key qualifications and vocational skills: - Internships - Practice in a safe environment - Practical vocational experience - Role plays - Case studies - Observation - Guest lecturers from the field

Table 7

Classic Forms of Curriculum Integration

1) The most natural and most classic form is a linear construction of the curriculum, that is, the consecutive flow in which each course builds upon the preceding course(s), and each educational phase builds upon the one before. The logic is simple and for much content unavoidable. The basics must precede the more advanced material. Where there is no foundation,

no super-structure can be added. When it comes to languages, including the biblical languages, this is irrefutably the case. Other linear curriculum plans may be highly recommended and yet may fall victim to any number of factors or priorities, especially in modular, flexible educational plans.

For the biblical courses, the sequential logic is: a) Bible introduction, languages, history. b) Exegesis. c) Topical courses and biblical theology. To what extent and at what cost this order should be abandoned must be negotiated in each case.

For practical theology, the following sequence is logical: a) Bible. b) History and theology. c) Current practice. Applied specifically to the church: a) A biblical theology of the church. b) Models of ecclesiology throughout the centuries. c) Church growth principles and practice today. Here, too, it may be questionable to depart from this sequence. For the study of church history, a chronological overview precedes more detailed study of specific eras or periods.

2) What is called a "spiral" curriculum is somewhat more complex. Like a spiral, the course of study moves ever higher by handling the same topics and questions again and again, each time in more depth. The curriculum plan of primary and secondary schools follow this principle.

It is important here to distinguish between increased quantity and increased quality. This is relevant in theological education when, for example, at the master's level the same topics and material are addressed as at the undergraduate level. It cannot simply be more of the same. There must be a distinctly higher quality and depth. It is the noticeable shift to a higher level of critical thinking that distinguishes a master's degree program from a bachelor's program.

In this situation, integration means that a student grows in relation to the same topic. The student is able to apply knowledge acquired earlier on this subject, can draw upon knowledge from other subjects and can reason at a higher level.

Programs which simply provide more of the same, additional knowledge at the same level year after year, show that curriculum planning has been weak. The same can be said of programs that attempt to begin at the highest level, without first providing the lower levels of the spiral.

3) A further model of curriculum integration works with "clusters" – bundles or groups of courses. A number of courses – possibly sorted according to the classical disciplines (Bible, theology, praxis, history) – are grouped under one topic. In each course, this topic is studied but from a unique perspective. This method demands a knowledge of the basics and is therefore only suited to the more advanced stages of a curriculum.

4) In view of current developments in theological education, the following is worth noting: the growing flexibility and modularity in education today along with the trend toward a more open admissions process results in an individualized educational experience. In this environment it is difficult to create consistently integrative curricula.

As understandable as this student-oriented (or shall we say "market-oriented"?) approach may be, serious thought must be given to the price paid for such an approach. It is certainly pedagogically irresponsible to leave such decisions completely in the hands of the students themselves, who lack the bigger picture and who therefore may not see the need for integration.

When, based on flexibility and modularity, a curriculum allows a student to take "Principles of Church Leadership" in the first semester, prior to any courses in ecclesiology, and when a student therefore doesn't take Greek until the seventh semester, something has gone awry. This is not an integrated curriculum. And it does not serve the student well.

It is, however, possible to build mechanisms into a curriculum, even one that is quite flexible and market-oriented, that are conducive to sequential and spiral integration: (a) Courses are ordered sequentially in three phases. Students can take the first courses of the next phase when they have completed a predetermined minimum number of courses in the previous phase. (b) Courses in the next higher phase have prerequisites, that is, they can only be taken when the prerequisite courses have been completed. (c) Each student is required to have a faculty advisor who assists the student in devising a good, balanced, curriculum tailored to the student's needs.

Such measures can only be taken by larger seminaries that are able to offer a wide variety of courses at all levels of study. Smaller schools do not have this luxury, which means that students have to take courses when they are offered, even if the sequencing is not ideal.

Emphasizing the "Dimension" of the Curriculum

Earlier we introduced the concepts of "dimension" and "intention." A curriculum should embody certain values, content and aspirations that cannot be simply relegated to courses or other organizational forms. Every component of the curriculum must "breathe" this dimension, like music that sets the tone and creates an emotional atmosphere.

It's important at this point to mention once again what these "dimensions" are. They can exist at several levels:

- An institution's motto implies dimensions of the curriculum. If the motto of a seminary is "To Know Him and to Make Him Known,"[54] it must be evident in every fiber of the curriculum. Sometimes it may be particular denominational or theological accents or a specific mission which shapes a seminary or a program. These must become dimensions of the curriculum. Core values, identity markers, and theological emphases cannot simply be assigned to specific courses or events. They must permeate the entire curriculum.
- The educational goal may determine dimensions for the entire course of study. A school that explicitly trains people for cross-cultural missions will want to make its intercultural emphasis a dimension of every part of its program. Everything – every course and every other organizational structure – should serve this dimension. A school focused on training pastors will want to make pastoral ministry its "dimension."
- A holistic view of education calls for additional dimensions. If "learn – grow – pass it on" describes the pedagogical philosophy of a school, these elements must permeate every course and every component of the curriculum.

This can only be accomplished when these "dimensions" are frequently articulated, and when every teacher sees it as part of his or her job to incorporate these dimensions into every course.

This raises the question – Where and how are these dimensions evident in the individual courses offered?

---

54. Motto of Columbia International University in South Carolina.

Intentionally Creating Integrative Connections

There are a number of measures that can be undertaken to facilitate "dialogue" among various elements of the curriculum. The list that follows is certainly not exhaustive but may supply some instructive examples:

- Introduction of interdisciplinary courses. Example: During my master's program, I encountered a course called "The Life and Legacy of Jesus." It combined elements of New Testament exegesis, biblical theology, historical and systematic theology, ethics, and spirituality.
- Assigning homework that goes beyond the specifics of the course. Example: I did my master's program at an institution that encouraged students to write papers that could be submitted for two courses (with twice the length, of course). I still have the paper that I wrote in combination for courses in both The Gospel of John and The Theology of Missions.
- Group a number of courses together as a module with a common theme. Example: In the master's program at TDS-Aarau and TS Bienenberg three courses are always combined in a module with a theme for the semester. For example, for the semester theme "Ministry in the Church in Light of the Transforming Power of the Holy Spirit," the following three courses were offered:
  1) New Testament theology: the Holy Spirit and the church
  2) Church history: Church renewal in historical perspective
  3) Practical theology: Mission and ministries of the church

  A combined introductory lecture at the beginning of the semester shows the students the potential for integration. They are instructed to complete all of their assignments in a way that is not limited to one course but that integrates insights from all three courses.
- Experience gained during internships can be integrated into the homework assignments of courses in the following semester. I'm always amazed how infrequently this method is used. The internships are evaluated by means of interviews conducted by people specifically assigned to this task, yet very little of what is learned through this evaluation process is incorporated into courses that follow. It only takes a little thought and imagination to

formulate homework assignments in such a way that draws upon insights gained from internship experiences.

For example, in dogmatics class, students write a paper on a doctrinal question that they encountered during an internship. In addition to theological insights, the paper includes a presentation of the question as it was encountered in practice.

- Integration has long since been incorporated in primary and secondary schools under the name "project instruction."[55] This method has been used far too little in theological education. Project instruction dedicates a limited time (one week) to a relevant topic that is approached from different perspectives by teachers from a variety of disciplines. Why do we make so little room for this approach in our overloaded curricula?

For example: A project week is scheduled mid-semester. Students travel with several teachers and work on the topic: "Immigrants and Hospitality." It is not hard to integrate biblical, theological, historical and practical questions in such a setting.

Supporting Measures: Portfolio and Mentoring

Integration must not be limited to curriculum development. The goal must be that students learn to think and act in ways that demonstrate mastery of the concept of integration. That is not an easy thing for students to achieve. Recently two educational tools have proven successful in supporting this goal:

1) One method often used today both to encourage integration and to move the student toward higher levels of responsibility is the compiling of a portfolio. "In the world of education a portfolio is a collection of documents that describe or verify a course of study, a portion of a curriculum, or in some cases the entire educational history of an individual."[56]

2) There are different kinds of portfolios that fulfill distinct purposes:[57]

---

55. On the method of project instruction see Johannes Bastian and Herbert Gudjons, eds., *Das Projektbuch. Theorie – Praxisbeispiele – Erfahrungen* (Hamburg: Bergmann und Helbig, 1994).

56. http://www.stangl-taller.at/ARBEITSBLAETTER/PRAESENTATION/portfolio.shtml. This website also offers an expanded bibliography on this topic. Helpful insights on compiling a portfolio can also be found at http://www.ph-freiburg.de/schreibzentrum.

57. The list here is taken from http://www.stangl-taller.at/ARBEITSBLAETTER/PRAESENTATION/portfolio.shtml.

The Working Portfolio

- A selected collection of a student's papers and work on a specific topic.
- Can include completed assignments as well as those still in progress.
- Individual parts of this portfolio may also be included in the Status Report or Assessment Portfolio or also in the Showcase Portfolio.
- Can be used by a teacher or advisor providing curriculum or career counselling to the student. Enables such advice to be individually tailored.
- Provides experience in self-assessment and also in receiving evaluation from others and thus is generally not subject to grading or marking.

The Status Report or Assessment Portfolio

When portfolios are used as a measure of performance and are thus subject to grading, the criteria by which they are to be produced and ultimately judged must be spelled out clearly. This includes the scope, content, language, style, as well as the format and external appearance of the portfolio. Students should receive a written list that clearly and explicitly articulates the expectations.

- Documented completion of specific assignments based on clearly outlined objectives, clearly defined scope, and a specific instructional sequence.
- Proof that certain study processes have been followed (for example, research, writing, creative processes, etc.)
- For the sake of objectivity and comparison in the evaluation process, criteria must be developed – ideally with input from students – that are specific, practical, and achievable. These criteria, which include the portfolio's external form, should be established and communicated before the portfolio assignment is given.
- Completion with evaluation/grading.
- Tests and papers of the traditional sort, designed to measure achievement in specific aspects of learning, are not in conflict with the concept of an assessment portfolio. Rather, they can serve as a meaningful complement to the portfolio.

The Showcase, Display, or Best Works Portfolio
- A careful and thoughtful selection of a student's best work, or samples of the work a student is most pleased with.
- Used most often with the arts but can be used in other fields as well.
- The works selected document a student's performance over a longer period of time – an entire school year or longer.

The Time Sequenced or Process Portfolio
- A collection of a student's work over a longer period of time.
- Includes assignments done at the beginning of a course of study as well as those done at the conclusion.
- Builds a foundation for self-evaluation by the student as well as evaluation by others, based on predetermined objectives.

The Interdisciplinary Unit Portfolio
- Documentation of work that transcends a specific subject and/or connects diverse subject matter (different fields of learning).
- A collection of a student's work on general topics such as learning how to learn, methods of study, or organizing one's study habits, as well as interdisciplinary topics such as AIDS, addiction, right-wing extremism, or new media.

The Celebration Portfolio
- A collection of a student's work on a particular topic from one or more specific perspectives chosen by the students themselves.
- Development of a line of questioning, demonstrating self-study and the use of feedback from a student's peer group as well as from the teacher.

The Job Application Portfolio
- Documentation of an individual's schooling, including certificates, diplomas and degrees, and selected samples of a student's work in a variety of areas, which give the reader insight into the individual's personality, character, skills and strengths and which go beyond information to be gleaned from a typical job application form.
- Includes such items as a letter of introduction, C.V., school certificates (demonstrating a student's involvement in extra-

curricular activities, school committees, etc.), academic record, course completion certificates, letters of recommendation, etc. May also include a personal letter, self-produced videos, letters to the editor, etc.

The Presentation Portfolio
- What should be included in a presentation portfolio must be clearly defined so that it can fulfill its purpose in documenting a student's learning and accomplishments. Because the specific elements may vary according to specific preferences, agreements, and requirements, it is not possible to give a definitive list here. The criteria used, however, should correspond to the nature of this particular portfolio, which seeks to present a blend of process and results.

---

3) The important thing about the portfolio concept is that it goes beyond earlier methods such as the keeping of a homework assignment journal. The use of portfolios is part of a new culture of learning designed to help students to achieve new levels of learning based on their own initiative. Gerd Bräuer lists the following characteristics of a well-designed portfolio approach:[58]

Portfolio Assignments Must Be Given under the Premise of "Learning as Process."
- Institutional, results-oriented performance assessments must not be allowed to play more than a minor role.
- Rough drafts and assignments that are still in progress should definitely be included.
- Standards for self-assessment must be modifiable (or modified) for each group of students and their particular learning situation.

---

58. See http://www.ph-freiburg.de/schreibzentrum. The summary which follows is taken from http://www.stangl-taller.at/ARBEITSBLAETTER/PRAESENTATION/portfolio.shtml.

Portfolio assignments must form a bridge between personal and group study.

- Materials included should give evidence of the interplay between the world of the individual learner and the world of general knowledge.
- The evaluation of the portfolio should take into consideration to what extent the student has been successful in adapting personal forms of communication (e.g. research notes) to public forms of communication (e.g. a project report).
- For a portfolio assignment, both in the personal and public forms of communication, the learning process is just as important as the learning outcome, and these should be weighted equally in any assessment.

Portfolio assignments should be designed to enable students to express themselves meaningfully and articulately.

- Portfolio assignments involve more than merely collecting materials for the folder (portfolio). Ultimately they should equip students to more easily complete other learning and work processes (journals, diaries, research, etc.)
- Items included in a portfolio are ideally content-specific (they may, for example, include personal impressions gleaned from an article in a magazine) and sharpen a student's communication skills. (They could, for example, equip a student to write a book review in the student newspaper.)
- The ability to evaluate and assess one's own work is a complex skill not easily honed, and requires therefore regular practice. Peer review should occur frequently and be seen as a chance for mutual learning.

Portfolio assignments work best with interdisciplinary coordination and advisors.

- Ideal for this purpose are centres for reading and writing that are external to the classroom – extra-curricular structures with peer tutors – which offer advice and encouragement.
- Such school-sponsored reading and writing centres, through the involvement of a wide breadth of teachers, ensure that portfolio

assignments retain an interdisciplinary character. These centres oversee the content and assist with organization and coordination.

Portfolios can be used as an alternative means of assessing achievement.

- Because of the subjective elements involved in assessing the quality of a portfolio, more than one teacher should participate in the evaluation.
- The evaluation of a portfolio must go beyond assigning a grade or point value. It must include an oral evaluation (student-teacher conference) or a detailed written commentary.

Portfolio assignments are a tool of quality control and a measure of a school's progress.

- If portfolios are thoroughly and continuously evaluated, conclusions can be drawn concerning the quality of learning that is being achieved.
- Because portfolio assignments require significant cooperation and interaction between students and teachers, their use can reveal something about the efficiency of learning at the school, and where appropriate, adjustments/improvements can be made.

---

4) The use of portfolio assignments is most effective when it is accompanied and supported by mentoring. I am aware that the term "mentoring" is widely used but perhaps less widely understood. The distinction between mentoring and other terms such as coaching, supervision, or counselling is often unclear. Although there are many forms and definitions, the potential for mentoring within theological education should be addressed.[59] As a starting point, we can use the definition of mentoring provided by the Martineum, an educational institution for the church and diaconal ministries:[60]

---

59. Cf. Müller, "Persönlichkeitsprägung als Herausforderung," 123–152.
60. http://www.martineum.de/dozenten.html

> A member of the Martineum is chosen by the student as a mentor. This mentor accompanies the student from the onset of studies until that student is installed in a place of ministry. Mentors are specially trained for their task. They assist the student in building personal and professional relationships, in ensuring the quality of their educational experience, and in setting ministry goals.

According to this definition, mentoring includes the following elements:
- Mentoring is a voluntary relationship between an experienced person and a person who wants to learn (from the mentor's experience).
- Mentoring is a process that continues throughout the entire duration of a person's training.
- Mentoring provides a relationship that is outside the normal student-teacher relationship.
- Mentoring integrates – facilitates connections, networks, and relationships within the educational arena, in the professional world, and in one's private life as well.

In summary: Through regular conversations with a mentor, an individual's entire learning experience is consciously, intentionally reflected upon, assessed, evaluated, and directed. It is the mentor's job to encourage their students and help them to take responsibility for shaping their own educational experience.

Portfolio assignments and mentoring are two outstanding methods by which students can learn how to learn. And this applies not only to what they are learning at school but also to the whole of life, particularly with regard to their profession/ministry. This significance of tools like this becomes clear when one realizes that in view of *lifelong learning*, learning how to learn is a key competency of the highest priority.

The importance of mentoring for integration and the learning experience has become so clear that mentoring programs are now part of the quality standards for theological education. The EEAA expects its member schools to implement appropriate mentoring programs. These are valued so highly that academic credits can be earned for participation in structured mentoring.[61] Similarly, mentoring has become an integral element of pastoral education in the Reformed Church in Switzerland.[62]

Additional Literature

Tobias Faix and Anke Wiedekind. *Mentoring: Das Praxisbuch: Ganzheitliche Begleitung von Glaube und Leben* [Mentoring: An Experiential Handbook: Holistic Oversight in Faith and Life]. Neukirchen-Vluyn: Neukirchener Aussaat, 2010.

See also the "Christliche Mentoringnetzwerk" [Christian Mentoring Network], initiated by the same two authors (http://www.c-mentoring.net/).

6.6 Two Examples

I will conclude this chapter on integration and curriculum development with two examples.

6.6.1 "Reenvisioning the Theological Curriculum as If the Missio Dei Mattered"

Andrew Kirk proposed an integrative, missions-oriented curriculum that incorporates many of the elements discussed in this chapter. Kirk presented the basis for his work in *The Mission of Theology and the Theology as Mission*. In "Reenvisioning the Theological Curriculum as If the *Missio Dei* Mattered" he takes his thinking a step farther and gets more specific.

Kirk suggests that theological education needs a radically new orientation. As a first step, he proposes that the goal and purpose of theological education be redefined with the following two statements:[63]

- To make sense of the whole life by reference to God.
- To be an agent of transformation, so that the whole of life may reflect God's intentions.

Three things are noteworthy here: (1) The first statement emphasizes thought, reflection, theory. ("To make sense of" involves the task of

---

61. Cf. EEAA Manual 2011, Chapter 3.2.8 (http://www.eeaa.eu/downloads-and-tools/the-eeaa-manual/).
62. See "Mentorat" at http://www.konkordat.ch/htm.ausbilding.htm
63. Kirk, *Mission of Theology*, 31, 39.

interpretation.) The second statement involves behavior, practice, action (the task of transformation – "be an agent of"). The two stand in relation to one another. Theory and practice are integrated. (2) Both statements – theory and practice – are missions oriented. That is, they are *missional*. This missional orientation is holistic. It has the whole of life in view. (3) Both statements (and the theological work they undergird) are utterly theocentric. The world is to be interpreted in reference to God, and transformation has to happen in accordance with God's intentions.

Kirk proposes an educational path consisting of three phases:[64]

(1) Seeing, observing, perceiving	Observing what students believe, know, understand, and have experienced Cultural and social analysis
(2) Assessing, evaluating	Biblical and theological criteria Becoming familiar with history and tradition Evaluating past experience and current situation
(3) Taking action	Concrete experience in pastoral, missionary and social (compassion and justice) ministries

Table 8

For Kirk, the three steps of "see" – "judge" – "act" are important. These are steps that theology students will have to master in ministry after graduation. Observe the situation – form a reasonable judgment – take action. This proposal would ensure that the curriculum is analogous to what ministry will be like after graduation. Even though students are not yet living in the world of praxis and indeed may be intentionally separated from praxis in order to have time and space for adequate thought and reflection (theory), this educational model seeks to pave the way for students to gain familiarity with steps and skills they will later use in ministry. Traditional curricula often fail to provide this preparation.

In his book *The Mission of Theology and Theology as Mission*, Kirk ended with a brief but concrete curriculum proposal. He expanded this proposal in "Reenvisioning the Theological Curriculum as if the *Missio Dei* Mattered":

---

64. Ibid., 53–59.

Phase 1 (up to 6 months)	Exploring contexts (personal, cultural, social and political)
Phase 2 (up to 1 year)	Studying the church's mission
Phase 3 (3 months)	Engaging in interaction and consolidation
Phase 4 (15 months)	Dealing with issues that emerge

Total time required – approximately 3 years.

Table 9

Kirk remains quite flexible about the way the time is structured and the specifics of content. It is not his intention to predefine the details of the curriculum. He wants to retain freedom to respond to needs as they arise. Yet this proposed structure provides a workable framework upon which an entire curriculum can be developed.

Kirk circulated this proposal at a conference held at the Baptist seminary in Prague with the hope of stimulating thought and discussion about the reform of theological education. He is aware that accomplishing change in traditional theological institutions is not easy. Yet we must ask, what is keeping us from implementing his suggestions and traveling new directions that are more holistic, more missions oriented, and ultimately more relevant as well? It's not about simply copying his plan. It's about understanding the underlying principles and taking steps to implement them.

6.6.2 The Concordat Reform of the Reformed Church in Switzerland

The training of pastors in the Reformed Church of Switzerland, regulated cooperatively by several cantonal churches, was revamped as a result of the Bologna reform.[65] The revised plan was worked out in partnership between the theological faculties of the universities of Zürich and Basel and the Concordat churches.

---

65. For a description of the entire concept of pastoral education and continuing education in the Reformed churches of Switzerland see http://www.konkordat.ch/htm/ausbildung.htm.

The training regulations specify explicitly (section 2): "The training to become a pastor of a Concordat church consists of two segments – one through the university, and one through the church. Together they form a didactic whole." In carrying out this commitment to a holistic view of theological education, this new approach bids farewell to the traditional two-phase approach, which included a first phase of several years of academic theological education (theory) followed by the "second phase" of a vicariate (extended internship) in the church (praxis). The revised concept is a more integrated educational process, employing the following curriculum structure:[66]

University Component	Church Component
Bachelor's Program – 6 semesters Students acquire knowledge in all areas of basic theology through lectures, seminars, and writing papers and other assignments.	**Mentoring** Beginning with the first semester, students are mentored by trained individuals by the church.
	Ecclesiological-Practical Seminar A five-month internship outside the university setting combined with group supervision.
Master's Program – 4 semesters Students expand their knowledge and are able to present an overview of the central themes in their field and to articulate the state of current theological debate.	**Developmental Aptitude Assessments** Four evaluations interspersed throughout the entire four semesters.
	Study Internship A year-long training experience in a church, with supervision by a specially trained pastor. Includes twelve different week-long practical courses.
	Certification of Compentency Examination at the end of the course of study to determine skills acquired during training, using a recognized competency assessment grid.
	Continuing Education in the First Years of Pastoral Ministry

Table 10

---

66. Drawn from Hans Strub, "Der Weg zum Pfarramt," *Annex* 11 (magazine of the Reformed Press), (2006): 6–7.

Both of the educational models presented here must still prove that they can be effectively implemented. However, they are both certainly examples of the kind of paradigm shift that has been occurring in theological education over the past several years.

7

Ensuring Quality in Theological Education

The task of curriculum development must include evaluation – the constant examination of results. Only through adequate evaluation can it be determined whether the methods used are leading to the desired results. Only through evaluation can a feedback loop be established that makes ongoing improvement possible. This final step in curriculum development deserves its own chapter.

In the world of education, quality management has become a central concern. That can be seen everywhere. Globalization, liberalization, and a market-driven approach have become common factors within the educational sector. As a result, the quest for measurable, demonstrable quality in educational institutions and programs has become more urgent. Evaluation, certification, and accreditation have become everyday topics. This is new territory for European institutions of higher education, and a flood of new literature has been published in recent years.[1] The Bologna process also lent additional weight to the question of quality management. The establishment of nationwide systems of quality management was part of the Bologna reforms. As a result, any countries which were not yet familiar with quality management are now in the process of establishing nationwide

---

1. Cf. Mayer, Daniel and Teichler, *Die neue Verantwortung*, 95–111; Werner Fröhlich and Wolfgang Jütte, *Qualitätsentwicklung in der postgradualen Weiterbildung: Internationale Entwicklungen und Perspektiven* (Münster: Waxmann, 2004); Hedi Clementi, Andrea Hoyer and Judith Ziegler, eds., *Institutionelle Evaluierung an Fachhochschulen* (Vienna: Facultas wuv universitätsverlag, 2004); Holger Ehlert and Ulrich Welber, eds., *Qualitätssicherung und Studienreform* (Düsseldorf: Grupello Verlag, 2004).

systems of quality management and accreditation and indeed are learning lessons from their first attempts.

Even at the level of primary and secondary education, quality management has become a significant factor, especially in semi-autonomous schools.[2]

Theological schools – both those that are a part of the university system and those seminaries and Bible schools that are not associated with a university – are also involved in the process of quality management.

In North America and particularly in the United States, theological schools have a longer history of involvement with accreditation processes, whether through state and national recognition or within the framework of the ATS. Even so, the worldwide emphasis on quality and evaluation has led to the fact that *assessment* is now numbered among the top four topics being discussed by the leadership of institutions of theological education in North America.[3] A glance through the recent issues of the journal *Theological Education* provides ample confirmation.[4]

It is worth noting that evangelical theological schools on all continents have been interested in accreditation and quality management for decades and have established appropriate accreditation mechanisms and procedures. All of these accrediting associations from around the world are connected through ICETE. To the best of my knowledge this is the only place in theological education where accreditation and quality management are encouraged and coordinated in an international network.

The section that follows will take up the topic of quality management at the level of the individual educational institution. The principle that applies here is: Questions of quality are the responsibility of the leadership. Those in leadership must know the mechanisms and instruments of quality management and have the authority to ensure that they are appropriately used.

---

2. See Dubs, *Qualitätsmanagement für Schulen*.
3. See Warford, *Practical Wisdom*, 1–12
4. Of particular note are the following three issues: 39, no. 1 (2003) on the topic, "The Character and Assessment of Learning for Religious Vocation"; 39, no. 2 (2003) on the topic, "Institutional Assessment and Theological Education: Navigating Our Way"; 40, no. 2 (2005) on the topic, "Listening to Theological Students and Scholars: Implications for the Character and Assessment of Learning for Religious Vocation."

7.1 Quality Management, Evaluation, Accreditation – Definition of Terms

7.1.1 Terms and Concepts

When discussing quality management in the field of education, many terms are commonly used without being clearly defined. This has led to some confusion and misunderstanding. It is therefore essential to start by with some clear definition of terms. Some terms, however, are not defined and used in the same way by everyone. Thus all that can be accomplished here is to clarify how terms will be used here, in an effort to simplify communication throughout the rest of this chapter.[5]

Educational Control

The term *educational control* is used as an umbrella term for "ensuring that individual schools reach their goals." Dubs defines the term as follows:

> *Control* means: A body examines whether goals that are set are also achieved, and whether, when they are not achieved, the necessary corrective steps are undertaken. This body does not examine how the goals are achieved and does not intervene so long as the goals are reached, or, when they are not achieved, the institution itself takes the necessary corrective steps.

Educational control includes "all measures taken to assess the effectiveness of the educational process from a pedagogical and financial perspective." Thus it is clear that educational management includes two areas: (a) economical/fiscal responsibility and (b) quality management.

Dubs is addressing the situation in public schools. In that context, educational control is the job of the state.

Quality Management

This section deals with the aspect of educational control called quality management. This includes processes which define, improve and ensure quality in educational institutions.

---

5. Unless otherwise noted, I am drawing upon Dubs, *Qualitätsmanagement für Schulen*, 6–13. See also Rolf Dubs, *Die Führung einer Schule. Leadership und Management* (Stuttgart:

In order to institute a systematic approach to quality management, it is first necessary to develop a quality management concept which defines how quality management will be implemented. Such a concept may look something like the one suggested by Dubs and shown in figure 21.

Figure 21

The second level of the figure shows a divide between internally driven and externally driven quality management. In the former, the concept is developed within the school. In the latter, a third party (for example, an accrediting association) develops the plan.

Evaluation

On the lowest level of figure 21 the term *evaluation* is introduced. Evaluation entails the implementation of quality management. If the evaluation is conducted by the school itself, it is called internal evaluation. If the evaluation is done by a third party, it is referred to as external evaluation. A number of ideas can be deduced from this:

- Several agencies supervisory to a school (government, board, accrediting association) can prescribe a quality management program for the school. Such an externally generated quality management plan can require that the school conduct a self-evaluation and/or it can call for an external evaluation to be undertaken.
- The desire for quality management can arise from within the school, in which case the school would most likely develop its own quality management plan, which could include both internal and external evaluation. An internally driven quality management plan such as this could well follow the recommendations of an accrediting

agency, assuming the school sought to achieve accreditation through its quality management efforts.

When various forms of evaluation are used, both internal and external, the result is what is called *multiple quality management*. A further variation occurs when a quality management program is internally driven and developed, and evaluation is also internally done, but under the oversight of an external agency. Such a plan is called *metaevaluation*.[6]

Accreditation[7]

Accreditation, also called validation in the UK,[8] is the process by which an educational institution has the quality and level of its training certified by means of an external assessment of its educational program conducted by a recognized special authority (panel, committee or agency). A supervisory authority attests that the education provided by a school meets well defined, widely accepted standards.

The relationship between quality management and accreditation is obvious. An accreditation process consists of quality management and evaluation. There are a number of variations. Two basic forms are worth noting here:

1) In one model, accreditation is granted by a recognized accrediting agency. In most cases, the evaluation occurs through the process of multiple quality management. Often the accrediting agency prescribes the parameters, on the basis of which the school then develops a quality management plan and conducts an internal evaluation. The accrediting agency then verifies the work that the school has done through a metaevaluation, as well as conducting its own comprehensive, complementary evaluation. The accrediting agency then attests to the quality and academic level of the educational programs offered

---

6. At yet a higher supervisory level the entire evaluation process must itself be evaluated, which occurs through the use of appropriate scientific studies. The question must be addressed whether the evaluation and accreditation process really accomplishes what it alleges to accomplish. An example of such a study which examines and compares the evaluation process of twelve technical universities is Clementi, Hoyer and Ziegler, *Institutionelle Evaluierung*.

7. I addressed the topic of accreditation more thoroughly in an article entitled "Accreditation: Importance and Benefits for the Institution," in the handbook *Foundations for Academic Leadership*, eds. Fritz Deininger, Orbelina Eguizabal, International Council for Evangelical Theological Education (Nürnberg: VTR Publications, 2013).

8. Accreditation and validation are not precisely the same in Britain. We will not, however, go into the differences here.

by the school. There may be a number of variations of this basic format for an accreditation process. Depending on the context (country, state, public school system), accrediting agencies have the authority to give schools the right to confer degrees and academic titles (as in the US). In other cases, accrediting agencies only have the authority to examine (and attest) the equivalent value of degrees conferred (as is the case for the EEAA). In still other situations, accrediting agencies can attest that a school meets the quality standards and has the necessary academic level in order to apply to the government for the right to confer degrees and academic titles (as is the case according to the new regulations in Europe developed as a result of the Bologna reform process).

2) In a second accreditation model, a school seeking recognition is directly connected to an accredited university. In such a case, the university accredits or validates an external school or its program(s). In this scenario, the school submits to the quality management process of the university. The university must then provide the accrediting agency with documenting evidence that it (the university) has control over the quality of education offered by the external school and its program(s). The university fulfills this responsibility by establishing and enforcing a quality management plan which enables the university to examine and verify the school's academic level and quality.

The particular instruments used and measures undertaken by the university can be quite varied. In every case, however, the external school (seeking recognition) must comply with the quality management plan established by the university if it wants to be accredited by that university.

In this model, students at the external school are considered to be students of the parent university and receive, upon successful completion of their studies, degrees conferred by the university. A number of theological seminaries in German-speaking Europe have adopted this model in conjunction with American or British universities.

7.1.2 *Purpose and Goal of Quality Management, Evaluation and Accreditation*

The question may well be raised, of what value is all this? This question is particularly meaningful in view of the fact that the accreditation process requires a significant expenditure of time, energy and resources. Smaller theological seminaries find themselves quickly pushed to their limits.

The question of the purpose and value of accreditation is appropriate in view of the current accreditation boom in German-speaking Europe and the growing number of independent (free church and evangelical) educational institutions that offer recognized bachelor's, master's and doctoral programs.

Without insinuating anything about any particular school, it must be asked whether market pressures have contributed to this trend. School X will want to claim the same quality and offer the same degree as School Y and School Z. Such a mindset is in no way reprehensible, yet it may be too shortsighted when it comes to understanding and implementing a quality management plan.

Quality Management as an Ethical Obligation

A school must be profoundly interested in being a good school. What that means, how quality is defined – we will talk about that a bit later. For now, suffice it to say that to be good, a school must offer the very best that it can in view of its mission. It owes that much to its students. Students should be certain that they are getting what they have been promised. They should be confident that they are being optimally prepared for the vocational tasks that are represented in the educational goals.

Theological schools have an obligation to the church and to missions to be "good" schools. If theological education seeks to serve the church and its mission, and trains people to this end, then it has an ethical-moral obligation to deliver a good product.

However it is not enough to *want* to be good. A school that really wants to be good will do everything in its power to ensure – in ways that are concrete and measurable – that it is good and that it is constantly getting better. That is the role of quality management.

Quality Management and a School's Trust Factor (Public Confidence)

Quality management is also a means of building trust. By allowing the quality and level of its educational progam(s) to be openly evaluated and accredited by an outside agency, a school's quality becomes a matter of public record, plain for all to see. The qualities of the school become transparent and subject to inspection (and criticism). That creates trust. Such a school is building its authority on something more than its historic reputation and vague assumptions.

The fact that quality management and accreditation are directly related to a school's trust factor is well known in the world of secular education as well. Intensified efforts in quality management are a response to the loss of public trust in the universities. These noble old institutions can no longer base their good reputation on their notable history alone. Universities are, for the most part, no longer seen as the guardians of truth. That makes essential a rigorous quality management plan which openly examines whether an educational institution is (still) making an important contribution to the development of society.[9]

It is not a given, however, that quality management and accreditation will be able to strengthen public trust in institutions of theological education. Especially in the case of independent, denominational, and evangelical seminaries and schools, academic certification is not the only trust building factor. Other things such as the quality of the faculty, the work and reputation of the graduates, and the trustworthiness of the (theological) content are equally important. That means that an appropriate quality management plan must assess these factors as well.

This leads us to the question of what quality management can and should accomplish.

The Specific Functions of Quality Management

Drawing upon Rolf Dubs, we can identify the following four functions of quality management:

Directional Function: Evaluation results form an indispensable basis for making decisions about the future. A good evaluation will reveal trends and expose weaknesses. These insights should be seen as valuable for planning the future. It should not be taken for granted, however, that this will be the case. A good quality management program will ensure that a feedback loop is implemented, which will give ample weight to such insights. That is one mark of a good organization – that quality management is not seen as a means to

---

9. The increased importance of evaluation and accreditation in the world of higher education is a direct response to the crisis of trust between science and society. Universities no longer automatically enjoy a good reputation based on their history and tradition. They must submit to open evaluation in order to establish trust. See Ehlert and Welber, *Qualitätssicherung und Studienreform*, especially "Paradigmenwechsel in der Bildungspolitik: Evaluation und Akkreditierung als Instrumente der Qualitätssicherung," 80–103.

an end (evaluation simply in order to achieve accreditation) but rather as a tool used to achieve ongoing improvement.

Control Function: Evaluation results are useful for external control. Evaluations give accrediting agencies insights into deficiencies that may require intervention.

Vindication Function: The quality management process may give resource providers a sense of an institution's legitimacy. Two basic questions can be answered: "Is the educational mandate being fulfilled?" and "Are resources being used effectively?"

PR Function: Quality management and accreditation attest quality to the outside world and the marketplace. Anyone who is interested can receive from an independent external source the assurance that a school is delivering what it promises.[10]

7.2 Which Quality Management Model Should Be Used?

There is wide agreement in the world of education that quality management is of strategic importance. When it comes to identifying the appropriate quality management plan for any given situation, however, there are often hefty disagreements.

Some quality management plans, introduced with great enthusiasm and fanfare, have failed simply because they consumed too much time and energy. Quality management can quickly require enormous sums of personnel time, paperwork, and ultimately money. The cost-benefit ratio must be carefully analyzed.

In addition to this, it has proven to be quite challenging to take quality management principles from the marketplace and apply them directly to an educational setting. Because this kind of direct transfer has often not worked well, the concept of quality management has encountered opposition in the world of education, often from teachers and professors.

Therefore it is important to choose, after careful consideration, the most effective approach to quality management for any given context.

---

10. Dubs, *Qualitätsmanagement für Schulen*, 12–13.

The situation in public schools and state universities is different from that in private schools. In the case of the former, government agencies often prescribe the parameters for quality management. In the case of the latter, they are often implementing quality management plans of their own in an effort to achieve accreditation.

In the section that follows, we will deal primarily with seminaries and Bible schools that are privately funded and which operate apart from public or state universities.

7.2.1 Basic Categories and Basic Decisions

There have been a number of developments in the field of quality management within the past few decades. Different philosophies are occasionally at odds with one another. There are at least three basic categories which must be considered:

Control or Evaluation

Two differing approaches to quality management are sometimes contrasted with one another: the control paradigm and the evaluation paradigm.[11]

> The **control paradigm** assumes a static environment in which there are long-term qualities which must be controlled in order to determine whether the prescribed qualities are being maintained. If this is not the case, an appropriate authority intervenes.

> The **evaluation paradigm** assumes a dynamic environment in which constant adjustments are necessary, which means that no long-term qualities are possible. Therefore internally driven evaluations are essential, and improvements are made voluntarily as a result of organizational learning.

In the early history of quality management, the control paradigm was dominant. Today the trend is clearly in the direction of the evaluation paradigm. The control paradigm is seen as authoritarian, undemocratic, disempowering, and counter-productive to the life processes of a school. By contrast, the evaluation paradigm strengthens a school's self-determination,

---

11. The definitions that follow are taken from Dubs, *Qualitätsmanagement für Schulen*, 79.

takes the life processes of a school seriously, and encourages dynamic, lasting improvements in quality.

Experts warn, however, against an either-or mentality. Rudolf Dubs' assessment seems to me to be both wise and realistic:

> The evaluation paradigm serves as a foundation for every individual school. But it is not enough on its own. The effectiveness of quality management is ensured through the complementary implementation of the control paradigm.[12]

The implications for theological schools are clear: In order to continually improve the quality of education, it is not enough to undergo regular measurements by an accrediting agency. There must be an evaluation system integrated into the school philosophy and the everyday life of the school that is not primarily aimed at satisfying the requirements of an external agency, but which instead has in view the continuous, ongoing development and improvement of the school. Yet to ensure that this fundamental and continual evaluation process is not left up to the goodwill of the school, the use of an external control function is also needed.

Internal or External Quality Management

The terms internal and external quality management were already introduced, along with the concepts of self-evaluation and evaluation by a third party. The possible variations were represented in figure 22. Which approach is best for (independent, privately funded) theological schools? The answer can be found by considering the following facts:

- These seminaries and schools are not subject to any predetermined quality standards or enforcement mechanisms imposed by the government. Thus they are free to choose the model most suited for them.
- However, because most of these institutions seek some form of accreditation, they submit themselves voluntarily to an externally developed quality assurance system (an accrediting agency or a recognized university).

---

12. Dubs, *Qualitätsmanagement für Schulen*, 79.

Thus most of these schools adopt a quality management concept that combines internal and external elements:

1) The school voluntarily decides to submit to the *externally developed quality management plan* of an accrediting agency or institution.

2) In most cases this *externally developed quality management plan* requires a *self-evaluation*. The questions and categories covered by the self-evaluation generally demand a high degree of *internally developed quality management*. This internally developed quality management is intended to have the character of the *evaluation paradigm*. This means its evaluations should be systems- and process-oriented and encourage the continuous, ongoing development and improvement of the school. The self-evaluation process usually concludes with a written self-study report.

3) The accrediting agency takes a supervisory role which may encompass any of four dimensions:[13]
   - *Metaevaluation*, that is, an evaluation of the internal quality management process.
   - *Peer Review*, that is, an external assessment conducted by persons from similar educational institutions (Audit Teams).[14]
   - *External Evaluation*, in which external experts (Audit Team) conduct evaluations which go beyond the self-study report (interviews, surveys, observations, document review, etc.).
   - *Control Authority* (control paradigm), which ultimately must decide whether the school will be accredited and which can require that corrective steps be taken where minimum standards have not been met.

A combination of internal and external elements of quality management such as those just described seems to have carried the day. One-sided plans – purely external or purely internal – have not proven successful.

An external-external approach (externally developed plan coupled with external evaluation) disempowers the educational institution, creates

---

13. Cf. Dubs, *Qualitätsmanagement für Schulen*, 50; who speaks of a "subsidiary external evaluation" and refers to metaevaluation and peer review.

14. On the concept of peer review, see Ibid., 76.

resistance and opposition, which leads to minimal cooperation and also therefore to poor results. It also impedes internally driven quality management aimed at improvement and development, rather than encouraging it.

An internal-internal approach has deficiencies of its own. Organizational blindness, internal self-congratulatory evaluations, and a weariness factor in the face of a continuous evaluation process are all things that have shown that a purely internal quality management process is ineffective. Thus a "subsidiary external evaluation" (Dubs) can be helpful.

Internal evaluations submitted to an external accrediting agency have not always proven to be unproblematic. It is easy for such internal evaluations to be overly positive, in an effort to achieve accreditation. It is a much more challenging task to conduct a rigorous, honest, self-critical evaluation that truly aims at improving the quality development of the school.

That is why an external supervisory function is so important – one which can help to ensure that the internal quality management processes are optimized. The four mechanisms listed above (Metaevaluation, Peer Review, External Evaluation, and Control Authority) are appropriate tools that can be used to this end. These tools will be described in greater detail later in this chapter.

First, however, yet another basic decision must be considered.

Total Quality Management or "Focus Evaluations"

Total Quality Management is a term that is now commonly used to describe comprehensive quality management concepts such as have become the norm in the marketplace and have been standardized worldwide (International Standards Organization [ISO] and European Foundation for Quality Management [EFQM]).[15]

If and to what extent such comprehensive plans can and should be implemented in the educational sector has been a subject of debate. It would appear that the use of ISO norms adapted for the educational sector coupled with Total Quality Management is more widespread in higher education (tertiary level) than at the primary or secondary level.[16] Dubs recommends

---

15. Cf. Dubs, *Qualitätsmanagement für Schulen*, 41.
16. See Walter Brückner, Jürgen Heene and Karsten Koitz, "Nicht für die Schule, für's Leben. Neue Qualitätsstandards für Bildungsunternehmen," *Qualität und Zertifizierung* 49, no. 9 (2004): 24–25. The authors present the Norm DIN PAS 1037:2004 which was developed

that a comprehensive quality management plan not be used for primary and secondary education.[17] For one thing, it has not been scientifically proven that ISO or EFQM quality management actually leads to an improvement in quality. Indications are that quality management of this sort would lead to organizational improvements but not to improvements in the quality of instruction or in the overall atmosphere of the school. Furthermore, according to Dubs, these kinds of comprehensive quality management plans would tend to place an unsustainable bureaucratic strain on the school. The cost-benefit ratio is not positive.[18]

Instead, Dubs suggests "thoroughly analyzing individual schools with 'focus evaluations' in order to gather a sufficient amount of data to determine selected, targeted quality improvements."

For privately funded theological schools some of the implications may be:

- Neither the public schools at the primary and secondary levels nor the state universities are comparable to the theological schools that are the subject of this book. Nevertheless a number of helpful insights can be drawn from this discussion:
- Because they want to be accredited, privately funded theological schools find it necessary to submit themselves to the quality management processes required by accrediting agencies. In most cases, these requirements take the form of a comprehensive plan (both internal and external evaluations). Such schools thus implement a comprehensive approach to quality management.
- Because most of these schools are relatively small, the problems cited by Dubs tend to surface: a high quality, ongoing (not just once to achieve accreditation) comprehensive quality management plan is resource intensive, consuming enormous amounts of money, energy, and time. The result in too many cases is that after a time the implementation of the quality management plan becomes more and more superficial, simply because the strength and resources to do more are exhausted.

---

specifically for the educational sector.
17. Cf. Dubs, *Qualitätsmanagement für Schulen*, 45–46.
18. Dubs gives a number of additional reasons for his position. In regard to theological schools that are in view here, I do not find it necessary to list them.

- It is, therefore, worth considering whether the accrediting agencies (e.g. the EEAA) couldn't require more targeted focus evaluations. With this approach, a limited area within a school could be thoroughly evaluated and real improvements identified and implemented. The areas of school life that Dubs suggests as suitable for focus evaluations seem to me to be worth considering for theological education as well (see table 11).[19]

We can summarize the basic decisions as follows:

1) Quality management is about much more than judging a school's quality on the basis of a single "still photograph." It is more about a process, in which the people in the institution are engaged in a systems-oriented evaluation with the goal of constantly improving quality. That there are also external control mechanisms, especially when it comes to accreditation, is understandable, but this should not become the primary focus.

2) Internal and external perspectives must go hand in hand. A worthwhile evaluation – such as that just described in point 1 – can only be internally driven, supported by everyone in the organization. External control mechanisms are nevertheless important, to ensure that the internal quality management does not become lazy, blind, or biased. A school that wants an internal quality management that truly fosters improvement will welcome external supervision.

3) The accreditation process demands quality management plans that examine every aspect of the school. This can be extremely complex and costly. Smaller schools can often not afford the resource expenditure over the long haul. It makes sense, therefore, to invest targeted energy in doable and effective focus evaluations.

---

19. Dubs, *Qualitätsmanagement für Schulen*, 57.

Segments of the school	Sub-elements of these segments
Culture, goals of the school	School motto. Innovative energy. Responsibility toward the world outside the school. Order and discipline. Care for the students. The school as an element in the society and life in the region. School atmosphere.
Instruction	Quality of teaching plans/curricula, quality of instruction, quality of educational outcomes. Teaching loads of the instructors. Student satisfaction with the quality of instruction.
Leadership	Quality of school leadership. Student, faculty and staff satisfaction with the leadership.
School life	Quality of care provided to students. Interaction within the school. Extra-curricular activities. Scholarships, student aid, tutoring, and other assistance available to students.
Organization	Quality of organization and work processes in the school. Student, faculty and staff satisfaction with school's organization.
Resources	Quality of resource investment.

Table 11

When it comes to quality management at privately funded theological schools, a plan like that depicted in figure 22 is most often employed.

Now that these foundational questions have been handled, the individual elements can be examined more in detail. Particular attention will be given to practical implementation.

7.2.2 Handling Externally Developed Quality Management Plans

As has been stated previously, in most cases, as a result of efforts to achieve accreditation, an externally developed quality management plan is prescribed. The accrediting agency – whether it is the EEAA, a government accrediting agency, or a university – will establish a procedure that must be followed. The quality management plan is externally developed.

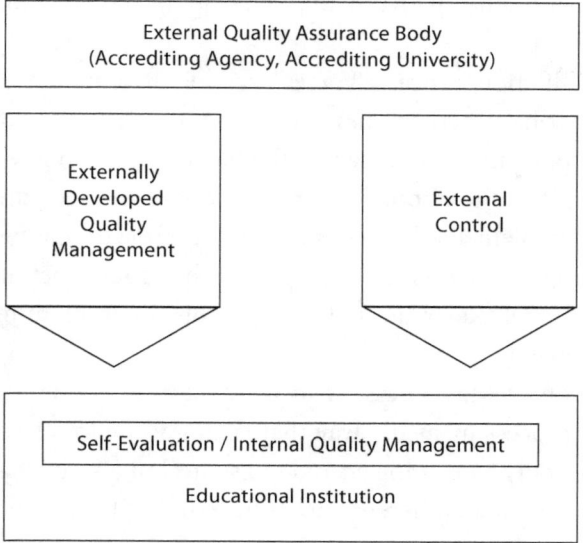

Figure 22

In dealing with an externally developed quality management plan, a number of factors must be considered:

Seeing the Accreditation Evaluation Process as an Opportunity

An evaluation process helps a school do what it wants to do at a higher level of quality. That's why evaluations should be viewed positively as tools of institutional learning. Too often they are seen as a necessary evil along the way toward achieving accreditation. Such a perspective short-circuits the potential benefits of the evaluation process. If the results of an internal evaluation are dishonest, positively skewed in the hopes of achieving accreditation, the work is being done for the sake of the accrediting agency instead of being done for the good of the school. In such cases, the long-term benefit to the school's development is minimal. Once the pressure of the accreditation process is removed, the willingness to engage in ongoing self-evaluation is gone as well. A commitment to ongoing evaluation and improvement for the sake of the school and its students has clearly not yet become part of the DNA of the school.

A good accrediting agency will recognize this and assist the school in learning to see the evaluation process not merely as a means to achieving accreditation, but rather as an tool that can help the school improve its quality year after year.

The accreditation process "forces" schools to conduct evaluations in a way that they have perhaps never done before. That should be seen as a tremendous opportunity. That can be the beginning of an integrated quality management plan. If a school doesn't come out of the accreditation process with a newly implemented or substantially improved quality management plan, something in the accreditation process has gone woefully wrong. Not only has the school leadership not done its job. The accrediting agency has not done its job either.

It is the job of the leadership to conduct evaluations required by the accreditation process in such a way that lasting value for the school itself is achieved – not only by gaining accredited status but also by making ongoing quality management an inherent part of the ethos of the institution.

Coordinating Internal Quality Assurance and External Questions

Usually when a school decides to pursue accreditation, it is already familiar with various forms of evaluation. If this is not the case, the accreditation process can be quite painful. Experience has shown that schools are best equipped to deal with an externally developed quality management plan when they are already comfortable with internally developed quality management.[20]

It is important to weave together the measures required by the accreditation agency with those quality management mechanisms already in place as a result of an existing internal plan. "Evaluation mechanisms that lead to duplication and double work are to be avoided."[21]

An effective, dynamic accreditation process will always want to see and evaluate the quality management structure already in place, in order to avoid unnecessary duplication and to give meaningful recommendations for improvement.

Creating Acceptance and a Positive Attitude in the Institution

Quality management measures will be most effective when all participants do the work required with a positive attitude. If the mindset (of many or most) is that the process is one of gathering, organizing, and presenting mountains

---

20. Ibid., 77.
21. Ibid.

of useless data under duress for an outside agency in order to achieve accreditation – clearly most of the benefits of the process are entirely lost.

An accrediting agency has not yet done its job when it has gathered all the data and conducted all the assessments necessary to make a decision on accreditation. Its final goal must be to establish an ongoing quality management system in the school being evaluated. Unfortunately the accreditation process often falls short at just this point.

For the educational institution, this means that the school's leaders have the responsibility of taking what the accrediting agency gives them and doing everything within their power to ensure that the externally developed evaluation process is well received and ultimately results in an internally developed (and internally welcomed) quality assurance system that lasts.

The following points should be taken into consideration:

1) It is advisable to implement targeted and systematic evaluations as tools for quality assessment and program development long before beginning the process of pursuing accreditation.

2) It is important to communicate clearly with all those affected (professors, students, administration) about the purpose and significance of quality management. Conducting evaluations always means additional work, and the justification for this is not always readily apparent.

3) It is also wise to start by introducing only a few quality management instruments. These should be well prepared and the insights gained from them should be used to create direct and visible improvements in the school. People will more readily support quality management when they see that the process results in improvements that help them in practical ways.

4) When a school enters the accreditation process, it is best when everyone involved (professors, academic administration) is involved in and supports the decision. It is scarcely feasible to successfully achieve accreditation when those most closely affected are opposed. Thus it is essential that the leadership takes seriously its responsibility to inform and to motivate.

5) When extraordinary time and effort is needed in order to conduct the necessary evaluations, the school's leaders must ensure that additional resources are provided (hiring additional personnel, reducing teaching loads,

etc.). In an institution where everyone is already overworked, it is unrealistic to add yet more work in the form of institutional self-evaluations and expect an acceptable level of quality.

7.3 Quality, Indicators and Standards

When quality management is introduced, the question of standards quickly arises. How is quality defined? What is a "good" school? Who sets the standards? What should be evaluated? We will turn our attention now to a number of these questions.

7.3.1 Definitions and Concepts

First let us clarify the categories and terms used:
- **Quality** is ultimately the "assessed condition of a school." This includes both efficiency and effectiveness. **Efficiency**, on the one hand, has to do with the question of "how well the goals identified in the teaching plans are accomplished" (sometimes called "output"). **Effectiveness**, on the other hand, has to do with question of "how well students perform in subsequent educational experiences, in their vocational experience, and in life" (sometimes called "outcome").[22]
- In order to assess the quality of a school, quality standards are needed. These are understood to be "requirements that must be met in order to determine that sufficient quality exists in the area under consideration."[23] Expressed another way: In order to attest that a school possesses a certain level of quality, it is necessary for the school to meet defined standards in the area under consideration.
- In order to measure quality, one must have **quality indicators**. These are characteristics "which help to determine quality."[24] Experts speak here of **variables** and **criteria**. These terms refer to

---

22. Ibid., 15–16. On the term "Total Quality Management" see also John West-Burnham, "Understanding Quality," 313–324. West-Burnham explores the origins of the concept of Total Quality Management in industry and business and has reservations about the application of the term in the education sector.
23. Dubs, *Qualitätsmanagement für Schulen*, 80.
24. Ibid.

aspects of an education that determine quality (and that can vary) and which must therefore be examined and evaluated.

An example: The "educational level of the teaching faculty" can be called a quality indicator. It is a criterion which is decisive for quality. The educational level of the teaching faculty can vary. It is therefore a variable. This indicator must be assessed, and that can only happen when there is a standard against which reality can be measured.

7.3.2 Defining the Quality of Education

Defining quality in education is, scientifically, a problem.[25] Objective norms are difficult to define, and long-term measurements are costly to compile (especially effectiveness as a long-term outcome). Some aspects drawn from the current debate may help us to better understand the question of quality:

Quality Defined by the Extent to Which Goals are Reached

Those who specialize in the scientific research into school quality now operate on the assumption that quality cannot be objectively defined. What constitutes a "good" school has to be measured against the goals that are set, and these, in turn, (at least in public schools) are subject to political negotiation. Dubs, therefore, arrives at the following definition:

> In the final analysis therefore, the quality of a school system or of individual schools or classrooms is determined by the extent to which goals that are set are actually achieved.[26]

"The extent to which goals are achieved" is the key concept here. In order to determine to what extent goals have been reached, goals must first be formulated. These are either established by a governing body (board) in the form of a productivity assignment, or they must be established by the school itself in consultation with is partners (see section 6.4.2 on defining educational goals).

Such an output-oriented definition of quality, targeting the results of education, is not an adequate basis for implementing quality management,

---

25. On the problem of defining quality in education, see Dubs, *Qualitätsmanagement für Schulen*, 14–35. See also John West-Burnham, "Understanding Quality," 313–324.
26. Dubs, *Qualitätsmanagement für Schulen*, 14–15.

however. The quality of results depends upon the foundational qualities upon which the educational system is built. These must be taken into account.

Input Quality – Process Quality – Output Quality

This broader perspective is opened up as soon as the following three levels are taken into consideration:[27]

1) **Input Quality** – The quality of the various factors that are inputted into the program. These include:
- The school's environment
- The qualifications of the teaching faculty
- The entrance requirements for the students
- Financial resources
- Infrastructure
- Other resources (e.g. library)
- Technology

2) **Process Quality** – The quality of the various factors that shape the educational process. These include:
- Curriculum
- Teaching methods
- Pedagogical, didactic performance of the instructors
- The school's leadership

3) **Output Quality** – The quality of the results, differentiating between:
- Outputs (= students' overall academic performance at the point of graduation or completion of their studies)
- Outcomes (= students' success in vocational practice or in further/advanced studies)

Quality management has all three levels in view. Empirical studies indicate that it is not enough to evaluate these three dimensions separately. Educational quality depends on how these three dimensions relate to one another. Caution is advised before assuming simple, linear causal relationships. Dubs points out, for example, that financial resources are an important input quality, but that a school that has an abundance of money is not necessarily

---

27. Ibid., 15–16.

a good school. It could also be said that neither highly qualified teaching faculty, nor an extensive library, nor a fantastic curriculum nor outstanding technological resources can, by themselves, guarantee the quality of a school. It really does depend on the connections and relationships:

- In what ways are financial resources invested to improve and ensure quality instruction?
- In what ways can the academic qualifications of the teaching faculty positively affect their didactic, pedagogical performance in the classroom?
- How can an extensive library best be used?
- How can available IT resources positively impact the learning process?

It is much more difficult to get a handle on these kinds of process-oriented indicators of quality than on more quantitative indicators, as we will see in the next chapter relating to measures and instruments.

The complexities involved in determining a school's quality lead inevitably to the conclusion that a realistic quality assessment can only be made by using a high number of indicators. That is the subject of the next section.

7.3.3 Indicators, Variables, Criteria

Next we must consider what are called indicators. As already defined at the beginning of this chapter, indicators are aspects and elements of a school (or educational system) that are relevant to its quality. They are criteria that must be examined if insights into a school's quality are to be gained. They are elements and aspects that can vary (thus variables) and that must, therefore, be measured and assessed.

We learn from research into the effectiveness of schools which criteria and variables can be seen as determinative of quality and which therefore must be examined. There are several useful studies:

School Environment, Teaching Faculty, Instruction

A study by the Americans Mayer, Mullens and Ralph lists thirteen variables, grouped under the three categories of school environment, teaching faculty, and instruction:[28]

---

28. Cited by Dubs, *Qualitätsmanagement für Schulen*, 19–20.

1) School Environment
    - School leadership
    - School goals
    - School community
    - Discipline
    - Intellectual orientation

2) Teaching Faculty
    - Expertise in their field(s) of study
    - Educational background
    - Teaching experience
    - Continuing education

3) Instruction
    - Content
    - Pedagogical convictions
    - Use of available technology and tools/resources
    - Classroom size

Nine Indicators of Quality according to Dubs

Based on a multitude of international studies, Dubs suggests the following nine characteristics (criteria/variables) of a "good" school:[29]

- A clear vision for the school with pedagogically sound guiding principles (schools with a clearly articulated profile which leads in turn to an identifiable school culture).
- High academic expectations placed on students based on a strong performance orientation at the school.
- An enthusiasm for teaching among the faculty and a purposeful, intentional atmosphere in the classroom.
- High level of cooperation among the faculty with an emphasis on continuously improving the school and goal-oriented self-evaluation.
- Ensuring basic standards of discipline and order throughout the school.
- Good leadership qualities in the school's leaders.

---

29. Ibid., 20.

- Effectively functioning organization and work processes evident throughout the school.
- Good relationships between the school, the families, and the community.[30]
- A climate of mutual trust.

With good reason Dubs points out that the results of research into school effectiveness tend to emphasize so-called "soft" characteristics, which are, as we know, more difficult to define and identify than "hard" qualities. That makes good quality management very challenging. Evaluations must go beyond snapshot analysis and "hard" factors that can be easily quantified. What is needed are evaluations that can be described as **dynamic quality management** and which use qualitative methods to identify "soft" factors, processes, and trends.

Input and Process Variables and Criteria

In order to accomplish this, Dubs proposes an additional list that includes the following variables and criteria:[31]

1) Input Criteria
   - Motto and curriculum
   - Organization (leadership and development)
   - Plan for cooperation/relationship between school and church, mission, or other non-profits
   - Support and continuing education for teaching faculty (ethos, performance expectations)
   - Exam culture
   - Budgetary system
   - Students (background, academic potential)
   - Goals for discipline and order

2) Process Criteria beyond Teaching and Classroom

---

30. Dubs is speaking about primary and secondary schools in the public sector. However his point is relevant for theological schools as well, thinking of the relationships between school and church or mission agency.

31. Dubs, *Qualitätsmanagement für Schulen*, 24. I am restricting myself to two of the categories proposed by Dubs. The third category has to do with input qualities particular to public schools. That seems to me to have little or no relevance for our consideration of privately funded theological schools.

- Processes for developing and improving the school
- Leadership

All of these categories ignore output criteria. That is because an evaluation of outcomes (the impact of education on students' later life and vocation) simply cannot be captured through evaluations of and at the school. Such studies are difficult to say the least. Determining the causal relationship between a person's (or a generation's) way of life and that person's (or generation's) educational experience requires complex sociological studies that cannot be included as part of quality management.

It is possible, however, using the lists of indicators/criteria cited above, to derive a catalogue of factors and elements that are relevant to the quality of theological education. To conduct evaluations, detailed lists of questions are essential. These can be developed using the framework of categories named above. And they will in any case be provided by the accrediting agency and are also available in the relevant literature.[32]

7.3.4 Quality Standards

Quantitative and Qualitative Standards

In the world of educational research and evaluation, a differentiation is made between two categories of quality standards:[33]

> *Qualitative Standards*: These describe the quality looked for in subjective, qualitative terms. For example, the criterion of good school leadership can be measured by a quality standard that seeks to determine if there are problems between the school leaders and the instructors, and if so, what problem-solving processes have been implemented. Qualitative standards are more difficult to define in absolute terms and are certainly more difficult to measure. But they are crucial, because they address the "soft" factors.

---

32. For example, the catalog of questions provided by the European Evangelical Accrediting Association (available at http://www.eeaa.eu). See also Dubs, *Qualitätsmanagement für Schulen*; and Walvoord, *Assessment Clear and Simple*.

33. Dubs, *Qualitätsmanagement für Schulen*, 80–81.

Quantitative Standards: These are defined using numbers, metrics, or other similarly clear, objective values. In most cases these standards can be assessed by counting or measuring. What percentage . . . ? How many books . . . ? How often . . . ? How long . . . ? These kinds of standards are simple to define and easy to ascertain. Their evidential power is not unimportant, but it is at times somewhat limited.

Norms and Benchmarks

A further differentiation is made when it comes to the relationship between the prescribed norms and the realities of the school.[34]

Norms define quality standards without regard to the performance of the school being evaluated. Based on experience and research, goals to be achieved (the qualities desired) are defined as standards. These values remain the same, no matter how any particular school being evaluated may perform. A redefinition of these standards occurs as a result of new scientific insights or educational policy decisions.

Benchmarks, on the other hand, are tied to the current performance of other schools. Thus a school is not judged against the standard of a "neutral" measuring stick but rather against the actual performance of other comparable schools. Either a median value or a top performance value can be used as a benchmark. If a top value is used for an evaluation, a school is assigned a ranking relative to the benchmark. There is a lively debate raging over the value of benchmarking and ranking in the educational sector.

Goal, Ideal, and Optimization Standards

Within the evolution of quality management in the educational sector, a further development in the formulation of quality standards is worth noting. Initially in business and industry, absolute standards or minimum standards or tolerances were defined. Using quantitative measurements, doing so is relatively simple and in many cases appropriate. It is easy to establish an absolute minimum standard for the number of volumes in a library. It is not hard to determine whether such a standard is being met. What it says about the quality of a school, however, is relative. For one thing, it would be

---

34. Ibid., 81, 85.

important to consider the quality (not just the quantity) of those volumes. For another, it would be important to know what other nearby libraries are available to the students. Such quantitative measurements are also static. They only give a snapshot of the situation at a given moment. They only call for improvements when a minimum standard is not met.

With a view to achieving continuous improvement, and in light of quantitative factors, current thinking differentiates among three levels of standards:

- A **goal** (also called an ideal or an orientation value) sets a very high standard to be aimed for, and thus establishes the direction in which the school must develop in order to improve its quality. For example, it could be determined that all instructors and professors must have an academic degree one level higher than the degree which will be awarded to their students upon completion of their program of study. (For example, in a bachelor's program, all instructors must have at least a master's degree. In a master's program, at least a doctorate.) In addition, all courses must be taught by professors who have specialized in the field they are instructing (In the case of theological education that generally includes at least specialties in Old Testament, New Testament, systematic theology, church history, and practical theology.) Values such as these, however, are not viewed statically, but rather defined as ideals to be strived for. They define the direction and goal for the school's development and improvement.
- A **minimum standard** must be established, especially if accreditation is involved. It defines a minimum level of quality that is necessary for entry into the accreditation process. To stay with the example above, it could be stated, for example, that at least 75 percent of instructors must achieve the goal established above, and in at least three of the five classical disciplines of theology the goal must be reached.
- An **optimizing standard** is decisive for any qualitative measurement. This defines the next steps to be taken toward ultimately fully reaching the goal. These optimizing standards must be accompanied by dates and deadlines, and the implementation must be documented and verified. In the example above, this could

mean that two instructors are engaged in advanced studies in an effort to achieve the goal. They will finish their studies in two or three years respectively. In addition, the school plans to hire an additional teacher within the next year for one of the areas in which there had thus far been no instructor available with sufficient academic qualifications. This sort of evaluation process does more than measure the present situation at any given moment. It aims at furthering the growth and development of the school. When this level of development has been attested, it means that a quality of development has been achieved that is worth far more than could ever be represented by any static snapshot measurement.

Differentiating between goals, minimum standards and optimizing standards is an approach that not only makes sense in the context of external evaluation (such as accreditation). It has also proven to be valuable for schools that are intent upon undertaking internal evaluation and improvements.

7.4 Implementation: Evaluation Instruments

In conclusion, it may be helpful to mention the individual tools and methods that may be used when conducting evaluations.

7.4.1 Instruments for Internal Quality Management

To implement a quality management program in a school, the appropriate use of social science research methods will be essential. The first step will be to collect data, which will then be analyzed in a second step.

Document Analysis
At this first level the documents that are needed are not ones that are written for the evaluation process. Rather it is about those which verify the carrying out of the educational mission.
- Texts in which the school has defined its mission and its goal(s): profile, mission statement, and the formulation of educational goals.
- Texts in which the school has defined the execution of its mission: teaching plans, rules and regulations, handbooks, notebooks, etc.
- Texts in which the school represents itself to the outside world: advertising, brochures, web presence, press releases, in-house newspaper/magazine, etc.

- Texts in which the organization of the school is defined: org charts, job descriptions, staff and student handbooks, etc.
- Administrative files: job applications, minutes of board or faculty meetings, student applications, students' grade records, certificates, diplomas, etc.
- Business and operational files: finances, budgets, invoices, property and real estate, cost projections, infrastructure projects, etc.

These documents are analyzed at two levels:

Quantitatively the information in these documents can be compared with norms or benchmarks. Quantitative assessments are made primarily using the measurable data of a static snapshot – data that can be measured against a recognized standard.

Qualitatively attention is given to relationships, connections, accord or discord, processes, developments, etc. For example: What was decided (and documented) where and by whom? Were decisions also carried out? This is called *tracking*. The footprints (or tracks) of decisions are followed, all the way through to their implementation and results. Qualitative assessments are primarily used in connection with processes, giving evidence of development and relationships.

Data Collection

A second level of analysis is based on data produced especially for the evaluation. This may include:
- Surveys and questionnaires
- Interviews (individual and group; structured and unstructured)
- Reports
- Assessment of data mentioned above done in faculty meetings or committees, business meetings, retreats, etc., and documentation of evaluations made and steps taken

Collecting such data is not without its problems. Good qualitative data will only be produced when those involved (faculty, students, staff) understand the purpose of quality management and have a positive attitude toward it. That can be the case when:

Ensuring Quality in Theological Education

- Everyone involved understands that it is not (just) about achieving accreditation. It is about becoming a "learning organization" and fostering ongoing improvements. When participants produce documents just for the accreditation process, these tend to be idealized. In addition, it is actually counter-productive to a true developmental process when people produce evaluation data unwillingly for an external agency.
- The timeframe given for collecting the data seems reasonable to those involved. If people have the impression that they are wasting valuable time collecting data that will be of little use, the quality of the data collected sinks dramatically.

Evaluation of Teaching and of Teachers

An area deserving special attention is the evaluation of instruction and of those instructing, that is, of teaching faculty and other instructional personnel. Dubs writes that "probably the most difficult question in quality management is the evaluation of teachers."[35] The reason, he says, is that "evaluating teachers is very demanding and a superficial approach does not do justice to the expectations of correct human behavior."[36] We cannot begin to adequately address the topic of teacher evaluation here; what follows, however, are a few basic considerations on the subject:[37]

1) A distinction should be made between the evaluation of instruction and the evaluation of teachers.
- An evaluation of instruction seeks to determine whether, in a particular subject or class, the learning goals were achieved. The results are largely but not entirely dependent upon the instructor. To what extent instructional goals are achieved does not rest solely upon the qualifications of the instructor. Other factors come into play as well, for example, the entrance qualifications of the students, the group dynamics, the support given by the institution, the availability of resources, etc.

---

35. Ibid., 93.
36. Ibid., 94.
37. On this subject, see Ibid., 96 and Dubs, *Die Führung einer Schule*, 277–298.

- An evaluation of the teacher focuses attention on the quality of the instructor's work.

2) An additional distinction must also be made: Evaluation of instructors can be done for a variety of purposes, and it is important that these be communicated.
- Evaluation for the purpose of improving the quality of instruction (measures taken for the development of teaching personnel in their didactic/instructional skills).
- Evaluation for the purpose of improving the school as a whole (measures taken for the development of the organization and/or its systems).
- Evaluation for the purpose of providing a basis for making personnel decisions (the results of which have direct impact on teaching personnel in terms of their assignments, promotion, pay, and continued employment).

With each of these three kinds of evaluations there is a different purpose, and teachers should know in advance which kind of evaluation they are undergoing.

3) The following evaluation tools are normally used when assessing teaching personnel:
- Self-assessment by the teachers themselves (including the use of the teacher portfolio).
- Assessment by students. Such evaluations may be collected by the teachers themselves or by the school administration.
- Assessment by third parties (school board, outside specialists or consultants, employers).
- Feedback from colleagues.
  - Reciprocal discussion and evaluation by teachers of their colleagues concerning instructional content.
  - Reciprocal discussion and evaluation by teachers of their colleagues concerning instructional quality (involves classroom visits).
- Discussions with the school's leadership (open discussion, structured discussion, discussion based on classroom evaluations, discussions based on teacher reports or teacher portfolios).

The data from these evaluations can be collected in a number of ways:
- As a report without any prescribed structure
- As a structured report with predetermined questions and categories
- By means of a questionnaire

4) Whatever form the evaluation may take, it must be kept in mind that scientific studies in the area of teacher evaluation advise an abundance of caution, for the following reasons:[38]
- The validity of self-assessments is generally overestimated.
- Comparing self-assessments with assessments by students leads to the conclusion that teachers tend to overrate themselves.
- Teachers who have been trained in self-assessment are able to evaluate themselves more realistically.
- The results of teacher evaluations done by students are quite controversial.
- Some studies show that students with high academic performance in a class rate the teacher higher than do students whose academic performance in the same class is lower.
- Well-crafted assessment questionnaires tend to provide useful data.
- Subjective factors (bias) affect the results of teacher evaluations. (This has not been exhaustively researched, however.) For example, teachers who praise their students tend to receive better evaluations from their students, and students who receive good academic grades tend to rate their instructors higher.)
- Evaluations done by outside third parties are generally less useful than evaluations done by students. This is in part because the results of these evaluations are affected not only by the quality of instruction but also by the quality of interpersonal contact between the instructors and the third parties. Nevertheless, assessment by third parties can be a meaningful contribution to an overall evaluation.

5) In conclusion, it may be said that the following factors should be considered when assessing data from such evaluations:

---

38. All the reasons named here are taken from Dubs, *Qualitätsmanagement für Schulen*, 100–103.

- Based on all the considerations above (and others which cannot be listed here), those who are skilled and experienced in educational quality management conclude that only a multi-faceted approach to teacher evaluation can provide appropriate results. A variety of tools must be used and their results must be compared and integrated. A teacher should never be evaluated solely on the basis of a single assessment tool.
- A method known as a **discrepancy evaluation** has proven helpful. The results of various assessment tools (self-evaluation, assessments by students, assessments by outside third parties) are compared with one another. In this way, differing perspectives can be identified, discussed, and weighed.
- Finally, when it comes to the development (ongoing improvement) of the school as a whole, it is important to use evaluations in a way that is developmental. That means that judgments made and conclusions reached are not seen as static. Instead the goal is to indicate paths to improvement and development. The evaluation of teachers should be part of the developmental plan for the school. The goal is not judgment but improvement. Evaluations of teachers should be used as tools to help those teachers grow and improve. "Good" teachers are always interested in every possible form of feedback, because they are constantly evaluating themselves and want to get better at their craft.[39]

7.4.2 Instruments of External Control

At the conclusion of this chapter it may be helpful to briefly mention the common tools of external control. As was said earlier, external control occurs when an outside agency or authority (such as an accrediting body) defines and monitors a school's quality management program. That is not strictly an external evaluation of quality, but rather an external evaluation of internal quality management. In the accrediting process, the following instruments are commonly used:

---

39. Cf. McKeachie, *Teaching Tips*, especially the chapter "Vitality and Growth Throughout Your Teaching Career," 319–332.

Requirements for Self-Evaluation
The outside agency sets requirements for self-evaluation by:
- Defining criteria, indicators and standards for self-evaluation
- Prescribing questions which must be answered in the self-evaluation report

How the self-evaluation was conducted and what results it achieved are then assessed. By taking samples and conducting discrepancy analyses (comparing the results obtained through the use of different tools) the quality of the self-evaluation can then be measured.

Requirements for Internal Quality Management
The outside agency sets requirements for internal quality management by:
- Prescribing or requiring a quality management plan.
- Prescribing tools and/or methods of evaluation.
- Requiring that evaluations and assessments follow predetermined forms.
- Defining standards.

Reporting System
Regular monitoring of internal quality management is often ensured by a reporting system. For example, by use of the following:
- Brief reports (either free-form or using predetermined questions) submitted with relative frequency (at least once a year).
- Intermediate evaluations which document mid-term or long-term progress (every 1–3 years).
- Thorough self-evaluation (often in conjunction with an audit) used as a basis for renewing accreditation (every 3–6 years).

Auditing
During the accreditation process an audit is usually conducted through a visit by an outside group of experts. An audit generally performs the following tasks:
- A report of the physical realities of the educational institution (personnel and infrastructure).
- The situation as presented in the documents submitted by the institution is compared with the observed reality.

- This is accomplished by studying files and documents. Of particular interest are all documents pertaining to the mechanisms of quality management and processes for improvement (tracking earlier recommendations and their implementation).
- The audit team also forms impressions based on conversations (with individuals and with groups, structured and unstructured).
- Insights into the school being audited are also gained by participation in academic classes, meetings, chapels, devotionals, etc.

Peer Review and External Testing

To ensure that appropriate academic standards are maintained, schools must undergo external evaluation by schools that are at the same academic level. This prevents an "in-house" academic culture and ensures that standards are open, public, and scientific. Methods employed include:
- Students' papers and assignments being read and evaluated by professors from other schools.
- Exams being administered while experts from other schools are present.
- Theses and dissertations being evaluated by outside appraisers.

All of the measures, tools, and steps of quality management discussed in this chapter serve one purpose: the ongoing improvement and transformation of the educational institution for the benefit of its students and ultimately for the benefit of the church and its mission in the world. All steps, all methods must be measured against this criterion, otherwise they can easily devolve into an inhumane bureaucracy, a misguided zeal to attain accreditation, or even a misrepresentation of facts.

Additional Literature

Herbert Buchen and Hans-Günther Rolff, eds. *Professionswissen Schulleitung* [Professional Knowledge, School Leadership]. Weinheim and Basel: Beltz 2006. Chapter 6 on "Qualitätsmanagement" [Quality Management].

Christoph Burkard and Gerhard Eikenbusch. *Praxishandbuch Evaluation in der Schule* [Practical Handbook: Evaluation in the School]. Berlin: Cornelsen Scriptor, 2005, 4th edition.

Guy Kempfert and Hans-Günther Rolff. *Qualität und Evaluation: Ein Leitfaden für pädagogisches Qualitätsmanagement* [Quality and Evaluation: A Guide for Pedagogical Quality Management]. Weinheim and Basel: Beltz, 2005, 4th edition.

Norbert Landwehr and Peter Steiner. *Q2E – Qualität durch Evaluation und Entwicklung: Konzepte, Verfahren und Instrumente zum Aufbau eines Qualitätsmanagements an Schulen* [Quality through Evaluation and Development: Concepts, Processes and Instruments for Constructing a Quality Management System in Schools]. Bern: Hep-verlag, 2008, 2nd edition.

8

Leading Theological Education with Head, Hand, and Heart

The paradigm shift cited frequently in this book creates an enormous challenge for the leadership of educational institutions. We referenced this early on, in chapter 2, and once chapters 2–7 are understood to describe leadership qualifications, it becomes unmistakably clear. To put it rather simply: In traditional schools, whose processes are conventional, institution centred and largely static, leadership is largely an administrative function. Today's schools, however, have to be forward looking, dynamic, and able to respond nimbly to market demands. Entrepreneurial skills are required.

In his research on *Führung pädagogischer Hochschulen* [The Leadership of Pedagogical Universities], Peter Thomas Senn distinguishes between leadership that is administrative and geared toward educational policy and that which is entrepreneurial and geared toward the demands of the market. He demonstrates that the deregulation and liberalization of the educational system require a significant shift in the job description of those who lead institutions of higher learning.

I have previously asserted that all of this is relevant to theological education as well, and in what follows I will attempt to present some questions and principles that may be significant for theological schools.

8.1 What Leaders of Theological Schools Must Accomplish

This chapter will provide an overview of what leaders of theological schools must do and how they can get it done. It is not my intention to present *the* definitive list of tasks or *the* one effective organizational model. There are too many variables (differences in school size, traditions, cultures) to prescribe a single formula. A look at several suggested concepts, however, can provide us with building blocks that can be contextualized into any given situation. I will differentiate three levels, which of course are closely connected:

- First it is essential to develop a list of tasks to be accomplished by those who are in leadership in an educational institution (leadership tasks). A description of leadership competencies can be derived from this list.
- Next it is important to become familiar with a variety of approaches to exercising leadership in the educational arena (leadership theories).
- Finally we will identify a number of ways to implement organizational and structural commitments (organizational models).

8.1.1 Leadership Tasks

What exactly do the leaders of theological schools do? What special tasks are involved? The answer is: there is nothing special really – nothing other than the competencies of good leadership. Required are the skills of a manager – what is often called strategic management.[1] Although strategic management has been defined in various ways, one thing remains constant: Those with the responsibility to lead will always have to move a group of people (and an organization) from point A to point B. In other words, leaders will always be responsible to motivate people to reach a goal.

In order to do that, leaders need specific competencies:[2]

---

1. A foundational resource is Roman Lombriser and Peter A. Abplanalp, *Strategisches Management: Visionen entwickeln, Strategien umsetzen, Erfolgspotenziale aufbauen* (Zurich: Versus, 1998). A helpful overview of the most important leadership tasks can also be found in Fredmund Malik, *Führen, Leisten, Leben* (Stuttgart: Deutsche Verlags-Anstalt, 2000).
2. Cf. Lombriser and Abplanalp, *Strategisches Management*, 43–48.

- First among these is the ability to lead processes of goal definition and articulation. This includes articulating vision and mission statements as well as mottos. This is about the question: *Where are we going?*
- It is not enough, however, to know where you are going. You also have to find ways to get there. A second competency involves defining and implementing the strategies needed. This is about the question: *How do we get there?*
- In order to formulate goals and initiate strategies, a third question must also be answered: *Where are we now?* An additional competency is the ability to conduct "state of the organization" assessments.
- Because no organization is static but is always in flux, an additional question must also be answered: *Where have we come from, and in what direction are we headed?*
- It is also true that no organization operates in isolation but rather within a culture, alongside other organizations – in other words, in interplay with many other factors and forces. A fifth competency is found in answer to the questions: *What terrain are we on? In what context are we operating? What challenges are we facing?*
- Finally, the five competencies listed above can only be of use when a sixth competency is also present. Basic and thorough theoretical knowledge – in our case, in the field of theological education – is required in order to be able to formulate goals, develop strategies, etc. The question to be answered is: *What* is *theological education in the first place?*

If you ask the experts about the specific, concrete leadership tasks needed in the educational arena, you will receive the following answers:

1) According to the foundational work of Bush and Bell in *The Principles and Practice of Educational Leadership,* the following six tasks are essential:
    - Strategic Management
    - Human Resource Management
    - Managing Learning and Teaching
    - Managing Finances and Resources
    - Managing External Relations
    - Managing Quality in Education

2) Katharina Cortolezis-Schlager and Reinhart Nagel propose viewing the school's leader as "General Manager." Instead of being a "Director of Everyday Happenings," a person in leadership should assume responsibility for overall leadership including the following:[3]

> a) Intentional pedagogical positioning: Proactive use of newly won freedom as partially autonomous institutions; developing an organizational profile.
> b) Responsibility for the quality of the school: Ensuring a customer orientation in every aspect of the school; introducing an appropriate quality management process.
> c) Human resources management: Responsibility for the leadership capabilities (and readiness) of teaching faculty; hiring of new personnel, leadership of the staff; continuing education and career development.
> d) Internal organizational development: Shifting the change process from a "hierarchical-bureaucratic system to a decentralized organization equipped with differentiated areas of responsibility."
> e) Resource management: Budget planning, controlled finances, benchmarking, developing sources of financial support.

3) Stefan G. Huber refers to a "complex spectrum of tasks" for a school's leadership. He outlines these as follows:[4]

> a) "In the work done with and for the people in the school, the leader is the organizational developer and change agent. He or she is responsible for the entire process of the school's development – for its initiation, implementation, institutionalization, and evaluation."
> b) "This work includes the development of a school profile, with input from the teaching faculty and staff, as well as the development and implementation of the curriculum and the entire school program."

---

3. Cortolezis-Schlager and Nagel, "'Und sie bewegt sich doch!?'," 8–9.
4. Stephan G. Huber, *Qualifizierung von Schulleiterinnen und Schulleitern im internationalen Vergleich* (Kronach: Link, 2003), 50–51.

c) "The leader is responsible for creating structures and conditions conducive for these tasks."
d) "Closely intertwined with this is the leader's role as 'personnel developer.'"
e) "In addition, the school's leader is a 'people person' who offers encouragement, counsel, and affirmation to teaching faculty, students, and parents alike."
f) Moreover s/he is a teacher. A leader's credibility is enhanced when s/he is seen as an "expert in the skills required of an instructor."
g) The leader must also be a "political animal" who can function "diplomatically and effectively amid the politics of educational committees and agencies."
h) The leader is the face of the school to the outside world.
i) Both internally and externally, the leader must be "mediator and agent."
j) Increasingly the leader is also responsible for finances, budget and "stewarding the resources" of the school.

Huber draws his list from a variety of international studies and thus provides an accurate picture of the current thinking.[5]

4) Richard Bessoth makes a strong case for those in leadership not to be consumed by administrative and management tasks but to keep the pedagogical dimension of leadership in clear focus.[6] Based on the assumption that school leadership is primarily a pedagogical function, he proposes the following areas of responsibility:[7]

5) Even more insistently than Bessoth, Peter Thomas Senn demands that task(s) of leadership must be centred in pedagogy. Using the motto of Heinrich Pestalozzi – education with head, heart, and hand – Senn outlines

---

5. Various classifications of the tasks of a school's leader are compared country by country in Huber, *Qualifizierung,* 52–53.
6. Richard Bessoth, *Pädagogische Leitungsfunktionen in der Schule* (Mannheim: DSE, ZGB, 1985), 5–7.
7. Ibid., 15–19.

384   Understanding and Developing Theological Education

a model for school leadership that is instructive for theological education as well:[8]

Leading with the *Head*:	Strategy → Orientation function e.g. formulation of mission, vision and goals
Leading with the *Hand*:	Structures → Coordination function e.g. building organization, providing resources
Leading with the *Heart*:	Culture → Motivation function e.g. developing school culture, values, relationships

Table 12

6) Rolf Dubs sees three elements within a school that provide basic categories for the tasks of leadership: Strategy, Structures, and Culture.[9] Within these basic categories Dubs defines the tasks of leadership as follows:[10]

1) Responsibility for the school's direction and goals
   - Constantly communicate the school's vision in order to stimulate innovation and application
   - Articulate the purpose of all steps taken in order to strengthen the school's culture
   - Set high standards and expectations for the school's everyday activities as well as for measures for the school's improvement and development
   - Encourage, capture, assess and support initiatives from the faculty

---

8. Senn, *Führung Pädagogischer Hochschulen*, 18, 127–128, 174.
9. Dubs, *Die Führung einer Schule*, 57–126.
10. Ibid., 393–394.

Improvement of the Educational Program	Execution: Ensuring the effective implementation of the existing program
	Evaluation: Constant monitoring and evaluation of program quality
	Revision: Plan and test changes in program, and incorporating those that are successful
Selecting and Developing Personnel	Provide opportunities for career development and skill sharpening
	Influence hiring decisions and staff transitions
	Inter-personal relationships
	Orientation and continuing education
	Student-teacher conflicts
Public Relations	Familiarity with donor development, grant writing, etc.
	Participation in and/or interaction with oversight boards, governmental agencies, civic organizations, etc.
	Representing the school to the outside world (media, etc.)
Ongoing Administration of the School	Organization of the teaching faculty
	Identification of needs / equipping and supplying
	Facility use and maintenance
	Systems of information: handbooks, personnel records, student records

Table 13

2) Pedagogical leadership of the school
   - Teach a few semester hours in the classroom each year in order to stay in touch with life in the classroom
   - Encourage pedagogical innovation and initiate innovative processes
   - Propose and implement a plan for continuing education
   - Support faculty in problems they face

3) Human resources
   - Develop and implement a human resources plan for the hiring, evaluation, compensation, and promotion of personnel
   - Establish constructive relationships with faculty and staff and a healthy school climate through clear job expectations, transparency, proactive problem solving and conflict resolution

- Ensure an open and effective feedback culture

4) Management/Administration
    - Ensure good organizational structures and effective work processes
    - Provide for excellent facility maintenance
    - Propose an effective budget and ensure responsible financial management throughout the organization
    - Provide teachers with resources and support for innovation, creativity and self-initiative
    - Create good working conditions for teachers and students
    - Implement a quality management system with teeth

5) Communication
    - Publicize the school's profile (vision, mission, goals, etc.) as broadly as possible in the community, including civic leaders, parents, etc.
    - Be an advocate and a lobbyist on behalf of the school
    - Develop an external communication plan and implement it without excess, in balance with other priorities
    - Develop an internal communication plan and communicate honestly and openly within the organization every day
    - Provide the school with symbols (symbolic leadership)

6) Personal requirements
    - The ability to open problems up to discussion, to create a positive culture of disagreement, to allow teachers to fully participate, and to make decisions at the right moment
    - The ability to create a climate of identification and trust
    - The ability to set priorities

This list of tasks is based on a philosophy of leadership that Dubs defines using the following terms:
- Not administrators but shapers
- Not dictators but leaders
- Not moderators but direct supervisors

7) Summary and preview: I can see parallels between the ideas of Senn (Head, Heart and Hand) and Dubs (Strategy, Structures and Culture). They seem to use different words to say similar things. Their entire lists of tasks are organized under their three-part overview. I suggest going back to the categories *Dimension* and *Intention* in order to combine these two three-part concepts together with their lists of tasks. The result can be found in table 8:

Dimension Intention	Head: Strategy → Orientation WHAT: Do the right things	Hand: Structures → Coordination HOW: Do things right	Heart: Culture → Motivation WHY
Strategic Management[11]			
Human Resources Management			
Management of Teaching and Learning			
Management of Finances and Resources			
Management of External Relations			
Quality Management			

Table 14

Based upon this table, I will further explore in the following sections the various tasks of leadership.

8.2 *Head*: Strategy → Orientation

This section deals with the *WHAT?* question.[12] Leadership with the head must formulate goals and thereby give people a sense of orientation. It is about

---

11. I have inserted here the list according to the table of contents in Bush and Bell, *Principles and Practice*. However, any parallel list can be inserted here, adapted to the situation.
12. Cf. Senn, *Führung Pädagogischer Hochschulen*, 18. Also the chapter "The Strategy of a School," 57–78.

doing the right things. In addition, leadership must ensure that these goals are actually reached, that is, strategies must be developed to reach the goals established. Normally these things are captured in the school's profile. That's what this section is about.[13]

The use of the word "head" must not be understood in such a way as to imply that we are talking purely about rational thought. A person, a leader, approaches work with heart, mind and soul. Here, however, we refer to the activity that is undertaken through quiet reflection. Here, it is not actions which are foremost, but rather thinking and reflecting about what needs to be done. That is a basic function of leadership.

Vision, mission, motto – these and related terms that are quite popular now. What they actually mean too often remains vague and unclear. First, therefore, we need some clarification.

Experts have defined these terms in various ways, none of which are normative.[14]

Dubs applies the terms to the leadership of a school as follows:

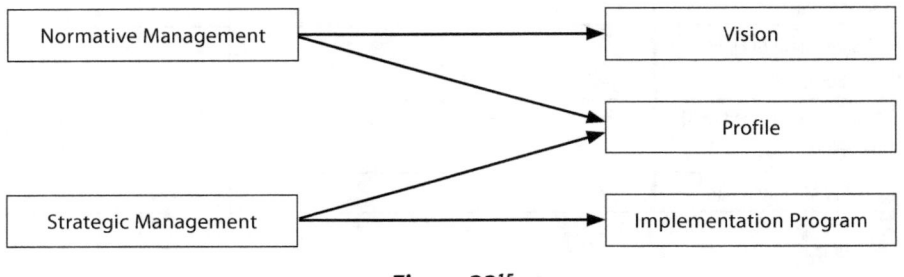

Figure 23[15]

---

13. The question is often asked, whether methods of business management can be used in the realm of education and in the realm of church and theology as well, and if so, with what modifications? It is impossible to give a thorough answer to this question in this context. I am assuming here that business management principles certainly can be used both in education and the church, and thus in theological education as well, if appropriate corrections are made. What that means for educational institutions can be found in Senn *Führung Pädagogischer Hochschulen*, 18–147. Concerning the integration of management principles in the church, see Abromeit, *Spirituelles Gemeindemanagement*, and Zindel, *Geistesgegenwärtig führen*.
14. See various definitions in Lombriser and Abplanalp, *Strategisches Management*, 231.
15. Dubs, *Die Führung einer Schule*, 59–60. It seems clearer to me, however, to use the term "Implementation Program" where Dubs uses "School Program."

The **vision** paints a broad but realistic picture of the school's future, indicating the direction in which the institution should develop.

The **profile** captures the goals, values and principles drawn from the vision. The profile provides a transition from the normative (orientation) to the strategic (management).

The implementation program states in concrete form what has been formulated in the vision and the profile, including the specifics of what will be accomplished by whom and in what time period.[16]

The following section will explain more clearly how to develop vision, profile and implementation program.

8.2.1 The Vision

1) A company's vision, according to Lombriser/Abplanalp, consists of "thoughts and ideas that determine the future direction of the business." Such a vision has three functions:[17]

- To give orientation
- To provide motivation
- To create meaning

2) Vision is more than a statement of what an institution does. Vision describes the greater cause to which the institution seeks to make a contribution by carrying out its mission. The vision of a theological school is not merely the delivery of theological education. Instead it may be the ushering in of the Kingdom of God or the growth of the church or a more just world, etc. The power of vision lies in the fact that it gives meaning and identity to the relatively limited activity of a specific institution by painting a picture of its contribution to something far greater. Fredmund Malik strikes the right tone when he says:

> To contribute to a greater cause creates the kind of motivation that an organization needs – namely, motivation that is not

---

16. Lombriser and Abplanalp understand the relationship between vision and profile to be such that the vision is anchored in the profile (*Strategisches Management*, 219). This yields the following distinction: Vision = a picture that can be perceived as a whole, including emotionally, which provides basic orientation. Profile = a more precise, more cognitive definition of the path into the future.

17. Lombriser and Abplanalp, *Strategisches Management*, 214.

dependent upon any incentives or motivating behavior of supervisors. An awareness of the greater cause, serving that cause, the sense of contributing something important to its creation, its continuation or its success – these things are not dependent upon the highs and lows of motivational tactics. A greater, higher, and more constant motivation is created throughout the rank and file than can be generated by most of those who are motivational speakers or motivational coaches.[18]

3) Vision is about painting a picture. Vision – the word itself says it – has a visual dimension. A vision consists of a picture. Its contents are pictures. Or its words generate pictures. Vision statements are therefore more than rational definitions. They speak to the whole person. They touch the heart and set things (and people) in motion.

4) In connection with the articulation of vision statements, the following anecdote is often told:

A passerby stops at a construction site and asks one of the workers: "Pardon me. May I ask what it is that you are doing?" Answer: "I'm building a wall." A second worker responds to the same question by saying, "I'm earning a living." The passerby asks yet a third worker, who responds by saying, "We are building a cathedral to the glory of God."[19]

A vision describes the "cathedral." It communicates the greater cause to which a specific task or activity is contributing.

5) The vision is often transcribed into a succinct mission statement, such as the one here from Columbia International University:

CIU educates people from a biblical worldview to impact the nations with the message of Christ.[20]

---

18. Malik, *Führen, Leisten, Leben*, 95. The entire chapter entitled "The Contribution to the Whole" is worth reading.
19. The story has been told many times, including in Malik, *Führen, Leisten, Leben*, 88–89.
20. From CIU's homepage: www.ciu.edu

All the elements of a good vision statement are present here. It identifies (a) what the institution does, as well as (b) its contribution to the greater cause.

The statement of Fuller Theological Seminar is more detailed: [21]

Beyond the immediate purpose of the nurture and training of students for the ministries of Christ, the faculty and Board of Trustees of Fuller Theological Seminary see a further mission. In 1983 they adopted a statement entitled "The Mission Beyond the Mission," which sets forth the vision that will give further direction to the seminary's planning and priorities. The statement is organized around five imperatives:

- Imperative One: Go and make disciples.
- Imperative Two: Call the church of Christ to renewal.
- Imperative Three: Work for the moral health of society.
- Imperative Four: Seek peace and justice in the world.
- Imperative Five: Uphold the truth of God's revelation.

These imperatives form an important part of the seminary's long-range planning process.

The mission statement of the Walt Disney Company is nothing short of masterful:

"We engage our imagination to make millions of people happy."[22]

It would be impossible to state more succinctly what every Disney employee does to contribute to the greater cause.

8.2.2 The Profile

1) As we've already said, the profile can be seen as the application, elaboration and anchoring of the vision. What is broadly, pictorially, and emotionally expressed in the vision becomes concrete, rationally understandable, and practical in the profile, which must answer these questions:[23]

1. Who are we?
2. What do we do?
3. Why do we do it?
4. How do we do it?

---

21. From their website: www.fuller.edu
22. Quoted in Lombriser and Abplanalp, *Strategisches Management*, 216.
23. Lombriser and Abplanalp, *Strategisches Management*, 219.

2) The profile of an educational institution can follow this checklist for the content of a profile:[24]

1. The Essence of the School
   - What theology and what values are the underpinnings of our work?

2. The Mission of the School
   - What strategic task is foundational for our school (outlined in the vision, possibly determined by the founders or board of trustees)?

3. The Structure and Leadership of the School
   - How is our school's leadership structured? What is our concept of leadership?

4. The Future Development of the School
   - How do we plan for the future expansion and development of our school?
   - What is the relationship between development and quality management?

5. Continuing Education for the Teaching Faculty
   - How important to us is the continuing education of our faculty?
   - How do we ensure that it happens?

6. The Organization of the School
   - How is our school structured and organized?

7. Finances and Investments
   - How do we determine the school's budget?
   - How do we plan for future investments?

8. Cooperation and Partnerships
   - How do we relate to various interest groups, similar/neighboring schools, etc.?

---

24. This checklist is taken from Dubs, *Die Führung einer Schule*, 71, which has been slightly modified for theological education.

9. Quality Management
   - How do we ensure that quality management happens at our school?

10. Teaching Faculty
    - How do we define the role and the task(s) of our teaching faculty?
    - What efforts do we make to ensure the wellbeing of our faculty?

In developing a profile, effort should be made to keep the formulation precise and succinct. A profile should be limited to 2–3 pages. Anything longer, and a profile looses its effectiveness. And that brings us to the question of the value of a profile.

3) A good profile is effective on several levels:[25]
   - It provides employees with clarity and orientation about where the organization is headed.
   - It gives the institution a sense of identity.
   - It serves as the "guiding star" for everything that is done.
   - It heightens awareness of existing problems and provides impetus for necessary change processes.
   - It creates a higher level of commitment and stability.
   - It enhances communication and coordination among the various departments.

4) A profile can be considered "good" when it fulfills the following requirements:[26]
   - *Achievable and practical*: A profile must be achievable and deliver practical advantages to all concerned. Theoretical utopias always end in failure.
   - *Future-oriented*: A profile must address the demands and conditions of the future. Simply capturing the realities of the present diminishes the usefulness of a profile.
   - *Capable of achieving a consensus*: A profile has to be written in such a way that it gains the support of the entire teaching faculty and

---

25. Lombriser and Abplanalp, *Strategisches Management*, 219.
26. Dubs, *Die Führung einer Schule*, 68.

administrative personnel. It has to be more than empty phrases derived from meaningless compromise. Instead, it must be the result of significant and profound thought and discussion.
- *Subject to modification*: A profile should be constructed in such a way that it can be modified to adapt to new trends or the input of relevant interest groups – while avoiding the pitfall of constant, never-ending revision. There should be a periodic review of what modifications may be appropriate, and when.
- *Concrete and implementable*: A profile should be formulated in such a way that it is clear in what areas changes should be implemented. Mere abstract declarations are ineffective.

8.2.3 The Implementation Program[27]

1) The implementation program (Dubs calls it the school program) is intended to turn the ideas expressed in the profile into concrete reality. The primary questions are:
- What must be done in what areas in order to reach the goals set out in the profile?
- Who is responsible for doing what, and in what time frame?

It is important to be this specific and concrete. Too many well-written profiles are consigned to a desk drawer or a file folder and never again see the light of day. In that case, they serve no useful purpose.

2) An implementation program is developed by comparing the profile (where we want to go) with an honest situational analysis (where we are now). Therefore the first step is to record the discrepancy between the present situation and the goals expressed in the profile, point by point. The result will be a **catalogue of actions needed.**

3) This catalogue forms the basis of the next step, which is to develop a catalogue of measures to be implemented. Table 15 can illustrate the process:[28]

---

27. On "school program" see Dubs, *Die Führung einer Schule*, 75–77.
28. Taken from Dubs, *Die Führung einer Schule*, 77.

Elements of the Profile	Strategic Goal	To Be Achieved By	Those Responsible
The profile states, for example, that it is the school's job to train pastors for churches	The school's graduation requirements must be tailored to correspond to the hiring criteria of churches	End of 2007	Academic Dean
The profile states that teaching faculty are given time to pursue continuing education and professional development	A plan for creating time for this purpose must be developed, including the necessary financial resources	June 2007	Board of Trustees
The profile states that the school has an internal quality management in place that encourages the school's ongoing development and improvement and meets the criteria of the accrediting agency	A system of quality management that corresponds to this description must exist	End of the 2006/2007 school year	Project Group
Etc.			

Table 15

The catalogue of measures must be specific and realistic. The resources needed for implementation (personnel, time, finances) must be provided.

And now we have introduced the three components of effective school leadership: vision, profile, and implementation program. We have placed all of this under the category "head" because it all involves thinking. But the question may be asked: Who's doing the thinking? Who decides and formulates what the vision is going to be, what the profile will look like, and what measures will be included in the implementation program?

8.2.4 The Process of Developing Vision, Profile, and Implementation Program

1) How an institution goes about the process of formulating its vision and profile depends in large part on its philosophy of leadership. And here, taken to the extremes, there are two opposing approaches. On one extreme, great importance is assigned to the vision of a single individual. In this view,

vision starts in the heads and hearts of visionary leaders. The other extreme holds that vision is achieved through a collective process. The emphasis here is on the creative, reciprocal inspiration of a team. Which perspective is correct is a question which has not been finally answered. Corresponding to these two different approaches, some speak of "democratically led" schools and "leadership led" schools. Depending on the leadership philosophy of the school, the profile will be developed primarily by the leader or by collective effort.

2) Most experts in the field agree that in the educational arena, there are a number of reasons for advocating processes in which everyone who is affected also has the opportunity to participate. There are at least two reasons for this:

- Teachers are generally highly interested in being actively involved in thinking through how to shape the future. They are likely to feel disenfranchised when they are simply told, top down, what direction is being taken.
- It is just as true in the educational sphere as in the business world that "a profile that is developed by the group is much easier to implement."

In what follows, therefore, it is assumed that the development process is clearly led but also distinctly participatory.

3) Such a process for developing a profile can take several forms. Whatever form the process takes, it is important that all those affected have the opportunity to participate. It has proven helpful to set aside sufficient time outside the normal work rhythm (retreats, training days) for this task. Christian organizations will not only seek to find ways to arrive at a profile that has the support of the entire group. They will also include biblical-theological considerations in the process and will want to listen for and respond to God's leading. Such a process could include the following sections:

Preparation Phase: (a meeting of the leadership team)
The school leadership or board decides to develop a profile.
The steps for developing a profile are outlined.
In larger schools, it may make sense to form a profile "project group."

Information and Consultation: (a plenary session)   Informing and motivating all participants.   Introducing the methods to be used.   Providing good examples.
Biblical Orientation: (sufficient time, ideally in a retreat, otherwise in smaller groups)   Reading biblical texts related to education/training (see ch. 4).   Prayer – listening to God.   Discussion – arriving at a biblically based vision of theological education.
Where Have We Come From: (a plenary session)   Our history, our heritage, the profile that has evolved.   Our ecclesiological and theological distinctives.
The "Cathedral" – The Greater Cause We Serve: (a plenary session)   The kingdom of God – our vision of church and mission.   Our specific role within the framework of our constituency (church, denomination, donors, alumni).
Formulating a Vision: (groups and plenum; retreat)   Collecting ideas, dreams, pictures of the future – primary question: What would our school look like if it were the school we're envisioning?   Finding a concise, meaningful, expressive formulation, endorsed by all.
Developing a Profile: (groups and plenary session; retreat)   Develop a statement for each of the topics in the "Checklist" (see table 9). A group works on each point and brings a suggestion to the plenary session.   Revision by the project group or school leadership, with ratification by the plenum.
Consultation: Vision and Profile are distributed to other circles for their evaluation and input (alumni, church leadership, school boards)   Inclusion of input from the consultation (school leadership or project group)
Developing an Implementation Program: (prepared in groups of those affected, then revised in plenary session and/or by school leadership or project group)   For each topic of the Checklist define where we are and where we want to be.   Define action needed and develop catalogue of measures to be taken.

4) All too often profiles that have been developed in this manner land in a desk drawer or file cabinet of school leaders and thus never have the impact that was intended. Therefore a number of additional steps must be taken, steps which involve "anchoring" or "applying" the profile.[29] We can only briefly outline such steps here:

---

29. Cf. Lombriser and Abplanalp, *Strategisches Management*, 228–229.

- Careful formulation of vision and profile using precise, contemporary and understandable language.
- Formulating a memorable motto – with graphics, symbols, or picture if possible.
- Attractive graphic presentation.
- Publicity – Vision and profile must be visible internally and externally.
- Inclusion in all publications – logo, motto, symbols, etc, must be visible everywhere.
- In staff meetings, training sessions, internal communiqués, etc., vision and profile should always be the reference points.
- The implementation program should be tracked, evaluated, and where necessary adjusted. There must be accountability connected with the implementation program.

Now we come to the end of the first task of leadership, to which we gave the title "head." The work of thinking is done. Now action must follow.

8.3 *Hand*: Structures → Coordination

Whereas the previous section was about thoughtful reflection on vision, profile and implementation program (i.e. about goals and direction), this section is about getting moving. "Hand" represents action in the broadest sense. It is now about getting "it" done – the "it" that has been so well expressed in the vision and profile.

Senn describes this facet of school leadership with the question: "What means must I employ in order to create the optimal environment for reaching our goals?"[30] Whereas the word "strategy" is about doing the right things, the word "structure" is about doing things right.[31]

Specifically, for the leadership of an educational institution, the following tasks are paramount:[32]

---

30. Dubs, *Die Führung einer Schule*, 18.
31. Ibid., 28.
32. Of course there is a broad spectrum of leadership tasks that must be accomplished by a school's leadership which cannot be addressed in detail here: setting goals, planning, organizing, delegating, communicating, making decisions, evaluating, initiating and/or guiding change processes, etc. There is ample literature which gives a thorough introduction to these tasks.

- Creating appropriate organizational structures
- Providing the necessary resources (personnel, finances, and infrastructure)
- Recruiting students

We will now examine each of these tasks in more detail.

8.3.1 Creating Appropriate Organizational Structures

Leadership Theories and Organizational Models

1) The actual organizational structures are closely related to the leadership theory or philosophy being lived out in the life of the school.[33] For our purposes here, we will draw attention to three approaches, presented in table 16.[34]

	Democratically Led School	Team Led School	Leader Led School
Decision Making	Democratic consensus building through discussion within the faculty and where necessary through voting in faculty meeting	In predetermined areas consensus building through discussion within the faculty and where necessary through voting in faculty meeting *and* in predetermined areas mutual decision by the leadership team	In predetermined areas consensus building through discussion within the faculty and where necessary through voting in faculty meeting *and* in predetermined areas decision by the school president (especially where there is lack of consensus)
Responsibility	All teaching / instructional personnel	The whole of the school's leadership team	The school's leader (president/ CEO)
Role of the School's Leader	Moderator	Team leadership	Leadership

Table 16

---

33. It lies beyond the scope of this book to present the various leadership philosophies in detail. An overview of the most common leadership philosophies in the educational arena is presented in Bush and Bell, *Principles and Practice*, 15–33.

34. Drawn from Dubs, *Die Führung einer Schule*, 84.

2) No matter what the leadership philosophy and, derived from that, no matter what the organizational structure or the leadership style, it will be impossible for educational institutions in our culture to avoid two facts:

- On the one hand, teachers (individuals with academic and pedagogical training) want to be included in the decision-making process as mature, responsible, and competent people.
- On the other hand, the effectiveness and success of an educational institution in today's marketplace call for clear, purposeful and strong leadership.[35]

3) These two factors – strong leadership on the one hand and broad-based participation on the other, do not have to be mutually exclusive. In fact, I suggest that the ideal philosophy of leadership will be found in a combination of the two. Figure 24 shows what this can look like in relation to the other leadership theories.

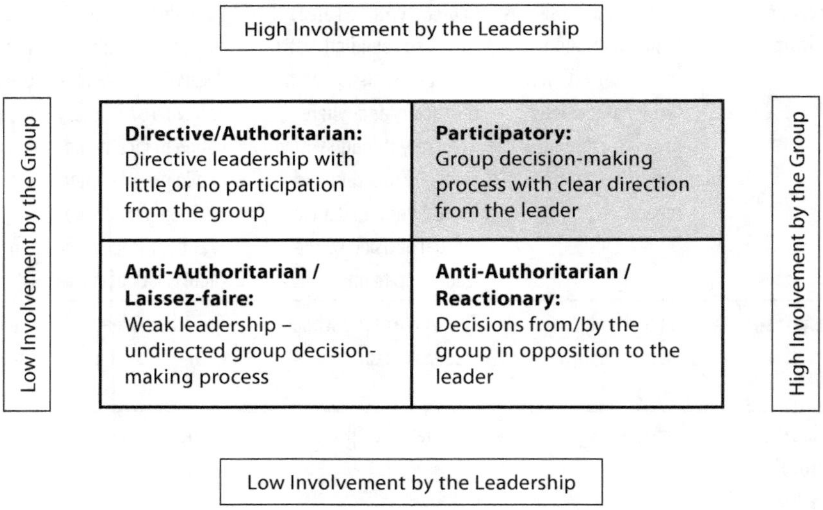

	High Involvement by the Leadership	
Low Involvement by the Group	**Directive/Authoritarian:** Directive leadership with little or no participation from the group	**Participatory:** Group decision-making process with clear direction from the leader
	Anti-Authoritarian / Laissez-faire: Weak leadership – undirected group decision-making process	**Anti-Authoritarian / Reactionary:** Decisions from/by the group in opposition to the leader
	Low Involvement by the Leadership	High Involvement by the Group

Figure 24

---

35. That's why Dubs argues for the leader-led model. He cites studies that show that democratically led schools generally do not demonstrate better decisions or better results. He cautions, however, that the leader-led model should not be understood as a return to authoritarian or dictatorial leadership styles (Ibid., 85).

To be specific, this means living by the following values and principles:
- Clear leadership is wanted and respected and is exercised.
- All of the faculty and staff, and the students as well, are seen as mature, responsible, competent people.
- It is assumed that faculty, staff, and students, in those areas which affect them, have valuable input that should be made a part of the decision-making process.
- The climate of all communication is marked by dialogue, consultation, and participation.
- High value is placed on teamwork, team decisions, and consensus building.
- Everyone affected by a decision is heavily involved in the decision-making process.

Based on this foundation, I will, in what follows, reflect upon specific organizational models for schools. By organizational models, we mean the specific structuring of leadership and organization within an institution, as expressed in organizational charts. Within the organizational structure there are functions, groups, jurisdictions/responsibilities, and their interrelationships.

It should be obvious that it is impossible to propose a single, ideal organizational model. Cultural differences, traditions, and the differing size of schools are all factors that will lead to varying solutions. That is as it should be. Nevertheless there are some basic considerations and possible solutions, which can inform any school's approach.

It is especially important to understand certain distinctions expressed in the organizational chart.

Separation of Powers: Legislative and Executive

For the organization and leadership of an educational institution it is important to distinguish between the internal operational leadership of the school and the external supervisory/regulatory bodies. Lack of clarity on this point can lead to confusion regarding responsibility and authority, which will quickly lead to conflict.

402 Understanding and Developing Theological Education

The differing tasks and responsibilities of these two groups can be defined using the table 17.[36]

Board	Leadership
Governance, Direction → Legislative	**Management, Program → Executive**
Principles, Strategies (Policy)	Execution, Administration (Implementation)
Determine, Decide (Discern)	Carry Out, Do (Act)
Goals, Results (Ends)	With the resources (Means)
What	How

Table 17

Boards define the guidelines and parameters within which the school will operate. They verify whether these are being maintained, implemented, and followed. It is not a board's responsibility to intervene in the operational life of the school. In most cases, board members are accountable to a broader constituency, which elects and commissions them.

School leaders (individuals and teams) lead the school according to the guidelines and parameters set by the board. They are accountable to the board. It is not their responsibility to define these guidelines and parameters.

What has been said above can be summarized as follows:

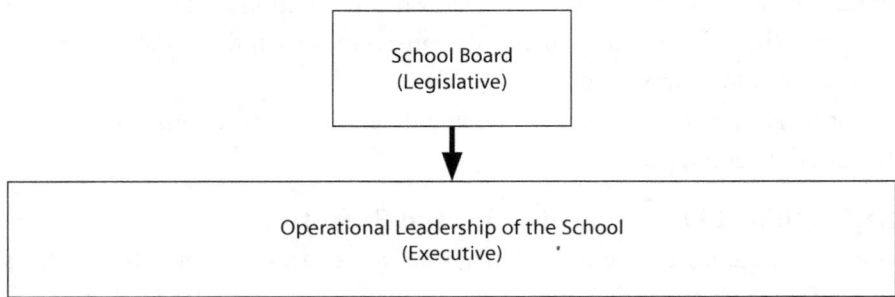

Figure 25

---

36. Edgar Stoesz and Chester Raber, *Doing Good Better: How to Be an Effective Board Member of a Nonprofit Organization* (Intercourse: Good Books, 1997), 13–16.

Operational Areas:

1) Within the operational life of the school, it is important to differentiate between "academics" and "administration."

- The academic leadership is responsible for the planning and implementation of the educational offerings (curriculum) and is in contact with the students about academic matters.
- The administration is responsible for providing and maintaining the necessary infrastructure (finances, facilities, technical equipment and support) and is in contact with the students as users of the infrastructure.

2) For any number of reasons it is wise and advisable to establish and maintain clear boundaries between these two areas, and as it pertains to accreditation, it is absolutely essential:

- A school can only attain accreditation if the academic side is supported by a solid administration, so that the long-term stability of the institution is ensured.
- Above all, when it comes to achieving academic recognition, the academic functions and the administrative functions must be clearly separated in order to maintain academic freedom. The administration has to make the academic operations possible, but it must never be allowed to influence academic content.

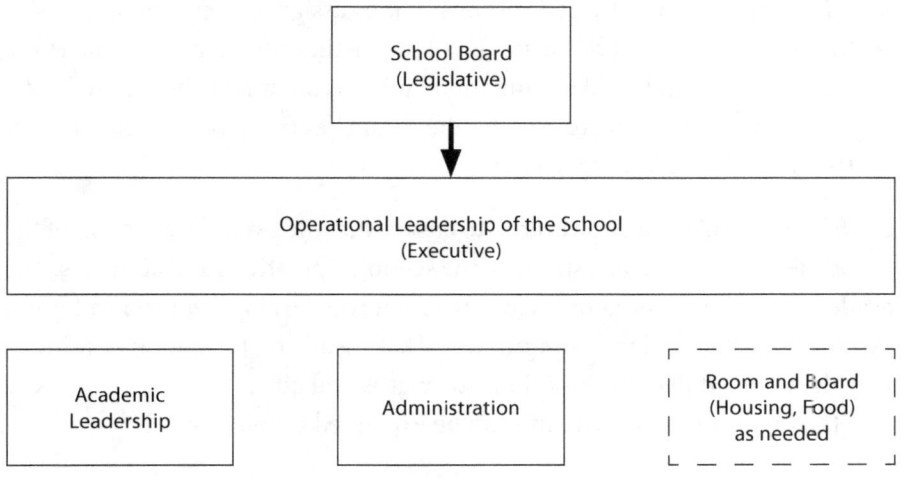

Figure 26

3) Schools that have resident students may have to establish a separate leadership area for the oversight of issues related to providing living accommodations and in some cases meals. This can be useful because it makes sense to separate academics and private life, work and free time, a student's school community and his or her life community, and to find creative, constructive, healthy ways for them to be connected.

School Leadership vs. Academic Leadership

1) Because of these distinctions within the organizational structure, schools often make a distinction between the overall leadership of the school and the academic leadership. Normally these two central leadership functions are carried out by two different people. Not all institutions give these two positions the same title, nor do they necessarily all divide the responsibilities in the same way. Nevertheless, the following comparison can be made:

Function / Areas of Responsibility	Title
1. Operational leadership for the entire institution	Rector, Director In North America: President, Principal, Provost
2. Academic leadership for the entire institution or for individual academic programs	Dean, Director of Studies In North America: Dean, Academic Dean

Table 18

2) How the tasks are divided responsibilities assigned depends on the size of the school and the overall structure of the institution. Some seminaries are connected to a church or denomination and thus are under the umbrella of a larger organizational structure with other branches (mission agencies, retreat centres, church headquarters, etc.).

3) The essential thing, however, is to ensure that the overall leadership of the school keeps an eye on all aspects of the school's operations and activities. The academic dean must be allowed to concentrate on development, planning and execution of the academic program(s). That means that these two positions may demand a different set of skills, strengths and gifts.

The organizational structure can be expanded as follows:

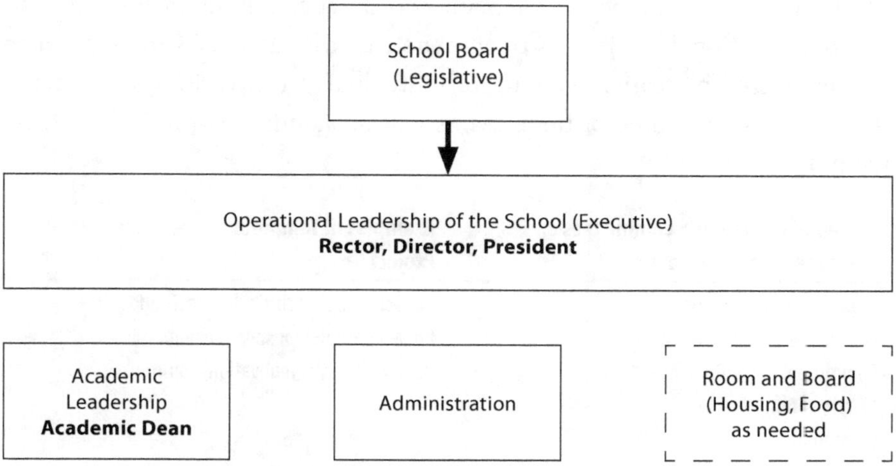

Leading Theological Education with Head, Hand, and Heart 405

```
                    ┌─────────────────────┐
                    │    School Board     │
                    │    (Legislative)    │
                    └──────────┬──────────┘
                               ▼
┌─────────────────────────────────────────────────────────────┐
│     Operational Leadership of the School (Executive)        │
│              Rector, Director, President                    │
└─────────────────────────────────────────────────────────────┘

┌──────────────┐      ┌──────────────┐      ┌──────────────┐
│   Academic   │      │              │      │ Room and Board│
│  Leadership  │      │Administration│      │(Housing, Food)│
│Academic Dean │      │              │      │  as needed    │
└──────────────┘      └──────────────┘      └──────────────┘
```

Figure 27

Additional Organizational Levels and Structural Forms

In addition to the basic categories of school organization that have already been introduced in these pages, there are a number of additional organizational forms to be considered, which are utilized according to the nature and size of the school.[37]

1) Curriculum and department leadership: Especially in larger institutions, people are given responsibility for academic departments or portions of the curriculum. These are often teachers who, in addition to their classroom responsibilities, assume leadership of departments or other areas, such as the following:
- Leadership of degree programs (bachelor program, master's program, extension program, continuing education offerings, correspondence courses)
- Library
- Information Technology
- Internship offerings
- Publications
- Public relations and publicity

---

37. Cf. Dubs, *Die Führung einer Schule*, 85–98.

2) Project groups: Some tasks demand coordination among various interests and organizational levels. It is often beneficial for such tasks to be planned and organized by teams made up of individuals from various segments of the organization. Some of these teams will be standing committees, others temporary (ad hoc).[38]

Examples of Standing Committees or Permanent Project Groups	Examples of Temporary Committees or Project Groups
Departmental committees	Project group for curriculum revision
Committee for oversight of internships	Project group(s) for special events
Committee for spiritual formation	Building (and/or renovation) committee
Library committee	
IT committee	

Table 19

Project groups and committees receive clearly defined tasks from the leadership (a single individual or a leadership team) and are responsible to the leadership for the completion of their assigned tasks. Depending on the tasks assigned, a committee may be given parameters for decision-making authority and/or spending authority.

3) School administration: The clear definition of the role of the administration is of particular importance. In many cases the administration is considered to be staff under the authority of the school president (or leadership team). In this case, the administration may not appear in the organizational chart (i.e. it has no decision-making or directive authority). The tasks of a school administration may include:

- Initial contact to applicants or inquirers; sending of requested information and other relevant material
- Ensuring and overseeing the production of printed materials of various kinds
- Providing, organizing, and archiving student files from initial application to transcripts to graduation records
- Preparing materials in advance of staff or committee meetings and afterwards organizing and filing such records

---

38. Cf. Ibid., 90.

- Collecting, organizing, and archiving all information needed for quality management, school development, and accreditation.
- Providing and administering all forms and regulations necessary for the running of the school
- Organizing, maintaining and archiving personnel files
- Maintaining mailing lists and distribution lists as well as the dissemination, mailing, or other distribution of information (weekly, monthly, or quarterly newsletters, etc.)

When dealing with files and documents, there are two things which must be kept in mind: (a) the policy for archiving files (what has to be kept, and for how long?) and (b) confidentiality (who has access to which files and documents?). The answers to these two questions must be clearly defined and articulated.

Providing Resources

In order for a school to function, it needs resources as well as organization. An organized school system has to be provided with three categories of "material":

- People who fill various roles to enable the school to function (personnel)
- Finances that make the running of the school possible
- Infrastructure in the form of facilities (buildings), equipment and technology.

Each of these areas is in itself such a large topic as to deserve its own detailed treatment. Here we are only able to list a few basics, which may serve as a checklist.

Human Resources Management[39]

1) The first task of human resources management is **human resources planning**. The tool for this work is the position plan. This plan documents specifically which positions will need to be filled over the next several years. It is based on two factors that often stand in conflicting relationship

---

39. See the chapter "Human Resource Management" in *The Principles and Practice of Educational Management*, eds. Tony Bush and Les Bell (London: Sage Publications, 2002), 101–150, and the chapter "Prozesse der Personalarbeit," in *Die Führung einer Schule* ed. Rolf Dubs (Stuttgart: Steiner, 2005).

to one another: first, the need for personnel, and second, the finances that are available.

Because the tendency is to constantly expand the position plan (an increasing number of personnel will be needed for "good" and "important" tasks), those in leadership (including at theological schools) will likely need to keep tight reins on the position plan. A number of evangelical schools have landed in serious financial difficulty because personnel costs got out of control.

That means, of course, that boards and leaders will sometimes be faced with difficult choices and will, when necessary, have to make painful decisions: concentrating on the "core business," reducing services, cutting some programs or courses, increasing efficiency, eliminating positions, etc.

On the other hand, expanded vision, which can lead to new areas of activity and thus to additions to the position plan, will require the leadership to address the question of the finances required.

2) One basic question affecting human resources planning is whether a school's teaching faculty will be composed primarily of full-time teachers or primarily of part-time teachers, guest lecturers, and adjunct faculty. Both approaches have advantages and disadvantages, reflected in the following three factors:

- Integration and continuity in the faculty-student relationships
- Expertise of the teaching faculty including research, advanced degrees, and writings published
- Praxis orientation
- Diversity and breadth of courses offered

The model of a faculty that is primarily permanent and full-time has the advantage that teachers are engaged with students over a longer period of time. Full-time faculty are also more likely to be granted time and encouragement to pursue further studies in their area of expertise, to do research, and to write and publish.

The model of a faculty that is primarily made up of part-time, adjunct or guest instructors is likely to be deficient in these two areas: Teachers come and go and have little opportunity for ongoing contact with students. The increasingly modular and flexible curricula tend to increase fragmentation (lack of integration) because continuity with the same instructors is missing.

In addition, guest lecturers are often people who are engaged in their professions. Their days are normally filled with responsibilities at and for their churches (or other places of employment), and they have little time in their schedules to pursue research, writing, or advanced study.

On the other hand, a small full-time faculty team will necessarily place limits on diversity and breadth because a limited number of instructors teach almost all of the classes. Particularly in smaller schools, which may only have one professor for a particular discipline or subject, this may result in narrowed scope or diminished quality. Full-time teachers may also be lacking in connection to praxis, because their whole world revolves around theological education. Guest lecturers and adjunct faculty are often able to bring more of this dimension to their teaching. The diversity and variety inherent in lecturers from various church and ministry professions can be an enrichment for the students and can provide a higher level of praxis orientation.

As is the case in many other areas, a combination of the two models is possible and can provide the best of both worlds, maximizing advantages and minimizing disadvantages.[40]

3) Once the position plan has been clarified, the next steps are **identifying, recruiting and hiring** of personnel. The common practices of posting open positions, receiving and screening applications, determining a "short list" of candidates, interviewing, and hiring are now employed. There is no need to discuss these here.

When it comes to hiring teachers in theological education, however, there are some critically important questions to consider:

- Because the quality of education received and the reputation of the school are closely tied to the quality of the teaching faculty, it is important to make faculty hiring decisions with the greatest of care. There will likely be a high price to pay for hasty decisions or careless compromises. The quality of education and the school's reputation can be quickly destroyed and are difficult to rebuild.

---

40. See the thinking of Strübind, "'Pastoren bilden Pastoren aus.'"

- For this reason, it is essential to have precise qualification criteria. At a theological school, the following points must be taken into consideration:[41]
    - Personal and spiritual qualifications, with a view to the church or churches which make up the school's constituency or provide the school's finances.
    - Academic and educational qualifications appropriate for the academic level (e.g. requirements laid down by accrediting agencies).
    - Practical (e.g. pastoral experience) and possibly cross-cultural qualifications consistent with the identity and goals of the institution.
    - Pedagogical, didactical qualifications.
    - Willingness to identify with the vision and profile of the school (i.e. a willingness to give oneself to the common educational mission, the school's culture and direction).

In some Christian organizations, especially in the pioneer phase, little attention was given to formal hiring agreements. Some schools and organizations may not have gotten started if these questions were the first issues faced. Yet over the long term, it is essential that hiring and personnel processes be professionally conducted and legally correct. Amateurism and superficiality have no place in a serious theological school.

4) Finally, a word about **personnel evaluations and career development**. It can be said that these topics are a part of quality management, and they were indeed discussed in the chapter on that subject. Within the context of human resources management, however, it is appropriate to comment on a few of the dimensions of a professional approach to providing personnel with opportunity for career development. I will concentrate here on teaching faculty, which is not to say that employees with other tasks and responsibilities will not have corresponding opportunity for career enhancement.

---

41. I am speaking here of seminaries and schools which are outside of the (German/European) university system. Hiring for positions within the university system is subject to other mechanisms.

The goals to be achieved by providing members of the teaching faculty with opportunities for career enhancement have been defined as follows:[42]

- Teachers should be given the chance to reflect upon their own performance and abilities in the classroom.
- They should be in a position to teach using the benefits of "the latest developments from the world of research, scientific theory, and educational philosophy."
- Teachers should be in a position, working together with their faculty colleagues, to constantly improve the quality of the school.

To accomplish these goals, a host of measures can be taken, depending on a school's individual situation:[43]

	Internal Measures	**External Measures**
Individual Measures	Teacher Evaluations Performance Reviews Self Development Reciprocal School Visits Internal Mentoring	Continuing Education Advanced Study Sabbatical (Study Year) External Supervision Educational Travel
Collective Measures	Continuing Education Events Seminars Workshops	External Continuing Education Educational Travel Visits to Other Schools

Table 20

Career enhancement and continuing education opportunities should be governed by a clear and transparent policy. In particular it must be clear what costs are carried by the employer and employee respectively.

Financial Management[44]

1) Professional financial management is indispensable for the stability and credibility of the school. The leadership must keep a few simple economic realities in view at all times:

---

42. Dubs, *Die Führung einer Schule*, 315.
43. The following list is drawn largely from Dubs, *Die Führung einer Schule*, 316–326, but also adds a few elements.
44. Cf. Lesley Anderson, "Resource Acquisition and Allocation," in *The Principles and Practice of Educational Management*, eds. Tony Bush and Les Bell (London: Sage Publications, 2002), 207–221.

- Income and expenditures must be kept in balance. You can't spend what you don't have. Or, to put it another way, whatever resources you want to spend, you must first acquire.
- Normally a school has two sources of income: (a) tuition and school fees (and other income generated through services provided) and (b) grants and donations (i.e. income that is not self-generated). The ratio between these two sources of income should be constantly monitored, especially to note changes that occur over time.
- Expenses tend to fall into one of these categories: (a) personnel costs – wages and salaries, (b) other educational costs (library, IT, school materials), (c) administration, (d) infrastructure (facilities), and (e) public relations. Here, too, the percentages should be regularly monitored. Unplanned or unaccounted for shifts should trigger a careful evaluation.
- Finally, a distinction is to be made between operating costs and investments. If the line between these two categories is blurred, it can have serious consequences, especially if investment funds are used to cover operational costs or if there is no long-term investment plan in place.

These are very general categories, and they are simple as well. They may suffice here, however, to mark the key points that a school's leader (or leadership team) must always have under control.

2) Since spending money is much easier than acquiring it, the financial management of the school is of utmost importance. It is not uncommon for the weight of this responsibility to rest heavily on the shoulders of those in leadership. As stated above, there are generally two sources of income:
- Tuition, fees, and other income generated through services provided.
- Grants and donations (income that is not self-generated).

3) We will not spend much time on income generated through services provided (beyond tuition and student fees). Examples, which will vary from school to school, may include income from faculty (teaching) services rendered on behalf of other schools or institutions, from publications, from renting or leasing facilities to third parties, etc. Of course, every theological school is well advised to fully utilize these means of generating income.

4) It will be helpful to reflect at length about tuition and student fees. The cost of an education is affected, if not dictated, by a number of contributing factors. It can be safely said that, for a number of reasons, the money that students pay for theological education will never cover the real costs. Very few students would be able to pay the entire cost, nor would they want to. Thus the calculation will always involve a combination of income from students and income from grants, donations or other external sources (not self-generated). What the calculation looks like depends on a number of factors, not the least of which is the context in which the school operates:

- In most cases tuition and fees must be comparable with those of other schools. The cost-benefit ratio must be competitive within the educational marketplace.
- Some seminaries are associated with denominations or associations of churches. These churches or denominations may determine what students preparing for church ministry must pay for their training.

Regardless, the school must have other sources of income beyond tuition and fees.

5) The generation of financial resources beyond those received from students (tuition and fees) is an essential part of a school's responsible financial management. There are several basic categories of these "external" sources of income. One classification differentiates between the recipients of the money:

> **Type A:** The funds go directly to the student in the form of grants or loans that enable the student to pay more for tuition and fees than would otherwise be possible.
>
> **Type B:** The funds go directly to the school in the form of grants from the government or the church, which enable the school to charge less for tuition and fees than would otherwise be possible.
>
> **Type C:** The funds go directly to teaching faculty (in cases where teachers are financed by external sources).

In most cases, there will be a combination of Type A and Type B. There will be a few cases where Type C also comes into play.

6) A second manner of classification has to do with the source of the funds:
- The funds come from the government
- The funds come from church associations or denominations
- The funds come from local churches
- The funds come from donors
- The funds come from foundations or endowments

Here, too, a combination of these sources will usually be the case.

7) All of these factors make the calculation of costs very complex, as shown in figure 28. The amounts represented by the elements in this figure will vary from school to school. It is important, however, for the school's president (and leadership team) to have a clear understanding of the school's financial structure. The leaders should have this figure for their own institution, for every fiscal year, so that changes and trends can be observed. Such a tool can create awareness of undesired, unhealthy developments and thus trigger the implementation of corrective measures.

8) And now we turn to some thoughts about fundraising. Fundraising is a form of acquisition of income by nonprofit organizations. This practice, common in North America, has now also become a significant factor in Europe. The flood of literature on this topic is an indication of this reality. Apparently there is a lot of money in the pockets of people in the Western world, and when the approach is made in the right way, many of these people are willing to part with some of these funds. It is, of course, possible (and all too common) that people can be persuaded to part with their money by aggressive and ethically questionable methods. That is why serious nonprofit organizations have banded together in many countries to form fundraising associations and agree upon ethical standards of behavior.[45] Without going into the details of fundraising, I mention here two essential elements of fundraising: (a) fundraising philosophy and (b) fundraising tools.

---

45. See http://www.fundraising-verband.de and http://www.swissfundraising.org. See also the honor code of the Swiss Evangelical Alliance at http://www.each.ch/dienste/projekte/ehrenkodex/ehrenkodex.html.

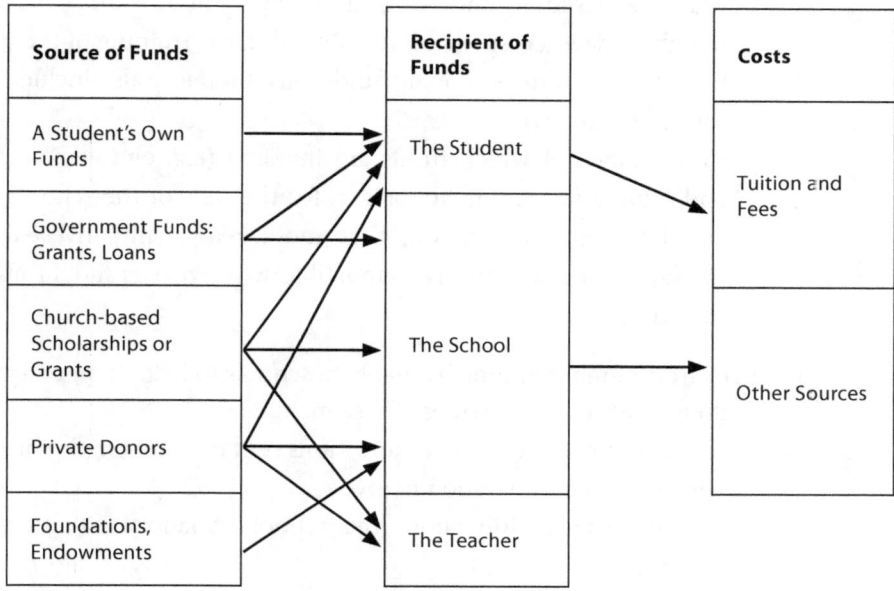

Figure 28

a) Every institution that has to engage in fundraising should define its own philosophy of fundraising. Such a philosophy should address the following topics and questions:
- How should monies obtained through fundraising be used?
- Which sources of funding should be sought?
- How can we ensure (and communicate) that funds are actually used for the purposes designated?
- How can we communicate openly and transparently about finances and their use?
- To what ethical values and norms are we committed (e.g. through membership in an association or being granted a certification through external evaluation)?

There are a number of considerations in this regard which are particularly pertinent in the world of theological education:
- In the case of theological education, the motivation for giving cannot be reduced to an appeal to the conscience and the challenge to acts of compassion. The motivation for supporting theological education with financial donations

must be based in the realization that churches and their members have a responsibility to invest in the training of their teachers and pastors. Raising funds must therefore also include raising awareness.
- In situations in which funds are invested (e.g. endowments and foundations), it is important, for the sake of the school's credibility and reputation, that monies are only invested in ways that are ethically compatible with what is taught at the school.

b) There are a number of tools available to schools to help them carry out their fundraising activities. These include:
- Regular or one-time communications sent to potential donors with an explicit invitation to give
- Specific information about the school's financial situation and needs
- Regular open communication about the use of donated funds and what these funds helped to accomplish
- A breakdown of the total need into smaller specific items with which donors can readily identify
- Project-based fundraising
- Cultivating relationships with donors (thank you letters, personal contacts, events)
- Gifts to donors in the form of books or admission tickets to an event
- Targeted work with new segments of potential donors (e.g. a new generation) using methods specially adapted and customized to appeal to the group targeted
- Creating access to online giving
- Allowing a person, group, or church to "adopt" or sponsor a particular student (or student profile) and designate their giving accordingly
- Creating volunteer opportunities at the school for donors (e.g. helping with a construction or renovation project can increase a donor's sense of identification and ownership)
- Encouraging the creation of foundations

- Communicate about possibilities for including the school in one's will
- Various forms of sponsoring[46]

Thus far under the topic of "Providing Resources" we have talked about people (human resources) and finances. There is only one element that remains:

Managing Infrastructure and Support

Theological education happens within visible structures. Some refer to this as hardware. The infrastructure in mind here can be classified under three headings:

- Facilities (buildings and grounds)
- Technology
- Library and other study resources

1) Depending on the kind of education and training offered, there are varying needs in terms of facilities. Table 13 indicates some of the categories:

Educational Form	Space for Instruction and Study	Space for Administration	Space for Living
Traditional educational model with residential facilities	Space on campus	Space on campus	Space on and off campus
Traditional educational model without residential facilities	Space on campus	Space on campus	
Alternative decentralized, mobile models of education	Decentralized classrooms, rented	Centralized space for administrative functions	
Internet-based models with virtual campus	At most, decentralized rented space for occasional events/gatherings	Centralized space for administrative functions	

Table 21

When schools and seminaries make decisions about their buildings, these decisions are made with an awareness of the following factors:

---

46. In contrast to pure giving, sponsoring is based on the principle of reciprocity, i e. the sponsor receives something in return, e.g. being able to place an advertisement in a school publication or receiving reduced admission to events.

- Schools with a long and storied history and a centralized presence, but perhaps with too little flexibility and functionality as well, and with excessive facility costs; in contrast to schools that are decentralized, mobile, possibly with rented facilities that can be adapted to the current needs, but have no historical centralized presence.
- Owning your own property which the school is free to build (or renovate) for its own purposes, which generates high costs, however, and is stationary; in contrast to rented facilities to which the school is not bound long term, but which also limit the construction or renovation options, and which may not be ideal for school facilities.
- And in all of these considerations, the question is always: invest funds in buildings or in people? In other words, there has to be clarity on the point that buildings are not an end in themselves but are subservient to a higher value – the students and their education.

2) Closely connected to facilities is the matter of technology. This includes any and all technical aides that provide support for study. Organizing and running a school includes the task of providing and maintaining technology in a way that facilitates study rather than hinders it. There are three basic categories of supporting technology:
- Classroom and instructional aides such as whiteboards, flipcharts, and various kinds of projectors
- Information technology: computers and internet access, in sufficient numbers and capacity (bandwidth and speed)
- Copiers and printers

The responsibility of the leadership in this regard includes the following elements:
- Keeping the school's expenditures for technology balanced between two extremes: on the one hand, those who haven't yet discovered the wonders of technology themselves and who therefore begrudge any funds spent on technology, even though these could foster improvements in learning; and on the other hand, technology freaks who always insist on having the latest technology, even when

these would not necessarily bring any significant improvements in learning.
- Training teachers and students in the use of technology for facilitating learning, because the availability of technology in no way guarantees its use to improve learning. One principle could be: new technology will be purchased only if it can be shown to facilitate learning.
- Curbing the excessive use of technology that generates costs but adds no value (e.g. photocopies and the power point boom).

3) Last but not least – the library, which remains an outstanding resource for every course of study. The library places the small world of the individual school into the larger world, giving students access both to other voices of the present and to the voices of history. Education can only happen in dialogue with this larger world. Education that is weak in this dimension is fundamentally weak overall.

Library development must be high on the priority list of school improvements and investments. Every accreditation process rightfully asks questions about this area. That being said, critical questions and clarifying comments are appropriate here:
- Traditionally, theological seminaries have invested heavily in the development of their own libraries. The assumption has been that the school must provide its students with adequate library resources. This assumption in turn was based on a classical residential educational model. Building and improving the school's own library remains an essential part of a school's development; however, there are now other factors that come into play.
- The pragmatic changes in education that have been described again and again in this book (student-centred education, flexibility, mobility, internet, distance learning, etc.) have caused a shift in the approach to ensuring the availability of adequate library resources. The question is no longer primarily formed from the point of view of the school but from the point of view of the student. The issue is no longer what the school has to offer but rather what is available to the student.

- Seen from this perspective, the question must then be: What access can we give students to adequate library resources, whether inside our institution or outside? (This, again, is one of the challenges facing school leaders.) Along with the development and expansion of the school's own library, which remains an important task, the expansion of students' access to other libraries becomes increasingly important – whether by providing lists of academic libraries in the area, by membership in an association of libraries (inter-library loans), or via online catalogues.

On our journey to get to know the responsibilities of the leaders of institutions of theological education, we have now taken two steps: Under "Head" we discussed the development of strategy (the WHAT question), and under "Hand" we discussed the development of structure (the HOW question). There is just one more step to go.

8.4 *Heart*: Culture → Motivation

Under the heading of "Heart" Senn talks about the culture of a school – a culture that motivates teaching and learning. His opening question is: "How can I motivate people to achieve goals?"[47] Dubs also sees the culture of a school as a third essential element, along with strategy and structure.[48]

The importance of the organizational culture of a school as a factor in facilitating teaching and learning is prominent in virtually all the relevant literature today. There is a broad consensus among experts that the shaping of a school's culture is one of the most significant tasks of a school's leader. "Leaders are responsible for building and maintaining organizational culture."[49] Dubs cautions, however: "It is still controversial among the scientific community whether the culture and climate of a school can be influenced and intentionally changed, and whether changes actually lead to improvements in quality."[50]

---

47. Senn, *Führung Pädagogischer Hochschulen*, 18.
48. Dubs, *Die Führung einer Schule*, 107–126.
49. Clive Dimmock and Allan Walker, "School Leadership in Context – Societal and Organizational Cultures," in *The Principles and Practice of Educational Management*, eds. Tony Bush and Les Bell (London: Sage Publications, 2002), 78.
50. Dubs, *Die Führung einer Schule*, 107.

If we assume that the culture of a school makes a qualitative difference, then it seems certain that the effects of "paramessages," "metacommunication," and "implicit messages" play a significant role. To put it more plainly, this means that implicit cultural factors drown out any explicitly taught content that stand in contradiction to the implicit culture.[51] T. J. Sergiovanny expresses it this way: "To be successful at culture building, school leaders need to give attention to the informal, subtle, and symbolic aspects of school life."[52]

For all of these reasons, it can no longer be seen as a luxury to engage in culture building in an educational institution. It is essential for the quality of the school.

8.4.1 *What Do We Mean by Culture?*

When it comes to defining culture, Geert Hofstede and others reference charts that differentiate between four levels of culture, in concentric circles.[53]

The inner circle is "Values." Next is "Rituals." Third is "Heroes." And the outer circle is "Symbols." If you group the three outer circles under the heading of "Practices," then you have a two-level model – values and practices. Some experts speak about the *surface culture* and the *deep culture* and point out that practices (behaviors) lie on the surface and are observable, whereas values lie deeper and are not directly visible.[54] Surface culture includes elements such as language, behavior, clothing, customs, rituals, and ceremonies. Deep culture includes values, beliefs, and convictions.[55]

---

51. Cf. Thomas R. Yoder Neufeld, "The Invisible Curriculum – On Being Wisdom's Schools," in *Mennonite Education in a Post-Christian World*, ed. Harry Huebner (Winnipeg: CMBC Publications, 1998), 129–143.

52. T. J. Sergiovanny, "The Lifeworld at the Centre: Values and Action in Educational Leadership," in *Effective Educational Leadership*, eds. Nigel Bennett, Megan Crawford, and Marion Cartwright (London: Sage Publications, 2003), 14.

53. Hofstede, *Interkulturelle Zusammenarbeit*, 22.

54. These terms come from the field of organizational development. Cf. Constantin Peer, "Was kann die OE von der Kulturentwicklung lernen?," *Organisationsentwicklung* 2 (2001): 48–57.

55. Ibid., 49. Without differentiating two categories in this way, Dimmock and Walker, "School Leadership in Context," 71, refer to "the enduring set of beliefs, values, ideologies and behaviors that distinguish one group of people from another."

422 Understanding and Developing Theological Education

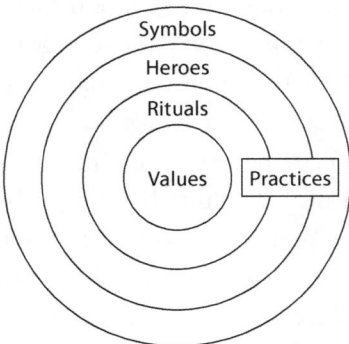

Figure 29

Similarly, Dubs distinguishes between the culture and the climate of a school. By culture he means "the common assumptions and values" and by climate he means "the shared perceptions of a school community."[56] In the past three to four decades a variety of studies have been done in a number of countries on the topic of school culture and climate. Categories, factors, and variables have been identified, tested, and refined, and tools have been developed to determine the climate of a school.[57]

In the following section I will attempt to summarize some of the factors that have proven to be significant in the shaping of a school's culture.

8.4.2 What Determines the Culture of an Educational Institution?[58]

1) Symbols: The basic premise here is that "many routine everyday actions have strong symbolic character to the extent that they are consciously undertaken in accord with the desired culture. If applied consistently over time, they induce a tendency toward imitation, and the effect becomes culture building and strengthening."[59] That happens when teachers and leaders demonstrate behaviors like these:

---

56. Dubs, *Die Führung einer Schule*, 108–109.
57. Various research findings, models, and measurement tools – Ibid., 109–126.
58. The five points outlined here follow those in the study by Deal and Peterson, described by Dubs, *Die Führung einer Schule*, 120.
59. Ibid., 121.

- Time management – actually making time for the important things, having time for eople, being available and accessible[60]
- Valuing people – speaking to and about others in a way that expresses their value
- Conscientiousness – in dealing with people, infrastructures, regulations and agreements
- Ensuring that the physical space of the school is space that is there for the people – space for being (esthetics) and for working (functionality)

Over and above the impact that these symbolic behaviors have, words, gestures, pictures, and objects also contribute to creating an unmistakable culture at a school, as long as they are typical for this institution.[61]

2) **Rituals**: These include shared or representative actions which make the values of the school visible and encourage or reinforce identification with those values. Such rituals include:
- Ceremonies and celebrations, such as graduation ceremonies and graduation parties
- Concerts and other cultural events which communicate something of the school's spirit
- The giving of awards and every form of expressing public appreciation for special efforts and achievements embodying the school's culture
- Devotionals, communal worship, and other spiritual activities and events (e.g. at the beginning or end of the day or week)
- Parties and celebrations marking holidays and other special dates
- Training days, retreats, day trips
- Inauguration ceremonies for people in special roles
- Memorial services or remembrance celebrations, giving special weight to events and people of note in the history and tradition of one's own school, church, or denomination and beyond

---

60. Cf. Gretchen E. Ziegenhals, "Faculty Life and Seminary Culture – It's About Time and Money," in *Practical Wisdom on Theological Teaching and Learning*, ed. Malcolm L. Warford (New York: Peter Lang, 2005), 49–66.
61. Cf. Michael Russenberger, *Führungskultur in der Schweiz. Eine sozio-historische Studie* (Giessen: Brunnen, 2005), 34.

Such events do not automatically have a culture shaping impact. They achieve this level of influence only if they truly embody the institutional culture, are planned and executed carefully, and practiced regularly.

3) **Language**: Vocabulary, language and communication style have an extraordinarily strong impact on an institution's culture and climate. If they are in accord with the explicitly communicated values of the school, they strengthen the influence of those values through their implicit messaging. If, however, they stand in contradiction to explicitly articulated values, they create confusion, undermining the explicit messaging and thus eroding or destroying what might otherwise be a positive culture. The following factors may merit specific consideration:

- Respectful interaction by teachers and leaders with and about students
- Open and trusting communication
- The consistent use of inclusive language
- Respectful speech about persons not present, especially those with whom we may be in (theological) disagreement
- Addressing conflicts and problems openly and constructively, in a solution-oriented way
- A passion for the values of the institution
- Open and respectful interaction with guests and visitors

4) **Appearance**: This is about the importance of teachers and leaders being present at significant times and places. This is not about asserting their dominance or putting them in the limelight. Nor is it about projecting a directorial mannerism that creates rather than removes a sense of distance.

- At moments and at events that are significant in the life of the school, leaders and teachers are present and visible. This is especially important at times of celebration as well as times of crisis
- At events and gatherings which students are expected or required to attend, teachers and leaders are also present
- In crisis situations, leaders and teachers exercise leadership and take responsibility in an appropriate manner
- The school's leader(s) makes official appearances as appropriate (giving words of greeting, opening the semester or school term,

graduation ceremonies and conferring of degrees, important communiqués, disciplinary interventions, etc.)

It's not just that these things must be done. It's *how* they are done. The presence of the school's leaders and teachers helps shape the institutional culture, as long as it is in accord with the school's stated values.

5) **Supporting Changes**: Every institution is evolving. Change is an everyday reality. Whether changes succeed, and how well they succeed, depends largely upon the culture and climate of the institution. The following measures can help produce a culture that is open to change, and thus also to improvement and development:[62]

- Loving people – demonstrating that it's about people and their development and not about institutional changes or change for the sake of change
- Valuing accessibility – seek people out, listen to them, find out what is important to them, and avoid retreating into the (apparent) security of the ivory tower of offices and conference rooms
- Encourage and implement innovative ideas and suggestions for improvement
- Integrity and reliability – especially in times of change, when many things are in flux, people must be able to count on the word of those in leadership
- Sensitivity – taking criticism seriously
- Clear and open communication
- Honoring the past – no reactive response to the history of the institution
- Willingness to learn on the part of the school and its leaders. Admitting mistakes and taking corrective steps
- Planning change processes carefully and competently
- Persistence and determination in pursuing stated goals. Not getting sidetracked by headwinds or crosswinds

---

62. I am using material here that I have used again and again in any number of seminars on the topic of change management. In these seminars and in the material here, I have incorporated material from a multitude of sources on this subject, as well as my own personal experience.

- Give people challenging goals that will stretch them – this honors them
- Celebrate successes
- Trust people. The implicit message should not be: "We will see to it that you measure up" but rather "We trust you to do it well."

Now that we have outlined the elements of a school's culture with the five characteristics above, the question arises, what impact does the institutional culture have on the learning process.

8.4.3 The Pedagogical Significance of the Institutional Culture

The pedagogical significance of the institutional culture can be defined at several levels:

1) The culture of an educational institution provides the community of teachers and students with a common core. In the face of many centrifugal, fragmenting forces, the shared culture has a centripetal effect. In today's world, education is shaped by a shift toward flexibility, modularity, and individualization. Part-time students and part-time faculty meet in constantly changing constellations. In such an environment, a strong institutional culture can create identification and integration. This must be purposefully desired and intentionally fostered, however – now, more than in the past. This starts with team building within the faculty and staff and builds in concentric circles throughout the entire school community. In other words, culture building at a seminary or theological school begins with culture building among the faculty and staff.[63]

2) The culture of a school will have either a conducive (accelerating) or a restrictive (limiting) effect upon the institution's declared educational goals. Every school speaks two languages: the explicit language in formal classroom settings, and the implicit language expressed through the life of the school. This "*invisible* or *hidden* curriculum"[64] communicates a "paramessage" which

---

63. Cf. The inspirational article by Stephen Ellington, "From Cordiality to Candor – an Ethnographic Study of a Faculty Forming Its Life Together," in *Practical Wisdom on Theological Teaching and Learning*, ed. Malcolm Warford (New York: Peter Lang, 2005), 67–86.

64. The term "hidden curriculum" can also have negative connotations in the sense of training goals not openly expressed and therefore hidden. That is not what is meant here.

may speak louder than everything taught formally in the classroom. This reality must be taken very seriously in shaping theological education since a great deal of what is formally taught in the classroom can be destroyed by a negative school culture. Here are some areas to be considered:

- If grace and freedom in Christ are taught, that should be observable in the school culture.
- If the fear of God and the value of creation (and humanity) are taught theologically, that should impact the spirituality and the interpersonal relationships on campus.
- If the value and responsibility of human beings is taught, that should be visible in the life of the school.
- If stewardship of creation is taught, that ought to be lived out throughout the institution.
- If the importance of relationships for church growth is taught, that too should be lived out throughout the life of the school.

3) Finally, the school's culture radiates beyond the limits of its own community in ways that should not be underestimated. It is embedded in the design and the content of school publications. It is reflected in those who represent the school to the outside world (teachers and students alike). Outsiders quickly notice the culture, which usually speaks louder than what they may hear when visiting a class or a campus-sponsored event.

Additional Literature

Comprehensive foundational work on the topic of school leadership:
Herbert Buchen and Hans-Günther Rolff, eds. *Professionswissen: Schulleitung* [Professional Knowledge: School Leadership]. Weinheim and Basel: Beltz, 2006.

See also Yoder Neufeld on this topic in "The Invisible Curriculum," 129, as well as Shirley Showalter, "The Invisible Curriculum II," in *Mennonite Education in a Post-Christian World*, ed. Harry Huebner (Winnipeg: CMBC Publications, 1998), 145–153.

A classic volume for a systematic approach to organizational development. Important insights on school management with emphasis on a learning organization:
Peter M. Senge. *The Fifth Discipline: The Art and Practice of the Learning Organization.* New York: Doubleday, 1990.

On the integration of Christian spirituality and leadership principles:
Friedrich Assländer and Anselm Grün. *Spirituell Führen mit Benedikt und der Bibel* [Leading Spiritually with Benedict and the Bible]. Münsterschwarzach: Vier-Türme-Verl., 2010, 3rd edition.
Peter Böhlemann and Michael Herbst. *Geistlich leiten: Ein Handbuch* [Leading Spiritually: A Handbook]. Göttingen: Vandenhoeck & Ruprecht, 2011.

Bibliography

Magazines

Evangelical Review of Theology
Evangelikale Missiologie [Evangelical Missiology]
International Review of Mission
Jahrbuch für Evangelikale Theologie [Almanac for Evangelical Theology]
Pastoraltheologie [Pastoral Theology]
Magazin Schule [School Magazine]
Ministerial Formation
Missiology
Mission Focus
Organizationsentwicklung [Organizational Development]
Panorama
Personal [Personnel]
Porta
Qualität und Zertifizierung [Quality and Certification]
Reformierte Presse [Reformed Press]
Theologische Beiträge [Theological Contributions]
Theological Education
Transformation
Zeitschrift für allgemeine Wissenschaftstheorie [Magazine for General Scientific Theory]
Zeitschrift für Theologie und Gemeinde [Magazine for Theology and Church]

Dictionaries and Lexicons

Enzyklopädie Erziehungswissenschaft (Handbuch und Lexikon der Erziehung). 11 volumes. Edited by Dieter Lenzen. Stuttgart: Klett-Cotta, 1982 ff.
Evangelisches Lexikon für Theologie und Gemeinde (ELThG). 3 volumes. Edited by Helmut Burkhardt and Uwe Swarat. Wuppertal: SCM R. Brockhaus, 1992/1993/1994.
Kleines Pädagogisches Wörterbuch. Edited by Josef A. Keller and Felix Novak. Freiburg: Herder, 1991.

Lexikon der Philosophie. Edited by Heinrich Schmid. Zürich: Buchclub Ex Libris, 1974.

Philosophielexikon. Edited by Anton Hügli and Paul Lübcke. Reinbek: Rowohlt Taschenbuch, 2000.

Religion in Geschichte und Gegenwart (RGG). 8 volumes. Edited by Hans Dieter Betz et al. Tübingen: Mohr Siebeck, 1998–2005 (4th edition, fully revised).

Theologisches Begriffslexikon zum Neuen Testament (TBLNT). Edited by Lothar Coenen et al. Wuppertal: Neukirchener, 2005 (rev. edition).

Theologisches Handwörterbuch zum Alten Testament (THAT). Edited by Ernst Jenni and Claus Westermann. Munich: Kaiser; Zürich: Theologischer Verlag, 1978.

Literature

Abromeit, Hans-Jürgen et al., eds. *Spirituelles Gemeindemanagement*. Göttingen: Vandehoeck & Rupprecht, 2001.

Aebli, Hans. *Zwölf Grundformen des Lehrens*. Stuttgart: Klett-Cotta, 1995.

Ahme, Michael. *Der Reformversuch der EKD 1970–1976*. Stuttgart: Kohlhammer, 1990. (The EKD is the *Evangelische Kirche Deutschland*, the Evangelical Church in Germany.)

Ahme, Michael and Michael Beintker. *Theologische Ausbildung in der EKD. Dokumente und Texte aus der Arbeit der Gemischten Kommission/ Fachkommission zur Reform des Theologiestudiums 1993–2004*. Leipzig: Evangelische Verlagsanstalt, 2005.

Allen, Diogenes and Eric O. Springsted, *Philosophy for Understanding Theology*. Louisville: Westminster John Knox Press, 2007.

Amirtham, Samuel and Robin Pryor. *Resources for Spiritual Formation in Theological Education: The Invitation to the Feast of Life*. Geneva: World Council of Churches, 1989.

Amirtham, Samuel and Ariarajah S. Weley. *Ministerial Formation in a Multifaith Milieu*. Geneva: World Council of Churches, 1986.

Ammann, Christoph. "Die Flucht vor dem 'Ich.' Kritische Bemerkungen zur theologischen Ausbildung." *Fakultativ* 01 (2004): 8–11.

Andrews, Roy A. "The Pastorate as a Metaphor for the Seminary Presidency: A Focus Study in the Theological Education Journal." *Theological Education* 40 (2005): 115–127. (Supplement).

Associated Mennonite Biblical Seminary. "Theological Education in the Free Church Tradition." In *The People of God*, edited by Ross T. Bender, 166–207. Scottdale: Herald Press, 1971.

———. "Theologische Ausbildung in der freikirchlichen Tradition." In *Das Leben wagen. Die Zukunft gewinnen,* edited by Daniel Geiser, 123–138. Weisenheim: Agape Verlag, 1986.
Banks, Robert. *Reenvisioning Theological Education.* Grand Rapids: Eerdmans Publishing, 1999.
Barrett, Louis Y. et al. *Treasures in Clay Jars: Patterns in Missional Faithfulness.* Grand Rapids: Eerdmans Publishing, 2004.
Barth, Karl. *Evangelical Theology: An Introduction.* Grand Rapids: Eerdmans, 1992.
Barz, Heiner and Susanne May, eds. *Erwachsenenbildung als Sinnstiftung.* Bielefeld: Bertelsmann, 2001.
Bastian, Johannes and Herbert Gudjons, eds. *Das Projektbuch. Theorie – Praxisbeispiele – Erfahrungen.* Hamburg: Bergmann und Helbig, 1994.
Baumgart, Franzjörg, ed. *Erziehungs- und Bildungstheorien.* Bad Heilbrunn: Klinkhardt, 1997.
Beaver, Pierce R. "The American Protestant Theological Seminary and Mission: An Historical Survey." *Missiology* 6, no. 1 (1976): 75–87.
Beck, Andreas J. "Der Bologna-Prozess und das Theologiestudium." *Evangelikale Theologie – Mitteilungen* 10, no. 2 (2004): 7–12.
Beck, Horst W. *Marxistischer Materialismus im Schafspelz.* Wuppertal: Aussaat Verlag, 1975.
Beer, Ulrich. *Methoden der geistigen Arbeit.* Tübingen: Katzmann, 1978.
Bender, Ross T. "Indoctrination." In *Harper's Encyclopedia of Religious Education,* edited by Iris V. Cully, 321–322. New York: Harper, 1990.
———. *Education for Peoplehood: Essays on the Teaching Ministry of the Church.* Elkhart, IN: Institute of Mennonite Studies, 1997.
Bennett, Nigel, Megan Crawford, and Marion Cartwright, eds. *Effective Educational Leadership.* London: Sage Publications, 2003.
Bessoth, Richard. *Pädagogische Leitungsfunktionen in der Schule.* Mannheim: DSE, ZGB, 1985.
Bittlinger, Arnold. *Gemeinde im Kraftfeld des Heiligen Geistes.* Marburg 1972.
Bockmühl, Klaus. *The Challenge of Marxism.* Downers Grove, IL: InterVarsity, 1980. Translated from German, original title *Herausforderungen des Marxismus.*
———. *Das größte Gebot.* Giessen: Brunnen, 1980.
———. *Theologie und Lebensführung.* Giessen: Brunnen, 1982.
———. *Leben mit dem Gott der redet.* Giessen: Brunnen, 1998.
Bohren, Rudolf. *Einführung in das Theologiestudium.* Munich and Hamburg: Siebenstern Taschenbuch Verlag, 1969.

———. "Die Krise der Predigt als Anfang der Exegese." In *Dem Wort folgen. Predigt und Gemeinde,* edited by Rudolf Bohren, 65–96. Hamburg: Siebenstern Taschenbuch, 1969.

Bosch, David. *Transforming Mission.* Maryknoll: Orbis Books, 1991.

———. "Reflexionen über das Neue Testament als missionarisches Dokument." In *Mission im Wandel: Paradigmenwechsel in der Missionstheologie,* edited by David Bosch. Giessen: Brunnen-Verlag, 2012.

Bouillon, Hardy and Gerard Radnitzky, eds. *Die ungewisse Zukunft der Universität.* Berlin: Duncker & Humblot, 1991.

Bourdieu, Pierre. *Entwurf einer Theorie der Praxis.* Frankfurt: Suhrkamp Verlag, 1979.

Brändl, Werner. "Descartes und seiner modernen Kritiker." In *Descartes und das neuzeitliche Denken,* Porta Studien 13, edited by Edith Gutsche and Hermann Hafner, 25–28. Marburg: SMD, 1993.

Brandt, Erwin. "Akzente und Perspektiven der ökumenisch-missionarischen Ausbildung an einer freikirchlichen Ausbildungsstätte." In *Impulse für eine Kirche von morgen. Beiträge zur ökumenisch-theologischen Ausbildung,* edited by Evangelisches Missionswerk, 102–107. Hamburg: Evangelisches Missionswerk, 1997.

Breitmaier, Isa. *Lehren und Lernen in der Spur des Ersten Testaments.* Münster: LIT Verlag, 2004.

Brereton, Virginia L. "Protestant Fundamentalist Bible Schools: 1882–1940." Unpublished doctoral dissertation, Columbia University, 1981.

Briggs, Ann R. J. "Monitoring and Evaluating Learning." In *The Principles and Practice of Educational Management,* edited by Tony Bush and Les Bell, 170–184. London: Sage Publications, 2002.

Brubacher, Ray. "The Globalization of Theological Education and of Mission." *Mission Focus* 8 (2000): 5–22.

Brynjolfson, Robert, and Jonathan Lewis, eds. *Integral Ministry Training: Design and Evaluation.* Pasadena: William Carey Library, 2006.

Buber, Martin. *Reden über Erziehung.* Gütersloh: Gütersloher Verlagshaus, 2005.

Brückner, Walter, Jürgen Heene, and Karsten Koitz. "Nicht für die Schule, für's Leben. Neue Qualitätsstandards für Bildungsunternehmen." *Qualität und Zertifizierung* 49, no. 9 (2004): 24–25.

Bukowski, Peter. "Rückfragen an die akademische theologische Ausbildung." *Pastoraltheologie* 89 (2000): 474–482.

Bush, Tony and Les Bell, eds. *The Principles and Practice of Educational Management.* London: Sage Publications, 2002.

Caldwell, Brian J. "Autonomy and Self-Management: Concepts and Evidence." In *The Principles and Practice of Educational Management*, edited by Tony Bush and Les Bell, 34–48. London: Sage Publications, 2002.

Cannell, Linda. "Opportunities for 21st Century Theological Education." In *Theological Education as Mission*, edited by Peter Penner, 153–170. Schwarzenfeld: Neufeld, 2005.

———. *Theological Education Matters*. Charleston: BookSurge publishing, 2008.

Carroll, M. Daniel. "Perspectives on Theological Education from the Old Testament." *Evangelical Review of Theology* 29, no. 3 (2005): 228–239.

Cheesman, Graham. "Competing Paradigms in Theological Education Today." *Evangelical Review of Theology* 17, no. 4 (1993): 484–499.

———. *The Bible College Movement in the UK: A History and Interpretation*. Saarbrücken: VDM Verlag, 2009.

Clementi, Hedi, Andrea Hoyer, and Judith Ziegler, eds. *Institutionelle Evaluierung an Fachhochschulen*. Vienna: Facultas wuv universitätsverlag, 2004.

Coelen, Thomas, ed. *Grundbegriffe der Ganztagsbildung*. Wiesbaden: VS Verlag für Sozialwissenschaften, 2004.

Conn, Harvie and Samuel F. Rowen, eds. *Missions and Theological Education in World Perspective*. Farmington: Associates of Urbanus, 1984.

Cortolezis-Schlager, Katharina, and Reinhart Nagel. "'Und sie bewegt sich doch!?' Steuerung und Organization der Schulprozesse." *Organizationsentwicklung* 2 (1999): 4–15.

Crittin, Jean-Pierre. *Erfolgreich Unterrichten*. Bern: Haupt, 2004.

Daniel-Rops, Henri, and Sigrid Stahlmann. *Die Umwelt Jesu: der Alltag in Palästina vor 2000 Jahren*. Munich: Deutscher Taschenbuch Verlag, 1980.

Danzig, Arnold B., et al., eds. *Learner-Centred Leadership: Research, Policy, and Practice*. Mahwah: Lawrence Erlbaum Associates, 2007.

Dearborn, Tim. "Preparing New Leaders for the Church of the Future." *Transformation* 12, no. 4 (1995): 7–12.

Dehnbostel, Peter, Werner Markert, and Hermann Novak, eds. *Erfahrungen in der beruflichen Bildung – Beiträge zu einem kontroversen Konzept*. Neusäss: Kieser, 1999.

De Vaux, Roland. *Ancient Israel*, Vol. 1: Social Institutions. New York: McGraw Hill, 1965.

Dieterich, Michael. *Auf dem Weg zum Beruf. Ein pädagogisches Fachbuch für Ausbilder und Lehrer*. Hamburg: Handwerk und Technik, 1991.

———. *Persönlichkeitsdiagnostik*. Witten: Brockhaus Verlag, 1996.

Dimmock, Clive and Allan Walker. "School Leadership in Context – Societal and Organizational Cultures." In *The Principles and Practice of Educational Management*, edited by Tony Bush and Les Bell, 70–85. London: Sage Publications, 2002.

Dinter, Astrid, Hans-Günther Heimbrock, and Kerstin Söderblom, eds. *Einführung in die empirische Theologie*. Göttingen: Vandenhoeck & Ruprecht, 2007.

Döring, Klaus W., and Bettina Ritter-Mamczek. *Lehren und Tranieren in der Weiterbildung*. Weinheim: Beltz, 1999.

Dreyer, Jaco S. "Theological Normativity: Ideology or Utopia." In *Normativity and Empirical Research in Theology*, edited by Johannes A. van der Ven and Michael Scherer-Rath, 3–16. Leiden: Brill, 2004.

Dubs, Rolf. *Qualitätsmanagement für Schulen*, 1st edition. St. Gallen: University of St. Gallen Institute, 2003.

———. *Die Führung einer Schule. Leadership und Management*. Stuttgart: Steiner, 2005.

Early, Gene. *Leadership Expectations: How Executive Expectations Are Created and Used in a Non-Profit Setting*. Oxford: Regnum, 2005.

Ebeling, Gerhard. *The Study of Theology*. Translated from German by Duane A. Priebe. Philadelphia: Fortress, 1978.

Edgar, Brian. "The Theology of Theological Education." *Evangelical Review of Theology* 29, no. 3 (2005): 208–217.

EEAA Manual 2011. Available at http://www.eeaa.eu/downloads-and-tools/the-eeaa-manual/

Ehlert, Holger, and Ulrich Welber, eds. *Qualitätssicherung und Studienreform*. Düsseldorf: Grupello Verlag, 2004.

Ellington, Stephen. "From Cordiality to Candor – An Ethnographic Study of a Faculty Forming Its Life Together." In *Practical Wisdom on Theological Teaching and Learning*, edited by Malcolm Warford, 67–86. New York: Peter Lang, 2005.

Ellis, E. Earle. *Prophecy and Hermeneutics in Early Christianity*. Grand Rapids: Eerdmans Publishing, 1978.

Engel, Lothar. "Ökumenische Impulse und die Wirklichkeit von Fakultäten und kirchlichen Hochschulen" in Evangelisches Missionswerk. *Impulse* (1997): 52–57.

Engel, Lothar and Werner Dietrich, eds. *Ökumenische Perspektiven theologischer Ausbildung*. Beihelft zur Ökumenischer Rundschau Nr. 60. Frankfurt: Verlag Otto Lembeck, 1990.

Enns, Marlene. *Toward a Theoretical Model of Mutuality and Its Implications for Intercultural Theological Education: Holistic and Analytical Cognition*. PhD dissertation Trinity International University, 2003.

———. "'Now I Know in Part': Holistic and Analytical Reasoning and Their Contribution to Fuller Knowing in Theological Education." *Evangelical Review of Theology* 29, no. 3 (2005): 251–267.

———. "Theological Education in Light of Cultural Variations in Reasoning: Some Educational Issues." In *Theological Education as Mission*, edited by Peter Penner, 137–151. Schwarzenfeld: Neufeld Verlag, 2005.

———. "Recovering the Wisdom Tradition for Intercultural Theological Education." *Journal of European Baptist Studies* 5, no. 3 (2005): 5–23.

Euler, Dieter. "Schlüsselqualifikationen zwischen Idee und Wirklichkeit." *Panorama* 6 (2002): 15 [also at http://www.panorama.ch].

Evangelisches Missionswerk. *Impulse für eine Kirche von morgen: Beiträge zu ökumenisch.theologischer Ausbildung* (Weltmission heute 27). Hamburg: Evangelisches Missionswerk, 1997.

Faix, Tobias, Wilhelm Faix, Klaus W. Müller, and Klaus Schmidt, eds. *Theologische Ausbildung zu Beginn des 21. Jahrhunderts*. Bonn: Verlag für Kultur und Wissenschaft, 1998.

Faix, Tobias. *Mentoring. Chancen für geistliches Leben und Persönlichkeitsprägung*. Neukirchen-Vluyn: Neukirchener, 2000.

Faix, Wilhelm. "Die Bedeutung der Pädagogik in der Theologischen Ausbildung." *Jahrbuch für evangelikale Theologie* (1993): 73–97.

———. "Theologische Ausbildung im Umbruch." In *Theologische Ausbildung zu Beginn des 21. Jahrhunderts*, edited by Tobias Faix, Wilhelm Faix, Klaus W. Müller, and Klaus Schmidt, 31–37. Bonn: Verlag für Kultur und Wissenschaft, 1998.

———. "Die Bedeutung von Schlüsselqualifikationen für die theologische Ausbildung." *Jahrbuch für Evangelikale Theologie* (2005): 191–210.

Farley, Edward. "The Reform of Theological Education as a Theological Task." *Theological Education* 17, no. 2 (1981): 93–117.

———. *Theologia: The Fragmentation and Unity of Theological Education*. Philadelphia: Fortress Press, 1983.

———. *The Fragility of Knowledge: Theological Education in the Church and the University*. Philadelphia: Fortress Press, 1988.

Ferris, Robert W. *Renewal in Theological Education: Strategies for Changes*. Wheaton: The Billy Graham Center, 1990.

———. "Renewal of Theological Education: Commitments, Models and the ICAA Manifesto." *Evangelical Review of Theology* 14, no. 1 (1990): 64–77.

———. *Establishing Ministry Training: A Manual for Programme Developers.* Pasadena: William Carey Library, 1995.

Ferris, Robert W., and Ralph E. Enlow. "Reassessing Bible College Distinctives." American Association of Bible Colleges, unpublished lecture manuscript, 1995.

Fiedler, Klaus. *Ganz auf Vertrauen. Geschichte und Kirchenverständnis der Glaubensmissionen*, Giessen: Brunnen-Verlag, 1992.

Finsterbusch, Karin. *Weisung für Israel. Studien zu religiösem Lehren und Lernen im Deuteronomium und seinem Umfeld.* Tübingen: Mohr, 2005.

Flechsing, Karl-Heinz. *Kleines Handbuch didaktischer Modelle.* Eichenzell: Neuland, Verlag für Lebendiges Lernen, 1996.

Foster, Charles R., et al., eds. *Educating Clergy: Teaching Practices and Pastoral Imagination.* San Francisco: Jossey-Bass, 2006.

Foster, Richard. *Streams of Living Water: Celebrating the Great Traditions of Christian Faith.* San Francisco: HarperSanFrancisco, 1998.

Frazer Evans, Alice, Robert A. Evans, and David A. Roozen, eds. *The Globalization of Theological Education.* Maryknoll: Orbis Books, 1993.

Freire, Paulo. *Pedagogy of the Oppressed.* Translated by Myra Bergman Ramos. New York: Bloomsbury, 2015.

———. *Erziehung als Praxis der Freiheit. Beispiele zur Pädagogik der Unterdrückten.* Reinbek: Rowohlt, 1977 (1st edition Stuttgart: Kreuz, 1974).

Frieden, Monika. "Konkordatsreform: Kulturwandel in der Ausbildung." *Annex* (Magazine of the Reformed Press) 11 (2006): 3–5.

Friedenthal-Haase, Martha and Ralf Koerrenz, eds. *Martin Buber: Bildung, Menschenbild, und Hebräischer Humanismus.* Paderborn: Schöningh, 2005.

Frische, Reinhard. *Theologie unter der Herrschaft Gottes.* Giessen: Brunnen, 1979.

Fröhlich, Werner, and Wolfgang Jütte, eds. *Qualitätsentwicklung in der Postgradualen Weiterbildung: Internationale Entwicklungen und Perspektiven.* Münster: Waxmann, 2004.

Gäbler, Ulrich. "Universität Basel: Forschungspolitik und Universitätsleitung." In *Die neue Verantwortung der Hochschulen* edited by Evelies Mayer, Hans-Dieter Daniel and Ulrich Teichler, 82. Bonn: Lemmens, 2003.

Gage, Nathaniel, and David C. Berliner. *Pädagogische Psychologie*, Vol. 1. Weinheim and Basel: Beltz, 1983.

Gilmore, Alec, ed. *An International Dictionary of Theological Colleges 1997.* London: SCM Press; Geneva: WCC Publications, 1997.

Giesekus, Hanswalter. *Glaubenswagnis. Leben und Erkennen aus der Sicht des Blaise Pascal.* Wuppertal: Brockhaus, 1997.

Gonon, Philipp. "Neue Studien zum Thema Schlüsselqualifikationen." *Panorama* 6 (2002): 11 [also at http://www.panorama.ch].

Götz, Klaus, and Peter Häfner. *Didaktische Organisation von Lehr- und Lernprozessen. Ein Lehrbuch für Schule und Erwachsenenbildung.* Weinheim: Dt. Studien-Verl, 1999.

Götzinger, Albrecht and Ekkehard W. Stegemann, eds. *Das Christentum an der Schwelle zum 3. Jahrtausend.* Stuttgart: Kohlhammer, 2002.

Grassi, Joseph. *A World to Win: The Missionary Methods of St. Paul the Apostle.* Maryknoll: Orbis, 1965.

———. *The Teacher in the Primitive Church.* Santa Clara: University of Santa Clara Press, 1973.

Greenleaf, Robert K. *Servant Leadership: A Journey into the Nature of Legitimate Power and Greatness.* New York: Paulist Press, 1977.

Greinacher, Norbert. "Das Theorie-Praxis-Problem in der Praktischen Theologie." In *Praktische Theologie Heute,* edited by Ferdinand Klostermann and Rolf Zerfaß, 102–115. Munich: Kaiser, 1974.

Griffith, Michael. "Theological Education Need Not Be Irrelevant." Unpublished lecture manuscript, 1989.

Gruber, Hans. "Hinführung zum wissenschaftlichen Arbeiten. Ein Leitfaden," 8. Available at https://www.uni-frankfurt.de/48891434/Hinfuehrung-zum-wiss-Arbeiten.pdf

Grün, Anselm. *Menschen führen – Leben wecken.* Münsterschwarzach: Vier-Türme-Verlag, 2001.

Guardini, Romano. *Die Lebensalter. Ihre ethische und pädagogische Bedeutung.* Würzburg: Werkbund Verlag, 1967.

Guder, Darrell, et al. *Missional Church: A Vision for the Sending of the Church in North America.* Grand Rapids: Eerdmans Publishing, 1998.

Haacker, Klaus, ed. *Lernen und Leben. Ansprachen an Theologiestudenten.* Wuppertal: Aussaat Verlag, 1981.

———. "Warum und wozu (noch) kirchliche Hochschulen?" *Theologische Beiträge* 33 (2000): 356–362.

Haddad, Wadi D. "Tertiary Education Today: Global Trends, Global Agendas, Global Constraints." Unpublished lecture manuscript, 2003 [also at http://www.icete-edu.org].

Hanselmann, Heinrich. *Andragogik. Wesen, Möglichkeiten und Grenzen der Erwachsenenbildung.* Zürich: Rotapfel Verlag, 1951.

Hauschildt, Eberhard. "Theologische Bildung und pastorale Kompetenz." *Pastoraltheologie* 89 (2000): 483–489.

Heimbrock, Hans-Günter and Matthias von Kriegstein, eds. *Theologische Bildungsprozesse gestalten. Schritte zur Ausbildungsreform*. Frankfurt: Spener, 2002.

Heisey, Nancy R. and Daniel S. Schipani, eds. *Theological Education on Five Continents*. Strasbourg: Mennonite World Conference, 1997.

Hempelmann, Heinzpeter. *Kritischer Rationalismus und Theologie als Wissenschaft. Zur Frage nach dem Wirklichkeitsbezug*. Wuppertal: Brockhaus, 1980.

———. *Wahrheit ohne Toleranz – Toleranz ohne Wahrheit*. Wuppertal: Brockhaus, 1995.

———. *Wie wir denken können*. Wuppertal: Brockhaus, 2000.

———. *Gott erleben in der Gemeinde. Kernsätze zum Wesen evangelischer Spiritualität nach 1. Kor 12*. Birsfelden: ArteMedia, 2004.

———. *Glauben wir alle an denselben Gott? Christlicher Glaube in einer nachchristlichen Gesellschaft*. Bad Liebenzell: VLM, Verl. der Liebenzeller Mission, 2005.

———. "Streiten für den Streit um die Wahrheit?" In *Glauben wir alle an denselben Gott? Christlicher Glaube in einer nachchristlichen Gesellschaft,* edited by Heinzpeter Hempelmann. Bad Liebenzell: VLM, Verl. der Liebenzeller Mission, 2005.

Herbst, Michael. *Missionarischer Gemeindeaufbau in der Volkskirche*. Stuttgart: Calwer, 1987.

———. "'Mission' in der theologischen Ausbildung." *Theologische Beiträge* 36 (2005): 202–216.

Herrlitz, Hans-Georg. "Geschichte der gymnasialen Oberstufe." *Enzyklopädie Erziehungswissenschaft* 9, no. 1 (1982): 89–107.

Herrmann, Wolfgang, and Gerd Lautner. *Theologiestudium. Entwurf einer Reform*. Munich: Kaiser, 1965.

Hertig, Paul. "Transforming Theological Education through Experiential Learning in Urban Contexts." *Mission Studies* XIX, no. 1 (2002): 56–76.

Hess, H. E., and H. E. Tödt. *Reform der theologischen Ausbildung,* Vol. 1: Untersuchungen, Berichte, Empfehlungen. Munich: Kreuz, 1967.

Hicks, Peter. *Evangelicals and Truth: A Creative Proposal for a Postmodern Age*. Nottingham: Apollos, 1998.

Hiebert, Paul G. *Missiological Implications of Epistemological Shifts: Affirming Truth in a Modern/Postmodern World*. Harrisburg: Trinity Press International, 1999.

Hillers, Delbert R. *Covenant: The History of a Biblical Idea*. Baltimore: Johns Hopkins Press, 1969.

Hofstede, Geert. *Interkulturelle Zusammenarbeit. Kulturen – Organisationen – Management*. Wiesbaden: Gabler, 1993.

Hollenweger, Walter. "The World Is the Agenda." In *Die Kirche für andere*, edited by Walter Hollenweger, 23–30. Geneva: World Council of Churches, 1967. (first published: Concept XI, Geneva: WCC, 1966).

Hough, Joseph C. Jr., and John B. Cobb Jr., eds. *Christian Identity and Theological Education*. Chico: Scholars Press, 1985.

Hough, Joseph C. Jr., and Barbara G. Wheeler, eds. *Beyond Clericalism: The Congregation as a Focus for Theological Education*. Atlanta: Scholars Press, 1988.

Huber, Stephan G. *Qualifizierung von Schulleiterinnen und Schulleitern im internationalen Vergleich*. Kronach: Link, 2003.

Huebner, Harry, ed. *Mennonite Education in a Post-Christian World*. Winnipeg: CMBC Publications, 1998.

Janzen, Waldemar. "Education in the Old Testament and in Early Judaism." In *Still in the Image: Essays in Biblical Theology and Anthropology*, edited by Waldemar Janzen, 92–108. Newton: Faith and Life Press, 1982.

———. *Werden was wir sind. Biblische Menschenbilder und ihre Bedeutung für uns*. Weisenheim: Faith and Life Press, 2001.

Jaspers, Karl. *Die Idee der Universität*. Berlin: Springer, 1980. (Reprint of the 1946 edition).

Johns, Cheryl Bridges. *Pentecostal Formation: A Pedagogy Among the Oppressed*. (*Journal of Pentecostal Theology*, Supplement Series 2). Sheffield: Sheffield Academic Press, 1993.

Johnstone, Patrick. *Viel größer als man denkt: Auftrag und Wachsen der Gemeinde Jesu*. Holzgerlingen: Hänssler, 1999.

Kähler, Martin. *Schriften zu Christologie und Misison*. Munich: Kaiser, 1971.

Karle, Isolde. "Pastorale Kompetenz." *Pastoraltheologie* 89 (2000): 508–523.

Kasdorf, Hans. *Missiologie und theologische Ausbildung*. Giessen: Freie Theologische Akademie, 1995.

Keegan, John. "Der Krieg ist keine Frage der Moral." *Die Weltwoche* 51, no. 52 (2002).

Kelsey, David H. *To Understand God Truly: What's Theological about a Theological School?* Louisville: Westminster John Knox Press, 1992. Available and accessed at http://www.religion-online.org/showbook.asp?title=379.

———. *Between Athens and Berlin: The Theological Education Debate.* Grand Rapids: Eerdmans Publishing, 1993. Available and accessed on http://www.religion-online.org/showbook.asp?title=437.

Kemp, Roger, ed. *Text and Context in Theological Education.* Springwood: International Council of Accrediting Agencies for Evangelical Theological Education, 1994.

Kinsler, F. Ross. *The Extension Movement in Theological Education.* Pasadena: William Carey Library, 1981.

———. *Ministry by the People: Theological Education by Extension.* Geneva: WCC, 1983.

Kinsler, F. Ross, and James F. Emery, eds. *Opting for Change: A Handbook on Evaluation and Planning for Theological Education by Extension.* Pasadena: William Carey Library, 1991.

Kirk, J. Andrew. *The Mission of Theology and Theology as Mission.* Valley Forge: Trinity Press International, 1997.

———. "Reenvisioning the Theological Curriculum as if the Missio Dei Mattered." In *Theological Education as Mission,* edited by Peter Penner, 39–51. Schwarzenfeld: Neufeld, 2005.

Klein, Günter, and Jürgen Ripper. "Schlüsselqualifikationen im Blickpunkt." *Magazin Schule* 9 (2003): 10–11 [also at http://www.km-bw.de].

Klein, Stephanie. *Erkenntnis und Methode in der praktischen Theologie.* Stuttgart: Kohlhammer, 2005.

Klostermann, Ferdinand and Rolf Zerfaß, eds. *Praktische Theologie heute.* Munich: Kaiser, 1974.

Knoll, Jörg. *Kurs- und Seminarmethoden.* Weinheim: Beltz, 2007.

Knowles, Malcolm S. *The Adult Learner: The Definitive Classic in Adult Education and Human Resource Development.* 8th edition. New York: Routledge, 2015.

Köberle, Adolf. *Descartes und die Folgen. Ein Weltbild in der Krise* (EZW-Informationen Nr. 92/IX). Stuttgart: Evangelische Zentralstelle für Weltanschauungsfragen, 1984.

Krajnc, A. "Andragogy." In *Lifelong Education for Adults: An International Handbook,* edited by Colin J. Titmus, 9–22. Oxford: Pergamon Press, 1989.

Kyrer, Alfred, ed. *Integratives Management für Universitäten und Fachhochschulen.* Vienna: Neuer Wissenschaftlicher Verlag (NWV), 2002.

Lehmann, Karl. "Das Theorie-Praxis-Problem." In *Praktische Theologie heute,* edited by Ferdinand Klostermann and Rolf Zerfaß, 84–89. Munich: Kaiser, 1974.

Lenzen, Dieter. *Orientierung Erziehungswissenschaft.* Vol. 3. Reinbek: Rowohlt-Taschenbuch-Verlag, 1999.

Leinemann-Perrin, Christine. *Training for a Relevant Ministry: A Study of the Work of the Theological Education Fund*. Geneva: WCC, 1981.

Lombriser, Roman, and Peter A. Abplanalp. *Strategisches Management: Visionen entwickeln, Strategien umsetzen, Erfolgspotenziale aufbauen*. Zürich: Versus, 1998.

Longenecker, Richard. *Biblical Exegesis in the Apostolic Period*. Grand Rapids: Eerdmans Publishing, 1975.

Loretan, Adrian, ed. *Theologische Fakultäten an europäischen Universitäten. Rechtliche Situation und theologische Perspektiven*. Münster: LIT Verlag, 2004.

Löwen, Heinrich and Hans Kasdorf, eds. *Gemeinsam im Auftrag des Herrn*. Bornheim/Bonn: Puls Verlag, 1999.

Lynn, Robert W. "Notes Toward a History: Theological Encyclopedia and the Evolution of Protestant Seminary Curriculum 1808–1868." *Theological Education* 1 (2002): 118–144.

MacBeath, John, ed. *Effective School Leadership*. London: Sage Publications, 1998.

Mallau, Hans-Harald. "Das Theologiestudium im BEFG und seine 'akademische Anerkennung'." *Zeitschrift für Theologie und Gemeinde* 6 (2001): 9–18.

Malik, Fredmund. *Führen, Leisten, Leben*. Stuttgart: Deutsche Verlags-Anstalt, 2000.

Marsden, George M. *The Soul of the American University: From Protestant Establishment to Established Unbelief*. New York: Oxford University Press, 1994.

———. *The Outrageous Idea of Christian Scholarship*. New York: Oxford University Press, 1997.

Martin, Ariane. *Sehnsucht – der Anfang von allem. Dimensionen zeitgenössischer Spiritualität*. Ostfildern: Schwabenverlag, 2005.

Marx, Karl. *Die Frühschriften,* edited by Siegfried Landshut. Stuttgart: Kröner, 1963.

Mayer, Evelies. "Dekane als Akteure der Hochschulentwicklung." In *Die neue Verantwortung der Hochschulen,* edited by Evelies Mayer, Hans-Dieter Daniel and Ulrich Teichler, 155–156. Bonn: Lemmens, 2003.

Mayer, Evelies, Hans-Dieter Daniel, and Ulrich Teichler, eds. *Die neue Verantwortung der Hochschulen*. Bonn: Lemmens, 2003.

McGrath, Alister, *Christian Spirituality*. Oxford: Blackwell Publishers, 1999.

McKeachie, Wilbert J. *Teaching Tips: Strategies, Research, and Theory for College and University Teachers*. Boston: Houghton Mifflin, 2002.

Mertens, Dieter. "Schlüsselqualifikationen. Thesen zur Schulung für eine moderne Gesellschaft." In *Wirtschaft – Arbeit – Beruf – Bildung: Dieter Mertens: Schriften und Vorträge 1968–1987,* edited by Friedrich Buttler and Lutz Reyher, 564–572. Nürnberg: Institut für Arbeitsmarkt- und Berufsforschung, 1991.

Mertes, Klaus. *Verantwortung lernen. Schule im Geist der Exerzitien*. Würzburg: Echter, 2004.

Mildenberger, Friedrich. *Theorie der Theologie: Enzyklopädie als Methodenlehre*. Stuttgart: Calwer Verlag, 1972.

Möller, Christian. *Der heilsame Riss. Impulse reformatorischer Spiritualität*. Stuttgart: Calwer, 2003.

Morgner, Christoph. *Geistliche Leitung als theologische Aufgabe*. Stuttgart: Calwer Verlag, 2000.

The Mud Flower Collective, Katie G. Cannon, et al. *God's Fierce Whimsy: Christian Feminism and Theological Education*. New York: Pilgrim Press, 1985.

Mulholland, Kenneth B. "Presbyterian Seminary of Guatemala: A Modest Experiment Becomes a Model for Change." In *Ministry by the people: Theological Education by Extension*, edited by Ross F. Kinsler, 33–41. Geneva: WCC, 1983.

———. "TEE Come of Age: A Candid Assessment after Two Decades." In *Cyprus: TEE Come of Age*, edited by Robert L. Youngblood, 9–25. Exeter: Paternoster, 1986.

Müller, Klaus W. "Persönlichkeitsprägung als Herausforderung: Mentoring als Aufgabe." In *Theologische Ausbildung zu Beginn des 21. Jahrhunderts*, edited by Tobias Faix, Wilhelm Faix, Klaus W. Müller, and Klaus Schmidt, 123–152. Bonn: Verlag für Kultur und Wissenschaft, 1998.

Müller, Klaus W. and Thomas Schirrmacher, eds. *Ausbildung als missionarischer Auftrag*. Bonn: Verlag für Kultur und Wissenschaft, 2000.

Müller-Böling, Detlef. *Die entfesselte Hochschule*. Gütersloh: Bertelsmann-Stiftung, 2000.

Müller-Böling, Detlef, ed. *Hochschule weiter entfesseln – den Umbruch gestalten*. Gütersloh: Verl. Bertelsmann-Stiftung, 2005.

Murphy, Nancy. "A Theology of Education." In *Mennonite Higher Education in a Post-Christian World*, edited by Harry Huebner, 1–16. Winnipeg: CMBC Publications, 1998.

Murray, Stuart. *Post-Christendom*. Carlisle: Paternoster, 2004.

Nanz, Philipp, ed. *Der Erneuerung von Kirche und Theologie verpflichtet*. Riehen: ArteMedia, 2005.

Newbigin, Lesslie. *Foolishness to the Greeks: the Gospel and Western Culture*. Grand Rapids: Eerdmans Publishing, 1986.

———. "Theological Education in a World Perspective." *Ministerial Formation* 4 (1987): 3–10.

Nicol, Martin. *Grundwissen Praktische Theologie*. Stuttgart: Verlag W. Kohlhammer, 2000.

Nicole, Jacques. "Brief History of the So-called 'Classical' Model for Theological Education." *Ministerial Formation* 67 (1994): 33–34.

Niebuhr, H. Richard. *The Purpose of the Church and Its Ministry: Reflections on the Aims of Theological Education*. New York: Harper, 1956.

Noelliste, Dieumeme. *Toward a Theology of Theological Education*. Seoul: World Evangelical Fellowship Theological Commission, 1993.

Nouwen, Henri J. M. *Wohin du mich führen willst. Notizen aus Lateinamerika*. Freiburg: Herder, 1983.

———. *Seelsorge, die aus dem Herzen kommt*. Freiburg: Herder 1989.

———. *Schöpferische Seelsorge*. Freiburg: Herder, 1991.

Nussberger, Cornelia. "Keine Pfarrerausbildung." *Reformierte Presse* 46 (1999): 7.

Ott, Bernhard. "Die KBA-Schulen im Licht globaler Veränderungen in theologischer Ausbildung." In *Theologische Ausbildung zu Beginn des 21. Jahrhunderts*, edited by Tobias Faix, Wilhelm Faix, Klaus W. Müller, and Klaus Schmidt, 38–76. Bonn: Verlag für Kultur und Wissenschaft, 1998.

———. "Denken und Handeln im Kontext einer nachchristlichen Gesellschaft. Eine Tagesordnung für Theologie und theologische Ausbildung an der Schwelle zum 21. Jahrhundert." In *Gemeinde mit Zukunft : Herausforderungen und Perspektiven an der Schwelle zum 21. Jahrhundert : Symposium zur Eröffnung des Theologischen Seminars Bienenberg, 11.–13. September 1998*, edited by Bernhard Ott et al., 8–30. Liestal: Ausbildungs- und Tagungszentrum Bienenberg, 1999.

———. "Missionstheologie in evangelikaler theologischer Ausbildung." In *Gemeinsam im Auftrag des Herrn*, edited by Heinrich Löwen and Hans Kasdorf, 123–139. Bornheim/Bonn: Puls Verlag, 1999.

———. *Beyond Fragmentation: Integrating Mission and Theological Education*. Oxford: Regnum Books International, 2001.

———. "Mission Oriented Theological Education." *Transformation* 18, no. 2 (2001): 87–98.

———. "Theologische Ausbildung im Spannungsfeld von Theorie und Praxis." *Jahrbuch für evangelikale Theologie* (2003):149–196.

———. *Wurzeln und Flügel. Schritte zu ganzheitlichem Wachstum*. Birsfelden: arteMedia, 2004.

———. "Accreditation: Importance and Benefits for the Institution." In *Foundations for Academic Leadership*, edited by Fritz Deininger, Orbelina Eguizabal,

International Council for Evangelical Theological Education. Nürnberg: VTR Publications, 2013.

Otto, Gunter, and Wolfgang Schulz. "Der Beitrag der Curriculumforschung." In *Enzyklopädie Erziehungswissenschaft*, Vol. 3, 49–62.

Overwien, Bernd. "Informelles Lernen, eine Herausforderung an die internationale Bildungsforschung." In *Erfahrungen in der beruflichen Bildung – Beiträge zu einem kontroversen Konzept*, edited by Peter Dehnbostel, Werner Markert, and Hermann Novak, 295–314. Neusäss, 1999.

———. "International Sichtweisen auf 'informelles Lernen' am Übergang zum 21. Jahrhundert." In *Grundbegriffe der Ganztagsbildung,* edited by Thomas Coelen, 51–73. Wiesbaden: VS Verlag für Sozialwissenschaften, 2004.

Padilla, C. René, ed. *New Alternatives in Theological Education*. Oxford: Regnum, 1988.

Peer, Constantin. "Was kann der OE von der Kulturentwicklung lernen?" *Organisationsentwicklung* 2 (2001): 48–57.

Penner, Peter, ed. *Theological Education as Mission*. Schwarzenfeld: Neufeld Verlag, 2005.

Peterßen, William H. *Lehrbuch Allgemeine Didaktik*. Munich: Oldenbourg, 2001. Completely revised and expanded 6th edition.

Pierard, Richard V. "'Pax Americana' and the Evangelical Missionary Advance." In *Earthen Vessels: American Evangelicals and Foreign Missions 1880–1980*, edited by Joel A. Carpenter and Wilbert R. Shenk, 157–160. Grand Rapids: Eerdmans Publishing, 1990.

Piper, Hans-Christoph. *Kommunizieren lernen in Seelsorge und Predigt*. Göttingen: Vandenhoeck & Ruprecht, 1981.

Plueddemann, James E. "The Future of Evangelical Theological Education." *Evangelical Review of Theology* 14, no. 1 (1990): 14–24.

Pöhlmann, Horst Georg. *Abriss der Dogmatik*. Gütersloh: Gütersloher Verlagshaus Mohn, 1972.

Prigodich, Raymond P. "Geistliches Leben und Hochschulbildung." *Evangelikale Missiologie* 18, no. 3 (2002): 106–111.

Printz, Markus. *Grundlinien einer bibelorientierte Gemeindepädagogik*. Wuppertal: Brockhaus, 1996.

Prokop, Ernst and Karlheinz A. Geissler. *Erwachsenenbildung. Modelle und Methoden*. Basel: E. Reinhardt, 1974.

Raber, Mary and Peter F. Penner, eds. *History and Mission in Europe: Continuing the Conversation*. Schwarzenfeld: Neufeld Verlag, 2011

Radnitzky, Gerard. "Die Universität als ordnungspolitisches Problem." In *Die ungewisse Zukunft der Universität,* edited by Hardy Bouillon and Gerard Radnitzky, 16–18. Berlin: Duncker & Humblot, 1991.

Reinalda, Bob and Ewa Kulesza. *The Bologna Process – Harmonizing Europe's Higher Education.* Opladen: Barbara Budrich Publishers, 2006. 2nd revised edition.

Riecker, Otto. *Mission oder Tod.* Wuppertal-Elberfeld: Verlag und Schriftenmission d. Evang. Ges. f. Deutschland, 1973.

———. *Bildung und Heiliger Geist.* Neuhausen-Stuttgart: Hänssler, 1974.

———. *Universitäts-Theologie und Gemeinde-Frömmigkeit.* Neuhausen-Stuttgart: Hänssler, 1984.

Riesner, Rainer. *Jesus als Lehrer.* Tübingen: Mohr, 1981.

Röd, Wolfgang. *Kleine Geschichte der antiken Philosophie.* Munich: C. H. Beck, 1998.

Rommen, Edward. *Die Notwendigkeit der Umkehr.* Giessen: Brunnen-Verlag, 1987.

Rooy, Sidney. "Historical Methods of Theological Education." In *New Alternatives in Theological Education,* edited by René C. Padilla, 50–72. Oxford: Regnum, 1988.

Ropohl, Günter. *Technologische Aufklärung.* Frankfurt: Suhrkamp Verlag, 1991.

———. "Technologische Bildung." In *Technologische Aufklärung,* edited by Günter Ropohl, 216–237. Frankfurt: Suhrkamp Verlag, 1991.

Rössler, Martin. *Schleiermachers Programm der Philosophischen Theologie.* Berlin: Walter de Gruyter, 1994.

Ruhbach, Gerhard. "Spiritualität." *ELThG,* 1880–1883.

Russell, Bertrand. *Philosophie des Abendlandes.* Zürich: Europaverlag, 1979 (1st edition 1950).

Russenberger, Michael. *Führungskultur in der Schweiz. Eine sozio-historische Studie.* Giessen: Brunnen, 2005.

Samuel, Viney. "Models and Directions of Theological Education in the Two Thirds World." Unpublished manuscript, Oxford 1996.

Sapsezian, A., S. Amirtham, and F. Ross Kinsler. *Global Solidarity in Theological Education.* Geneva: World Council of Churches, 1981.

Schäfer, Heinz. *Hört ein Gleichnis.* Stuttgart: Christliches Verlagshaus, 1971.

Schindler, Alfred, ed. *Kirche und Staat.* Zürich: TVZ, 1994.

Schipani, Daniel S. "The Church and Its Theological Education." In *Theological Education on Five Continents,* edited by Nancy R. Heisey and Daniel S. Schipani, 3–33. Strasbourg: Mennonite World Conference, 1997.

Schirrmacher, Thomas. "Ausbilden wie Jesus und Paulus." In *Ausbildung als Missionarischer Auftrag,* edited by Klaus W. Müller and Thomas Schirrmacher, 7–45. Bonn: Verlag für Kultur und Wissenschaft, 2000.

Schlatter, Wilhelm. *Die Geschichte der Basler Mission*, Vol. 1. Basel: Verlag der Basler Missionsbuchhandlung, 1916.

Schleiermacher Friedrich. *Theologische Enzyklopädie 1831/32* (postscript by David Friedrich Strauß, edited by Walter Sachs). Berlin: Walter de Gruyter, 1987.

Schmid, Johannes H., ed. *Unterwegs zu biblisch erneuerter Theologie.* Giessen and Basel: Brunnen, 1984.

Schnabel, J. Eckhard. *Urchristliche Mission.* Wuppertal: Brockhaus, 2002.

Schneider, Norbert. *Erkenntnistheorie im 20. Jahrhundert. Klassische Positionen.* Leipzig: Reclam, 1998.

Schottroff, W. "jd erkennen." THAT (*Theologisches Handwörterbuch zum Alten Testament*) I, 685.701.

Schröer, Henning, ed. *Einführung in das Studium der evangelischen Theologie.* Gütersloh: Gütersloher Verlagshaus Gerd Mohn, 1982.

Schroll-Machl, Sylvia. "Kulturbedingte Unterschiede im Problemlöseprozess." *Organisationsentwicklung* 1 (2000): 76–91.

Sedmak, Clemens. *Theologie als "Handwerk": Eine kleine Gebrauchsanweisung.* Regensburg: Pustet, 1999.

Seiß, Rudolf. *Dynamik der geistlichen Entwicklung. Schritte und typische Verlaufsformen geistlichen Wachstums.* Giessen and Basel: Brunnen-Verlag, 1994.

Seitz, Manfred. *Erneuerung der Gemeinde. Gemeindeaufbau und Spiritualität.* Göttingen: Vandenhoeck & Ruprecht, 1985.

Senn, Peter Thomas. *Führung Pädagogischer Hochschulen.* Zürich: Rüegger, 2004.

Sergiovanny, T. J. "The Lifeworld at the Centre: Values and Action in Educational Leadership." In *Effective Educational Leadership,* edited by Nigel Bennett, Megan Crawford, and Marion Cartwright, 14–24. London: Sage Publications, 2003.

Shaw, Ian. *Best Practice Guidelines for Doctoral Programs.* Carlisle: Langham Global Library, 2015.

Showalter, Shirley. "The Invisible Curriculum II." In *Mennonite Education in a Post-Christian World,* edited by Harry Huebner, 145–154. Winnipeg: CMBC Publications, 1998.

Siebert, Horst. *Der Konstruktivismus als pädagogische Weltanschauung.* Frankfurt: VAS, 2002.

———. *Pädagogischer Konstruktivismus.* Landsberg: Beltz, 2005, 3rd edition.

Sohm, Kurt. *Praxisbezogene Ausbildung auf Hochschulniveau. Eine pädagogisch-didaktische Herausforderung.* Vienna: Facultas wuv universitätsverlag, 1999.

Sprenger, Reinhard K. *Vertrauen führt. Worauf es im Unternehmen wirklich ankommt.* Frankfurt: Campus-Verlag, 2005.

Stachowiak, Herbert. *Allgemeine Modelltheorie.* Vienna and New York: Springer, 1973.

———. "Der Modellbegriff in der Erkenntnistheorie." *Zeitschrift für allgemeine Wissenschaftstheorie* 21, no. 1 (1980): 53–68.

Stackhouse, Max L. *Apologia: Contextualization, Globalization and Mission in Theological Education.* Grand Rapids: Eerdmans Publishing, 1988.

Stadelmann, Helge. *Grundlinien einer bibeltreuen Schriftverständnisses.* Wuppertal: Brockhaus, 1985.

Stadelmann, Helge. *Den Sinn biblischer Texte verstehen.* Giessen: Brunnen, 2006.

Stegemann, Ekkehard, and Ulrich Gäbler. "Früh Kontakt mit den Kirchen suchen." *Basler Zeitung*, April 3 (1995): 7.

Stenschke, Christoph. "Das Neue Testament als Dokumentsammlung urchristlicher Mission: Alter Hut oder neue Perspektive?" *Jahrbuch für Evangelikaler Theologie* (2005): 167–190.

Stewart, Bruce C. "Tensions in North American Theological Education." *Evangelical Review of Theology* 14, no. 1 (1990): 42–49.

Stoesz, Edgar, and Chester Raber. *Doing Good Better! How to Be an Effective Board Member in a Nonprofit Organization.* Intercourse: Good Books, 1997 (revised edition).

Stollberg, Dieter. *Therapeutische Seelsorge. Die amerikanische Seelsorgebewegung.* Munich: Kaiser, 1969.

Stollberg, Dieter, and Isolde Karle. "Über den Pfarrberuf. Ein Briefwechsel zwischen Dieter Stollberg und Isolde Karle." *Pastoraltheologie* 89 (2000): 524–528.

Strub, Hans. "Der Weg zum Pfarramt." *Annex* (Magazine of the Reformed Press) Nr. 11 (2006): 6–7.

Strübind, Kim. "'Pastoren bilden Pastoren aus' – Ein Entwurf für eine zeit- und sachgemäße theologische Ausbildung im Bund Evangelisch-Freikirchler Gemeinden in Elstal." *Zeitschrift für Theologie und Gemeinde* 6 (2001): 204–217.

Studer, Felix. "Christliche Erziehung als Erziehungshandeln." *Was geht bei uns?* Informationsblatt des TDS-Aarau Nr. 197 (1997): 4–14.

Stuhlmacher, Peter. *Vom Verstehen des Neuen Testaments.* Göttingen: Vandenhoeck und Ruprecht, 1986.

Taylor, William D., ed. *Internationalizing Missionary Training: A Global Perspective.* Exeter: Paternoster Press; Grand Rapids: Baker Book House, 1991.

Thielicke, Helmut. *A Little Exercise for Young Theologians.* Translated from German by Charles L. Taylor. Grand Rapids: Eerdmans, 1962.

Titmus, Colin J., ed. *Lifelong Education for Adults: An International Handbook.* Oxford: Pergamon Press, 1989.

Tournier, Paul. *The Seasons of Life.* Eugene, OR: Wipf and Stock Publishers, 2012.

Ventur, Birgit. *Martin Bubers pädagogisches Denken und Handeln.* Neukirchen: Neukirchener, 2003.

Volf, Miroslav. "Dancing for God: Challenges Facing Theological Education Today." *Evangelical Review of Theology* 29, no. 3 (2005): 197–207.

Walvoord, Barbara E. *Assessment Clear and Simple: A Practical Guide for Institutions, Departments, and General Education.* San Francisco: Jossey-Bass, 2004.

Warford, Malcolm L. *Practical Wisdom on Theological Teaching and Learning.* New York: Peter Lang, 2005.

Weber, Beat. *Werkbuch Psalmen I.* Stuttgart: Kohlhammer, 2001.

———. "Psalm 1 und seine Funktion der Einweisung." In *Der Erneuerung von Kirche und Theologie verpflichtet,* edited by Philipp Nanz, 175–212. Riehen: ArteMedia, 2005.

Weber, Otto. *Grundlagen der Dogmatik II.* Neukirchen-Vluyn: Neukirchener Verl. d. Erziehungsvereins, 1977.

Wehr, Hermann. "Die hohe Schule. Hochschul QM heute: Chancen und besondere Herausforderung." *Qualität und Zuverlässigkeit* 50, no. 9 (2005): 28.

Weidenmann, Bernd. *Erfolgreiche Kurse und Seminare.* Weinheim and Basel: Beltz, 1998.

Weinert, Franz E. *Leistungsmessungen in Schulen.* Weinheim and Basel: Beltz, 2002.

Wenk, Matthias. *Community-Forming Power: The Socio-Ethical Role of the Spirit in Luke-Acts.* Sheffield: Sheffield Academic Press, 2000.

———. "Do We Need a Distinct European Pentecostal/Charismatic Approach to Theological Education?" Unpublished, undated manuscript.

Werner, Dietrich. "Ecumenical Renewal of Congregations." *International Review of Mission* 71 (1992): 73–78.

———. *Theologie zum Leben bringen. Anforderung an eine zukunftsorientierte Ausbildung* (EMW Information 105). Hamburg: Evangelisches Missionswerk, 1995.

Werner, Dietrich, David Esterline, Namsoon Kang, eds. *Handbook of Theological Education in World Christianity.* Eugene, OR: Wipf and Stock Publishers, 2010.

West-Burnham, John. "Understanding Quality." In *The Principles and Practices of Educational Management*, edited by Tony Bush and Les Bell, 313–324. London: Sage Publications, 2002.

Wheeler, Barbara G. and Edward Farley, eds. *Shifting Boundaries: Cultural Approaches to the Structure of Theological Education*. Louisville, KY: Westminster John Knox Press, 1991.

Wick, Peter. "Ein Text, viele Auslegungen." In *Das Christentum an der Schwelle zum 3. Jahrtausend*, eds. Albrecht Grözinger and Ekkehard Stegemann, 77–90. Stuttgart: Kohlhammer, 2002.

———. "Verborgenes und Befohlenes: Schriftgelehrsamkeit und Jüngerschaft bei Matthäus." In *Der Erneuerung von Kirche und Theologie verpflichtet*, edited by Philipp Nanz, 259–271. Riehen: ArteMedia, 2005.

Wilkey Collison, Sylvia. *Making Disciples: The Significance of Jesus' Educational Methods for Today's Church*. Carlisle: Paternoster, 2004.

Willard, Dallas. *Aus dem Herzen Leben*. Giessen: Brunnen-Verlag, 2004.

Winter, Ralph D., ed. *Theological Education by Extension*. Pasadena: William Carey Library, 1969.

Witmer, S. A. *The Bible College Story: Education with Dimension*. New York: Channel Press, 1962.

Wood, Charles M. *Vision and Discernment*. Atlanta: Scholars Press, 1985.

Wood, W. Jay. *Epistemology: Becoming Intellectually Virtuous*. Downers Grove: InterVarsity Press, 1998.

Woodberry, J. Dudley, Charles Van Engen, and Edgar J. Elliston, eds. *Missiological Education for the 21st Century*. Maryknoll: Orbis Books, 1996.

World Council of Churches. *Europäische Konsultation über theologische Ausbildung* (EMW Information 20). Hamburg 1981.

———. *Spiritual Formation in Theological Education* (Iona document). Geneva: World Council of Churches, 1987.

Woschnak, Ute, and Peter M. Frischknecht. "Schlüsselqualifikationen – vom Arbeitsmarkt verlangt! Von der Hochschule gelehrt?" *Personal* 54, no. 10 (2002): 26–30 [also at http://e-collection.ethbib.ethz.ch/ecol-pool/incoll/incoll_761.pdf].

Yoder Neufeld, Thomas R. "The Invisible Curriculum – On Being Wisdom's School." In *Mennonite Education in a Post-Christian World*, edited by Harry Huebner, 129–144. Winnipeg: CMBC Publications, 1998.

Youngblood, Robert L. *Cyprus: TEE Come of Age*. Exeter: Paternoster, 1986.

Zehr, Paul M. and Jim Egli, eds. *Alternative Models of Mennonite Pastoral Formation*. Elkhart: Institute of Mennonite Studies, 1992.

Zenger, Erich, et al. *Einleitung in das Alte Testament*. Stuttgart: Kohlhammer, 2001.

Ziegenhals, Gretchen E. "Faculty Life and Seminary Culture – It's About Time and Money." In *Practical Wisdom on Theological Teaching and Learning*, edited by Malcolm L. Warford, 49–66. New York: Peter Lang, 2005.

Zimmerling, Peter. *Die charismatischen Bewegungen*. Göttingen: Vandenhoeck & Ruprecht, 2002.

———. *Evangelische Spiritualität. Wurzeln und Zugänge*. Göttingen: Vandenhoeck & Ruprecht, 2003.

Zindel, Daniel. *Geistesgegenwärtig führen – Spiritualität und Management*. Schwarzenfeld: Neufeld, 2003.

Zippert, Thomas. "Die Bedeutung der Fortbildung in den ersten Amtsjahren (FEA) für die Stärkung pastoraler Kompetenz." *Pastoraltheologie* 89 (2000): 490–497.

Zumstein, Jean. "Theologische Fakultäten an staatlichen Universitäten." In *Kirche und Staat*, edited by Alfred Schindler, 82–100. Zürich: TVZ, 1994.

ICETE is a global community, sponsored by nine regional networks of theological schools, to enable international interaction and collaboration among all those engaged in strengthening and developing evangelical theological education and Christian leadership development worldwide.

The purpose of ICETE is:
1. To promote the enhancement of evangelical theological education worldwide.
2. To serve as a forum for interaction, partnership and collaboration among those involved in evangelical theological education and leadership development, for mutual assistance, stimulation and enrichment.
3. To provide networking and support services for regional associations of evangelical theological schools worldwide.
4. To facilitate among these bodies the advancement of their services to evangelical theological education within their regions.

Sponsoring associations include:

Africa: Association for Christian Theological Education in Africa (ACTEA)

Asia: Asia Theological Association (ATA)

Caribbean: Caribbean Evangelical Theological Association (CETA)

Europe: European Evangelical Accrediting Association (EEAA)

Euro-Asia: Euro-Asian Accrediting Association (E-AAA)

Latin America: Association for Evangelical Theological Education in Latin America (AETAL)

Middle East and North Africa: Middle East Association for Theological Education (MEATE)

North America: Association for Biblical Higher Education (ABHE)

South Pacific: South Pacific Association of Evangelical Colleges (SPAEC)

www.icete-edu.org

Langham Literature and its imprints are a ministry of Langham Partnership

Langham Partnership is a global fellowship working in pursuit of the vision God entrusted to its founder John Stott –

to facilitate the growth of the church in maturity and Christ-likeness through raising the standards of biblical preaching and teaching.

Our vision is to see churches in the majority world equipped for mission and growing to maturity in Christ through the ministry of pastors and leaders who believe, teach and live by the Word of God.

Our mission is to strengthen the ministry of the Word of God through:
- nurturing national movements for biblical preaching
- fostering the creation and distribution of evangelical literature
- enhancing evangelical theological education

especially in countries where churches are under-resourced.

Our ministry

Langham Preaching partners with national leaders to nurture indigenous biblical preaching movements for pastors and lay preachers all around the world. With the support of a team of trainers from many countries, a multi-level programme of seminars provides practical training, and is followed by a programme for training local facilitators. Local preachers' groups and national and regional networks ensure continuity and ongoing development, seeking to build vigorous movements committed to Bible exposition.

Langham Literature provides majority world preachers, scholars and seminary libraries with evangelical books and electronic resources through publishing and distribution, grants and discounts. The programme also fosters the creation of indigenous evangelical books in many languages, through writer's grants, strengthening local evangelical publishing houses, and investment in major regional literature projects, such as one volume Bible commentaries like *The Africa Bible Commentary* and *The South Asia Bible Commentary*.

Langham Scholars provides financial support for evangelical doctoral students from the majority world so that, when they return home, they may train pastors and other Christian leaders with sound, biblical and theological teaching. This programme equips those who equip others. Langham Scholars also works in partnership with majority world seminaries in strengthening evangelical theological education. A growing number of Langham Scholars study in high quality doctoral programmes in the majority world itself. As well as teaching the next generation of pastors, graduated Langham Scholars exercise significant influence through their writing and leadership.

To learn more about Langham Partnership and the work we do visit **langham.org**

www.ingramcontent.com/pod-product-compliance
Lightning Source LLC
Chambersburg PA
CBHW060416300426
44111CB00018B/2874